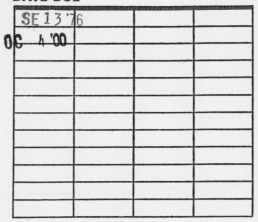

MATHEMATICAL
PSYCHOLOGY

Clyde H. Coombs

The University of Michigan

Robyn M. Dawes

University of Oregon and Oregon Research Institute

Amos Tversky

The Hebrew University of Jerusalem

PRENTICE-HALL SERIES IN MATHEMATICAL PSYCHOLOGY
Clyde H. Coombs, Editor

MATHEMATICAL PSYCHOLOGY

An Elementary Introduction

PRENTICE-HALL, INC., ENGLEWOOD CLIFFS, NEW JERSEY

MATHEMATICAL
PSYCHOLOGY
Coombs, Dawes and Tversky

Current printing (last digit):
10 9 8 7 6 5 4 3 2 1

13-562157-7

Library of Congress catalog card number:
73-101580

Printed in the United States of America

Prentice-Hall International, Inc., London
Prentice-Hall of Australia, Pty. Ltd., Sydney
Prentice-Hall of Canada, Ltd., Toronto
Prentice-Hall of India Private Ltd., New Delhi
Prentice-Hall of Japan, Inc., Tokyo

PREFACE

This book grew out of our joint teaching experiences at the University of Michigan. In the course of introducing our students to mathematical psychology, we felt the need for a general introductory textbook for advanced undergraduates and beginning graduate students. We also felt that such a book should cover the diversity of work in the field and that it should demand a minimum of mathematical sophistication, so that it could be of use for students with only a little knowledge of statistics or college mathematics.

To present the diversity of both methods and areas of application, we have chosen to write ten largely independent chapters. We have attempted to write the book in such a way that each chapter may be read and studied without reference to other chapters. Yet, we have tried to bring out some of the more interesting interrelations among the chapters by discussing general principles shared by various models and by referencing across chapters. The reader who wishes to study any of the topics in greater depth may consult the general bibliography for details on those authors, articles, and books referenced in the chapter section of interest. In addition, we have written a mathematical appendix in which the major mathematical ideas used in the book are defined and discussed.

The nine chapters following the introduction may be grouped into three parts: Chapters 2, 3, and 4 are concerned with measurement and models; Chapters 5, 6, and 7 are concerned with decision processes; and Chapters 8, 9, and 10 deal with sequential processes and information theory.

Although we have all worked on the book together, Chapters 3, 6, and 9 were primarily written by Clyde H. Coombs; Chapters 4, 8, 10, and the appendix by Robyn M. Dawes; and Chapters 2, 5, and 7 by Amos Tversky.

C.H.C.

R.M.D.

A.T.

ACKNOWLEDGMENTS

It is virtually impossible to fully acknowledge the many students, friends, and colleagues who have contributed to our writing of this book. Because of the scope of the material covered many people commented only on a particular chapter and sometimes on only a part of that chapter; but the benefit to the book cannot be measured in terms of the amount of material covered. Hence we have tried to be as generous as space permits and include all who have voluntarily contributed a substantial amount of their own time in helping us to make the book more accurate and readable.

Harley Bernbach	David H. Krantz	Harold L. Rausch
Robert Bjork	Sarah Lichtenstein	Leonard G. Rorer
Ward Edwards	James Lingoes	Richard Rose
Terry Gleason	Melvin Manis	Edward Roskam
Lewis R. Goldberg	Jay Millman	Philip J. Runkel
Noel J. Hicks	Richard Millward	Roger Shepard
Paul J. Hoffman	Ronald M. Pickett	Paul Slovic
Ray Hyman	Irwin Pollack	Gordon Wilcox
Richard R. Jones	Michael I. Posner	Benjamin B. Winter

CONTENTS

part **II**

DECISION

part **III**

**LEARNING AND
INFORMATION THEORY**

INTRODUCTION

We are writing this book to introduce the reader to the field of mathematical psychology. When we asked some colleagues for a brief characterization of this field, we received replies ranging from the "last best hope of scientific psychology" through "a useful bag of tricks" to "a sophisticated formulation of the obvious." Our own view is that the field may be characterized by the attempt to use mathematical methods to invesigate psychological problems; thus it is not defined in terms of content but rather in terms of an approach. Unlike the fields of learning, perception, or social psychology, which are characterized by substantive areas of investigation, the field of mathematical psychology is characterized by a style of investigation—a style that is employed in a diversity of substantive areas.

Moreover, this style is not uniform. Just as mathematical psychologists investigate a wide range of substantive problems, they use a variety of mathematical methods.

The attempt to employ mathematical methods in psychological investigation dates back to the middle of the 19th century, in particular to the work of Fechner (1860). Fechner was concerned with the relation between the mind and the body, and he believed that this relation could be understood by specifying mathematically the way in which sensation (e.g., perceived brightness) varies as a function of physical input (e.g., luminance measured in foot candles); thus Fechner sought a mathematical function relating amount of physical input to a measure of intensity of sensation; such a function has been called a psychophysical function. The attempt to specify the relationship between sensation and physical input in a mathematical form continues today, although most psychologists no longer think that this research sheds light on the mind-body problem.

Since Fechner, many psychologists have investigated both the possibility of measuring psychological variables and of expressing psychological relationships in mathematical form. In particular, there has been a great deal of work on the measurement of intelligence (e.g., Spearman 1904) and attitude (e.g., Thurstone 1928); in addition, there have been well-known attempts to represent mathematically the basic principles of learning (e.g., Hull 1943) and social psychology (e.g., Lewin 1936). Since the early 1950's, work in mathematical psychology has increased rapidly and followed some new directions. This recent work was greatly facilitated by new work in mathematics—in particular by the development of information theory, the theory of games, and statistical decision theory, as well as by the growing field of computer sciences. The emphasis of this book is on this recent work.

One of the characteristics of much of this recent work is the use of mathematical models to represent psychological phenomena. This representation process is not a simple one. It involves isolating a particular set of empirical phenomena, selecting a particular formal system, and then establishing a correspondence between them. Just as many languages can be used to express the same idea, many formal models can be used to represent the same empirical phenomenon. Indeed, mathematical psychologists have employed a variety of models differing in structure and form. Some models are geometric, others algebraic, whereas some have a probabilistic character. Similarly, some models are stated as computer programs, some as systems of equations, and some in an axiomatic form. Numerous examples of various types of models are discussed and studied in the following chapters.

The basic defining characteristics of all models is the representation of some aspects of the world by a more abstract system. In applying a model, the investigator identifies objects and relations in the world with some elements and relations in the formal system. Consequently, the model is regarded as an abstract representation of the world and the modeling process is called abstraction. When the model has been constructed, its consequences may be derived using the rules of logic and the available mathematical machinery.

It is important to realize that the process of derivation is a purely formal one, independent of the interpretation of the model. Given a specific inter-

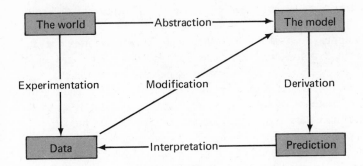

Fig. 1.1 Schematic illustration of a scientific investigation.

pretation of the model, its logical consequences are taken as *predictions* to be compared with the *data* to determine the degree of correspondence between the model and the world. This stage of the process involves a conceptual interpretation of the predictions as well as a statistical interpretation of the data. Typically, the data lead to revisions or extensions of the original model, and the model is then modified in order to incorporate new data. A schematic illustration of this process is depicted in Fig. 1.1 (adapted from Coombs, Raiffa, and Thrall 1954).

It should be noted that Fig. 1.1 does not purport to describe the actual modeling process. Rather, it attempts to summarize, in schematic fashion, some of the relations among the various phases of this process. The portrayed schema is clearly an oversimplification. The stages of research are typically interdependent and the directions of the arrows are often reversed. The essence of this schema is the characterization of the investigation as an attempt to construct a model of the world which is then tested by comparing its consequences to the observed data. The problem of evaluating models by testing their empirical consequences has both statistical and logical aspects. The statistical problems involved in the verification process are those of determining how well the model fits the data and how likely it is to be correct given the empirical evidence. Although these problems belong in statistics rather than in mathematical psychology, they are extremely important for the understanding of models and the interpretation of data.

From a logical viewpoint it should be noted that a model can only be rejected on the basis of data, not proved. If a model (M) implies certain characteristics (C) of the data, then the absence of these characteristics (not-C) is sufficient to reject the model, but the presence of these characteristics does not imply the model—although this presence does give the model some inductive support. For example, if a particular learning model predicts that teaching method X is superior to teaching method Y, then the finding that Y is superior to X would lead us to reject the model; however, the finding that X is superior is not sufficient to establish the validity of the model, because this finding may be predicted by a variety of otherwise different models.

When *A* implies *B*, *A* is often termed a *sufficient condition* for *B*, whereas *B* is termed a *necessary condition* for *A*; these terms are self-explanatory, for *A* alone implies *B*, whereas *B* is necessary for *A* in that the negation of *B* implies the negation of *A*. In our context the model is a sufficient condition for the existence of the data characteristics, whereas these data characteristics are necessary conditions for the validity of the model.

Similarly, we say a model M_1 is weaker or more general than M_2 (M_2 is called stronger or a special case of M_1) if M_2 implies M_1—or, equivalently, if the rejection of M_1 implies the rejection of M_2. General models have the important property that if they are rejected, all their special cases are rejected.

The advantage of mathematical models over other forms of theories lies in their generality, their precision, and their deductive power. By using the language of mathematics, psychological theories can often be stated in a form that is both general and precise. Moreover, by using logical derivations, the investigator can discover the consequences of his assumptions, some of which may not be apparent at all.

The importance of mathematics in the history of science cannot be overestimated. On the other hand, not every application of mathematics in science has proved fruitful. A useful application of mathematics to psychology results from identifying a lawful phenomenon and selecting an appropriate mathematical system that reflects this lawfulness. It is our hope that a better understanding of the variety of investigations in the field of mathematical psychology will lead to deeper and more fruitful applications. We have attempted to represent this variety in the following chapters.

MODELS

part ▌

2

PSYCHOLOGICAL MEASUREMENT THEORY

2.1 INTRODUCTION

Science attempts to explain and predict observable phenomena in terms of a few general laws. In the more advanced sciences, such laws express quantitative relationships among several fundamental properties of the objects under investigation. Examples of such properties are velocity and mass in physics, supply and demand in economics, or utility and subjective probability in psychology. In order to formulate quantitative laws, however, the relevant properties must be expressible by numbers. The process by which the scientist represents properties by numbers is called *measurement*.

Some properties, such as length and weight, are measured using methods that have evolved for centuries and seem, at present, very natural. Other properties, such as utility and intelligence, are measured using methods of much more recent origin that may seem less natural and more arbitrary. In fact, some have argued that psychological attributes such as utility or intelligence cannot be measured in the same sense that one measures physical attributes such as length and weight. Others have maintained that although it is possible to measure utility or intelligence it is impossible to measure happiness or creativity. The justification for these positions is often unclear. Do they reflect the fact that the measurement of psychological attributes is more complicated, in some sense, than that of physical attributes? Are they based on the higher degree of accuracy that can be attained in physical measurements? Or do they simply express the belief that some (or most) psychological properties cannot be properly quantified?

Without discussing these issues in any depth, it seems that there are different kinds of measurement that vary in the amount of information they provide, the types of structure they reveal, and the degree of accuracy with which they can be carried out. The delineation of the various types of measurement and the explication of their meaning are the subject matter of measurement theory.

It is interesting to note that although measurement is as old as science itself the logical foundation of measurement had not been studied before the turn of the century, when Hölder (1901) developed his classic axiomatization for the measurement of mass. Over the years the measurement process has been studied extensively by physicists, logicians, and psychologists. Although the importance of measurement has never been questioned, the analysis of its status and justification has not been free from controversy. This chapter is an introduction to measurement theory. The goal of measurement theory is the logical analysis of the measurement process. More specifically, it is concerned with the justification of various measurement procedures and with the meaningfulness of their results. To illustrate these problems, we first introduce two examples of measurement, one from physics and one from the social sciences.

The Measurement of Weight

The procedures involved in measuring weight, or mass, are simple and familiar. They are based on an order relation $\gtrsim$ meaning "at least as heavy as," which is established by placing objects on the pans of a balance and observing which pan descends. In addition to the comparisons between single objects, denoted x, y, z, etc., one can concatenate objects by placing them together on the same pan of the balance. Thus $x \circ y$ denotes the concatenation of x and y, and $x \circ y \gtrsim z$ denotes the observation that the combined weight of x and y is at least as great as that of z. Given this information, one wishes to construct a measurement scale w that assigns a number $w(x)$ to each object x such that

1. $w(x) \geq w(y)$ if and only if $x \gtrsim y$.
2. $w(x \circ y) = w(x) + w(y)$.

The weight scale, therefore, is required to reflect the heaviness order between the objects and to satisfy additivity, in the sense that the weight assigned to the concatenation of objects equals the sum of the weights of the concatenated objects.

The Measurement of Utility Intervals

The measurement of utility intervals, like the measurement of weight, is based on an ordering of objects with respect to the attribute to be measured. Unlike the measurement of mass, however, the ordering, denoted $\succsim$, is established by observing preferences or judgments of an individual rather than the pans of a balance. Consider a situation where an individual has to evaluate a set of candidates. The individual might be a judge in a beauty or a diving contest, or he might be a voter evaluating a set of political candidates. Suppose the individual orders the candidates, according to his preferences, and let $x \succsim y$ denote the judgment that candidate y is not preferred to candidate x. Furthermore, suppose the individual can order not only candidates but also (positive) differences between candidates, and let $(x, y) \succsim (z, w)$ denote the judgment that the difference between z and w does not exceed that between x and y. Note that although the same symbol, $\succsim$, is used to denote both orderings, they are, in fact, different relations that reflect different types of judgments. The former is an ordering of candidates, whereas the latter is an ordering of differences between candidates. Given these orders, one wishes to construct a utility scale u for the given individual that assigns a number $u(x)$ to each candidate such that

1. $u(x) \geq u(y)$ if and only if $x \succsim y$.
2. $u(x) - u(y) \geq u(z) - u(w)$ if and only if $(x, y) \succsim (z, w)$.

The utility scale, therefore, should reflect the ordering of the candidates as well as the ordering of differences, or intervals between candidates.

If we examine these as well as other examples of measurement systems, we are naturally led to a series of questions that constitute the basic problems of measurement theory.

(1) *The representation problem.* Can all attributes be measured? If not, what are the conditions under which measurement scales can be established? For example, what are the necessary (or sufficient) conditions for the construction of a weight or a utility scale? (2) *The uniqueness problem.* Given a particular measurement procedure, how much freedom is there in assigning numbers to objects? Are the numbers determined uniquely by the measurement process, or are they chosen arbitrarily? (3) *The meaningfulness problem.* Given a particular measurement scale, what inferences can be made from it? What assertions can be meaningfully made on the basis of a numerical measurement scale? (4) *The scaling problem.* How do we go about the actual construction of the numerical scales? How do we convert ordinal information into statements about numbers? Finally, how do we deal with errors of

measurement that may be caused by the inaccuracy of the balance or the inconsistency of the preference judgments?

The representation, uniqueness, and meaningfulness problems are discussed in turn in the next three sections and examples of psychological measurement models are presented. The scaling problem is discussed and illustrated in Chapter 3. For a more detailed discussion of the foundation of psychological measurement, see Krantz (1968) and Suppes and Zinnes (1963).

2.2   THE REPRESENTATION PROBLEM

To introduce the representation problem in full generality, let us have another look at the relationships between theory and data, as portrayed in Fig. 1.1. A careful examination of this schematic diagram reveals that although the processes of experimentation and derivation (denoted by vertical arrows) seem well understood the processes of abstraction and interpretation (denoted by horizontal arrows) call for further discussion. What do we mean when we say that a particular formal system is a model or a representation of our world? When are we justified in interpreting a logical consequence of the model as an assertion about the world?

Before trying to answer these questions, note that the representation problem of measurement theory is a special case of a more general representation problem. Whenever we measure some property, we construct, in a sense, a simple numerical model of our world. Hence, measurement may be viewed as a numerical model, that is, a model based on the familiar system of the real numbers. Although such models are indispensable, there are many important nonnumerical models in the various branches of science. Examples of psychological models of a nonnumerical nature are discussed in Chapter 4.

Loosely speaking, a formal system (numerical or otherwise) is regarded as a model of the world if it reflects the structure of the world or represents its essential features. To give precise definitions to these intuitive notions, we introduce some elementary constructs from the theory of relational systems. The language of this theory provides a precise way of characterizing the nature of the correspondence between the world and its model.

A relational system is simply a collection of objects along with one or more relations defined among them. Formally, a relational system is a sequence $\langle A, R_1, \ldots, R_n \rangle$ where A is a (non-empty) set and $R_1, \ldots, R_n$ are relations defined on the elements of A. A relational system is called empirical if its objects are of empirical nature, such as people or weights, or it is called formal if its objects are formal entities such as numbers or points.

Let us first consider simple relational systems of the form $\langle A, R \rangle$ with one binary relation, that is, a relation defined on pairs of points. For example, A may be a set of objects and R may be the relation "heavier than." That is, for any pair of objects x, y in A, we define:

$$x \, R \, y \quad \text{if and only if} \quad x \text{ is heavier than } y.$$

Note that R can be defined either by a balance or by psychophysical experiments using an observer to compare the weights. The two procedures yield similar empirical relational systems with the same object set. The interpretation of the relation "heavier than," however, is physical in the former system and psychological in the latter. For an example of a simple formal relational system, let A be the set of all real numbers and let R be the relation "greater than." In this case R is defined for all real numbers x and y by:

$$x \, R \, y \quad \text{if and only if} \quad x > y.$$

The generality of the concept of a relational system suggests that the domain of investigation may be conceived of as an empirical relational system, whereas models may be conceived of as formal relational systems. It should be emphasized, however, that the characterization of the field of study as an empirical relational system is in itself a process of abstraction in which the raw data of our experience are classified and structured as objects and relations.

Although the process of setting up the empirical relational system is an essential aspect of any scientific investigation, the explication of this process lies beyond the scope of this chapter.

The relation between the world and its model may thereby be viewed as a correspondence between an empirical and a numerical relational system. Put differently, the processes of modeling and measurement are described as representations of empirical systems by formal ones.[1]

More formally a system $\alpha = \langle A, R \rangle$ is said to be *represented* by another system $\beta = \langle B, S \rangle$ if there exists a function f from A into B (which assigns to each x in A a unique $f(x)$ in B) such that for all x, y in A

$$x \, R \, y \quad \text{implies} \quad f(x) \, S \, f(y).$$

Thus α is represented by β if there exists a correspondence f that maps A into B in such a way that if the relation R holds between some x and y in A then the relation S holds between $f(x)$ and $f(y)$ in B, where $f(x)$ and $f(y)$ are the images of x and y, respectively. If both β represents α and α represents β, the two systems are called *isomorphic*.

A simple example illustrates the definition. Let $\alpha = \langle P, > \rangle$, where P denotes the set of all positive integers and $>$ denotes the relation "greater than"; and let $\beta = \langle N, < \rangle$, where N denotes the set of all negative integers

---

[1] The present definition of the representation relation is closely related though not identical to Suppes and Zinnes' definition (1963) of a homomorphism between relational systems.

and $<$ denotes the relation "less than." To show that α is represented by β we have to find a function f from P into N such that for all positive integers x, y in P, $x > y$ implies $f(x) < f(y)$. If we let $f(x) = -x$, for all x in P, it is easily seen that the above assertion is always satisfied, and hence α is represented by β. Furthermore, because f is one to one, β is represented by α and the two systems are therefore isomorphic.

The measurement of weight, discussed in Sec. 2.1, provides a good example of a representation of an empirical relational system by a numerical system. To reformulate this example as a representation problem, let $\alpha = \langle A, \circ, \succ \rangle$, where A denotes a set of empirical objects, $\circ$ denotes a physical concatenation operation between the objects, and $\succ$ denotes the relation "heavier than." Similarly, let $\beta = \langle R, +, > \rangle$, where R denotes the positive real numbers, $+$ denotes the usual addition operation between real numbers, and $>$ denotes the usual inequality relation between real numbers. The measurement of weight is essentially a representation of α by β. It consists of mapping A into R in such a way that the number assigned to the concatenation of two objects equals the sum of the numbers assigned to the two separate objects and such that the number assigned to one object is greater than that assigned to a second object whenever the first object is heavier than the second.

As the above example suggests, the notion of a representation of a relational system is not limited to a simple system with one binary relation, and it can be naturally generalized to systems with any number of relations of any order. A system $\alpha = \langle A, R_1, \ldots, R_n \rangle$ is said to be *represented* by another one $\beta = \langle B, S_1, \ldots, S_n \rangle$ if there exists a mapping f from A into B such that whenever R_i holds among a sequence of elements in A, S_i holds among their images in B. Intuitively, α is represented by β if anything that "happens" in α is "reflected" in β: Every object in α has a corresponding object in β and every relation among objects in α has a counterpart among the corresponding objects in β. In this case f is said to be a representation of α by β.

At this point we can reformulate the problem of constructing a model of the world as that of representing an empirical relational system (the world) by a formal relational system (the model). If the model is numerical, the representation is called measurement. Hence, not any assignment of numbers to objects according to some rule can be properly viewed as measurement. It is essential that the relations among the objects of the world be properly reflected by the relations among the numbers assigned to them. After we have defined measurement as the representation of an empirical system by a numerical system, the problem arises as to how we represent a given empirical system by a numerical system.

Let us investigate a simple example. Suppose you plan to go to a foreign movie, and you are considering the following three alternatives: x, a British comedy; y, an Italian drama; and z, a French mystery. Suppose you consider all pairs of movies and decide that you prefer a British movie to an Italian one and an Italian movie to a French one but that you prefer a mystery to a comedy. Thus you prefer x to y, y to z, and z to x. (If you feel that such preferences are bizarre or irrational, see the discussion at the end of Sec. 5.3.) Aside from the question of which movie you would choose, one may wonder whether there exists a utility scale u that assigns a number to each of the alternatives such that the number assigned to one alternative exceeds the number assigned to another if and only if the first alternative is preferred to the second. Stated differently, one asks whether the empirical system consisting of the three movies together with the above set of preferences can be represented by a formal system consisting of any three numbers with the relation of "greater than."

The answer to this question is clearly negative because the given preference relation is not transitive. (A binary relation R is transitive if $x\,R\,y$ and $y\,R\,z$ imply $x\,R\,z$ for all x, y, z; see Sec. A.3 of the appendix.) Hence, any numerical representation of these preferences would have to satisfy the inequalities $u(x) > u(y)$, $u(y) > u(z)$, and $u(z) > u(x)$, which are obviously inconsistent.

The transitivity of the empirical relation, therefore, is a necessary condition for the representation of an empirical relation by the relation "greater than" between real numbers. It can also be shown that whenever the preference relation is transitive, the corresponding empirical system can be represented by a numerical system provided the number of alternatives is finite. The existence of the desired representation, therefore, is equivalent to the transitivity of the empirical relation. One of the major goals of measurement theory is the investigation of the conditions (or axioms) under which various numerical representations can be constructed. The results of such an investigation are typically summarized by a representation theorem stating that if certain conditions are satisfied then a given numerical representation can be obtained. The representation theorem for the above example can be stated as follows.

THEOREM 2.1

Let A be a finite set and let R be a connected binary relation on A (i.e., a relation defined for all pairs of elements in A). If R is transitive, then and only then there exists a function u from A into the real numbers such that for all x and y in A

$$u(x) > u(y) \quad \text{if and only if} \quad x\,R\,y.$$

The proof of theorem 2.1 is quite simple and may be sketched as follows. Assuming there are no ties, we can start by finding an element x_0 in A such that $x\,R\,x_0$ for all x in A. Because A is finite and R is transitive, there exists an

element with this property. To this element we assign the scale value 0.
That is, $u(x_0) = 0$. Next we consider the remaining elements of A and find
an element x_1 in A for which $x R x_1$ for all x in A excluding x_0. By the same
argument, based on the facts that A is finite and R is transitive, there exists
an x_1 with the above property to which we assign the scale value 1. In
general, we repeat the process as many times as necessary, setting $u(x_i) = i$
until we exhaust our object set A. It can be shown, then, that in the resulting
representation $u(x) > u(y)$ if and only if $x R y$. In some instances, however,
R may include ties; that is, it includes some elements for which both $x R y$
and $y R x$ hold. In these situations the choice of our x_i is not unique and the
same scale value is assigned to all the tied elements, which are referred to as an
equivalence class (or as an R-equivalence class, to be precise).

It is important to realize that the outlined proof relies heavily on the
fact that A is finite. If A is not finite (or countable), then the transitivity of R
is no longer sufficient to establish the desired representation. Because the
problem is of no great empirical interest, we do not discuss it here. Additional
examples of representation theorems for more elaborate measurement
models are discussed in Sec. 2.5.

An important feature of the outlined proof is the fact that it is constructive. That is, it provides a method of generating actual scale values.
Such proofs are of particular interest because they not only ensure the
existence of the scale but also provide effective methods for constructing it.
In many cases, in fact, the actual measurement procedures follow the proof
rather closely. This parallelism between the empirical and the formal methods
is by no means accidental. The formal analysis of the representation problem
leads to the formulation of the assumptions needed to justify a given
numerical representation and to the development of constructive procedures.
The empirical analysis of the representation problem is aimed at testing the
underlying assumptions and implementing the constructive methods to
obtain measurement scales. The importance of measurement in science is a
consequence of the fruitful interaction between the formal and the empirical
analyses.

2.3 THE UNIQUENESS PROBLEM

After the representation problem has been solved and the scale is constructed,
we wish to discover the status of the obtained scale. Stated differently, we
wish to determine how much freedom we have in constructing the scale
and to characterize the relationships among the various numerical scales
resulting from a given representation theorem.

To illustrate the uniqueness problem, let us return to the problem of
choosing between movies. Suppose, after careful consideration, you decide
that you prefer x to y, y to z, and x to z. Because these preferences are transi-

tive, they can be represented numerically by a utility function, according to theorem 2.1. In particular, if we set $u(x) = 3$, $u(y) = 2$, and $u(z) = 1$, we obtain a representation of the alternatives such that the order of the scale values coincides with the preference order. The actual scale values 3, 2, and 1, however, are not determined by the measurement model. We could set $u(x) = 17$, $u(y) = \sqrt{2}$, and $u(z) = 0$ and still satisfy the model. In fact, any three numbers satisfying the inequality $u(x) > u(y) > u(z)$ can be used as scale values. Conversely, any set of scale values would have to satisfy the above inequality. Such scales are called *ordinal* scales, and we say that the scale is unique up to an order-preserving transformation. That is, any transformation of the scale values that preserves their order yields another admissible scale, and any two admissible scales are related by an order-preserving, or a monotone, transformation.

Let us suppose now that in addition to stating the preference order $x \succ y \succ z$, you are able to order differences between alternatives (with respect to preference) and you perceive the difference between x and y as equal to that between y and z. Assuming the measurement model for utility intervals (discussed in Sec. 2.1), the scale values must satisfy the inequality $u(x) > u(y) > u(z)$ as well as the equation $u(x) - u(y) = u(y) - u(z)$, and hence $2u(y) = u(x) + u(z)$. It can easily be seen that the scale values $u(x) = 3$, $u(y) = 2$, and $u(z) = 1$ satisfy these conditions but that the scale values $u(x) = 17$, $u(y) = \sqrt{2}$, and $u(z) = 0$ do not. Not any order-preserving transformation is admissible, therefore, according to this model. An admissible transformation in this case must preserve not only the order of the scale values but the order of differences between scale values as well. The only transformation, however, that preserves the ordering of intervals (for any set of objects) is a positive linear one that consists of multiplying each scale value by a positive constant and adding to it another constant. Scales of this type are called interval scales, and they are said to be unique up to a positive linear transformation. Put differently, after two scale values are selected, all the others are uniquely determined. Thus, if we let $u(x) = a$ and $u(y) = b$, in the above example, it follows from the model that $u(z) = 2b - a$.

To state the uniqueness problem more precisely, the notion of an admissible transformation is defined formally. Let α be an empirical system with object set A that is represented by a numerical system β with object set B. That is, for any object x in A there exists a unique scale value $f(x)$ in B, where the relations between the objects are reflected by the relations between their scale values. A transformation of the scale values is called *admissible* if the numerical system obtained by replacing B by the transformed scale values also represents the empirical system α. Formally, let $\alpha = \langle A, R_1, \ldots, R_n \rangle$ be an empirical relational system, and let $\beta = \langle B, S_1, \ldots, S_n \rangle$ be a numerical relational system, where B denotes the set of real numbers. A transformation T from B into itself is said to be admissible, with respect to a given representation f, if the mapping f', defined by $f'(x) = T[f(x)]$ for all x in A, is also a representation of α by β. Thus a transformation of the scale values is called admissible whenever it preserves the representation relation between the empirical and numerical systems. The set of all admissible transformations determines the scale type or the degree of uniqueness of the measurement.[2] Scales are characterized, therefore, in terms of their admissible transformations.

The admissible transformations for the simple utility scale that is based on ordering of alternatives alone are the set of all order-preserving transformations. The associated scale type is called *ordinal* because only the ordinal properties of the numbers are employed in the measurement. Otherwise, the actual numerical values can be chosen in an arbitrary fashion. In the measurement of utility that is based on an ordering of intervals or in the measurement of temperature for example, the admissible transformations are limited to the set of positive linear transformations of the kind $T(x) = ax + b$ for $a > 0$. In this case the scale values are uniquely determined except for an arbitrary origin (b) and a unit of measurement (a). These scales are called *interval* scales because intervals between scale values can be meaningfully compared. Some models, such as those employed in the measurement of mass and length, impose even stronger constraints on the numerical scales. In these cases the only admissible transformations are the similarity transformations of the form $T(x) = ax$ for $a > 0$. Such scales are called *ratio* scales and the scale values are uniquely determined except for an arbitrary unit of measurement (a). Two other, commonly mentioned though less important, scale types are the *nominal* and the *absolute* scales. In the nominal scale (exemplified by the assignment of numbers to football players) any one-to-one transformation is admissible. Here, the numbers are used only as labels and hence only their distinctness has to be preserved. At the other extreme, in the absolute scale no transformation is admissible. Counting, viewed as measurement, provides an example of an absolute scale.

Although the five scale types mentioned are widely known and discussed, they certainly do not exhaust the variety of possible scale types. Because the scale type is determined by the admissible transformation, there is an infinity of scale types corresponding to the infinity of classes of admissible transformations. Furthermore, the determination of the scale type or the characterization of the class of admissible transformations is, in many cases, a nontrivial mathematical problem.

There is an interesting correspondence between the representation and the uniqueness problems of measurement theory and representation and uniqueness problems in mathematics in general. The problem of demonstrating the solvability of a given system of equations, for example, is a representation problem, whereas the problem of describing the relations among

---

[2]The general study of scale types originated with Stevens (1946, 1951). Further discussion can be found in Suppes and Zinnes (1963) and in Adams, Fagot, and Robinson (1965).

its various solutions is a uniqueness problem. Thus construction of scale values is analogous to solving the equations, whereas the determination of the scale type amounts to describing the degree of uniqueness of the obtained solution.

2.4 THE MEANINGFULNESS PROBLEM

The knowledge of the scale type is important for an adequate interpretation of the scale. Inferences based on scale values should be invariant with respect to admissible transformations of the scale. Similarly, the interpretation and the meaning of various descriptive statistics depend on the scale type. We cannot make justifiable inferences based on comparative statements about means, for instance, unless the relevant properties are measured on, at least, an interval scale. Otherwise, our conclusions will not be invariant with respect to admissible transformations of the scale. Our statements would be true relative to some admissible scales and false with respect to others.

Following Suppes and Zinnes (1963), we define a statement involving numerical values as *formally meaningful* only if its truth (or falsity) is invariant under all admissible transformations of the scale values. Note that this definition depends on the particular measurement models through which the numerical values are obtained. Thus a statement such as "the difference between x and y equals that between y and z" is a formally meaningful statement if the relevant property is measured on an interval scale because its truth value remains unchanged under any linear transformation. If, on the other hand, the relevant property is measured only on an ordinal scale, the statement is not formally meaningful because its truth value can be changed by an (admissible) order-preserving transformation.

A more difficult problem arises with respect to statements involving numerical values for which no explicit measurement model exists. The measurement of intelligence is a case in point. To justify the use of averages, some psychologists have argued that intelligence is measured on an interval scale. Others claimed that the IQ scale is essentially ordinal and that hence no averaging can be justified. A closer examination of the problem reveals that no measurement theory for intelligence is available. Consequently, no representation theorem can be established and no meaning can be given to the uniqueness problem. This does not imply that IQ scores are useless. On the contrary, they may provide an extremely useful and highly informative index. In the absence of a well-defined representation relation, however, the uniqueness problem is not well defined.

What justification can be given, then, to the assignment of numbers to objects that does not follow from some established representation theorem? Without discussing this unexplored issue in detail, three lines of argument are suggested.

1. Prediction. In many situations numerical indices are devised mostly in order to predict some dependent variable on the basis of some independent variables. In these cases one might wish to construct a numerical scale that would maximize the correlation with some external criteria. Thus one can view IQ scores as a weighted combination of several test scores designed to maximize the predictability of intellectual performance. The basic dependent variable, however, typically remains elusive. It seems difficult to define a single measurable dependent variable whose correlation with the IQ scale should be maximized. Thus any decision concerning what to predict involves some serious theoretical considerations. Furthermore, even if the dependent variable (say intelligence) can be properly defined, one would eventually wish to predict it on the basis of some psychological theory (about intelligence) rather than on the basis of some "blind" statistical procedure.

2. Description. In some situations the numbers assigned to the objects are regarded as descriptive statistics, with respect to some sample or population. IQ scores may thus be regarded as percentile ranks relative to the general population. Although such a usage may be both informative and fruitful, it restricts the interpretability of the scale and reduces its theoretical interest. One hopes that as the discipline progresses such scales will be replaced by scales based on explicit assumptions about the underlying psychological process.

3. Direct assignment. Many numerical scales in psychology are not arrived at by a well-established representation relation but instead are generated directly by the subjects according to some specified instructions. Rating scales, category scales, and magnitude estimation scales are examples. Although no measurement models for these scales are developed, they are usually treated as interval or ratio scales. That is, inferences about differences or ratios between stimuli are made, based on the numerical properties of the ratings or the magnitude produced by the subjects.

Consider the method of ratio estimation (Stevens 1951) for example. In this method the subject is presented with stimuli, say tones, and he is instructed to assign a number to each tone describing its loudness, so that if tone x sounds twice as loud as tone y, then the number assigned to x will be twice as large as the number assigned to y. Stated formally, the subject is asked to construct a scale which preserves ratios of the magnitude to be measured (e.g. loudness, utility, pain). The scales arrived at by this method, however, are based on the assumption that the subject can follow the above instructions in a consistent and an unbiased fashion. If the subjects can do so, then the numbers produced by them can be viewed as a valid measurement scale. Indeed, many useful measurement scales in psychology have been constructed in this manner (see Stevens 1957). If, on the other hand, the numbers produced by the subjects fail to preserve perceived ratios, they cannot be treated as a valid scale of ratios.

This assumption, concerning the numbers produced by the subjects, is very different from the assumptions usually made in measurement models. Nevertheless, it has testable consequences that can and should be tested in order to validate the procedure. For example, if x is felt to be twice as heavy as y, which in turn is felt to be three times as heavy as z, then according to the ratio estimation procedure, x should be felt to be six times as heavy as z. Hence, although numbers can be properly assigned to objects even in the absence of a well-defined measurement model, the meaningfulness of the results depends on the validity of the underlying assumptions.

2.5 PSYCHOLOGICAL MEASUREMENT MODELS

The ordinal measurement model described in Sec. 2.2 is weak in the sense that only a few of the properties of the real numbers are used in the representation. Indeed, it has been claimed (Campbell 1920) that measurement of psychological properties cannot advance beyond this stage. Campbell distinguished between two kinds of measurement, called intensive and extensive. The measurement is extensive if it is based on an empirical concatenation operation, such as the juxtaposition of objects in a balance, that corresponds to the arithmetical operation of addition. Otherwise, the measurement is intensive. Campbell argued that only extensive properties can be measured on an interval scale, and since psychological attributes are intensive in nature, no interval scale measurement in psychology is possible. The more recent research in measurement theory has shown, however, that the existence of an empirical concatenation operation is not necessary for an interval scale measurement, contrary to Campbell's views. Indeed, several psychological models that yield an interval scale measurement have been developed in recent years.

In this section we present three psychological measurement models: semiorder, bisection, and additive conjoint measurement. The axioms of each model are discussed, and the resulting representation and uniqueness theorems are stated (without proofs). Some general remarks concerning the axiomatic approach to measurement are postponed until Sec. 2.6.

Semiorders

Our earlier discussion revealed that in order to represent equality and inequality relations between objects by the corresponding relations between numbers both observable relations should satisfy transitivity. In many situations, however, observed equality relations fail to be transitive. An object x may be judged as heavy as object y, which, in turn, is judged as heavy as object z, yet x may be judged heavier than z. Such judgments are likely to occur whenever the differences (in weight) between x and y and between y and z are too small to be noticed, yet their combined effect is large enough to render the difference between x and z noticeable. Put differently, the pairs (x, y) and (y, z) are less than a just noticeable difference (or a jnd) apart. The difference between x and z, on the other hand, may very well exceed a jnd, thus giving rise to an intransitivity. Because any measuring instrument has a limited sensitivity, this phenomenon is as likely to occur in physical measurement based on a pan balance as in psychological measurement based on subjective judgments of equal weight.

To accommodate this reality, Luce (1956) introduced the concept of a semiorder as a natural generalization of a full order. The present discussion of semiorders follows the development of Scott and Suppes (1958). A *semiorder* is a relational system $\langle A, P \rangle$, where A is an object set and P is a binary relation on A (interpreted as a strict inequality) satisfying the following three assumptions for all x, y, z, w, in A.

S1
Not $x\,P\,x$.

S2
If $x\,P\,y$ and $z\,P\,w$, then either $x\,P\,w$ or $z\,P\,y$.

S3
If $x\,P\,y$ and $y\,P\,z$, then either $x\,P\,w$ or $w\,P\,z$.

In terms of our example, P is interpreted as the relation "heavier than." The first axiom asserts that no object is heavier than itself. The next two assumptions specify properties of P, which follow from interpreting $x\,P\,y$ as: x is greater than y by at least one jnd. A geometric illustration of S3 may clarify its meaning. Let x, y, and z be three points on a line that, according to the hypothesis of S3, are separated by at least one jnd from each other. It is required, then, that for any w whatsoever either $x\,P\,w$ or $w\,P\,z$. The four different positions that can be occupied by w are denoted in Fig. 2.1 by w_1, w_2, w_3, and w_4. It is quite easy to see that for w_1 and w_2 we obtain $w_1\,P\,z$ and $w_2\,P\,z$, whereas for w_3 and w_4 we obtain $x\,P\,w_3$ and $x\,P\,w_4$. The reader is invited to construct the similar geometric illustration for S2.

Note that the semiorder is defined in terms of the "greater than" relations

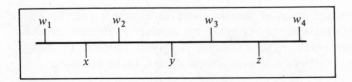

Fig. 2.1

(*P*) only. We can easily define the equality relation (*I*) in the semiorder by

$$x \, I \, y \quad \text{if and only if} \quad \text{neither } x \, P \, y \text{ nor } y \, P \, x.$$

This relation (*I*) is clearly reflexive (*x I x*) and symmetric (*x I y* implies *y I x*), but, as one might expect, it need not be transitive. It is possible, however, to define another relation (*E*), in terms of *I*, that is transitive. This can be done by defining

$$x \, E \, y \quad \text{whenever for any } z \text{ in } A \quad x \, I \, z \quad \text{if and only if} \quad y \, I \, z.$$

Stated in terms of the weight judgment example, an object *x* is said to stand in the relation *E* to an object *y* whenever all the objects (*z*) that are judged as heavy as *x* are also judged as heavy as *y*. It is easy to verify that the new relation (*E*) is, indeed, transitive. Hence, although the observed equality judgments are not transitive, it is possible to extract from them a transitive equality relation. Furthermore, by an appropriate selection of *z* one can obtain an arbitrarily fine ordering of the elements of *A* despite the fact that the given ordering orders only stimuli that are at least one jnd apart. Consequently, under the semiorder assumptions one can achieve practically infinite discriminability (in principle, at least) from apparently insensitive data. The numerical representation of a semiorder is described in theorem 2.2.

THEOREM 2.2

Let $\langle A, P \rangle$ be a semiorder, defined by S1–S3, with a finite object set *A*. Then there exists a function *f* and a positive number δ such that for all *x*, *y* in *A*

$$f(x) > f(y) + \delta \quad \text{if and only if} \quad x \, P \, y.$$

The interpretation of δ is as a single jnd unit. It is interesting to note that under the semiorder axioms one obtains a numerical representation where the size of the jnd unit is constant throughout the scale. The uniqueness properties of this representation are quite difficult to characterize. For a discussion of these problems, the reader is referred to the papers of Luce (1956) and Scott and Suppes (1958). An empirical application of the semiorder idea is discussed in Sec. 5.3.

Bisection systems Although no natural empirical addition operation arises in psychology, there are several contexts in which the subject is asked to produce a stimulus that is (subjectively) halfway between two given stimuli with respect to some specified attribute. The stimuli might be tones varying in sound intensity, for example, and the subject is asked to adjust a variable tone until its subjective loudness "bisects" the loudness of a fixed pair of tones. Alternatively, the subject can be presented with various variable tones and asked to judge whether the variable tone is above or below the bisection point between a fixed pair of tones. The stimulus which is judged to be above the bisection point and below it an equal number of times (i.e., the 50 percent point on the psychometric function) is taken as the bisection point. The next model, developed by Pfanzagl (1968) uses a psychological bisection operation, which is analogous to the physical concatenation operation used in the classical physical measurement of weight and length.

We start with an object set A, which is weakly ordered (by $\gtrsim$) with respect to some attribute, and such that for any x, y in A there exists a unique element $B(x, y)$ in A that is interpreted as the bisection point between x and y. Such a system is called a *bisection system* if, in addition, the following four axioms are satisfied for all x, y, z, w in A.

B1   REFLEXIVITY:

$B(x, x) = x.$

B2   MONOTONICITY:

$x \gtrsim y$ implies $B(x, z) \gtrsim B(y, z).$

B3   CONTINUITY:

B is continuous in both of its arguments.

B4   BISYMMETRY:

$B(B(w, x), B(y, z)) = B(B(w, y), B(x, z)).$

We turn now to the interpretation of the axioms. Reflexivity states that whenever the two end points coincide, their midpoint coincides with them. The monotonicity axiom asserts that if x is louder than y, for example, then the midpoint between x and z, $B(x, z)$, must be louder than the midpoint between y and z, $B(y, z)$, for any z. The third axiom is a continuity requirement. Its precise formulation calls for topological notions but its intuitive interpretation is rather straightforward.

The main assumption of this model is the bisymmetry axiom, which requires that the bisections of the respective bisection points coincide. A geometric illustration of the bisymmetry axiom is given in Fig. 2.2.

Note that this axiom is directly testable with any four distinct stimuli. To do so, one instructs the subject first to bisect the pairs (w, x) and (y, z) and then to bisect the resulting bisection points. The obtained stimulus should coincide with that obtained by first bisecting the pairs (w, y) and (x, z) and then bisecting the resulting bisection points. It is important to

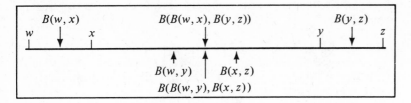

Fig. 2.2

note that the bisection operation need not be symmetric. That is, $B(x, y)$ need not coincide with $B(y, x)$. Consequently, the theory can handle order or position biases, called hysteresis effects, that are commonly found in bisection experiments (see Stevens 1957).

The following representation for bisection systems has been established by Pfanzagl (1968).

THEOREM 2.3

Given a bisection system, defined by B1–B4, there exists a function f such that for all x, y in A

1. $f(x) \geq f(y)$ if and only if $x \succsim y$.
2. $f[B(x, y)] = pf(x) + qf(y)$, where $p + q = 1$; $p, q \geq 0$.

The theorem guarantees that, given B1–B4, one can construct a numerical scale such that (1) the order of the stimuli is preserved by their scale values, and such that (2) the scale value assigned to the bisection point is a weighted average of the scale values of the end points. The weights (p and q) reflect a position bias toward the first or the second end point. Thus, if $p > 1/2$, the bisection point is biased toward the first end point, whereas for $p < 1/2$ the bisection point is biased toward the second end point. The uniqueness properties of the representation are described in the following uniqueness theorem.

THEOREM 2.4

f is an interval scale.

That is, for any function g satisfying the above representation theorem for a bisection system, there exist numbers b, and $a > 0$ such that for all x in A

$$g(x) = af(x) + b.$$

To shed some light on the meaning of the bisymmetry axiom, we show that it is a necessary condition for the existence of the desired representation.

Assume there exists a function f satisfying parts (1) and (2) of the representation theorem. Hence

$$
\begin{aligned}
f[B(B(w, x), B(y, z))] &= pf[B(w, x)]+qf[B(y, z)] \\
&= p[pf(w)+qf(x)]+q[pf(y)+qf(z)] \\
&= p^2f(w)+pqf(x)+pqf(y)+q^2f(z) \\
&= p[pf(w)+qf(y)]+q[pf(x)+qf(z)] \\
&= pf[B(w, y)]+qf[B(x, z)] \\
&= f[B(B(w, y), B(x, z))]
\end{aligned}
$$

and because f is order-preserving, by (1),

$$
B(B(w, x), B(y, z)) = B(B(w, y), B(x, z)),
$$

which is precisely the bisymmetry axiom. It can easily be shown that the reflexivity (B1) and the monotonicity (B2) axioms are also derivable from the desired representation. The most significant result, however, is that these three necessary conditions together with the continuity of the bisection operation are sufficient to obtain an interval scale measurement of the underlying psychological variable.

TABLE 2.1   Intensity (in decibels SPL) of Obtained Bisection Points for Subject 1

	Session			
	I	II	III	IV
$B(65, 75)$	72.3	74.4	74.0	74.3
$B(80, 90)$	87.3	87.0	87.4	87.6
$B(65, 80)$	74.6	78.6	77.3	76.8
$B(75, 90)$	84.5	86.8	86.3	87.1
$B[B(65, 75), B(80, 90)]$	83.0	84.0	83.5	83.7
$B[B(65, 80), B(75, 90)]$	81.5	84.5	83.7	83.5

	Session			
	V	VI	VII	VIII
$B(75, 65)$	70.9	70.4	72.3	72.2
$B(90, 80)$	86.1	86.3	85.5	85.5
$B(80, 65)$	72.9	74.0	75.6	75.9
$B(90, 75)$	81.3	83.5	84.4	81.7
$BB(90, 80), B(75, 65)]$	78.3	78.5	79.5	79.8
$B[B(90, 75), B(80, 65)]$	79.0	79.0	80.0	79.9

An empirical investigation of the bisection model, including a direct experimental test of the bisymmetry axiom, was conducted by Cross (1965). The stimuli were pure tones that vary in intensity only. The subject was presented with a pair of tones and was asked to bisect them by selecting a third tone produced by adjusting an appropriate knob. That is, the subject was instructed to set the knob such that the third tone would lie halfway between the two given tones. The subject first bisected several pairs of tones and the intensities of the obtained bisection points were recorded. These tones were then presented to the subject and bisected in order to test the bisymmetry axiom. In sessions I–IV the tones were always presented in an increasing order (i.e., the louder tone last), whereas in sessions V–VIII the order was reversed. The intensities (measured in decibels SPL) of the tones presented, as well as those of the bisection tones obtained in all eight sessions for one subject are shown in Table 2.1. Note that the last two values in each of the eight columns should be equal under the bisymmetry axiom. The data show that in every session, except for the first, bisymmetry holds to a satisfactory degree of approximation. Finally, a small but consistent hysteresis effect is observed in the data. The bisection settings were higher for increasing order than for decreasing order in all cases.

Additive Conjoint Measurement

The absence of a natural concatenation (or even bisection) operation in many areas of psychology has led to the development of measurement models of a different kind. These models are based on a paradigm where an ordering of a dependent variable is obtained under different combinations of two (or more) independent variables. Learning rate, for example, may be studied under various combinations of deprivation periods and reward magnitudes, loudness judgments may be obtained for tones varying in intensity and frequency, or preferences may be observed for alternative job offers varying in interest and salary. In all these examples one investigates the joint effects of several factors on some observed response measure. It turns out that for sufficiently rich empirical systems of this type a simple axiomatization in terms of the ordinal properties of the joint effects of two (or more) factors yields an interval scale measurement of the additive type. Luce and Tukey (1964) refer to such measurement as simultaneous conjoint measurement to emphasize the fact that the dependent and the independent variables are measured simultaneously.

Let $A \times P$ be a weakly ordered product set (obtained from a two-way factorial experiment, for example) with typical elements (a, p), (b, q), with a, b in A and p, q in P. Alternatively, $A \times P$ can be viewed as a data matrix, where $M(a, p)$ is some (ordinal) measure of the effect of the (a, p) treatment combination. Such a data matrix is said to be *additive* or to have an *additive representation* if there exist functions f, g, and ϕ defined on A, P and $A \times P$, respectively, such that

1. $\phi(a, p) = f(a) + g(p)$.
2. $\phi(a, p) \geq \phi(b, q)$ if and only if $M(a, p) \geq M(b, q)$.

Thus a data matrix is said to be additive if its cell entries can be rescaled such that their order is preserved and such that every rescaled entry is expressed as the sum of its row and column components. If such a representation exists, the two factors can be regarded as independent in the sense that they contribute independently (or additively) to produce the joint effect.

The notion of an additive representation is related to the absence of interactions in the analysis of variance. The essential difference is that in testing for the absence of a significant interaction in a two-way analysis of variance, for example, one asks whether the *given* scale values, or cell means, can be described as an additive combination of their row and column components. In the present additive model, on the other hand, one asks whether the given scale values can be monotonically *transformed* such that additivity would be satisfied by the transformed cell entries. In applying the present additive model, one is looking, in effect, for that order-preserving transformation of the data with respect to which additivity holds. In general, such a transformation need not exist; however, it does exist if the following two axioms are satisfied.

A1   CANCELLATION

For all a, b, c in A and p, q, r in P, if $M(a, q) \geq M(b, p)$ and $M(b, r) \geq M(c, q)$, then $M(a, r) \geq M(c, p)$.

A2   SOLVABILITY

If $M(a, p') \geq t \geq M(a, p'')$ for some real t, then there exists a p in P such that $M(a, p) = t$. Similarly, if $M(a', p) \geq t \geq M(a'', p)$ for some real t, then there exists an a in A such that $M(a, p) = t$.

A graphic illustration of the cancellation axiom is given in Fig. 2.3, where the arrows indicate the ordering. Fig. 2.3 suggests how to design an empirical test of the cancellation axiom. To clarify the meaning of A1, we

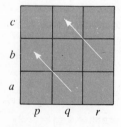
Implies
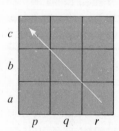

Fig. 2.3

show that it is a necessary condition for additivity. Assume additivity holds; hence, by the hypotheses of A1

$$f(a)+g(q) \geq f(b)+g(p)$$

and

$$f(b)+g(r) \geq f(c)+g(q).$$

Adding the two inequalities and subtracting $f(b)+g(q)$ from both sides yield

$$f(a)+g(r) \geq f(c)+g(p) \quad \text{or} \quad \phi(a,r) \geq \phi(c,p)$$

and because ϕ is order-preserving, by assumption, we obtain $M(a, r) \geq M(c, p)$ as required.

Further insight into the nature of the cancellation axiom can be gained by interpreting the model in terms of differences rather than sums. Under the additive model

$$M(a,q) \geq M(b,p) \quad \text{if and only if} \quad f(a)+g(q) \geq f(b)+g(p),$$

which is equivalent to $f(a)-g(p) \geq f(b)-g(q)$.

The observation $M(a,q) \geq M(b,p)$ may thus be interpreted as asserting that the psychological difference, or the interval, between a and p is at least as large as that between b and q. Under the same interpretation $M(b, r) \geq M(c, q)$ implies that the interval between b and q is at least as large as that between c and r, and, finally, the conclusion of the cancellation axiom, $M(a, r) \geq M(c, p)$, implies that the interval between a and p is at least as large as that between c and r. Hence, in this interpretation, the cancellation axiom reduces to the familiar transitivity axiom, applied to the ordering of intervals. (Note the similarity between the above interpretation of the additive model and the measurement model for utility intervals discussed in Sec. 2.1.)

The solvability axiom A2 requires both factors, A and P, to be sufficiently dense such that, for a fixed level (a) on one factor, if $M(a, p') \geq M(a, p'')$ and t is some number between them, then there exists a level p for which $M(a, p) = t$. Although solvability is not necessary for additivity, it is likely to be satisfied (to a sufficiently high degree of approximation) in a variety of situations, particularly where the dependent variable is regarded as a continuous function of the independent variables. Some minor modifications[3] of theorems of Debreu (1960) and Luce and Tukey (1964) yield the following result.

[3]The present axiomatization differs slightly from those of Debreu (1960) or Luce and Tukey (1964) in that it is formulated in terms of a numerical (ordinal) scale M rather than in terms of purely qualitative properties. Introducing such a numerical (ordinal) scale, however, simplifies the statement of the axioms.

THEOREM 2.5

Any data matrix satisfying A1 and A2 has an additive representation that is unique up to a positive linear transformation. That is, if A1 and A2 hold, there exist functions f and g such that for all a, b in A and p, q in P,

$$f(a)+g(p) \geq f(b)+g(q) \quad \text{if and only if} \quad M(a, p) \geq M(b, q).$$

Furthermore, given any f' and g' satisfying the above equation, there exist constants u, v, and $t > 0$ such that for all a in A and p in P $f'(a) = tf(a)+u$ and $g'(p) = tg(p)+v$ (i.e., f and g are interval scales with a common unit).

It is interesting to note that one obtains an additive measurement scale in the absence of any physical concatenation operation. The numerical addition represents the combination of the two treatments, which are, so to speak, added inside the organism.

The additive conjoint measurement model has been applied to several areas of psychology and in particular to the study of choice behavior as described in Sec. 5.2. A direct test of the cancellation axiom has been performed by Coombs and Komorita (1958) in studying preferences among gambles. In this experiment three subjects were asked to choose among gambles of the form (a, p) where one has a 50:50 chance of winning \$$a$ or losing \$$p$. The major purpose of the study was to test the hypothesis that preferences among such gambles can be expressed as an additive combination of their positive and negative outcomes (i.e., of their win and lose components). Four series of gambles were constructed and each subject chose among the gambles within each of the series. All the gambles (except two) used in the experiment are shown in Table 2.2, where each gamble is designated by a letter (from A to H) with a subscript indicating its series.

TABLE 2.2   FOUR SERIES OF GAMBLES USED IN THE TEST OF CANCELLATION CONDUCTED BY COOMBS AND KOMORITA (1958)

	Lose	0	0.60	1.20	1.80	2.40	3.00	3.60	4.20	4.80	5.40
	4.20								H_1	H_4	
	3.60							G_1	G_4	H_2	H_3
	3.00						F_1	F_4	G_2	G_3	
	2.40					E_1	E_4	F_2	F_3		
	1.80				D_1	D_4	E_2	E_3			
Lose	1.20			C_1	C_4	D_2	D_3				
	0.60		B_1	B_4	C_2	C_3					
	0	A_1	A_4	B_2	B_3						

(Win)

It is evident from Table 2.2 that if additivity (and hence cancellation) holds then some preferences must be determined by others. For example, if B_1 is preferred to C_1 and B_2 is preferred to C_2, then, by cancellation, A_4 must be preferred to C_4. These predictions were tested by comparing the preferences obtained in series 4 to the preferences predicted, via cancellation, from the other three series. The results showed that (except for a single violation) the subjects always preferred the less risky gambles (i.e., those with lower wins and losses) in all the series. Consequently, the cancellation axiom was satisfied in 29 out of 30 cases where it was tested. If one assumes that solvability is satisfied in this context, then these data provide strong support for the additive model.

2.6 CONCLUDING COMMENTS

Measurement is viewed as a representation of an empirical relational system by a numerical relational system. The essence of such a representation is the assignment of numbers to objects in such a way that the observed relations among objects are reflected by the corresponding relations among the numbers assigned to them. The two fundamental problems of measurement theory are (1) the representation problem of showing that a numerical representation exists and (2) the uniqueness problem of characterizing the relationships among the existing numerical representations.

The representation problem has two facets, a formal one and an empirical one. The formal problem is that of stating testable assumptions that are necessary and/or sufficient to obtain the desired numerical representation. The formal analysis of the representation problem produces axiom systems for measurement models and yields methods for constructing numerical representations, provided these axioms are satisfied. The empirical phase of the investigation is aimed at testing these axioms and constructing the scales.

One can distinguish between two general types of axioms, with respect to their experimental testability. Axioms of the first type are called *simple* (or universal) axioms, and they are necessary for the desired representation. They assert something about the relation among several observations and are directly testable. Transitivity, bisymmetry, and cancellation are examples of such simple (or universal) axioms.

Axioms of the second type are called *existential* axioms because they postulate the existence of elements with certain specified properties. Continuity and solvability are examples of existential axioms. Such axioms may be viewed as regularity conditions in the sense that they are not "essential" to the model although they play an important role in the proofs. Specific experimental investigations, therefore, are likely to focus on the examination of the simple axioms. The existential axioms are more likely to be accepted or rejected on the basis of general considerations.

The main contribution of the axiomatic method to the measurement problem lies in its ability to isolate critical properties for an experimental investigation and to reveal the structure that underlies a given numerical representation. One might further argue that the discovery of the structural assumptions underlying the phenomena is the basic goal of science and that measurement is "only" a consequence of these assumptions. In this sense measurement is a by-product of theory. Only when the assumptions of the theory are satisfied by the data can measurement be obtained.

chapter

3

SCALING AND DATA THEORY

3.1 RELATIONS TO MEASUREMENT THEORY

Measurement theory is concerned with the conditions under which various types of scales can be constructed. The actual process of assigning numbers to objects, or properties, is called scaling. There are three major reasons for discussing scaling in addition to but apart from measurement. First, the axiomatic analysis of measurement models does not always provide feasible methods for constructing scales. For example, one may verify the axioms of the additive conjoint measurement model (see Chapter 2) without knowing how to obtain the additive scales. To do so, special methods have to be devised.

Second, rarely (if ever) are measurement models satisfied exactly. Even in the absence of any systematic violations of the axioms, some departures from the model are almost always present. Such departures may be attributable to the imperfection of our observations or procedures or to some other uncontrolled factor. Such departures are referred to as error or noise. Their presence, however, renders the scaling problem considerably more complicated. To construct a scale from noisy data, one needs a scaling method that "removes" the error and provides means of estimating the "true" scale values.

Third, axiomatic foundations for many psychological measurement models have not been developed. These models are formulated, therefore, in terms of the desired numerical representation rather than in terms of axioms from which the representation is derived. To test such models, one attempts to construct the scales and test their internal consistency and their predictive power. Indeed, a scaling method can be treated in two ways: as a technique and as a criterion.

When a scaling method is applied as a technique, it assumes some particular measurement model. Departures from the model are regarded as random fluctuations or observational errors, and the purpose of the scaling is to find numbers that provide the "best" fit between the model and the data in the presence of some error. The concept of best fit is usually defined in terms of some error function to be minimized, e.g., the sum of squared deviations in the method of least squares. When a scaling method is applied as a criterion, it is employed as a method of testing the descriptive validity of some measurement model. The purpose of the scaling in this case is to discover whether the data can be fitted by the model.

Consequently, when a scaling procedure is used as a technique, it tends to be insensitive to error as it is designed to yield numerical scale values regardless of whether the measurement model is satisfied or not. In contrast, when a scaling procedure is used as a criterion, it tends to be sensitive to error because its main objective is to detect departures from the theory. A scaling method can, clearly, be used both as a technique and as a criterion.

It should be noted that although the terms *measurement* and *scaling* have been sometimes used interchangeably in the literature, we have chosen to distinguish between them. To structure the discussion of scaling and its relations to observational data and to measurement theories, we introduce a simple classification system called *data theory*. This system offers a suggestive organization of the domain of measurement and scaling and provides a basis for selecting representative scaling methods.

3.2 DATA THEORY

Many measurement models in the behavioral sciences are based on geometric representations of the observed behavior. Frequently this geometric representation is a one-dimensional scale but it need not be, and multidimensional representations are becoming more common. The points on these scales or in these spaces may represent individuals or stimuli or both, and the relations among the points reflect the observations according to some rule.

We shall now draw two distinctions, each of these a dichotomy, so in conjunction they yield four classes. Because all behavioral observations and scaling theories fall into one of these classes, certain similarities and differences become apparent. The first distinction we shall draw has to do with the kind of relation that is observed between objects.

An observation of a relation between two objects falls into one of only two classes: an order (dominance) relation or a proximity (consonance) relation. For example, order relations are exemplified by an individual's judgment that one tone is louder than another, or that one handwriting specimen is more legible than another or the observation that one chicken pecks another chicken or that one tennis player beats another tennis player. Proximity relations are exemplified by an individual's judgment that two tones match, that one color is like another color, and that a particular cigarette tastes like another and, in general, by responses that indicate two stimuli are similar or confusable.

Such observations as the above may be displayed in a square matrix with each object represented by a row and the corresponding column. A cell of the matrix would contain the observation, coded in some form, for example, a *one* to indicate that the row object dominated the column object and a *zero* to indicate the reverse. A consonant or dissonant relation could be similarly represented. Of course, the cell entries are not limited to such coarse categories; for example, the most common proximity matrix is a correlation matrix where the cell entry is a measure of proximity. There are also circumstances in which measures of amplitude or latency could be interpreted as proximity relations (for a fuller discussion of these measures, see Coombs 1964, p. 526).

We have made one dichotomous classification of real world observations into dominance and proximity relations, and we shall now see that independently of this classification we may make another dichotomous one.

Observations are sometimes made between members of the same set and sometimes are made only between members of different sets. All the instances above, for example, could be classified as reflecting relations between elements of the same set. As an illustration of an observation that may be represented as an order relation between elements of different sets, consider an individual's response, pass or fail, to an arithmetic problem. The two real world elements here are the difficulty of the problem and the individual's ability, and the observation, pass or fail, reflects an order (dominance) relation between them.

Attempts to measure an individual's sensory threshold may yield the same kind of data. The sensory input may be mapped into a point on an intensity axis and the subject's response indicating that he detected or failed to detect the signal is represented as an order relation between the input point and a point corresponding to the individual's momentary threshold. There are many other examples of behavior represented as an order relation between points from distinct sets, and we shall have another example later when we illustrate a scaling model for such data.

Examples of proximity (or consonance) relations between elements of distinct sets are also readily found. An individual's willingness to endorse certain attitude statements and not others may be represented this way. The individual and each of the attitude statements may be regarded as corresponding to points on an attitude continuum from pro to con. The point for the individual corresponds to a hypothetical ideal statement that precisely describes his attitude; his endorsement of an attitude statement implies that the point corresponding to the statement is in the proximity of his ideal point.

All instances of labeling are examples of proximity relations between objects in distinct sets, e.g., psychiatric classifications of patients, efficiency ratings of foremen, the classification of paintings as renaissance, modern, etc. In each such instance the correspondence could be between a set of points corresponding to the response categories and a set of points corresponding to the objects to be classified. The matching of a point in one set with a point in the other reflects their relative "nearness" or proximity.

Such observations as these could be entered into a matrix, but because the objects are from two distinct sets, the elements identifying rows and columns would be different, so of course the matrix would not necessarily be square, as, for example, if there were more individuals than arithmetic problems.

There is a relation between the data matrix for elements of one set and that for elements of two sets that is useful to recognize as it implies a relation between corresponding measurement theories and scaling models. If we took a square data matrix and divided the objects into two distinct subsets of m elements in one and n elements in the other, we could describe the submatrix formed with the m elements as rows and the n elements as columns as an $m \times n$ off-diagonal submatrix of the intact matrix (Fig. 3.1). Therefore, the data based on two sets of objects may be viewed as a special case of that based on one set of objects, as if, in a very particular way, all the data were not collected (i.e., no within-set relations were observed). As a con-

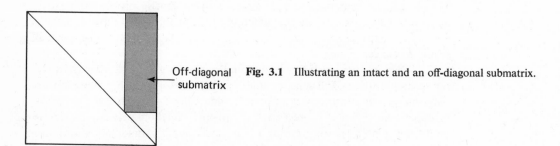

Off-diagonal   **Fig. 3.1**   Illustrating an intact and an off-diagonal submatrix.
submatrix

Intact matrix

	Dominance matrix	Proximity matrix
Two sets: the off-diagonal submatrix	Quadrant II Single stimulus	Quadrant I Preferential choice
One set: the intact matrix	Quadrant III Stimulus comparison	Quadrant IV Similarities

Fig. 3.2 Four quadrants of the theory of data.

sequence a model designed for one of these data matrices is potentially adaptable to the other kind.

At this point we have two kinds of matrices, dominance and proximity, and we see that either kind may be an intact or off-diagonal submatrix, corresponding, respectively, to whether the observed relation is between elements of the same set or between elements of two distinct sets.

In Fig. 3.2 we have portrayed this four-fold classification in terms of quadrants, and in each quadrant we have indicated the type of behavior with which it is commonly identified.

However, the same behavioral observations may be classified in different quadrants according to one's "theory" about the behavior. Suppose, for example, each member of a tennis club lists the other members he likes to play tennis with. One individual may list those he thinks he can beat and another may list those who would give him a good game—in one case the behavior is represented by a dominance relation and in the other by a proximity relation.

With respect to the other dimension of whether we wish to represent the real world elements with one or two sets of points, it might seem at first blush that there is only one set of points, the members of the tennis club. But some individual member's self-estimates may not match the estimates made by their fellow members, if, for example, they are overmodest or have an overinflated opinion of themselves.

In this case each individual should be represented by two points, one corresponding to his self-conception and the other corresponding to the evaluation of him by his fellow members, as a respondent and as a stimulus for others to respond to.

Therefore, the observations might all be recorded in a matrix but no analysis could be made until a theoretical position was taken as to whether there were one or two sets of points and whether the relation was one of dominance or proximity.

This version of the Theory of Data (Coombs 1964) is a simplified and abbreviated form which, though it leaves some gaps, does cover the most important kinds of data matrices in behavioral science. We have chosen to present below at least one representative and significant scaling model to illustrate the analysis of each kind of data matrix, but of course we have neglected some very important scaling theories. Fortunately more complete treatments are available in Torgerson (1958) and Coombs (1964).

Because of the small sample of existing scaling theories to be presented here, some wider perspective of the domain is in order. Until as late as the end of World War II the only kinds of data matrices for which scaling theory had been constructed are those described above. There were sporadic instances of observations that could be differently classified, but this possibility was generally unrecognized. Indeed it would be fair to say that only two of the above four kinds of data matrices had been given substantial attention. These two were the two kinds of dominance matrices—the intact and its off-diagonal submatrix, Quadrants III and II, respectively.

The predominant model for the analysis of the intact matrix, Quadrant III, with proportions in the cells, is Thurstone's law of comparative judgment (1927a), so it has been chosen for presentation here; but an alternative theory that appeared in 1959 (Luce 1959) should be mentioned because it is playing a substantial role in behavior theory (see Sec. 5.3). We have chosen to illustrate the application of Thurstone's model by repeating a study of social values he made 40 years earlier.

Interest in the dominance off-diagonal submatrix, Quadrant II, was most evident among psychometricians concerned with measuring abilities and aptitudes and psychophysicists concerned with measuring thresholds. During World War II, however, Louis Guttman (1944) developed what has come to be known as scalogram analysis for this Quadrant II data matrix, and his model has had very extensive use in the behavioral sciences, particularly the social sciences. We have chosen scalogram analysis for discussion here and shall illustrate it with an application made in World War II.

Before 1950 the only proximity matrix for which scaling theory had been constructed was the special case of the correlation matrix, an intact proximity matrix, Quadrant IV. Charles Spearman initiated the development of factor analytic theory in 1904 as a theory of intelligence and was followed by his countryman Cyril Burt, by Godfrey Thomson in Scotland, and by Kelley, Holzinger, and Thurstone in this country.

Since 1950 methods have been developed for the analysis of the off-diagonal submatrix of the proximity matrix, Quadrant I, preferential choice. The method that will be presented and illustrated here is unfolding theory. The crucial idea in this method, and in all the later developments of methods for analysis of proximity matrices, is the interpretation of proximity data as relations on *distances*.

Unfolding theory was designed initially as a theory of preferential choice behavior (Coombs 1950) and so it was concerned with the analysis of order relations in the data rather than metricized data such as test scores;

these order relations are on "distances." An individual and an attitude statement, for example, are represented in unfolding theory by points, an ideal point for the individual and a point for the item. The individual's endorsement of a statement is represented by the distances between the two points being less than some critical amount that is serving as the momentary threshold for the response. An individual's endorsement of one item in preference to another is represented as an order relation on the relative proximity of two points to the ideal point and hence an order relation on distances.

A data matrix with individuals as rows and with stimuli as columns and with cells containing a response measure representing a proximity measure will yield for each individual the rank order of the distances of the stimulus points from an ideal point, i.e., his preference ordering. This is why Quadrant I data are interpreted as preferential choice.

Unfolding theory is a scaling theory designed to construct a space with two sets of points, one set for the individuals and one set for the objects of choice, the stimuli; the individual's preference orderings are reflected in the order relations on the distances between corresponding points.

Since 1952 the development of methods for analysis of the intact proximity matrix, Quadrant IV, similarities data, has been intense. Torgerson's thesis in 1952 extended the application of factor analysis to a proximity matrix in which the cells contained interpoint distances presumed to be measured at the level of an interval scale, that is, distances are preserved or recoverable up to a linear transformation. The factor analysis of correlation coefficients is equivalent to measuring interpoint distances at the level of a ratio scale, i.e., distance is preserved up to multiplication by a positive constant. Note that a correlation matrix is symmetric and Torgerson's method requires that the matrix of interpoint distances be symmetric.

Then in 1962 Shepard presented the first computerized iterative procedure for the analysis of an intact proximity matrix in which the interpoint distances were measured only at the level of an ordinal scale, i.e. distances are recoverable only up to a monotone transformation. "Since then Torgerson and Meuser, Kruskal (1964), and Guttman and Lingoes have all developed what each considers to be an improvement over the original Shepard program" (Torgerson 1965).

Because of the rapid development and current fluid state of these methods, no one of them will be presented in detail but general characteristics and common properties and problems will be discussed and an application presented.

All these methods were originally designed for the intact symmetric proximity matrix. There is another and very common form of the intact proximity matrix called a conditional proximity matrix that is not necessarily symmetric. Both of these matrices will be discussed in detail in Sec. 3.4.

A method particularly designed for the analysis of the conditional proximity matrix was developed by Hays, who extended multidimensional unfolding for this purpose. The method is applicable to the symmetric proximity matrix and was illustrated by an application to such a matrix on Morse Code data by Coombs (1958). Hays's method has since been more fully developed and is described in Coombs (1964).

Hays's method is weaker than any of the computerized iterative procedures whenever they are applicable, as it preserves only the rank order of distances within triangles, i.e., for all triples of points, corresponding to a partial order of the interpoint distances that is more general than the simple order of the interpoint distances representing the symmetric proximity matrix. The partial order of distances, however, is the appropriate level of measurement for the conditional proximity matrix.

Hays's method will also be briefly described and illustrated with an application.

In Sec. 3.3 we shall begin with the simplest data, Quadrant II, and proceed through Quadrants III, I, and IV in that order.

3.3   THE DOMINANCE MATRIX

Guttman Scalogram Analysis for Quadrant II Data

This method may serve as a criterion to test the hypothesis of a one-dimensional latent attribute mediating the behavior, or, of course, it may serve as a scaling technique. Because it is a highly vulnerable method, the pure form is rarely observed with real data.

The data matrix has individuals as rows and stimuli or items as columns. Each cell of the matrix contains a 1 if the row individual "dominated" the column stimulus; otherwise it contains a zero. Figure 3.3(a) illustrates a hypothetical data matrix of six individuals and five stimuli.

Let c_i and q_j designate points associated with individual i and stimulus j, respectively. Then the model's basic axiom is

	B	C	A	E	D
2	0	0	1	0	0
4	1	1	1	0	0
1	0	0	0	0	0
5	1	1	1	0	1
3	1	0	1	0	0
6	1	1	1	1	1

	A	B	C	D	E
1	0	0	0	0	0
2	1	0	0	0	0
3	1	1	0	0	0
4	1	1	1	0	0
5	1	1	1	1	0
6	1	1	1	1	0

(a)   (b)

Fig. 3.3 Hypothetical data matrix and the scalogram solution.

$$c_i \geq q_j \quad \text{iff} \quad i \succcurlyeq j, \tag{3.1}$$

where $i \succcurlyeq j$ signifies the generic observation that "i is not dominated by j" in some empirical sense.

Clearly, if an individual passes one item, say j, and fails another, say k, then q_k, the point associated with the latter item, is "above" q_j by transitivity, $q_k \geq c_i \geq q_j$, and transitivity is a necessary condition for a one-dimensional attribute to mediate the behavior.

Of course, this condition of transitivity cannot be violated by one individual but must be tested across individuals. If there were another individual, for example, who passed item k and failed j, then this behavior would be inconsistent with the first individual's behavior and the model would be violated.

These conditions, *transitivity* and *consistency*, are necessary and sufficient to construct a joint ordering of the items and the individuals (strictly speaking, the elements of the ordering are equivalence classes based on identity of response patterns). This ordering reflects the fact that the weakest individual fails all the items, the one next in ability passes only the easiest item, and so on, to the strongest individual who passes them all. The algorithm Guttman provided for testing these conditions involves permuting the rows and permuting the columns of the data matrix to seek a triangular pattern, as in Fig. 3.3(b). Here the items would be in the order A to E from easy to difficult with the six classes of individuals alternating in the joint order as follows: 1 A 2 B 3 C 4 D 5 E 6.

In most instances of real data this pattern is at best only approximated. Some indication of the degree of approximation is given by a coefficient of reproducibility, the proportion of cells that fit the perfect pattern. The statistical theory of this coefficient is unfortunately quite incomplete and only rule-of-thumb standards are in common use, such as a coefficient of .90 being referred to as "good."

A significant instance of an application of the model is reported by Suchman (see Stouffer et al. 1950) in a study of the fear symptoms of U.S. soldiers when interviewed after being withdrawn from combat (World War II). The questions and instructions were as follows:

Soldiers who have been under fire report different *physical reactions to the dangers of battle*. Some of these are given in the following list. How often have you had these reactions when you were under fire? *Check one answer after each of the reactions listed to show how often you had the reaction.* Please do it carefully.

1. Violent pounding of the heart
2. Sinking feeling of the stomach
3. Feeling of weakness or feeling faint
4. Feeling sick at the stomach

5. Cold sweat
6. Vomiting
7. Shaking or trembling all over
8. Urinating in pants
9. Losing control of the bowels
10. Feeling of stiffness

For each of the items, administered in the above order, there were five categories:

a. Often
b. Sometimes
c. Once
d. Never
e. No answer

The five alternatives for each item were collapsed into a (0, 1) dichotomy as follows: for all items except 2 and 3, the answer categories a and b were mapped into a zero, and c, d, and e were mapped into a 1; for items 2 and 3, categories a, b, and c were mapped into zero, and d and c into a 1.

It was found that by deleting one of the items (5) a quasiscalogram pattern was obtained for the remainder with a coefficient of reproducibility of .92. The scalogram is shown in Fig. 3.4 with the zeros omitted for clarity.

The ordering of the columns from left to right orders the fear symptoms (as dichotomized) from least to most severe. Thus, according to the scalogram, the ordering of the symptoms from least to most severe is as follows:

1ab Violent pounding of the heart, sometimes or often
2ab Sinking feeling of the stomach, sometimes or often
7ab Shaking or trembling all over, sometimes or often
4ab Feeling sick at the stomach, sometimes or often
10ab Feeling of stiffness, sometimes or often
3ab Feeling of weakness or feeling faint, sometimes or often
6abc Vomiting, once, sometimes, or often
9abc Losing control of the bowels, once, sometimes, or often
8ab Urinating in pants, sometimes or often

A soldier reporting any one of these tended to report all those above it. The existence of a scalogram pattern would suggest the existence of a common mechanism reflecting degree of psychological stress.

Thurstone's Model of Comparative Judgment for Quadrant III Data

Thurstone was seeking a method of measuring subjective magnitude that was not dependent on manipulating a known physical correlate. The psychophysical methods common at that time were exactly what their name implies —methods for measuring a subjective response to a physical variable.

Unfortunately there is no known relevant physical variable for many

1 a, b	2 a, b	7 a, b	4 a, b	10 a, b	3 a, b	6 a, b, c	9 a, b, c	8 a, b	f
1		1		1			1		1
						1			1
					1				1
			1		1				1
	1			1					1
1									7
1		1							1
1			1						1
1				1					1
1						1			1
1							1		1
	1								1
1	1				1				1
1	1								7
1	1		1						2
1	1		1		1				1
	1			1					1
1	1			1		1			1
1	1		1			1			1
1	1		1			1	1		1
1	1		1				1	1	1
	1	1							1
1	1	1							3
1	1	1		1					3
1	1	1			1				1
1	1	1	1						2
1	1		1		1				2
1	1	1	1		1				1
1	1	1	1			1			2
1	1		1	1					2
	1		1	1					1
1	1	1	1	1					2
	1		1	1		1			1
1	1		1	1		1			1
1		1	1	1			1		1
1	1	1	1	1	1				1
1	1	1	1	1	1				6
1	1	1	1	1	1		1		1
1	1	1	1	1	1			1	1
1		1	1	1		1			1
1	1	1	1	1		1			1
1	1		1		1	1			1
1	1	1	1		1	1			1
1			1	1	1	1			1
1		1	1	1	1	1			1
1	1	1	1	1	1	1			5
1	1		1	1	1	1	1		1
1	1	1	1	1	1	1	1		7
1	1	1	1	1	1		1	1	1
1	1	1	1	1	1	1	1	1	6

Fig. 3.4 Scalogram of fear symptoms reported as experienced in combat.

psychological variables—attitudes, preferences, aesthetic quality, interests, etc. Throughout history, at least that of psychometrics, it is a common observation that the greater the difference between two stimuli on some physical magnitude, the more likely one will be judged greater than the other. Psychophysicists made use of this property of monotonicity only for experimental convenience in guiding the manipulations of the physical variable to seek a threshold (subjective equality of two points) or the subjective equality of stimulus differences.

In the absence of a known and manipulable physical variable it was perhaps natural to turn to the monotonicity property and assume a relation between the degree of consistency of judgment and the subjective difference between two stimuli.

Thorndike in 1910 proposed a procedure for converting the proportion of times one object is judged greater than another into a measure of the subjective difference between them. Thurstone provided a rationale and more fully developed the theory, which he called the law of comparative judgment.

The data matrix with which Thurstone worked is the intact dominance matrix based on data collected by the method of pair comparisons. This means that on each pair of stimuli a judgment is made as to which member of the pair "dominates" the other, e.g., lighter, longer, lovelier. Each pair is replicated, experimentally independently, and the proportion of judgments "j dominates k" is determined. The data matrix, then, is bordered by the same elements as rows and as columns, and in each cell is recorded the proportion of times the row element dominated the column element.

Thurstone constructed a model by means of which the data in such a matrix could yield a one-dimensional scale of the stimuli. He assumed that when an individual made a choice between two stimuli, e.g., a judgment about which was greater, each stimulus had given rise to a subjective experience of some degree of magnitude, and the subject's response reflected which stimulus had given rise to the greater subjective experience. He further assumed that in experimentally independent replications a stimulus did not necessarily give rise to the same magnitude of subjective experience but rather that there is a normal distribution of such "discriminal processes," as he called them, reflecting their relative probability of occurrence on any one trial.

Letting q_j be the magnitude of the discriminal process associated with stimulus j for an individual on a given trial, then a basic assumption of Thurstone's model is

$$q_k \geq q_j \Leftrightarrow k \succcurlyeq j \qquad (3.2)$$

where $k \succcurlyeq j$ signifies the (generic) response by individual i that k is not dominated by j.

Another way of putting it is that if the difference $q_k - q_j$ is not negative the individual i says that k is not dominated by j. There is assumed to be a

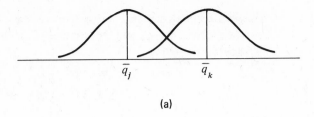

(a)

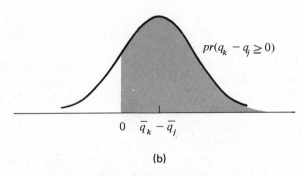

$pr(q_k - q_j \geq 0)$

$0 \quad \bar{q}_k - \bar{q}_j$

(b)

Fig. 3.5 Distributions of discriminal processes and their differences. (a) Subjective continuum of discriminal processes. (b) Continuum of differences between discriminal processes.

normal distribution of such differences between discriminal processes for stimuli j and k, and when our individual makes a judgment, he has drawn a "difference" at random from this distribution. Hence, for a number of experimentally independent replications we may write

$$pr(q_k - q_j \geq 0) = pr(k \geqslant j).$$

The proportion pr is an estimate of the area of the distribution above zero differences.

These relations are portrayed in Fig. 3.5, where $\bar{q}_j$ and $\bar{q}_k$ represent the means of their respective distributions. Part (a) illustrates the distributions of the discriminal processes for two stimuli, j and k. Drawing a point from each distribution and judging whether one point is beyond the other is equivalent to drawing a single point from the distribution of differences [shown in part (b) of the figure] and judging whether that difference is greater or less than zero. The observed proportion, then, is an estimate of the shaded area in the figure.

Tables of the normal integral may be used to obtain the standard score corresponding to zero, say z_{kj}. The mean of the distribution of differences is known from elementary statistics to be the difference between the corresponding means, $\bar{q}_k - \bar{q}_j$, and the variance of the differences is $\sigma_j^2 + \sigma_k^2 - 2r_{jk}\sigma_j\sigma_k$. Hence we may write

$$\frac{(\bar{q}_k - \bar{q}_j) - 0}{\sqrt{\sigma_j^2 + \sigma_k^2 - 2r_{jk}\sigma_j\sigma_k}} = z_{kj},$$

which may be more simply written in the form

$$\bar{q}_k - \bar{q}_j = z_{kj}\sqrt{\sigma_j^2 + \sigma_k^2 - 2r_{jk}\sigma_j\sigma_k}, \tag{3.3}$$

in which the left-hand side, $\bar{q}_k - \bar{q}_j$, represents the psychological distance between k and j.

Case I of the model of comparative judgment is that in which the probabilities are estimated from replications within an individual over occasions. As noted in the development of the model, the replications are required to be experimentally independent. This independence is not likely to be achieved if the stimuli are identifiable, as in scaling attitude statements, handwriting specimens, nationalities, etc.

When necessary to achieve experimentally independent replications, estimates of proportions are obtained by having each of a number of different individuals respond once. The same Eq. (3.3) applies, but in this case of replication over individuals it is referred to as Case II.

Equation (3.3) is an observational equation and there is one such equation for every pair of stimuli, of which there are

$$\binom{n}{2} = \frac{n(n-1)}{2}.$$

For n stimuli, however, there is a mean and sigma for each and a correlation for every pair. The total number of unknowns, then, is $2n + \binom{n}{2} - 2$, the -2 reflecting the fact that two parameters, such as one mean and one sigma, may be freely assigned to establish an origin and unit of measurement.

Clearly, with more unknowns than equations it is necessary to place restrictions on the unknowns to get a system of any interest. For this reason Thurstone constructed Cases III, IV, and V involving restrictions on the parameters. Case V is the simplest and most widely used in psychological scaling and is the only one described here.

For Case V the expression under the radical in Eq. (3.3) is assumed to be a constant for all pairs (j, k), and so for convenience may be arbitrarily set equal to 1 for the unit of measurement. Hence Eq. (3.3) becomes

$$\bar{q}_k - \bar{q}_j = z_{kj}. \tag{3.4}$$

There are n scale values for the stimuli, but as there is still one free parameter for the origin of the scale, there are only $n-1$ parameters to be determined. In view of the fact that the number of experimental observations goes up almost as n^2 and the number of parameters goes up as n, the model yields a substantial degree of data reduction.

In general, then, for each pair of stimuli there is an observational equation, Eq. (3.4), with the unknowns on the left and a numerical value on the right. The total number of equations, if the data are complete, is $n(n-1)/2$, which may be considerably more than the number of unknowns. Because the solution is overdetermined and the equations are almost certainly inconsistent (being based on empirical data), an averaging process is used to get some "best" estimate of the parameters.

Thurstone's procedure is based on the following idea. If stimulus points are in the order A, B, X on the subjective continuum, an estimate of the distance from A to B may be obtained by subtracting the distance from B to X from the distance from A to X. Such an estimate may be obtained from each X including $X = A$ and $X = B$. Thurstone averaged these to get a "best" estimate of the distance from A to B.

This procedure was shown later (Horst 1941; Mosteller 1951) to be a least-squares solution. The details of the procedure are covered in Torgerson (1958). Here it is only important to note that the assumption of the constancy of the unit of measurement in Case V is equivalent (for $n > 2$) to requiring that the discriminal dispersions of all stimuli be the same and that the correlational term be the same for all pairs.

We illustrate the method with a replication of a study Thurstone (1927*b*) made of the judged seriousness of offenses. He utilized 266 University of Chicago students and presented them with 171 pairs of offenses (all pairs of 19 offenses). His instructions to the subject were as follows:

> The purpose of this study is to ascertain the opinions of several groups of people about crimes. The following list of crimes has been arranged in pairs. You will please decide which of each pair you think more serious and underline it.
>
> An example: Cheating—Murder
>
> You would probably decide that murder is a more serious offense than cheating; therefore you would underline *Murder*.
>
> If you find a pair of crimes that seem equally serious, or equally inoffensive, be sure to underline one of them anyway, even if you have to make a sort of guess. Be sure to underline one in each pair.

The study was repeated, using the same stimuli and instructions, on 369 University of Michigan students in a number of sections of an elementary psychology course. An occasional student missed an item or a page in the list of pairs but no pair had less than 363 respondents. The number of

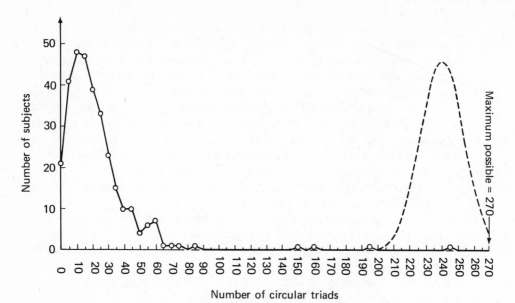

Fig. 3.6 Obtained frequency distribution of intransitivities (circles and solid lines) and a normal approximation to the expected distribution for random responses (dashed lines).

intransitive triples (circular triads) in each student's pair comparisons is an indication of the student's consistency, assuming that he is basically transitive except for random fluctuations. The frequency distribution of circular triads for the 311 subjects who responded to all 171 pair comparisons is shown in Fig. 3.6. If a student's choice on each pair were on a random basis with $p = 1/2$, the number of circular triads to be expected by chance is $(1/4) \binom{n}{3}$ and the variance of the distribution is $(3/16) \binom{n}{3}$ (Kendall 1955). In this case the expected value is 242 and the standard deviation is 13.5. The distribution for this number of triads is approximately normal and we see that there is only one student within three standard deviations of the chance expectation.

The 1966 data could be analyzed separately for males and females as well as for the total group, so altogether four scales were constructed[1] utilizing Case V of the law of comparative judgment. Figure 3.7 illustrates the four scales together, equated at both extremes (zero and 100)—the numerical code is the alphabetical order.[2]

[1]Thurstone's data were reanalyzed in order to ensure that exactly the same procedure was used on all data. There are no differences between his results and the reanalysis reported here.

[2]More complete data are presented in Coombs (1967).

Thurstone classified the offenses into three groups: sex offenses, injury to the person, and property offenses. For clarity of comparison, Figs. 3.8, 3.9, and 3.10 display the relative positions of the offenses in each group, respectively, for the different sets of data.

In interpreting these results it should be emphasized that it is not the college students' legal knowledge that is being tested but their attitudes toward the seriousness of these offenses, which they may know only through the daily newspaper. Also, the samples of subjects are only superficially matched. The students who went to the University of Chicago in 1926 probably represented a narrower segment of the society, socially and eco-

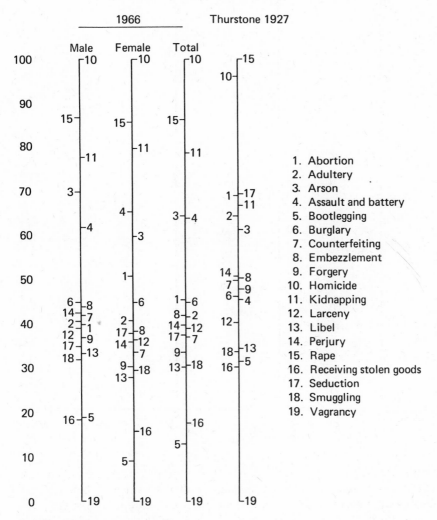

Fig. 3.7 Scales for all offenses.

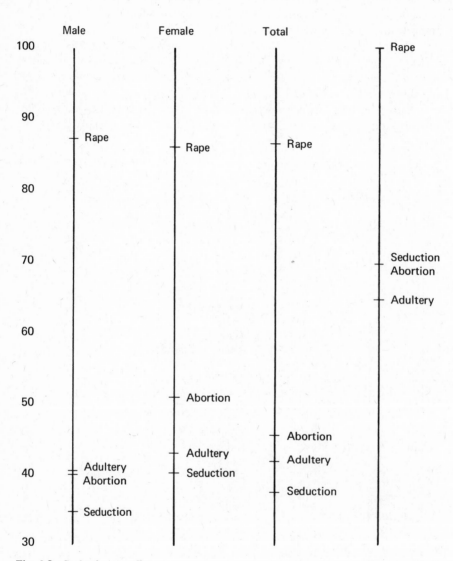

Fig. 3.8 Scales for sex offenses.

nomically, than do college students today when a larger portion of young people are attending college. It may also be conjectured that there are differences in the caliber of the students in the two samples, but it is not obvious what effect, if any, such a difference would have on the results.

It should be kept in mind that the origin and the unit of measurement

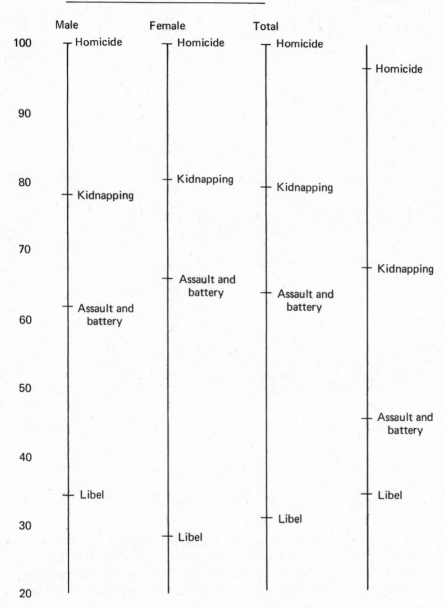

Fig. 3.9 Scales for injury to the person.

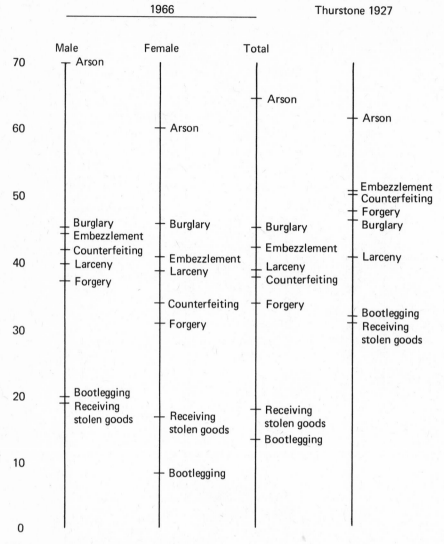

Fig. 3.10   Scales for offenses against property.

for each scale are arbitrary so that all changes are relative. For example, it cannot be said that crime x is regarded as more serious today than 40 years ago. There is no valid way to make such a comparison without equating two points on the 1927 scale with two points on the 1966 scale, which can be done only by making ad hoc assumptions.

   This method of scaling does permit a comparison of the discriminability of the offenses in the earlier and later data. In the initial Case V solution the unit of measurement is the standard error of the discriminal differences, called the comparatal variance and assumed to be a constant for all pairs of stimuli. The range of the original raw scale values, then, is a rough index of the relative discriminability of the stimuli.

In this context the term *discriminability* should be interpreted to mean the homogeneity of the subjects in their attitudes. The more uniformity or agreement among the subjects, the greater the range of the scale relative to the unit of measurement. For Thurstone's data the range is 3.28 and for the 1966 data, 3.02. In view of the number of subjects these data are based on, the difference is very significant and indicates greater homogeneity of attitudes toward the seriousness of offenses 40 years ago than now.

For males and females in the 1966 data, the range is 3.20 and 2.94, respectively, a difference of .26, which is as large as the mean difference between the 1927 and the 1966 data, but being obtained from smaller size groups turns out not to be significant.

The changes in judged seriousness for all offenses are shown together in Fig. 3.7 but are more easily interpreted from Figs. 3.8, 3.9, and 3.10. We see from these that offenses against the person are now judged relatively more serious and sex offenses less so. We see this most dramatically in homicide replacing rape as the most serious of all offenses.

Offenses against property, with the exception of arson, are judged less serious relative to the others than they were 40 years ago.

The principal sex difference is in the judged seriousness of abortion, women judging it more serious than men; and it is perhaps interesting that men judge rape somewhat more serious than women do. The other major sex difference is that, with one exception, men judge offenses against property to be relatively more serious than women do. The exception is burglary, for which there is almost no difference.

3.4 THE PROXIMITY MATRIX

Before we can discuss some of the procedures designed for analyzing proximity matrices, we must return to the study of proximity data as such and make another dichotomous classification, this time between two kinds of proximity data.

Symmetric and Conditional Proximity

Not unreasonably, at least at first glance, it would seem that a proximity measure on a pair of points ought to be transformed into their interpoint distance by a strictly monotonic function, i.e., for all x, y, u, v

$$M(x, y) \leqslant M(u, v) \Leftrightarrow d(x, y) \geq d(u, v) \tag{3.5}$$

where $M(x, y)$ represents an empirical proximity measure on the pair of stimuli x and y and $d(x, y)$ is their interpoint distance in the spatial representation. If, for example, the latency of discriminating x and y is less than that for u and v, one might seek to reflect this in a spatial representation in which the distance between the points corresponding to x and y is greater than that for the points corresponding to u and v (less "proximity" is interpreted as more "distance").

There is good reason, however, to suspect that in some circumstances this assumption, Eq. (3.5), is not a good one to make but needs to be generalized. The distinction between the assumption in Eq. (3.5) and its generalization rests on a distinction between two kinds of proximity matrices, the symmetric and the conditional. We shall discuss the symmetric proximity matrix very briefly, because of its relative simplicity, then turn to the conditional proximity matrix, and then present the generalization of the assumption expressed in Eq. (3.5).

The symmetric proximity matrix is one in which the entry in the (j, k) cell is the same as in the (k, j) cell and is interpreted as a measure of the similarity or proximity of the two stimuli. If, for example, an individual were presented with a pair of cigarettes, tasted them, and judged whether they were the same brand or not, the proportion of individuals making the "same" judgment could be interpreted as a symmetric measure of similarity if there were no constant error or bias caused by the order in which the two cigarettes were presented. In a similar manner, latency as a response measure could be interpreted to reflect a distance in a metric space. Perhaps the most common symmetric proximity matrix is the correlation matrix. In factor analysis, for example, the correlation between two variables is a monotonic function of the distance between the corresponding points.

Any method designed to construct a geometrical representation from order relations defined on distances will have no special problems with a symmetric proximity matrix. The property of symmetry in the proximity measure ensures symmetry of distance and the assumption of monotonicity in the transformation of the proximity measure into distance ensures transitivity of interpoint distances.

We turn, then, to the study of conditional proximity matrices, for which neither the property of symmetry nor the assumption of monotonicity obtains. Any method designed to handle such a proximity matrix will readily handle the symmetric proximity matrix.

What is a conditional proximity matrix? Generically speaking, it is a kind of matrix that arises when an individual is presented, say, with a row stimulus and responds to a degree or in a manner that indicates some degree of confusion with a column stimulus. The column stimuli, then, may be ordered in their degree of dissimilarity to the row stimulus. It is a matrix with rows and columns representing stimuli and with a proximity measure in the cells such that symmetry does not hold in general and monotonicity is assumed *within* rows (columns) but not *between* rows (columns).

Such data typically arise in studies of generalization, transfer, and identification. For example, an individual presented with stimulus A identifies it some proportion of the time as B, $M(B|A)$. When the individual is presented with B, it is in general *not true* that he identifies a B as an A with the same frequency, i.e., $M(A|B) \neq M(B|A)$. The data matrix is nonsymmetric.

In another context a group of individuals is conditioned to stimulus A and the average response decrement or latency when stimulus B is presented may be observed. A second group is conditioned to B and then A is presented. In general, one does not find that the response decrements are the same.

What is disturbing about this is that in a metric space distance is symmetric. So it would seem that the data are not in conformity with models that transform proximity measures into distances by a strictly monotonic function. A possibility, of course, which we do not consider here at all, is that a metric space is not a suitable representation for the data. Instead we rise to the challenge by seeking a rationale that makes such a nonsymmetric data matrix compatible with a metric space.

One alternative is to assume that the matrix should be symmetric but fails because of error and hence symmetrize it by averaging corresponding cells from the two sides of the diagonal—this averaging has sometimes been done.

A second alternative is to modify the function that transforms the proximity measures into distances. One way this can be done is to restrict the domain of the function, i.e., the set of interpoint distances to which the function is applied, to those distances that have a common terminus. A heuristic understanding of why this might be a suitable restriction may be obtained as follows.

Consider the following diagram of four stimuli in a two dimensional Euclidean space.

$$C$$
$$A \qquad\qquad B$$
$$D$$

When stimulus A is presented, we might expect that sometimes it will be identified as stimulus B in error, $M(B|A)$. But the presence and location of stimuli C and D as alternatives may well have a different effect on the errors made when B is presented than when A is presented. Specifically, B will not be identified with A as often as A will be with B, because C and D are nearer to B than is A, whereas B is the nearest stimulus to A. In other words we would not expect conditional confusions to be independent from other alternatives.

Such an explanation for the lack of symmetry in a conditional proximity matrix needs more complete exploration, both formally and experimentally, but its reasonableness (at least to some psychologists, e.g., Shepard 1958) has led to the more limited assumption that strict monotonicity of the function transforming proximity measures into distances applies only to distances from a common point; e.g., the rank order of the cell entries in a row of the matrix corresponds to the rank order of the similarity (or dissimilarity) of the column stimuli from the row stimulus and hence the rank order of the distances of the column stimuli from the row stimulus. In formal terms, the assumption expressed by Eq. (3.5) can be written in a more general form as follows; for all x, y, z

$$M(x, y) \leqslant M(x, z) \Leftrightarrow d(x, y) \geq d(x, z). \qquad (3.6)$$

To illustrate a possible instance of this assumption, suppose the proximity measure $M(x, y)$ were the number of times stimulus x was identified as stimulus y by mistake. Then this condition would require that in the geometrical representation the points for x and y would be farther apart than x and z if and only if stimulus x was more often called stimulus z than it was called stimulus y. Under this condition each row of the data matrix yields a rank order of the column points in order of their distance from the row point, an order relation on a set of distances from a common terminus.

This condition applies equally well, of course, to the off-diagonal and to the intact conditional proximity matrix. In the case of the off-diagonal matrix there are two sets of distinct elements represented by rows and columns, respectively. These sets could correspond, for example, to individuals and to stimuli or to two sets of stimuli such as articles and journals, in which instances the proximity measures lead to a rank order of the points in one set from each of the points in the other, corresponding to the preferential ordering of each individual over the set of stimuli or the relative suitability of an article for each of the several journals (Quadrant I, preferential choice data; cf. Fig. 3.2).

In the intact matrix the interpretation is made that there is *one* set of objects and each is identified with a row and a corresponding column, as in the case of a set of tones where the cell entry is the response decrement in the response to the column stimulus when the individual has been conditioned to the row stimulus. In this case the interpretation normally made is that the greater the response decrement, the less the proximity of the column point to the row point. This interpretation leads to a rank order of the distances of every point in the set from each point in turn, corresponding to the rank order of the response decrements in a row of the matrix.

We may summarize the distinction between the off-diagonal versus the intact conditional proximity matrix as follows: (1) We may have two sets of points, constituting an off-diagonal submatrix, in which case we have the rank order of the points in one set in order of increasing distance from each of the points in the other set. (2) We may have one set of points, constituting an intact matrix, and we have the rank order of the distances of all the points from each point in turn. Note in both these instances that we do not have the rank order of distances between the points x, y and the points *u, v,* where all four points are distinct, i.e., disjoint pairs of distances, but only between distances with a common terminus.

In the following discussion of methods for analyzing the rank order of interpoint distances, it does not matter to the methods how the particular rank orders were obtained. They may have been obtained from proximity matrices as above, but this is not necessary. They may have been obtained from the pairwise preferential choices of an individual or from judgments of the comparative similarity of two stimuli to another one. Such observations may be represented as order relations on pairs of interpoint distances and hence are elements of a dominance matrix.

The methods of analysis to be discussed are unfolding theory and computerized iterative procedures. The application of unfolding theory to the case of two sets of distinct points (Quadrant I, preferential choice) will be discussed first, and then we shall turn to the analysis of Quadrant IV (similarities data) after a discussion of certain aspects of metric spaces.

Unfolding Theory for QI Preferential Choice Data

The prototype real world situation to which unfolding theory applies, and the context in which it was originally developed (Coombs, 1950), is the analysis of preferential choice. In preferential choice the data consist of or are converted to each individual's rank order of preferences for a set of alternative stimuli.

The model associates a point with each stimulus, called a stimulus point, and a hypothetical stimulus point with each individual, called the ideal point of the individual. The hypothetical stimulus corresponding to an individual's ideal point is that which he would prefer to endorse over all the others in the stimulus set. An individual's preference ordering, then, is taken to correspond in the model to the rank order of the stimulus points from the individual's ideal point.

In the real world of preferential choice, an individual's preferences may depend on his consideration of many aspects of a stimulus, aspects that in the model would correspond to dimensions of the space. Any real stimulus may differ from the hypothetical stimulus that is the ideal in one or more aspects, and in the model these differences correspond to differences in the projections of the corresponding points on the dimensions of the space. What is meant by "consideration of many aspects" is captured in the model by the concept of a *distance* in a multidimensional space between the ideal point and a stimulus point.

Only unidimensional unfolding will be illustrated here but multidimensional theory for a Euclidean distance function has been developed by J. F. Bennett and William L. Hays (cf. Coombs 1964, Chapter 7).

Another feature of real world preferences that should also be mentioned is that for any given set of stimuli an individual may not have a clear concept of a hypothetical stimulus that would be his ideal in that set. Most college students, for example, have probably never formulated an exact statement of how they feel about athletic scholarships, and in the same vein a given statement might not be interpreted or perceived as corresponding to a precise position on the issue. This uncertainty or ambiguity about an ideal point or about a stimulus point is captured in the model by a probability distribution in the spirit of the distribution of discriminal processes hypothesized by Thurstone in his model of comparative judgment.

Although the above discussion brings out certain aspects of the generality of unfolding theory, we shall present the one-dimensional case under circumstances that do not require more than a simplified form of the theory.

Of interest in the application reported here is the effect of the number of children a mother has had on her subjective scale of preference for how many children she wants (Goldberg and Coombs 1962). The sample was selected from marriage and birth records to represent, on a probability basis, white couples in the Detroit metropolitan area who

1. had been married for the first time in July 1961 (102 couples, the zero parity sample)
2. had a first birth in July 1961 (372 couples, the first parity sample)
3. had a second birth in July 1961 (372 couples, the second parity sample)
4. had a fourth birth in July 1961 (369 couples, the fourth parity sample)

Extensive interviews were conducted during the months of January and February 1962 through the facilities of the Detroit Area Study of the University of Michigan Population Studies Center; 92 per cent of the selected women were interviewed.

Included in the interview was the following question:

> The number of children people expect and want aren't always the same. If you could choose and have just the number of children you want by the time your family is completed, how many children would that be?

This question was followed with

> Suppose you couldn't have that number, but had to choose between ——— and ———. Which would you choose?

and

> If you couldn't have that, would you choose ——— or ———?

The numbers put in the blanks depended on the previous response and were chosen so as to yield the individual's preference ordering on number of

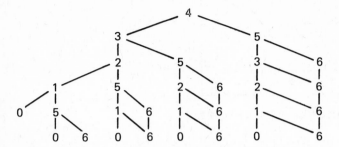

Fig. 3.11   An interviewer's tree of questions.

children. The interviewer had a "tree" for each ideal number. Thus, for example (see Fig. 3.11), if the respondent said four initially, the next question asked her to indicate her preference between three and five. If she chose three, then she was asked to choose between two and five, etc.

A respondent's rank order of preference is obtained, e.g., 4352160, from left to right, and is called an I scale. Respondents whose initial preference was for more than six children were assumed to have the preference ordering 6543210 for this set of alternatives and similarly those whose initial preference was for zero children were assumed to have the preference ordering 0123456. In unidimensional unfolding theory the stimuli and the ideals of the respondents are represented by two corresponding sets of points on a line representing an attribute continuum. This line is called a J scale, a joint distribution of two sets of points. Each respondent's I scale is obtained from the J scale by folding it at the ideal point of that respondent so the respondent's preference ordering of the stimuli is represented by the rank order of the stimulus points in order of increasing distance from the ideal point.

The objective of the method might in some instance be to test for the existence of one common latent attribute underlying people's preferences for a set of alternatives or in another instance to construct a one-dimensional space to account for the observed preferences. These objectives correspond to the two alternative functions or roles of a scaling theory discussed in Sec. 3.1, the role of criterion and of technique.

In this application we are not concerned with discovering whether there is a J scale that is ordered from 0 to 6; we were willing to assume that, as was apparent in the method of collecting the preference orderings. Instead the interest here is in the subjective differences between the stimuli on the J scale and how these change, if at all, with parity. So here we are utilizing unfolding theory as a technique to study the structure of a scale.

The analysis of data rests on the fact that the existence of a J scale places great constraint on the variety of I scales that can occur. Because an individual is assumed to prefer the nearer of any two stimuli, their midpoint divides the scale into two segments, as in Fig. 3.12. All individuals to

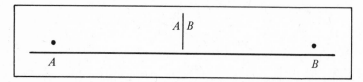

Fig. 3.12   Points corresponding to stimuli A and B and their midpoint $A|B$.

the left of the midpoint $A|B$ prefer A to B and all individuals to the right prefer B to A.

If this scale is picked up and folded at an individual's ideal point, the rank order of the stimuli on the folded scale is the individual's preference ordering. Clearly, with more stimuli there are more midpoints and the J scale is sectioned into more intervals, to each of which corresponds a unique preference ordering as if the J scale were folded at an ideal point in the interval.

The problem of analyzing such data requires unfolding the I scales and constructing a J scale. The algorithm for the unfolding is quite simple and is fully described elsewhere (Coombs 1964). Sufficient for our purposes here is to understand how metric information on the J scale is obtained.

Consider the two J scales of Fig. 3.13. Each has four stimulus points shown and the important difference is that for the one on the left the distance between A and B, $\overline{AB}$, is less than that between C and D, $\overline{CD}$; whereas the reverse is true for the J scale portrayed on the right. The effect of this is to reverse the order of just one pair of midpoints, $B|C$ and $A|D$,

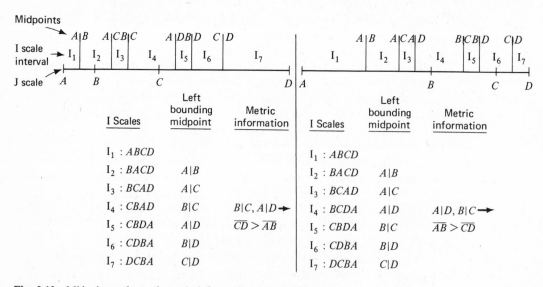

Fig. 3.13   Midpoint order and metric information in unfolding theory.

which may be shown as follows. As

$$A|D = \frac{A+D}{2} \quad \text{and} \quad B|C = \frac{B+C}{2},$$

then

$$A|D < B|C \Rightarrow A+D < B+C \Rightarrow D-C < B-A \Rightarrow \overline{CD} < \overline{AB}.$$

This difference in the metric relations of the two J scales of Fig. 3.13 causes a difference in the composition of the two sets of I scales. It will be noted that I scale 4 is different in the two sets. In going from I_3 to I_4, one crosses $B|C$ in one instance and $A|D$ in the other, generating different orderings for I_4. All ordered metric information reduces to this simple relation.

In general the composition of the set of I scales implies an ordering of the midpoints on the J scale, and this ordering has metric information in the form of order relations on certain pairs of distances. A necessary condition for an ordered metric J scale is that these order relations on distances must be transitive and satisfy the necessary partial order on the midpoints of a set of ordered points. The necessary partial order arises from the fact that for all triples A, X, Y,

$$A|X \text{ precedes } A|Y \quad \text{iff} \quad x \text{ precedes } y.$$

Given an ordered metric J scale, several methods have been devised for constructing a numerical representation, one of which is that of Frank Goode (cf. Coombs 1964, Chapter 5). His method reduces every interval to multiples of elementary units and then a simple version of the method is to assume that all these elementary units are equal, called the *equal delta solution*.

To return now to the actual analysis of the data obtained in the fertility study, we recall that there was a group of subjects at each of four parities. For each group the analysis consisted of finding a maximum subset of the subjects for whom the metric relations were transitive and then applying Goode's method. The results are portrayed in Fig. 3.14 in which the total interval between 0 and 6 is made the same for all parities, so that comparisons of changes across parities are comparisons relative to this common base.

For each parity the first interval, between zero and one child, is the largest, and across parities this first interval is largest for those mothers who have had exactly one child. One is tempted to say that the anticipated relative effect of having one child as represented by the $\overline{01}$ interval for the zero parity group is more than realized, as seen in the first parity group, by the relative increase in the $\overline{01}$ interval. The anticipated effects of having a second and a third child seem to be borne out by those parities that have had

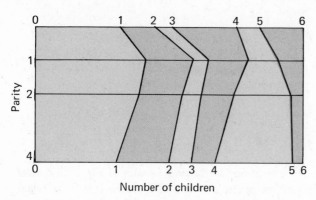

Fig. 3.14 Dominant J scale solutions by parity.

that number of children or more—in other words the $\overline{12}$ interval and the $\overline{23}$ interval appear relatively constant across parities.

Very great changes across parities occur in the metric of the preference structure on each side of the fourth child. The interval *before* the fourth child substantially decreases, and the interval *after* substantially increases, so that on the scale of those mothers with four children, as far as their preferences are concerned, the $\overline{45}$ interval is almost as large as that for the first child.

The interpretation is as follows. The difference between having four and five children appears relatively slight before the family has been started but with each succeeding child it appears increasingly large, and by the time the mother has had four children the subjective step to the next child is one of the largest in the scale.

This application of unfolding theory is an example of the analysis of an off-diagonal conditional proximity matrix, which is a particular subset of the data of an intact conditional proximity matrix, which itself is a particular kind of similarities data.

A discussion of certain aspects of metric spaces and multidimensional analysis follows, and then methods of analyzing intact proximity matrices are discussed.

Metric Distance and Psychological Theory

As mentioned in Sec. 3.2 on data theory, the current methods of analyzing proximity data involve transforming the proximity measures into measures of interpoint distances. Before proceeding with models for the analysis of such data, a brief discussion of the concept of distance in a metric space is in order. If one's theoretical interest lies in the decomposition of complex behavior, then the relation of this decomposition process to measurement and scaling theory must be understood. In brief, the decomposition process as a real world theory can correspond to a distance function in the measurement model.

As an illustration of the relation, if an individual's performance on a mental test problem were mediated by two component abilities and the performance reflected the square root of the sum of the squares of the differences between his ability and the problem's difficulty on each component, then a Euclidean metric would be a valid formal model of the process. This theory of the underlying process is certainly not the only possibility, however.

Alternative theories of the process, for example, might be that the performance reflected the simple sum of the component differences, or only the largest difference, or any of a host of possibilities. Many of these possibilities correspond to distance functions in the abstract model and permit a representation in what is called a metric space, but metric spaces form only a small part of the possible combination rules that are potential psychological theory.

The class of functions that permits modeling in a metric space satisfies the four axioms of a distance function, D1 to D4, given in the appendix.

A particular class of distance functions that has some interest for psychologists is known as the Minkowski r-metric (cf. Beckenback and Bellman 1961), brought to the attention of psychologists by Shepard (1964). This metric is a one-parameter class of distance functions defined as follows:

$$d_r(x, y) = [\sum_{i=1}^{n} |x_i - y_i|^r]^{1/r}, \qquad r \geq 1, \tag{3.7}$$

where x and y are two points in an n-dimensional space with components $i = 1, 2, \ldots, n$ and $d_r(x, y)$ is the distance between x and y under the distance function indexed by r. Let us consider some special cases that are of particular interest.

Clearly, the familiar Euclidean metric is the special case of $r = 2$, as in that case:

$$d_2(x, y) = [\sum_{i=1}^{n} |x_i - y_i|^2]^{1/2}. \tag{3.8}$$

The other special cases of interest are $r = 1$ and $r = \infty$. The case of $r = 1$ is known as the "city-block" model,

$$d_1(x, y) = \sum_{i=1}^{n} |x_i - y_i|, \tag{3.9}$$

i.e., the distance from one point to another is the sum of their differences on each component. It gets its name because it is the distance between two addresses in a city in which one can only follow streets parallel to the two axes of the city, as indicated in Fig. 3.15.

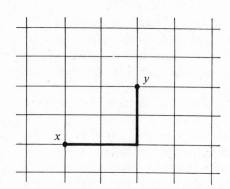

Fig. 3.15   Distance in the city-block model.

One way of characterizing a particular r-metric is in terms of the so-called "unit circle," which is the locus of all points a unit distance from another, say the point at the origin. Thus if we let $y = (0, 0)$, then the locus of all points a unit distance from y in the Euclidean model is given by the circle of radius 1 with center at the origin (see Fig. 3.16). The unit circle for the city-block model is given by the diamond-shaped contour shown in Fig. 3.16.

Before continuing with the special case of $r = \infty$, let us consider one psychological interpretation of r suggested by Cross (1965). Let the origin be $(0_1, \ldots, 0_n)$, and let the distance of a point from the origin be designated x; in the Minkowski r-metric then:

$$x = [\sum_{i=1}^{n} |x_i|^r]^{1/r}$$

and in the Euclidean metric

$$x^2 = \sum_{i=1}^{n} |x_i|^2.$$

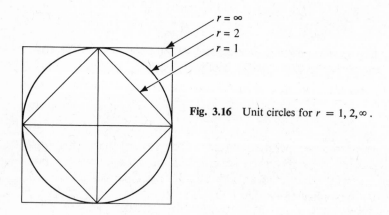

$r = \infty$
$r = 2$
$r = 1$

Fig. 3.16   Unit circles for $r = 1, 2, \infty$.

Dividing this expression through by x, we may write

$$x = \sum_{i=1}^{n} \frac{|x_i|}{x} |x_i|,$$

where $|x_i|/x$ may be interpreted as a *weight* to the ith component. Therefore we may interpret the Euclidean metric as one in which the components are weighted proportionally to the difference on them.

In general we have

$$x^r = \sum_{i=1}^{n} |x_i|^r$$

$$= \sum_{i=1}^{n} |x_i|^{r-1} |x_i|$$

$$x = \sum_{i=1}^{n} \left[\frac{|x_i|}{x} \right]^{r-1} |x_i|,$$

and we see that in the Minkowski r-metric the distance x of a point from the origin (and, of course, the distance between any two points) may be looked on as a sum of the component differences $|x_i|$, each weighted by its own magnitude raised to the power $r-1$.

Consider now the relative contribution of two dimensions, say $i = 1$ and $i = 2$. We may write the ratio of their weights as

$$\frac{|x_1|^{r-1}/x^{r-1}}{|x_2|^{r-1}/x^{r-1}} = \left[\frac{|x_1|}{|x_2|} \right]^{r-1}.$$

If we let $|x_1| < |x_2|$, then their ratio is less than 1, and as $r \to \infty$, the ratio approaches zero, which means that the component $i = 2$, being the larger, dominates the distance of x from the origin and the component $i = 1$ makes no contribution to this distance.

We may interpret r, then, as a parameter of *component weight*. If $r = 1$, then all components are weighted equally in their effect on the distance between two points, but as r increases, the components become increasingly differentially weighted according to the differences between the two points on the components, which in the limit at $r = \infty$, only the largest component difference matters, it alone determines the distance between two points.

The unit circle for this "dominance" metric ($r = \infty$) is the square contour shown in Fig. 3.16 in relation to the city-block and Euclidean unit circles. In general the unit circle for any fixed value of r contains those corresponding to smaller values of r.

It is important to note that although the distance between two points in the Minkowski r-metric is invariant under translation of the origin, it is not in general invariant under rotation of the axes. Only for the special case of $r = 2$, the Euclidean distance function, is distance invariant under rotation of axes. It can be shown that the Euclidean distance function is completely characterized by this property of rotational invariance and hence is the only distance that has this property.

Although the above has been largely a discussion of some of the mathematical properties of the Minkowski r-metric, there are corresponding psychological implications. Instances of each of the three distance functions, $r = 1$, 2, and ∞, are current in psychological theory.

Pavlov (1927) proposed that generalization was caused by a wave of excitation that radiated out from a central point in the brain in all directions, a theory sometimes referred to as the *excitation* model and leading to the Euclidean metric. Similarly, generalization in Hull's theory (1943) as the "spread of habit strength" also corresponds to a representation of the similarity of stimuli in a Euclidean metric. In such theories, then, one reference frame or set of axes is as good as another to describe and predict generalization and transfer. Each pair of stimuli defines a line in the space along which the flow occurs, and hence the Euclidean distance function is a valid representation of the process.

One alternative theory to this excitation model is the proposal of Lashley and Wade (1946) that generalization occurs because of an organism's failure to discriminate relevant aspects of stimuli because it was not trained to discriminate them or because of failure to attend. Guttman (1956) has pointed out that this theory, referred to as the *discrimination* model, implies that the total generalization decrement is a *sum* of the decrements occurring along each of the component dimensions, which we recognize as the city-block model. Restle (1959) has also advanced theoretical arguments for this combination rule.

Finally, the $r = \infty$ model corresponds to Lashley's principle of dominant organization (1942). He proposed that the mechanism of nervous integration may be such that when any complex of stimuli arouses nervous activity, that activity is immediately organized and certain stimulus properties become dominant for reaction whereas others become ineffective. This model is called the *dominance* model. The distance between two points in such a metric is the greatest of their differences on the component dimensions.

These three special cases are of particular interest but, of course, there are an infinite number of other combination rules corresponding to the possible values of r. The value of r may be interpreted, as we have seen, in terms of the relative differential contribution of each component to the total effect of the stimulus, and for any given combination rule, except $r = 2$, the dimensions are unique.

An interesting related application has been made by the Danish poet Piet Hein to the problem of designing an aesthetically pleasing highway intersection complex in the center of Stockholm. The family of unit circles generated by the Minkowski r-metric may themselves be considered a special case of a family of unit ellipses in which one axis is stretched relative to another. Piet Hein found that an exponent of $r = 2.5$ would yield a pleasing oval that would fit harmoniously into the rectangular area allotted for the intersection. The extension of these unit ellipses to three dimensions is now being utilized in other applied arts such as the design of furniture and jewelry. An interesting account of this is given by Gardner (1965).

The Minkowski r-metric, also called the power metric, defined by Eq. (3.7), exhibits three basic properties (see Beals, Krantz, and Tversky 1968):

1. Interdimensional additivity: The distance between x and y is a function of the additive combination of the contributions of their components.
2. Intradimensional subtractivity: The distance between x and y is a function of the absolute values of their component-wise differences.
3. Power: All component-wise differences are transformed by the same convex ($r \geq 1$) power function.

Note that property 1 is an interdimensional property as it refers to summation across the different dimensions, whereas property 2 is an intradimensional property as it refers to subtraction of values along the same dimension. If properties 1 and 2 alone are satisfied, we obtain the *additive difference model*, defined by

$$d(x, y) = F[\sum_{i=1}^{n} \phi_i(x_i - y_i)], \tag{3.10}$$

where $F, \phi_1, \ldots, \phi_n$ are increasing functions or scales. Although the additive difference model generalizes the power metric, it need not be a metric distance function for it may fail to satisfy the triangle inequality, axiom D4 in the appendix. Indeed, it has been shown by Beals, Krantz, and Tversky that the conditions under which an additive difference model is a proper distance function impose severe restrictions on the form and the interrelations among the various scales.

The analysis of proximity data has been based on both dimensional and metric assumptions. The dimensional assumption asserts that objects or stimuli can be properly represented in a dimensionally organized space. The metric assumption asserts that the psychological distance between objects or stimuli is expressable as a metric distance between points. An analysis of both assumptions, from the viewpoint of measurement theory, has been carried out by Beals, Krantz, and Tversky (1968). More specifically, they have investigated testable conditions that are necessary and/or sufficient for general classes of metric or dimensional models. This research illustrates the applicability of the measurement-theoretical analysis to the problem of discovering the basic empirical assumptions that underlie multidimensional scaling of similarities.

The Analysis of Similarities Data

In this subsection two methods of analyzing intact proximity matrices will be discussed and illustrated. The first to be discussed is Hays's nonmetric method for intact conditional proximity matrices and the second is the general class of computerized iterative procedures for intact symmetric proximity matrices. There will be no attempt here to prepare the student to carry out such analyses but merely to provide an understanding of the principles on which such analyses are based and some of the issues and alternative courses of action. This particular area is developing so rapidly that communication among the workers in the field is by manuscript and at scientific meetings. It is probably fair to say that what gets published was prime news two to three years before.

Hays's nonmetric analysis of similarities data. The objective of Hays's nonmetric similarity analysis is to find a reference frame for a psychological space given a partial order on the interpoint distances, obtained from the rank order of distances in all triangles, obtained, in turn, from the conditional proximity matrix. This reference frame is to consist of n linearly independent rank orders of the stimulus points, interpreted as the rank order of the projections of the points on n axes or dimensions of the space.

In a Euclidean space, which Hays's method assumes, there is no unique reference frame, because the distance between a pair of points is invariant under rotation of axes. The problem then is to devise criteria that will yield a space of the minimum dimensionality necessary to account for the observed data. One criterion for this purpose is to construct dimensions for the space that successively account for a maximum proportion of the variance of the interpoint distances. How shall we find such lines in the space?

It will be recalled that the conditional proximity matrix yields the rank order of all the stimulus points from each stimulus in turn. These orderings are like the preference orderings previously discussed, but now they are orderings from a stimulus point and not an individual's ideal point, so we shall call such orderings stimulus I scales. These play a critical role in determining the order of projections of points on a line in the space, as we see from the following theorem:

THEOREM 3.1

Given four points X, A, B, Y in an n-dimensional Euclidean space, if the order of the distances of the points from X is $XABY$ and from Y is $YBAX$, then the order of projections of the points A, B on the line joining X and Y is $XABY$.

Proof

With no loss of generality let the coordinates of the four points have the following nonnegative values on three orthogonal dimensions:

$$X = (0, 0, 0)$$
$$Y = (y_1, 0, 0)$$
$$A = (a_1, a_2, 0)$$
$$B = (b_1, b_2, b_3)$$

Therefore, for algebraic convenience we have placed the point X at the origin and passed the first dimensions through Y so that the distance from X to Y is y_1. We have permitted A to project on a second dimension and B to project on a third.

As the rank order of distances from X is $XABY$, then $\overline{XB} > \overline{XA}$.

The squares of these distances bear the same relation and by the Pythagorean theorem, and knowing the coordinates of the points, we may write

$$b_1^2 + b_2^2 + b_3^2 > a_1^2 + a_2^2$$

and therefore

$$b_1^2 + b_2^2 + b_3^2 - a_1^2 - a_2^2 > 0.$$

As the rank order of distances from Y is $YBAX$, we may, in the same manner as above, write the following:

$$\overline{YA} > \overline{YB}$$
$$\Rightarrow \quad (y_1 - a_1)^2 + a_2^2 > (y_1 - b_1)^2 + b_2^2 + b_3^2$$
$$\Rightarrow y_1^2 - 2a_1 y_1 + a_1^2 + a_2^2 > y_1^2 - 2b_1 y_1 + b_1^2 + b_2^2 + b_3^2,$$

cancelling y_1^2 from both sides and collecting terms in y_1,

$$\Rightarrow \quad 2(b_1 - a_1)y_1 > b_1^2 + b_2^2 + b_3^2 - a_1^2 - a_2^2,$$

and from our previous result above,

$$\Rightarrow \quad 2(b_1 - a_1)y_1 > 0,$$

and as all coordinates are positive, for this expression to be positive requires that

$$b_1 - a_1 > 0.$$

As these values are the coordinates, respectively, of B and A on the first dimension, this proves that A and B project on the line from X to Y, on the first dimension, in the order $XABY$.

As a consequence of this theorem, if we have two stimulus I scales that are mirror images of each other, there exists a line in the space on which the rank order of the projections corresponds to this pair of stimulus I scales.

Each pair of stimuli defines a line in the space and the basic idea of Hays's nonmetric similarity analysis is to choose the longest line in the space to define the first dimension. All the other stimulus points project between the two stimuli defining this longest line. The I scales of these two stimuli may be used to construct at least a partial order of the projections between the two end points.

That such a partially ordered scale resembles the order of projection on a line of least-squares fit to the space may be seen from the following argument. Every triple of points defines a triangle in the space. The order of projection of the vertices of a triangle on a line that is a least-squares fit to the triangle will necessarily have the vertex opposite the longest side project between the other two vertices.

By choosing the two points farthest apart in the space to define the first dimension, all the other points in the space project between these, and hence the order of projections required for a least-squares fit to the *largest* triangles in the space is satisfied. By having the order of projections of these points correspond to the common partial order of the stimulus I scales from the stimuli at the ends of the line, a maximum number of triangles are fitted that have exactly one of these extreme points for a vertex. A resolution of this partial order may be accomplished by fitting as many more triangles as possible.

Successive dimensions follow essentially the same procedure but with primary concern for fitting triangles not fitted by previous dimensions. Linear independence is accomplished by selecting points to define successive dimensions that project close together on the previous dimensions.

A simple one-dimensional example of this procedure is contained in the analysis of an intact conditional proximity matrix obtained in an experiment on paired associate learning by DeSoto and Bosley (1962). The stimuli were 16 names to be associated with freshman, sophomore, junior, and senior, four to each. There were 28 subjects, 7 from each college class level. In the course of learning the associations between names and classes the subjects sometimes made errors, calling a sophomore a freshman, junior, or senior. The subjects were run to a criterion of two successive errorless trials through the entire list and DeSoto and Bosley report the mean number of each kind of error for each correct response. The data are as shown in Fig. 3.17, with the correct responses as rows and the errors as columns.

Here we have a conditional proximity matrix. We shall assume that these errors are a proximity measure that satisfies Eq. (3.6); i.e., for each row stimulus we can rank order the column stimuli from nearest to farthest. Relabeling freshman, sophomore, junior, and senior as *A*, *B*, *C*, *D*, respectively, for convenience, we have the following stimulus I scales from the data matrix:

	Freshman	Sophomore	Junior	Senior
Freshman	–	3.48	2.74	1.72
Sophomore	2.36	–	4.77	3.29
Junior	2.23	3.54	–	3.29
Senior	1.78	3.00	4.08	–

Fig. 3.17 DeSoto–Bosley paired associate learning data.

$$ABCD$$
$$BCDA$$
$$CBDA$$
$$DCBA.$$

Each of these corresponds to a rank order of distances as follows:

$$ABCD \Leftrightarrow \overline{AD} > \overline{AC} > \overline{AB}$$
$$BCDA \Leftrightarrow \overline{AB} > \overline{BD} > \overline{BC}$$
$$CBDA \Leftrightarrow \overline{AC} > \overline{CD} > \overline{BC}$$
$$DCBA \Leftrightarrow \overline{AD} > \overline{BD} > \overline{CD}.$$

Each of these orderings of distances has a distance in common with every other ordering, so they may be merged together in a common partial order if there are no contradictions or intransitivities. In this case the data yield the following simple ordering:

$$\overline{AD}$$
$$|$$
$$\overline{AC}$$
$$|$$
$$\overline{AB}$$
$$|$$
$$\overline{BD}$$
$$|$$
$$\overline{CD}$$
$$|$$
$$\overline{BC}.$$

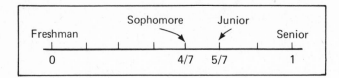

Fig. 3.18   Cognitive structure revealed by errors in a paired associate learning task.

Stimuli A and D are farthest apart so we take the line joining them as our first dimension. We see that A's I scale is $ABCD$ and D's I scale is $DCBA$, one the mirror image of the other; so the order projections on the line from A to D is $ABCD$, by theorem 3.1. As this dimension fits all the triangles, we have a one-dimensional solution on an ordered metric scale.

Using Goode's method, the scale values are as shown in Fig. 3.18. Having in mind that the subjects were performing a routine paired associate learning task with no reference to scaling at all, one finds that the cognitive structure shown by the scale in Fig. 3.18 represents the pattern of errors made in the course of learning.

Computerized iterative procedures.   We turn now to programs designed, at least originally, for the analysis of symmetric proximity matrices. These programs all have the property of seeking to preserve the original information in the data on interpoint distances only up to a monotone transformation as expressed by Eq. (3.5); that is, the interpoint distances in the representation are required to satisfy only the order relations in the data.

The principal programs include Shepard's original program (1962a, b), Kruskal's modification of it (1964a, b), and a set of programs developed by Guttman and Lingoes called smallest space analysis (SSA) (Lingoes 1965, Guttman 1969).

The program by Torgerson and Meuser has been developed further by Young (Young and Torgerson 1967, Young 1968) and its latest version is labeled TORSCA-9. There are a number of other programs that are worthy of mention but that cannot be discussed here; these include McGee's multi-dimensional analysis of "elastic" distances (1966).

Conceptually, all these iterative algorithms have a great deal in common. The first steps in the analysis of a data matrix are to specify the metric function, the number of dimensions, and an initial configuration. The programs then follow three successive steps.

1. The distances between points in the configuration are calculated on the basis of the prescribed metric function.
2. The rank order of these distances is then compared with the rank order of distances given by the data. A measure of discrepancy between these two rank orders is defined and this measure is calculated and used as a criterion to be minimized.

3. For each point the magnitude and direction of a "step jump" is calculated which is designed to reduce the measure of discrepancy, and a new configuration is generated.

The program then returns to the first step and iterates until the configuration converges in the sense that further changes do not sufficiently reduce the measure of discrepancy.

The analysis of similarities data is a new development, so changes in the current procedures and the construction of new ones are to be expected. None of the current methods have been widely used or adequately compared on the same data.

Because these methods are undergoing such rapid development and improvement to combat deficiencies and weaknesses, some of the differences between them, such as the freedom of choice in selecting an initial configuration, the freedom of choice in selecting a distance function, and the problem of missing data, may cease to exist or at least be greatly changed in the future. Hence only common characteristics and more important differences are discussed below.

An important characteristic of all programs is a measure of discrepancy between the distances in the configuration and what they should be if the order relations in the data are to be preserved. The programs of Kruskal and Guttman–Lingoes differ in their definition of "what the distances should be" in the above statement and in their respective measures of discrepancy. These differences are important to the measures of discrepancy and need to be described.

Kruskal's procedure uses a measure of discrepancy which he calls an index of normalized stress S, which for any configuration is given by

$$S = \sqrt{\frac{\sum_{i \neq j} (d_{ij} - \hat{d}_{ij})^2}{\sum_{i \neq j} d_{ij}^2}}, \qquad (3.11)$$

where d_{ij} is the formal distance between the points i and j in the configuration according to the specified metric function, and $\hat{d}_{ij}$ is a distance *least* deviant from d_{ij} that would satisfy monotonicity.

The Guttman–Lingoes system calls one of its measures of discrepancy *normalized phi*, which is closely related to Kruskal's S, the relation being

$$\phi = \tfrac{1}{2} S^2 \qquad (3.12)$$

except that $\hat{d}_{ij}$ is estimated somewhat differently.

As mentioned before, these methods were all designed initially for the analysis of the symmetric proximity matrix. Efforts are being made to adapt or modify them to handle the conditional proximity matrix, the off-diagonal submatrix of a proximity matrix, and matrices with data missing in arbitrarily selected cells (see Lingoes 1966).

There are varying degrees of claims and counterclaims of success in these attempts, and independent objective investigations are too few to justify comparative evaluations at this stage.

There are some common fundamental problems among these computerized iterative procedures that seem especially stubborn. One of these problems is called the local minimum problem. These programs, as we have said, seek a configuration that minimizes a measure of discrepancy, and they do this by making discrete jumps. The difficulty is that there may be configurations with less discrepancy than those configurations that are "close" to it but that have more discrepancy than some that are "farther" from it, like the altitude of a valley in the Alps. Such a configuration is called a *local minimum*, and, of course, there may be any number of such local minima.

If a program makes "small" changes, then, it is in danger of being trapped in one of these local minima; and if it makes "large" changes, it may be slow to converge. In spite of local minima, however, one has the qualitative impression that the solutions obtained by the different programs are substantially alike.

Another fundamental problem with these procedures is provided by the case in which the points may be partitioned into two or more non-empty subsets such that all distances between points within each subset are less than any distance to points outside the subset. In this case these programs yield a different configuration for the subset of points when embedded in the total set of which they are a part and when analyzed as a set in their own right. Torgerson, in discussing degenerate cases in which the iterative procedure failed, puts it neatly when he says, "the iterative procedures work best when the space is relatively well-filled" (1965).

The TORSCA-9 program appears to be a combination of Torgerson's 1952 method and a modified Kruskal program. The first stage of the program involves a factor analysis of derived distances and yields the starting configuration for the second stage, which proceeds in the same general manner as the Shepard–Kruskal procedures already described.

An example of similarities analysis. For an illustration of similarities analysis we have chosen to apply the Kruskal program and the Guttman–Lingoes program on a small body of data constituting a conditional proximity matrix.[3] For comparative purposes Hays's nonmetric method was applied to the same data matrix.

---

[3]We are indebted to Myron Wish for the application of the Guttman–Lingoes program and to Mike Fried for constructing a program to get a partial order out of a conditional proximity matrix and adapting that so Kruskal's program could be applied.

TABLE 3.1 NUMBER OF REFERENCES IN ROW JOURNAL TO COLUMN JOURNAL, 1964

	AJP	JASP	JAP	JCPP	JCP	JEdP	JExP	Pka	Total
American Journal of Psychology	119	8	4	21	0	1	85	2	240
Journal of Abnormal and Social Psychology	32	510	16	11	73	9	119	4	774
Journal of Applied Psychology	2	8	84	1	7	8	16	10	136
Journal of Comparative and Physiological Psychology	35	8	0	533	0	1	126	1	704
Journal of Consulting Psychology	6	116	11	1	225	7	12	7	385
Journal of Educational Psychology	4	9	7	0	3	52	27	5	107
Journal of Experimental Psychology	125	19	6	70	0	0	586	15	821
Psychometrika	2	5	5	0	13	2	13	58	98
Total	325	683	133	637	321	80	984	102	3,265

The question of interest here was whether the mutual dependencies and interactions of some psychology journals could be reflected in a metric representation. Eight journals were selected and are represented by the rows and columns of Table 3.1. A tally was made of the number of references made by each of these journals to the others during the calendar year 1964; these numbers are in the cells of the matrix.

The lack of symmetry in this matrix is notable and, of course, not surprising. The fact that the *American Journal of Psychology* made 8 references to the *Journal of Abnormal and Social Psychology* in 1964 is independent, in an experimental sense, of the fact that the *Journal of Abnormal and Social Psychology* made 32 references to the *American Journal of Psychology*. The question being asked here is whether there is any dependence, and if so, along what lines this dependence can be understood.

If these numbers could be taken as proximity measures, we could make the assumption of Eq. (3.6) for conditional proximity matrices and rank order the distances of each column stimulus from each row stimulus. But because journals differ in the number of articles for referral, and in the number of references their articles tend to make, the data in this matrix need to be corrected for these "bulk" effects. This correction was done by subtracting out row and column means. The resulting matrix of residuals was then analyzed as a conditional proximity matrix. A Euclidean distance function was assumed, and because Hays's method indicated that two dimensions are adequate, the results from the other methods are also reported for two dimensions.

The results are presented in Table 3.2 for easy comparisons. The first column contains the Hays analysis with the rank order of the journals on

TABLE 3.2 THREE ANALYSES OF THE 1964 JOURNAL
DATA

	Hays Nonmetric Analysis	Kruskal Analysis		Guttman–Lingoes Analysis	
	Rank Order	Rank Order	Projection	Rank Order	Projection
Dimension I	1. JASP	1. JASP	−1.382	1. JASP	−935
	2. JCP	2. JCP	−.924	2. JCP	−731
	3. JAP	3. JAP	−.261	3. JAP	−139
	4. JEdP	4. JEdP	−.180	4. JEdP	−109
	5. Pka	5. AJP	+.125	5. Pka	−33
	6. JExP	6. Pka	+.416	6. AJP	+232
	7. AJP	7. JExP	+.904	7. JExP	+592
	8. JCPP	8. JCPP	+1.302	8. JCPP	+1125
Dimension II	1. JASP	1. JExP	−.924	1. JExP	−791
	2. JCPP ⎫ tied	2. JASP	−.644	2. JASP	−613
	3. JExP ⎭	3. JAP	−.237	3. AJP	−215
	4. JCP	4. JCP	−.002	4. JCP	+127
	5. JEdP ⎫ tied	5. Pka	+.207	5. JCPP	+298
	6. Pka ⎭	6. JEdP	+.324	6. JEdP	+355
	7. JAP	7. JCPP	+.366	7. JAP	+411
	8. AJP	8. AJP	+.910	8. Pka	+427
	All triangles fitted	$S = .108$ 10 triangles left unfitted		$\phi = .00087$ 12 triangles left unfitted	

the first dimension and second dimension. The second column presents the results from the Kruskal analysis showing the actual projections on the first and second principal axes; and the third column gives the corresponding results from the Guttman–Lingoes analysis.[4] Figure 3.19 is provided to permit easier visual comparison of the configurations. It should be remembered that the configuration shown for Hays's method is merely a product of the simple orders. The correct configuration would be one that satisfied the rank orders of distances in all triangles, which would be some monotone transformation of these axes.

As is evident, there is exceedingly close correspondence among the three first dimensions and in general the configurations are similar. It is interesting to note that both of the metric methods violate order relations on distances within triangles of points—Kruskal's method fails to fit 10 of

[4]Hays's method, as applied here, represents the maximum number of the largest triangles by the first dimension; the second dimension represents all the remaining triangles. Kruskal's method, after converging on a configuration, reports out the projections on dimensions chosen in decreasing order of amount of variance each accounts for. The Guttman–Lingoes method begins with a principal components factor analysis as an initial configuration, so the dimensions of their final configuration would tend to be close to these principal axes. Hence, although the configurations are expected to match, one should also expect that at least the first dimension of all analyses would be closely matched.

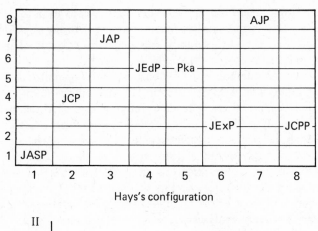

Hays's configuration

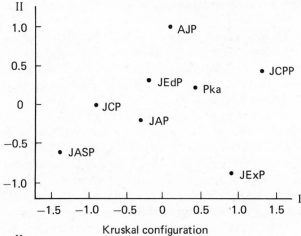

Kruskal configuration

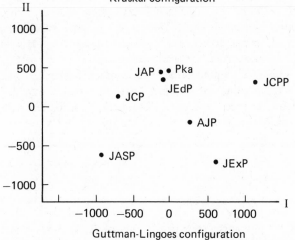

Guttman-Lingoes configuration

Fig. 3.19

the triangles and Guttman–Lingoes method fails to fit 12.[5] However, despite the fact that Hays's method fits all triangles with say r dimensions, it does not follow that a metric solution can necessarily be found in that number of dimensions.

Hays's method was previously applied to similar data for the calendar year 1960. This analysis is reported in Coombs (1964) and yields a very similar configuration. The interpretation suggested for the first dimension in that analysis included any or all of the following: soft-hard, real-artificial, field-laboratory, and significant-rigorous. The only change in the rank order on the first dimension in 1964 is the *Journal of Experimental Psychology*, which was at the extreme end in 1960. Either it has softened up or the *Journal of Comparative and Psychological Psychology* has moved farther out, if one takes the above analyses and interpretations seriously. Statistical theory for such analyses is almost totally undeveloped.

A look ahead. Recent research on multidimensional scaling models for similarity data has followed two major approaches, one aimed at the development of computer programs for multidimensional scaling and the other aimed at a theoretical analysis of the basic assumptions underlying the various similarity models.

The former approach, represented by the work of Shepard (1962*a*, *b*), Kruskal (1964*a*, *b*), Torgerson (1965), Lingoes (1966), and Guttman (1969), has led to the development of several general and efficient computer programs that have been applied to a wide variety of psychological data. The rapid progress that is being made in computer technology and numerical analysis, however, leads us to expect more general and more effective programs for obtaining geometric representations of similarity data.

The latter approach, exemplified by the work of Beals, Krantz, and Tversky (1968), has approached multidimensional scaling models from the viewpoint of measurement theory. It has led to axiomatizations of several classes of metric and/or dimensional similarity models and to the isolation of critical properties for empirical tests.

The development of new effective scaling procedures, combined with a theoretical analysis of similarity models, and an empirical investigation of their consequences will inevitably lead to a better understanding of the determinants of psychological similarity.

---

[5]Out of the 56 triangles there were two for which the distances within the triangles were intransitive [given Eq. (3.6)]; these were corrected before the data were analyzed, so all three methods were applied to the identical partial order.

NONNUMERICAL MODELS

4.1 INTRODUCTION

In Chapter 2 *measurement* was defined as the establishment of a correspondence between an empirical relational system and a numerical relational system; the numerical relational system was said to represent the empirical one in that elements in the empirical system are assigned numbers and the relationship between these elements is reflected by the relationship between the numbers. For example, an object a is assigned a weight of 8 pounds, an object b is assigned a weight of 4 pounds, and the fact that a outweighs b in a pan balance is represented by the numerical relation that 8 is larger than 4.

This chapter, in contrast, will deal with work in which a correspondence is established between empirical relational systems and nonnumerical relational systems, which are nevertheless formal. When such a correspondence is established, the formal, nonnumerical system is said to be a model of the empirical relational system it represents; hence, such a formal relational system is termed a *nonnumerical model*. This chapter will outline three types of nonnumerical models found in the psychological literature: (1) those provided by graph theory, (2) a specific model provided from the naive set theory of J. D. Gergonne, and (3) those provided by computer simulation.

4.2   GRAPH THEORY

When graph theory is used as a nonnumerical model in psychology, people and objects are represented by points and the relationships between people and objects are represented by lines between these points. For example, the relationship "John, who likes *Newsweek*, is in love with Mary, who doesn't like John but who shares his enthusiasm for *Newsweek*" may be represented as in Fig. 4.1.

The solid lines in Fig. 4.1 represent positive relationships; the dashed line represents a negative relationship. The entire collection of points and lines is referred to as a *graph*.

Of course, graphs need not be drawn on paper with actual lines and points. As formal relational systems, graphs simply consist of a set of entities and a set of one or more relations that may exist between some ordered pairs of these entities. (See the appendix for a rigorous definition of what is meant by a relation.) It is only when graphs are illustrated—as in Fig. 4.1—that the entities are represented as points and the relations are represented as lines. To be in accord with common usage, however, we shall henceforth refer to the entities of a graph as *points*.

Before proceeding with a discussion of the application of graphs to psychology, it is necessary to distinguish between the most common types of graphs. To do so, the points in graphs will be represented by letters and the relations by capital R's with appropriate subscripts. The fact that the relationship R_i exists between the ordered pair of points a and b will be represented by $a \, R_i \, b$.

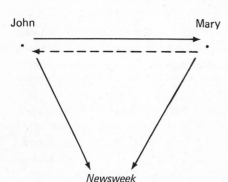

Fig. 4.1   Graph of the relations between two people and an object.

An *undirected* graph is one whose relations are symmetric. That is, a graph is undirected if and only if $a\,R_i\,b$ implies $b\,R_i\,a$ (note that then $b\,R_i\,a$ also implies $a\,R_i\,b$, as is proved immediately by interchanging a and b). In contrast, a *directed* graph is one in which $a\,R_i\,b$ may exist and $b\,R_i\,a$ does not exist.[1]

In undirected graphs, where $a\,R_i\,b$ if and only if $b\,R_i\,a$, it is unnecessary to distinguish between the two situations; hence, when undirected graphs are illustrated by points and lines, $a\,R_i\,b$ is illustrated by simply drawing a line between the points representing a and b, as in Fig. 4.2(a). In directed graphs, in contrast, it is important to distinguish between $a\,R_i\,b$ and $b\,R_i\,a$; hence, $a\,R_i\,b$ is illustrated by drawing an arrow from the point representing a to the point representing b, as in Fig. 4.2(b).

(a) a ——————— b
(b) a ——————→ b

Fig. 4.2   Undirected and directed graphs.

Undirected lines are commonly called *edges*, whereas directed lines are commonly called *arcs*. Thus, when $a\,R_i\,b$ in an undirected graph, we state that there is an *edge between a and b*, whereas when $a\,R_i\,b$ in a directed graph, we state that there is an *arc from a to b*; alternatively, we state that the arc is *oriented* from a to b.

In addition to the distinction between undirected and directed graphs, there is a basic distinction between *unsigned* and *signed* graphs. Briefly, an unsigned graph is one in which only one type of relation may exist between ordered pairs of entities. A signed graph is one in which two or more types of relations may exist between ordered pairs of entities. The most common type of signed graph is one in which there are two types of relations, one of which is termed a *positive* relation and one of which is termed a *negative* relation; these relations may be symbolized R_+ and R_-, respectively. Although it is possible to construct (i.e., conceptualize) graphs in which three or more types of relations may exist, it is rarely done—at least not in applications to psychology. Hence, such graphs will not be discussed in this chapter.

When signed graphs are illustrated with points and lines, the relation termed positive (R_+) is represented by a solid line, as in Fig. 4.3(a), whereas the relation termed negative (R_-) is represented by a dashed line, as in Fig.

---

[1]A directed graph is sometimes referred to as a *digraph*. The major text in which digraph is defined, however (Harary, Norman, and Cartwright 1965), includes in the definition the stipulation that no relations are reflexive, i.e., that it is never true that $a\,R_i\,a$. This stipulation seems unnecessarily restrictive for our purposes; hence, we shall not use the term *digraph* but shall continue to speak of "directed graphs."

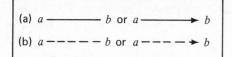

Fig. 4.3 Positive and negative relations in signed graphs.

4.3(b). It is, of course, arbitrary which relation is labeled positive and which negative; often, however, there is some semantically good reason for making the choice. In unsigned graphs the single relation is, by convention, illustrated by a solid line.

There are, then, four basic types of graphs that are generated from the undirected versus directed and unsigned versus signed dichotomies. Each of these four types will be illustrated briefly by example.

Types of Graphs   **An undirected unsigned graph.** Suppose that a supervisor a has conversations with three subordinates b, c, and d by interoffice telephone. Suppose, moreover, that a has interoffice phone connections to b, c, and d, but none of these subordinates has interoffice phone connections with each other. A graph representing this social situation may be constructed according to the following correspondence rule: $x\ R\ y$ if and only if x converses with y by interoffice telephone. Clearly, such a graph is undirected, because conversing (hence R) is a symmetric relation. And the graph is unsigned because it has a single relation. The graph representing the supervisor and his subordinates is illustrated in Fig. 4.4.

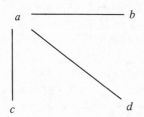

Fig. 4.4 Undirected unsigned graph.

When the graph of such an interpersonal communications network consists of a single point with lines to every other point, as in Fig. 4.4, the network is said to be in the form of a *star pattern*. The effect of the form of communication networks on group problem solving and satisfaction has been investigated by a number of social psychologists (for example, Festinger and Thibaut 1951; Shaw, Rothschild, and Strickland 1957).

An undirected signed graph. Suppose that a man M and his wife W have a male friend m and a female friend f to dinner. The wife wishes to seat the four of them around the dinner table in such a way that (1) she does not sit next to her husand and (2) no two males or females sit next to each

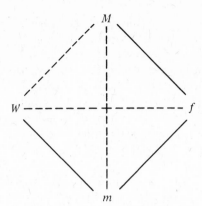

Fig. 4.5 Undirected signed graph.

other. A graph representing this seating arrangement may be constructed according to the following correspondence rule: $x\ R_+\ y$ if and only if x and y may sit next to each other, and $x\ R_-\ y$ if and only if x and y may not sit next to each other (according to requirements 1 and 2). Clearly, such a graph is undirected, because "sitting next to" (hence R_+) is a symmetric relation, as is "not sitting next to" (hence R_-). The graph representing the seating arrangement is illustrated in Fig. 4.5.

Note that we have constructed a graph representing a rule for seating arrangements despite the fact that this rule is impossible to implement.

A directed unsigned graph. A common structure represented by a directed unsigned graph is that of supervision in a business or governmental organization. Such supervision hierarchies may be represented by a graph according to the following correspondence rule: $x\ R\ y$ if and only if x supervises y. Clearly, the relation "supervises" (hence R) is not symmetric; in fact, it is never symmetric. Thus the graph is directed. It is also unsigned, because it has a single relation. Graphs representing various possible forms of supervision hierarchies are illustrated in Fig. 4.6. Such graphs are common.

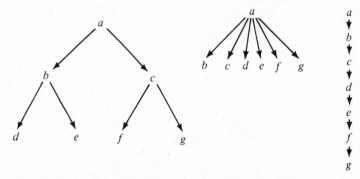

Fig. 4.6 Supervision hierarchies as directed unsigned graphs.

A directed signed graph. Maruyama (1963) has suggested that systems of processes may be studied in terms of whether a process a augments a process b, inhibits it, or does not act on it directly. A graph representing such a system studied in this manner may be constructed according to the following correspondence rule: $x\ R_+\ y$ if and only if process x augments process y, and $x\ R_-\ y$ if and only if process x inhibits process y. Clearly, such a graph is both directed and signed. Maruyama discusses the system of sanitation and garbage collection processes in a city; the graph representing his discussion is presented in Fig. 4.7 (adapted from Fig. 3 of Maruyama's 1963 article, p. 176).

Note that *cycles* exist in Fig. 4.7; that is, there are some series of arcs that begin and end at the same point. For example, $P\ R_+\ M$, $M\ R_+\ C$, and $C\ R_+\ P$. (The more people in a city, the greater the pressure toward modernization; the greater the modernization, the more appealing the city is to immigrate to; and the more immigration, the more people in the city.) Such a cycle represents *positive feedback*. A cycle representing *negative feedback* is $P\ R_+\ G$, $G\ R_+\ B$, $B\ R_+\ D$ and $D\ R_-\ P$. (The more people, the more garbage; the more garbage, the more bacteria; the more bacteria, the more disease; and the more disease, the fewer people.) The reader may verify for himself that a cycle represents positive feedback if and only if it contains an even number of R_-'s (counting zero as an even number), and it represents negative feedback if and only if it contains an odd number of R_-'s. Note that an overall system, such as that illustrated in Fig. 4.7, may contain both positive feedback and negative feedback.

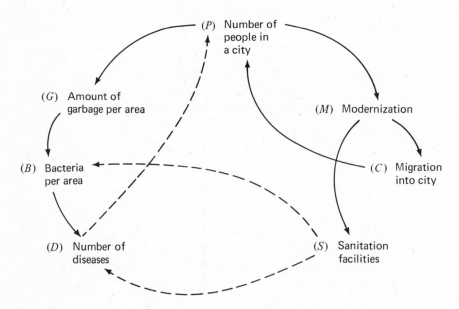

Fig. 4.7 Directed signed graph.

Maruyama, in the article from which the graph is taken, makes the point that scientists are prone to look for negative feedback systems at the expense of looking for positive feedback systems. Feedback is associated with cybernetics, which by definition means negative feedback—or rather steering accomplished by the use of negative feedback. Maruyama argues with particular vigor that positive feedback systems exist in great quantity in social interaction and individual psychology. Following are examples. (These examples are those of the present authors, not Maruyama's.)

1. SS men were required to serve as concentration camp guards, and immediately upon arriving at the camps, they were forced to perform acts of cruelty (Cohen 1953). The performance of such acts reinforced the belief that the inmates were subhuman, because this belief alleviated the guard's guilt. This reinforced belief, in turn, increased the probability that the guards would engage in further acts of cruelty, acts that in turn reinforced the belief.

2. An individual who is "mentally ill" may act in ways that cause other people to reject him, and this rejection leads to greater feelings of isolation and inferiority, i.e., exacerbates the "sickness."

3. Socially stressful situations result in a complex endocrine reaction, one of the results of which is to shrink gonads (Christian 1963). In chimpanzee groups, which are largely based on a dominance hierarchy of the members, the subordinate males are more likely than the dominant males to be placed in stressful situations. (Often this stress is provided by the dominant males.) But one effect of stress is to shrink gonad size, which presumably makes the male even less dominant, which would lead to a greater probability of being stressed (and hence even smaller gonads).

4. High-quality staff in an academic institution attracts high-quality students, who in turn make it easier to attract high-quality staff.

Platt (1966) discusses many other positive feedback systems in society.

Graph theory consists of theorems and proofs about the types of graphs described above. Like other mathematical theories, it is not a substantive theory about what the real world is like; rather the mathematician working with graph theory is concerned with certain properties of graphs and with the logical relationships among these properties—for example, which properties imply which other properties and which are independent of which. Often, however, a graph can be used to represent a real world system of interest to the psychologist; when such a representation is validly established, any theorems that may be asserted about the graph apply also to the system it represents; thus such theorems are of interest for their possible application as well as for their own sake. In the following sections, three such theorems will be asserted and their applications discussed briefly. One proof will be included in order to give the reader a familiarity with how such theorems are proved.

**Balance and the
Structure
Theorem**

Consider a finite undirected signed graph. A *path* is said to exist between points x and y of such a graph if and only if there is a sequence of edges beginning with point x that lead to point y. That is, a path exists between points x and y if and only if there exists a series of distinct points $(p_1, p_2, \ldots, p_i, \ldots, p_n)$ having the properties that (1) $p_1 = x$, (2) $p_n = y$, and (3) for all i there is an edge between p_i and p_{i+1}. When a path exists, we speak of the path as *containing* points $(p_1, p_2, \ldots, p_i, \ldots, p_n)$ and of these points as being *included* in the path. The path itself *consists of* the edges involved.

Note that the edges in a path may be either positive or negative. And in fact the number of negative edges in a path turns out to be crucial in defining an important property of a path. The *sign* of a path is said to be *positive* if and only if it contains an even number of negative edges; otherwise it is said to be *negative*. (Zero is considered to be an even number.) The sign of a path may be conceptualized as consisting of the product of the signs of its edges, where each positive edge is assigned the value $+1$ and each negative edge assigned the value -1; then, if there are an even number of negative edges, the product of all the numbers assigned to the edges will be $+1$; if there are an odd number of negative edges, the product of all the numbers assigned to the edges will be -1.

Finally, a particular type of path is defined. A *cycle*, loosely speaking, is a path that begins and ends at the same point. That is, a cycle exists if and only if there are a series of points $(p_1, p_2, \ldots, p_i, \ldots, p_n)$ having the properties that (1) $p_1 = x$, (2) $p_n = x$, (3) for all i there is an edge between p_i and p_{i+1}, and (4) all the points are distinct except for p_1 and p_n. Note that we do not state that a cycle exists "from" and "to" a particular point, because any point in the sequence $(p_1, p_2, \ldots, p_i, \ldots, p_n)$ could be used to define the cycle. As before, we speak of the cycle as containing the points $(p_1, p_2, \ldots, p_i, \ldots, p_n)$ and of these points as being included in the cycle. Also, we define the *sign* of a cycle as *positive* if and only if it contains an even number of negative edges, and as *negative* otherwise.

The concepts of path, sign, and cycle are illustrated in Fig. 4.8. There are paths from a to all other points except f, g, and h. Similarly, there are paths from b to every other point except f, g, and h, and so on. From f there are paths only to g and h, from g only to f and h, and from h only to f and g.

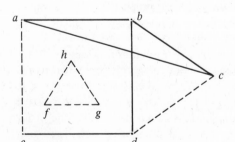

Fig. 4.8   Graph illustrating concepts of path, sign, and cycle.

Five cycles are apparent: (1) the cycle containing the points (a, b, and c), which has a positive sign; (2) the cycle containing the points (b, c, and d), which has a negative sign; (3) the cycle containing the points (a, b, d, and e), which has a negative sign; (4) the cycle containing the points (a, b, c, d, and e), which has a positive sign; and (5) the cycle containing the points (f, g, and h), which has a negative sign. The figure also contains a great many paths that are not enumerated here.

It may be asked if it is possible to construct paths and cycles that contain the same point and/or edge more than once; e.g., does the sequence of edges between a and b, b and c, c and a, a and b again, b and d, d and e, and e and a constitute a legitimate cycle? The answer is no. In the definition of *path* given in this book, there was the restriction that the same point may not appear more than once (i.e., the points in the paths were required to be distinct). And in the definition of *cycle* only the point defining it could appear twice. It follows that the same edge cannot appear more than once, for such an edge is between the same two points, and it would hence cause both of them to appear more than once. In insisting that the points in a path be distinct, we are following Cartwright and Harary (1956). Other authors (e.g., Berge 1962) do not have this requirement stated in their definition of *path*. Such authors, however, define a *simple path* as one not containing the same edge twice and an *elementary path* as one not containing the same point twice; they then often limit attention to elementary (hence simple) paths—paths of the type discussed in this book.

The two theorems to be discussed in this section concern conditions under which every cycle in a graph will have a positive sign, in which case the graph is said to be *balanced*. These conditions are described in the following theorems.

THEOREM 4.1

A finite undirected signed graph is balanced if and only if all paths joining the same pair of points have the same sign.

THEOREM 4.2 (termed the *structure theorem*)

A finite undirected signed graph is balanced if and only if its points can be separated into two mutually exclusive subsets having the property that each positive edge is between two points of the same subset and each negative edge is between points from different subsets.

Proof

The second theorem may be derived from the first, whose proof will be outlined here. First, it will be proved that if a graph is balanced all paths joining the same pair of points have the same sign. For suppose points x and y were joined with two paths having different signs; then one of these paths must have an odd number of negative edges and one an even number; hence the cycle formed by combining these two paths must have an odd number of negative edges (the sum of an even number and an odd number is an odd number); that is, the graph is not balanced, which is contrary to assumption. (If the two paths have a point in common, they do not form a legitimate cycle when combined; it can then, however, be proved that there is a cycle containing the point in common that has an odd number of negative edges.)

Now it will be proved that if all paths joining the same pair of points have the same sign, then the graph is balanced. For suppose the graph were not balanced; then there would be at least one cycle containing an odd number of negative edges. Now consider any two points x and y on such a cycle and consider the two paths joining them that make up the cycle; if both these paths had an even number of negative edges or both had an odd number of negative edges, the cycle itself would have an even number of negative edges, which is untrue; hence one path must have an even number of negative edges and one an odd number, which means that not all paths joining the same pair of points have the same sign.

Three balanced graphs are illustrated in Fig. 4.9, which is adapted from Cartwright and Harary (1956, pp. 286–287). Because these graphs are balanced, two subsets of points satisfying the stipulation of the structure theorem may be found in each. In Fig. 4.9(a) these two subsets are readily determined—$\{a, b, c, d\}$ and $\{e, f, g, h\}$—whereas in the other parts of the figure, the subsets may not be so obvious. In Fig. 4.9(b) they are $\{A, D, E, H\}$ and $\{B, C, F, G\}$; in Fig. 4.9(c) they are $\{A_1, B_1, A_3, B_3, A_5, B_5\}$ and

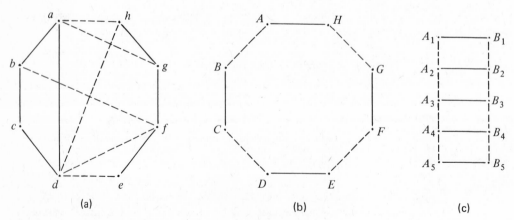

Fig. 4.9 Three balanced graphs illustrating the structure theorem.

$\{A_2, B_2, A_4, B_4\}$. It should be noted in passing that although the structure theorem asserts a property about edges rather than paths, it is also true that all paths joining points from the same subset are positive and all paths joining points from different subsets are negative.

The theorems in this section have application whenever a real world process may be represented by a finite undirected signed graph in such a way that the sign of a cycle has some empirical meaning. Consider, for example, a group of businesses some of which compete with each other, some of which cooperate with each other, and some of which neither compete nor cooperate with each other. These businesses may be represented as points in a finite undirected signed graph whose edges are determined according to the following rule: $a R_- b$ (i.e., there is a negative edge between a and b) if and only if a competes with b, and $a R_+ b$ (i.e., there is a positive edge between a and b) if and only if a cooperates with b. Now consider what happens in the business group whenever a negative cycle exists in the graph. All the businesses represented by points included in such a cycle are cooperating and competing in such a way that they might eventually hurt themselves (e.g., a competes with b, who cooperates with c, who cooperates with a). From the structure theorem we can tell immediately that such potentially self-defeating behavior will be avoided if and only if the businesses can be divided into two mutually exclusive groups having the property that competition exists only between businesses in different groups and cooperation exists only between two businesses in the same group.

Before concluding this section, one point of terminology should be mentioned. Throughout this chapter, when a graph represents a real world system or process of some sort, the graph has been referred to as a *model* of the process. Conversely, it is possible to refer to the process as a *realization* of the graph, and many authors do. In the above example, the system of businesses would be referred to as a realization of a finite undirected signed graph, and the fact that self-defeating behavior is avoided only if the subset condition is met would be referred to as a realization of the structure theorem.

A Theorem About Finite Directed Unsigned Graphs

As in the previous section, we first define certain properties of such graphs. A *path* is said to exist between points x and y of a directed graph if and only if there is a sequence of arcs beginning with point x that lead to point y. That is, a path exists between points x and y if and only if there is a series of distinct points $(p_1, p_2, \ldots, p_i, \ldots, p_n)$ having the properties that (1) $p_1 = x$, (2) $p_n = y$, and (3) for all i there is an arc from p_i to p_{i+1}. A graph is said to be *unilateral* if and only if for any two points x and y there is a path from x to y or from y to x (or both). A graph is said to have a *complete sequence* if and only if there exists some path in which every point is included; this path is termed *the* complete sequence.

The following theorem may now be stated.

THEOREM 4.3

A finite directed graph is unilateral if and only if it has a complete sequence.

This theorem is stated without proof, because it is trivial to prove that a finite graph with a complete sequence is unilateral and rather difficult to prove that a unilateral finite graph has a complete sequence.

One realization of this theorem involves rumor networks. Such a network may be represented by an unsigned directed graph according to the rule that $x \ R \ y$ (i.e., there is an arc from x to y) if and only if x tells rumors to y. Clearly then a rumor may reach y from x if and only if there is a path from x to y. A realization of the theorem just stated is that the following two properties of a rumor network are equivalent.

1. Given any two people in it, at least one can start a rumor that will reach the other (i.e., the graph representing the network is unilateral).
2. There exists at least one person who can start a rumor that will reach everyone else even though everyone transmits the rumor to only one person. (Such a person is one represented by the first point of a complete sequence, at least one of which exists.)

For a fuller discussion of the theorem and its realization concerning rumor networks, see Harary, Norman, and Cartwright (1965, p. 64).

Empirical Work Involving Graph Theory

The three theorems presented in the last two sections were presented as abstract graph theory theorems and some realizations were discussed. It would have also been possible to present the theorems directly in terms of their realizations; that is, instead of discussing points and positive and negative edges in the first two theorems, it would have been possible to discuss businesses and cooperation and competition between such businesses; the conclusions would have been exactly the same as those reached by first considering graphs and then regarding business activity as a realization. Further, to establish the equivalence of the two properties of a rumor network, it is not necessary first to discuss directed graphs. In both the theorem and its proof (which was omitted here) the word "person" could be substituted for the word "point" and the phrase "x tells rumors to y" could be substituted for the phrase "there is an arc from x to y." Again, the conclusions would be identical with those reached by first considering directed graphs in their abstract form and then regarding rumor networks as a realization.

The decision to consider graphs rather than each of the empirical relational systems they represent separately is one based on convenience and economy. Statements that are true of graphs may have a number of realizations; i.e., the graphs considered may represent a number of empirical relational systems. In addition, many people find it easier to reason about points, edges, arcs, etc., than to reason about more concrete entities and their relations. *Simply representing an empirical relational system as a graph does not, however, in and of itself, increase our knowledge of that system. Nor does illustrating the graph with points and lines.*

On the other hand, it is possible to represent certain properties of empirical relational systems as properties of graphs, and such a representation may allow the researcher to derive empirical implications of these properties that he might not have derived otherwise. For example, Heider (1946) proposed that people have a cognitive bias to perceive that people they like have attitudes toward other social phenomena similar to their own and to perceive that people they dislike have contrary attitudes toward other social phenomena. He termed this bias a bias to perceive *social balance*. Later, Cartwright and Harary (1956) showed how such a bias could be regarded as a bias to perceive social relationships in such a way that the graph representing the relationships is balanced (in the graph theory sense described earlier).

Consider, for example, graphs representing a situation discussed by Heider. There are two people, who will be labeled p and o, who either like or dislike each other, and there is some social phenomenon, which will be labeled x, toward which they have positive or negative attitudes. An undirected signed graph representing the eight possible situations is illustrated in Fig. 4.10. It is constructed according to the following correspondence rule: $a \, R_+ \, b$ if and only if a has a positive attitude toward b, and $a \, R_- \, b$ if and only if a has a negative attitude toward b. (Despite the fact that x does not properly have an "attitude" toward p or o, no harm is done by considering attitude as symmetric in this example.)

The four situations represented by the graphs illustrated in Fig. 4.10(a) are those that Heider would term to be in a state of social balance; people who like each other are holding similar attitudes toward the social phe-

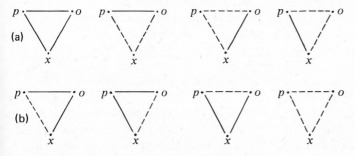

Fig. 4.10 Balanced and unbalanced social situations.

nomenon in question, or people who dislike each other are holding contrary attitudes. In contrast, the four situations represented by the graphs illustrated in Fig. 4.10(b) are not in a state of social balance. This social balance is represented perfectly by the balance of the graphs. The cycles in the graphs illustrated in Fig. 4.10(a) are positive, and those in the graphs illustrated in Fig. 4.10(b) are negative.

Cartwright and Harary (1956), noting that the graph theoretic property of balance perfectly represented Heider's notion of social balance in the p, o, x situation, proposed that much larger social situations could be defined as unbalanced or balanced. One simply represents the social situation with a signed graph and then notes whether the cycles of this graph are balanced or unbalanced. Moreover, this representation leads directly to two additional concepts; one of these, the *degree* of balance, refers to the proportion of cycles that are positive in sign; the other, *local balance*, refers to the balance and imbalance of cycles containing a given point; we refer to local balance as being *at* that particular point. Combining these concepts, we can speak of the degree of local balance at any given point.

The concepts of *cycle* and *balance* can be extended in a natural manner to directed graphs as well. We do not do so here for the reason that the literature to be discussed does not require an understanding of the technicalities involved in this extension. The interested reader is referred to the 1956 article of Cartwright and Harary of the 1965 book of Harary, Norman, and Cartwright.

(As noted earlier, when a graph represents processes that may augment or inhibit each other, cycles with an even number of negative relations represent positive feedback and cycles with an odd number of negative relations represent negative feedback; thus the above concepts of balance have applicability to systems other than those consisting of social interactions.)

Although the concepts concerning balance in a graph are quite broad and have numerous applications, the *experimental* literature on balance is, as of the writing of this book, primarily concerned with balance in the two person/single object or phenomenon situation discussed by Heider. (This object may be a third person.) It has been demonstrated that when subjects are told the sign of all but one relationship and asked to guess its sign they have a tendency to guess that sign that will result in balance (Morrisette 1958). It has also been shown that subjects will tend to judge that balanced relationships are more pleasant than unbalanced relationships —at least when the relation between p and o is positive (Price, Harberg, and Newcomb 1966).

Such studies show a cognitive bias only in that people tend to expect balance or judge it to be pleasant when there is no other information on which to base their judgments. If this bias disappears when other information is available, it is of limited interest to social psychology, because people are almost never placed in a situation of knowing nothing about a set of social relationships except whether a few are positive or negative. If, on the other hand, the bias exists in situations in which people have other information, it could result in misuse of this information in reaching conclusions. Then, as a source of social distortion, it would be of great interest.

A similar point is made by Rorer (1965) in his discussion of response bias in personality assessment; he distinguishes between a bias that exists in the absence of any other factors (e.g., a bias to guess true to a true-false item concerning which one has no knowledge) and a bias that exists in the presence of other factors (e.g., a bias to agree with personality items irrespective of their content).

This distinction between establishing a bias in the absence or in the presence of other information is crucial in the study of cognitive bias. If the experimenter wishes to establish that his subject has a bias to believe X, he may either (1) tell the subject nothing about whether X is true or not and ask him if he judges X to be true or (2) give the subject information indicating that X is not true and see if the subject nevertheless judges X to be true. These two operations for establishing bias are quite different, and the type of bias they establish is likewise different. Clearly, if the experimenter wishes to establish a bias that he believes is responsible for certain social distortions and misunderstandings, he must establish it by means of operations of type 2. Most experimenters investigating belief in balance as a cognitive bias have employed operations of type 1.

One exception is found in the work of Zajonc and Burnstein (1965). What these researchers did was to test the ease with which subjects could *learn* balanced and unbalanced situations. Their subjects were told directly whether certain relations were positive or negative and then asked to remember them. If there is a tendency to believe in balance despite information to the contrary, the subjects should have greater difficulty learning the relationships that exist in unbalanced situations. If, on the other hand, subjects judge situations to be balanced only in the absence of other information, this bias should not interfere with their learning of unbalanced relationships. They should have no greater difficulty in learning the relations in unbalanced situations than in balanced situations.

The actual social relationships that Zajonc and Burnstein had their subjects learn are illustrated in Fig. 4.11 (adapted from Zajonc and Burnstein, p. 155). In this figure an arrow signifies *likes* or *approves of* and a dashed arrow signifies *dislikes* or *disapproves of*. Note that Fig. 4.11 is drawn in such a way as to suggest that the relationships involved are represented by directed, rather than undirected, graphs. In the present context, however, there are no situations in which there is an arc from x to y as well as one from y to x. Hence, the relations may be treated, for all practical purposes, as symmetric, and in fact each situation is regarded as balanced or unbalanced depending on whether an undirected graph representing it is balanced or unbalanced.

The task was one of straightforward paired associates learning. The

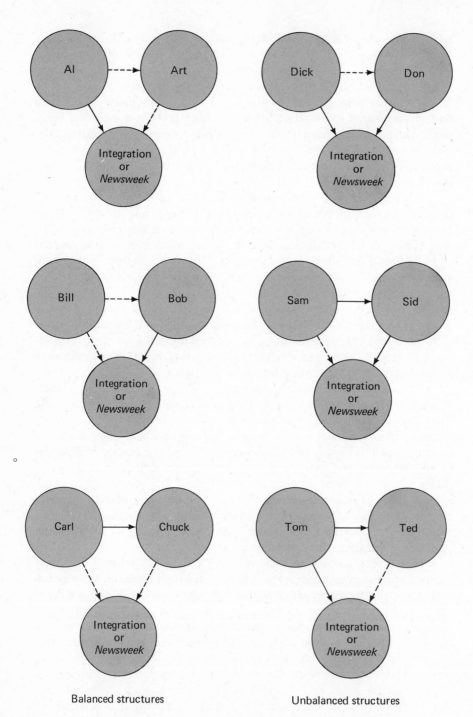

Balanced structures   Unbalanced structures

Fig. 4.11 Balanced and unbalanced structures used by Zajonc and Burnstein.

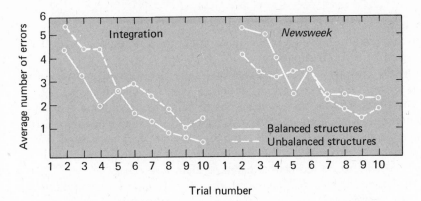

Fig. 4.12 Average number of errors in the learning of balanced and unbalanced structures.

subject was presented with a stimulus consisting of two names or a name and a social object (*Newsweek* or integration) printed on one side of an index card, and he was to anticipate whether a plus or minus sign was printed on the other side; a plus sign appeared whenever the first member of the stimulus pair liked or approved of the second member, and a minus sign otherwise. The meaning of these signs was explained to the subjects, all of whom were tested for a total of 10 trials through the entire set of 18 pairs. Of course, the actual names were counterbalanced across subjects. Care was also taken in constructing the task to have an equal number of correct plus and minus responses (as can be verified by inspection of Fig. 4.11).

The subjects in this study were 12 volunteers from among male undergraduates at the University of Michigan. The average number of errors they made in balanced and unbalanced contexts across the trials is presented in Fig. 4.12 (adapted from Zajonc and Burnstein, p. 157).

It can be seen that the hypothesis that there is greater difficulty learning relations in unbalanced than in balanced contexts is supported when the social phenomenon under consideration is integration but not when it is *Newsweek*. A second finding in the study, one not indicated by Fig. 4.12, is that negative relations are more difficult to learn than are positive ones. The authors conclude (p. 161):

> Two findings emerged from the experiment. First, an unbalanced structure was found more difficult to learn than a balanced one but only when the issue was an important one. Second, negative relationships were found to be more difficult to learn than positive ones. This finding was independent of whether these relationships exist between two people or between a person and an issue.

The findings of this study are quite provocative when it is realized that (1) the relationships were entirely hypothetical and were recognized as such by the subjects and (2) the subjects were presumably attempting to learn these relationships in a rote manner rather than attempting to form an impression of a social situation.

More recently, other investigators have investigated memory for balanced and unbalanced social situations (Gerard and Fleischer 1967; Lohrenz 1967). The tentative conclusions to be drawn from these investigations are that imbalanced situations are better remembered when short-term recall is required, that balanced situations are better remembered when long-term recall is required, and that at long-term recall unbalanced situations are more likely to be recalled as balanced than *vice versa*.

What constitutes the *source* of this bias is another question, one presently unanswered. Perhaps actual social relationships do tend to be balanced and the subject comes to believe in balance as a result of experience. Perhaps, on the other hand, the bias to believe in balance is simply a manifestation of the simplemindedness one discovers in people if he studies them carefully. Or, perhaps, a simpleminded belief in balance creates expectations that lead to the formation of balanced relationships, such formation in turn reinforcing the simpleminded belief (another instance of positive feedback). At the present time, experiments differentiating these possible sources are lacking, although some careful work on the formation of friendships and dislikes is available (Newcomb 1961).

4.3   ANALYSIS OF GROUP RELATIONSHIPS IN TERMS OF GERGONNE'S SET RELATIONS

Consider a number of groups each consisting of a finite number of objects, such as people. The relationship between any two of these groups corresponds to one of the four set relationships explicated by the French mathematician Gergonne (1817) in the early 19th century.

> EXCLUSION: The two groups have no objects in common.
> IDENTITY: The two groups consist of the same objects.
> INCLUSION: All the objects in one group are included in the other, but not *vice versa*.
> DISJUNCTION: The two groups have elements in common, but both groups also have objects not included in the other group.

These four possible relationships are represented by Venn diagrams in Fig. 4.13. Any two groups consisting of a finite number of objects have one of these relationships and only one; that is, Gergonne's taxonomy is exhaustive and exclusive. Gergonne's taxonomy, moreover, is different from that of Aristotle; for example, the Aristotelian relation "some X are Y" is true of all but the exclusion relation of Gergonne.

A belief about two groups of objects, such as people, may be repre-

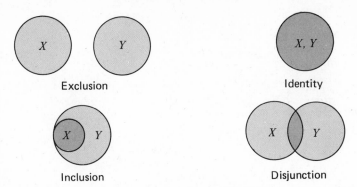

Fig. 4.13   Venn diagrams of Gergonne relations.

sented by a Venn diagram representing one of the Gergonne relationships. For example, a belief that all liberals are communists may be represented by a diagram illustrating the set of liberals included in the set of communists. Many beliefs about social relationships concern such group relations, and these beliefs may therefore be represented by the diagrams of the appropriate Gergonne relations.

Dawes (1964) has proposed that distorted beliefs about social groups may be studied within the framework of the Gergonne relations. He proposed that a distorted belief about the relationship between groups occurs whenever an individual is exposed to information that the relationship between the groups corresponds to one of the Gergonne relationships but the individual's beliefs about the relationship correspond to another.

Dawes further classified two basic types of distortions. The crux of this classification is that inclusion, exclusion, and identity are all *nested* relationships. If two sets have an exclusion relationship, each is nested in the complement of the other; if two sets have an inclusion relationship, one is nested in the other; finally, if two sets have an identity relation, they are mutually nested. In contrast, if two sets have a disjunctive relationship, neither is nested in the other.

According to Dawes's classification system, then, there are two basic types of relationships: nesting and disjunction. It follows that there are two basic types of distorted beliefs about groups: belief that a nested relation is disjunctive and belief that a disjunctive relation is nested. The former type of distortion has been termed *pseudodiscrimination*, because it involves the discrimination of a category that literally does not exist (a part of one set not nested in the other); the latter type of distortion has been termed *overgeneralization*, because it involves the belief that a set partially nested in another is totally nested. Overgeneralization and pseudodiscrimination are illustrated in Fig. 4.14.

Figure 4.14(a) illustrates an instance of overgeneralization; all members of a given group are believed to be communists despite exposure to informa-

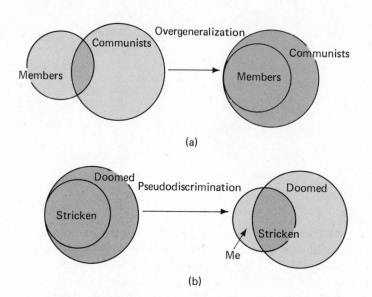

Fig. 4.14 Venn diagrams of overgeneralization and pseudodiscrimination.

tion indicating some are and some are not. Figure 4.14(b) illustrates an
instance of pseudodiscrimination; some people who are stricken with a
given disease are believed not to be doomed despite exposure to information
indicating all are doomed.

Simply explicating beliefs in terms of set relations and classifying
distortions in terms of these relations does not in and of itself increase our
knowledge about those beliefs—nor does illustrating this classification by
the use of Venn diagrams.

The relations and the classification of distortion can, however, be used
as a basis for framing psychological propositions. And just as Heider proposed that people have a cognitive bias to perceive social balance, Dawes
proposed that people have a cognitive bias to believe relations between
social groups are nested. Thus people have a cognitive bias to overgeneralize.
There are two rationales for this proposition, which are actually two ways
of stating the same principle. First, nested relations are conceptually simpler
than disjunctive relations in that fewer categories of objects exist; e.g., if
all members of a given group are communists, there is no category consisting
of noncommunist group members. If, as earlier, we accept the general
postulate that people tend to be simpleminded, we would expect distortions
to be of the type that makes the environment simple, i.e., of the type that
reduces, rather than increases, the number of categories of objects that exist.
(It should be remembered that this general simplemindedness postulate was
one possible explanation for the bias to perceive balance.) A second rationale
for Dawes's proposition is that nested relationships provide *structure* between

groups in that knowledge that an object is a member of one of two nested sets *may* immediately imply that it is or is not a member of the other. For example, if all members of a given group are communists, knowledge that someone is a group member implies that he is a communist. No such implication can be made when two groups have a disjunctive relationship. If, as Garner claims (1962, p. 339), "the search for structure is inherent in behavior," we would expect people to search for nested relations. (Garner discusses probabilistic structure, measured with the statistics of information theory, whereas the above discussion is concerned with logical structure.)

That the above two rationales are merely two ways of stating the same principle is evident when one realizes that *two sets will have a structured relation in the above sense if and only if some categories of objects do not exist.* Prediction is possible if and only if certain combinations are impossible.[2]

To test his proposition, Dawes wrote stories about hypothetical groups of people and then tested subjects' memory for these stories. These stories presented relations between groups that clearly corresponded to one of the Gergonne relations. Subjects' memory was tested by asking them which of the Gergonne relations in fact existed according to the stories. The errors of the subjects could then be classified as either overgeneralizations or pseudo-discriminations and the relative frequency of each type of error compared.

One such story read as follows.

> Circle Island is located in the middle of the Atlantic Ocean; it is a flat island with large grass meadows, good soil, but few rivers and hence a shortage of water.
> The main occupations on the island are farming and cattle ranching. While the majority of the islanders are farmers, the ranchers are much more prosperous, for they are less affected by the lack of water; thus, no ranchers farm in addition.
> The island is run democratically; all issues are decided by a majority vote of the islanders. The actual governing body is a 10-man senate, whose job is to carry out the will of the majority. Since the most desirable trait in a senator is administrative ability, the senate consists of the 10 best proven administrators—the island's ten richest men. For years, all the senators have been ranchers.
> Recently, an island scientist discovered a cheap method of converting salt water into fresh water; as a result, some of the island farmers wanted to build a canal across the island, so that they could use the water from the canal to cultivate the island's central region. Some of the farmers formed a pro canal association and even persuaded a few senators to join.
> The pro canal association brought the idea of constructing a canal to a vote. All the islanders voted, with all the members of the pro canal association and all the farmers voting for construction and everybody else voting against it. The majority voted in favor of construction.

[2]It is of interest to note that the logical errors involved in "affirmation of the consequent" and "reasoning according to the Von Domarus principle" (Arieti 1955) are also instances of overgeneralization (Dawes 1964).

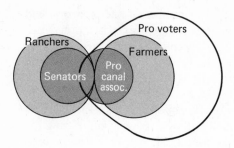

The senate, however, decided it would be too dangerous to have a canal that was more than 2 in. wide and 3 in. deep. After starting construction on such a canal, the island engineers found no water would flow into it, and the project had to be abandoned.

A Venn diagram of the set relations presented in the story is presented in Fig. 4.15.

It should be noted that half the relationships in this story are disjunctive and half are nested.

After reading two such stories, subjects were presented with questions of the following form:
Circle the correct alternative:

    a. No ranchers voted for construction of the canal.
    b. Not all, but some ranchers voted for construction of the canal.

All questions consisted of one alternative describing a nested relationship and one describing a disjunctive relationship. Thus each erroneous response could be classified either as an overgeneralization or a pseudodiscrimination. (Although the statement "not all but some X are Y" may be true of both a disjunctive relation and of the inclusive relation in which Y is nested in X, it was never used when the latter sort of relation was possible in the context of the story; rather the disjunctive alternative was worded "not all, but some Y are X.")

In his original study Dawes asked 12 such questions[3]; to 6 of these 12 questions the correct answers consisted of the nested alternative and to 6 the correct answers consisted of the disjunctive alternative. Hence, overgeneralizations and pseudodiscriminations should be equally likely if no cognitive bias exists. His college student subjects made, on the average, more overgeneralizations than pseudodiscriminations. This bias was not caused by any particular item being particularly easy or difficult, because analysis of all possible subsets of items revealed the same bias. The bias was highly reliable statistically.

[3]Actually, 12, 14, and 16 questions were given to different groups but only the 12 common items were scored. For an explanation of this variation, see the original article.

Another result of some interest is that only one of Dawes's 135 subjects correctly answered all the questions.

The finding that overgeneralization is the predominant type of erroneous response to the above type of question has several possible interpretations. It is possible that when subjects choose an incorrect nested alternative in response to a question they actually believe that alternative to be correct because they have distorted the story. It is also possible that when subjects choose an incorrect nested alternative they do so because they have forgotten the relationship and they have a response bias to choose nested alternatives when they are guessing. Finally, it is possible that subjects learn nested relationships with greater ease than they learn disjunctive alternatives and that they therefore have a greater possibility of making an erroneous guess on items in which the correct alternative is disjunctive, i.e., a greater possibility of making overgeneralizations.

To distinguish between these interpretations, Dawes (1966) ran a second study. In this study, rather than testing subjects' memory by presenting them with pairs of groups and asking them to choose which relation existed between these pairs, he presented his subjects with the Gergonne relations and asked them to pick any pair of groups they remembered as having these relationships. (Thus subjects were asked to list all the groups they could remember having the relationship that "all X were Y" and so on.) The groups were listed for the subject's reference, but he was under no obligation to specify that any two of them had a particular type of relationship. This study allows a differentiation between the subject's distortion of the material and his selectively remembering it, because it allows a distinction between being correct and making an error. A subject does not automatically assert an incorrect relation if he does not remember the correct one; he may assert no relation whatsoever.

Dawes found statistically reliable evidence for both (1) a greater tendency to assert that nested relationships are nested than to assert that disjunctive relationships are disjunctive and (2) a greater tendency to assert that disjunctive relationships are nested than to assert that nested relationships are disjunctive. Thus the overgeneralization in the previous study must have been caused both by selective memory and selective distortion. Consistent with the previous study, Dawes found memory to be exceedingly poor. In fact, the subjects in this study were just as apt to assert an incorrect relationship as to assert a correct one; an accuracy score, consisting of the number of correct assertions minus the number of incorrect assertions, was computed for each subject; the mean of these scores was not significantly greater than zero. In his pioneering work on memory of meaningful material, Bartlett had also found that accuracy of recall is "not a rule" (1932, p. 93).

Given that accuracy is not the rule, how confident do people feel of their recall? Bartlett had previously been surprised at the low level of accuracy in his subjects' recall, because both he and his subjects believed they recalled what they read much better than the evidence indicated they did. To explore the relationship between accuracy and confidence, Dawes asked 40 subjects in his first study to assign confidence ratings to their responses. It will be recalled that in this study subjects were to circle a nested relation or a disjunctive relation as the one holding between pairs of groups in the stories. The subject was to assign a rating of zero if he were purely guessing between the two alternatives and a score of 100 if he were absolutely certain. The findings on confidence are quoted from Dawes (1964, pp. 456–457). (It should be mentioned that accuracy was greater in this study than in the second study, apparently because the type of measure used to assess memory in this study was essentially a recognition measure whereas that used in the second study was essentially a recall measure.)

> For each S, the mean confidence rating assigned to each type of circled alternative was computed; there are, of course, four types: correct nested, correct disjunctive, incorrect nested (i.e., overgeneralization), and incorrect disjunctive (i.e., pseudo-discrimination). These mean ratings yield an over-all ordering of the four types of alternatives according to the criterion that one type is ordered above another if and only if over half the Ss have a higher mean confidence assigned to the former type. The order of these types— reading from the type engendering greatest confidence to that engendering least—is as follows: correct nested, overgeneralization, correct disjunctive, pseudo-discrimination.[4]

Furthermore:

> An unexpected statistic of interest is the number of confidence ratings of 100 given to erroneous responses. Twenty-one of the 40 Ss made at least one such response. Of these 21, one assigned the rating to a pseudo-discrimination, 5 assigned the rating to one overgeneralization and one pseudo-discrimination, and 15 assigned the rating to more overgeneralizations than pseudo-discriminations. A sign test permits rejection of the null hypothesis that such a rating is equally likely to be given predominately to over-generalizations or predominately to pseudo-discriminations; the level of confidence is well beyond .01. The erroneous ratings of 100 were given predominately to overgeneralizations.

Thus Dawes found considerable evidence for a response bias to perceive nested relationships in the stories his subjects read. This bias may be found in both selective memory and selective distortion. Furthermore, he found a high degree of association between belief that a relationship is nested and belief that one's memory about that relationship is correct. There is, however, a large conceptual jump from these findings to the

---

[4]The finding that subjects are more confident when they overgeneralize than when they correctly choose a disjunctive alternative was not found in a replication experiment by Michael O'Connor (personal communication).

assertion that there exists a general cognitive bias to believe that social groups have nested relationships. One can legitimately raise questions about whether some particular characteristics of the stories used may not account for the findings; further, one may ask by what particular mechanism the selective memory and distortion occur. It should be pointed out that the same questions may be raised about the assertion that a tendency to perceive balance is a general cognitive bias, although the research findings in support of the latter bias are far stronger than those in support of the nesting bias (at least more extensive).

Before we turn to another type of nonnumerical model, one peripheral aspect of Dawes's work may be mentioned. It has been emphasized earlier that demonstrating that subjects have a tendency to guess X in a situation where no information is available is different from demonstrating that subjects have a tendency to believe X despite information to the contrary. In Dawes's experiments, the subject is given clear information in the stories that certain relations are not nested; hence, he shows a bias to remember relations as nested despite information to the contrary.

In one additional experiment in the first study, Dawes asked subjects to guess whether relations were nested or disjunctive without having read the stories. These subjects were told that the experimenter was interested in determining whether some students did better than others on reading comprehension tests simply because they had a better idea of what a correct answer looks like. All but one subject accepted this explanation as a reasonable rationale for answering questions about stories he had not read. There was an overwhelming tendency for these subjects to circle the disjunctive alternative. Thus the bias found in the absence of information was precisely opposite that found in the presence of information. As pointed out earlier, the two methods for determining cognitive bias are quite different.

4.4 SIMULATION

Imagine that you have two secretaries, Miss Intuitive and Miss Plod. Miss Intuitive is an excellent secretary, bright and quick. She is particularly good at filing papers; she can retrieve any paper with almost unerring accuracy. She has no insight, however, into the rules she uses for filing, and even when you suggest to her a set of rules she may be using, she is unable to tell you whether in fact those are the rules she follows. Miss Plod, in contrast, cannot file any papers without being told explicitly what system to use; moreover, you must be very careful in telling Miss Plod how to file the papers, because she will interpret everything you say quite literally, even though her interpretation may lead to absurd results. Once, for example, when you asked her to "take a letter to Mr. Jones in Ypsilanti," she picked up a letter selected at random from her desk, took an airplane to Ypsilanti, and handed the letter to Mr. Jones. But Miss Plod's compulsivity has its advantages; she never makes an error in carrying out literally any instructions she is given.

One day you think you have figured out the rules Miss Intuitive is using implicitly when she files papers. You explain the rules to her and ask her whether these are in fact her rules. As usual, she replies that she simply cannot say, because she files without conscious awareness of how she does it. You are quite interested in determining whether you have discovered the correct rules, so you turn to a strategy for testing them that does not rely on Miss Intuitive's introspections.

The next time you get a set of papers that need to be filed, you make duplicate copies and ask Miss Plod, as well as Miss Intuitive, to do the job. She immediately objects that she has had no experience at filing papers and must be told how to do so. You then tell her to follow the rules you believe govern Miss Intuitive's filing; you state these rules explicitly, and you give her the papers to file. You know now that the papers will be filed according to these rules. What you wish to discover is whether Miss Plod and Miss Intuitive will file the papers in the same places. (Alternatively, you might have Miss Plod alone file the papers and ask Miss Intuitive to retrieve them.)

If the two secretaries do not file the papers in the same places, you will know that the rules you told Miss Plod to follow do not govern Miss Intuitive's filing. If, on the other hand, the papers are filed in the same places, you know that the set of rules *could* be governing Miss Intuitive's filing. (Of course, it is always possible that she is actually operating according to different rules that have the same results.)

Technically, what you have done is to *program* Miss Plod to *simulate* Miss Intuitive's filing behavior. A *program* consists of a set of rules for manipulating certain objects; these rules are often termed *instructions*; the "objects" manipulated according to these instructions may be concrete or symbolic. When we have an agent execute these instructions, we are said *to program* that agent (for example, Miss Plod). A program *simulates* a given process if its output is meant to match the output of that process; that is, a program is said to simulate a given process if the behavior of an agent following the instructions in the program is similar to that of the process studied.

Such simulation constitutes a nonnumerical model of behavior, because a correspondence has been established between an empirical process and a formal relational system consisting of the instructions of the program; *the program itself is the model*; the consequences of this model, rather than being determined through mathematical or logical analysis, are determined by having an agent carry out the program's instructions. Then these consequences are compared with the behavior (or output) of the process studied in order to determine how well the model fits the process. If this comparison demonstrates close agreement between the behavior of the process and that of the agent carrying out the program, the program is accepted as a reasonable model of how the process *could* be functioning. If the agreement is poor, it is concluded that the program cannot represent the process.

Theoretically, simulation of a given process can be carried out with any agent capable of following the instructions in the program; thus Miss Plod's simulation of Miss Intuitive's filing behavior is a perfectly valid example of simulation. In fact, however, most researchers in the area of simulation have a computer act as the agent that carries out the instructions in the program. The computer is capable of carrying out "simple" instructions involving symbolic manipulation with great speed and perfect accuracy; moreover, it is capable of carrying out "complex" instructions by breaking them down into simple instructions in a manner to be illustrated later in this section. (The actual way in which the computer goes about executing such instructions will not be discussed here, nor will the physical character- istics of the computer. It is not necessary to understand how the computer works in order to understand how it is used in the field of simulation.)

Many problems in simulation can be reduced to problems in symbolic manipulation. It is not necessary, for example, to have Miss Plod actually place the papers in the files in order to have her simulate Miss Intuitive's behavior. It is simply necessary to give her a set of symbols that describe the paper to be filed and she, by applying the instructions you have given her, can then give you a symbol indicating where the paper would be placed in the files. As noted above, however, such symbolic manipulations can be performed with much greater speed and accuracy by a computer; hence, you would be wiser to have a computer act as agent simulating Miss Intuitive's behavior than to have Miss Plod do it. Within a matter of seconds (or less) you would have a computer output telling you where each paper goes accord- ing to the instructions you've specified, and you would know that these rules have been applied perfectly. Moreover, if you have some sophisticated electronic gadgetry, you could even sit at your desk and continually modify your instructions in light of the output from the computer until you have a program that seems to be an adequate simulation of Miss Intuitive's behavior.

Thus the reason for using a computer as the agent of simulation is one of convenience—speed and accuracy. The importance of the speed, however, cannot be overemphasized, because the rapidity of a computer executing instructions is several orders of magnitude greater than the rapidity of a person executing the same instructions. The output of a program involving many steps might take a person a matter of years, or even lifetimes, to determine, whereas a computer could determine it in a matter of minutes. This rapidity has become particularly important to researchers who develop programs based on the repeated application of rather simple rules.

Thus Laughery and Gregg (1962, pp. 267–268) write the following about the advantages of using computers to execute instructions meant to simulate certain information-processing behaviors.

The power of the simulation technique is that it enables the theorist to see the behavioral results of the application of the model to a task. In general, this would not be possible in any other way, since the interactions of the elementary information processes become so complex that the amount of time required to trace through the branching network soon becomes prohibitive.

By "behavioral results" these authors refer to the consequences of the program that are meant to correspond to behaviors of interest.

Before giving an example of computer simulation, it is first necessary to answer the question of what constitutes a "simple" instruction. To do so, consider the solution of the following two simultaneous equations.

$$3x+6y = 15 \qquad (1)$$

$$2x+8y = 18 \qquad (2)$$

The solution may be found by executing the following simple instructions.

1. Divide each of the numbers occurring in Eq. (1) by the number found to the left of the symbol x. Refer to the result as Eq. (1′).
2. Divide each of the numbers occurring in Eq. (2) by the number found to the left of the symbol x. Refer to the result as Eq. (2′).
3. Form Eq. (3) by subtracting the number found to the left of the symbol y in Eq. (2′) from the number found to the left of the symbol y in Eq. (1′). Follow this number by a y; follow the y by an equals sign, and follow the equals sign by the difference between the number found to the right of the equals in Eq. (1′) and that found to the right of the equals in Eq. (2′).
4. Divide the number found to the right of the equals in Eq. (3) by the number found to the left of the y. The number so constructed is the value of y.

The solution for x is obtained in a similar manner.

These instructions would be carried out as follows:

Applying instruction 1, we obtain

$$x+2y = 5. \qquad (1')$$

Applying instruction 2, we obtain

$$x+4y = 9. \qquad (2')$$

Applying instruction 3, we obtain

$$-2y = -4.$$

Applying instruction 4, we obtain

$$y = 2.$$

Now, after we have obtained a series of instructions for solving simultaneous equations, we may conceptualize a new instruction that reads "solve the following simultaneous equations: _____ and _____" (where the equations to be solved are placed in the blanks). When the computer receives that instruction, it immediately switches to the previous set of instructions it has for solving such equations, solves, and returns to the instruction after the "solve simultaneous equations" instruction.

In general, after a particular instruction has been constructed from a series of instructions, it itself may be part of a new series of instructions. (The instructions of which it consists are technically said to constitute a *subroutine*.) This new series of instructions may then correspond to yet another single instruction of a new series. And so on.

Following the above procedure, more and more complex instructions may be constructed from simpler ones. The possibility of doing so is limited only by the ability and inspiration of the person writing a program. As a result, whereas the first instructions computers were capable of executing consisted only of simple numerical manipulations (of the sort one can perform with a desk calculator), now computers can execute much more complex instructions. As Newell and Simon (1963*a*, p. 283) write, "We have learned that a computer is a general manipulator of symbols—not just a manipulator of numbers. Basically, a computer is a transformer of patterns." In fact, the computer can even write computer programs.

An Example of Computer Simulation

As many psychologists have pointed out (e.g., Duncker 1945; Bartlett 1958), much human problem solving follows three steps. The first step is the specification of the goal, or desired state of affairs; the second step is the evaluation of the discrepancy between the present state of affairs and the desired state of affairs; the third step is the search for means to reduce this discrepancy. After this discrepancy is reduced, a new state of affairs exists, and its discrepancy from the goal may be evaluated and reduced. In complex or difficult problems the reduction of the discrepancy may involve attaining a series of subgoals, each of which in turn is attained by evaluating discrepancy and searching for means to reduce it.

Newell, Shaw, and Simon have developed a program called a *general problem solver* (GPS) that attempts to simulate the above type of problem solving. (The simplest description of this program may be found in the chapter by Newell and Simon in the *Handbook of Mathematical Psychology*, 1963*b*.) This program is succinctly summarized in the logical diagram, technically termed a *flow diagram*, or a *flow chart* (1963*b*, p. 404), displayed in Fig. 4.16.

Goal type 1: Transform object *a* into object *b*

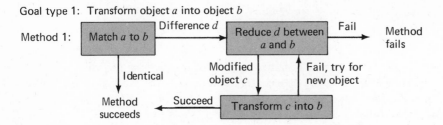

Goal type 2: Reduce the difference, *d*, between object *a* and object *b*

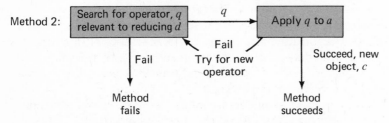

Goal type 3: Apply operator *q* to object *a*

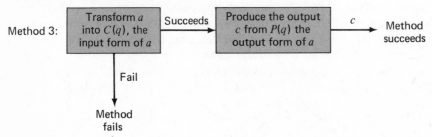

Fig. 4.16   Principal methods employed by the general problem solver.

Figure 4.16 should be interpreted as follows: *a* is the actual state of affairs and *b* the desired state (that is, goal or subgoal of a larger problem). *a* is matched with *b*. If there is no discrepancy, the problem is solved. If there is a discrepancy, *d*, an attempt is made to reduce it. This attempt involves carrying out the instructions in goal type #2; a discussion of its nature will be deferred briefly. (Note that the program described in goal type #2 constitutes a subroutine of the program described in goal type #1.) If the attempt succeeds in reducing the discrepancy between *a* and *b*, *a* will be transformed into a state of affairs more like *b*. The authors have labeled this state *c* in their diagram. If *c* can then be transformed to *b*, the problem is solved. If not, the procedure of reducing *d* is repeated until a suitable *c* is obtained.

The part of the diagram labeled goal type #2 describes how it is that *d* is reduced; it consists of an instruction to search for an operator that will reduce *d* and then to apply that operator to *d*. Finally, the part of the diagram labeled goal type #3 describes the subroutine of goal type #2 that involves applying the operator.

Thus the flow diagram in Fig. 4.16 illustrates the GPS at a rather abstract level. The GPS is meant to simulate solutions of problems of the sort described earlier.

Some problems actually invesigated by Newell, Shaw, and Simon consist of derivations from elementary symbolic logic. The premise in the derivation is regarded as an actual state of affairs, and the conclusion is regarded as the desired state of affairs. The derivation thus consists of moving from an actual state of affairs to a desired state of affairs.

Subjects are presented with these problems, and their solutions are recorded verbatim. The problems are presented to the computer, which attacks them according to the instructions of GPS. The steps the subject goes through in solving the problem are then compared with the steps the computer goes through in solving the same problem. (The list of the subject's steps is often termed the subject's *protocol*; the list of the machine's steps is often termed the program's *trace*.) If the protocol and trace are very similar, the program according to which the machine solves the problem is considered a successful model. If not, it is modified.

Following is a typical problem:

PREMISE: *R* implies not-*P* and not-*R* implies *Q*.
CONCLUSION: It is not the case that both not-*Q* and *P* are true.

The truth of this conclusion may be established by noting that either *R* or not-*R* must be true (by the law of the excluded middle); hence, either not-*P* (which is implied by *R*) or *Q* (which is implied by not-*R*) must be true; hence, it cannot be the case that both *P* (the negation of not-*P*) and not-*Q* (the negation of *Q*) are true.

The reader familiar with symbolic logic will know that the above type of reasoning is not the type used in solving such problems. Instead, certain rules, or *axioms*, are presented in symbolic form, the problem is presented in symbolic form, and the conclusion is derived from the premise by making symbolic transformations specified by the axioms. Thus the above problem is presented in the following form:

PREMISE: $(R \supset \sim P) \cdot (\sim R \supset Q)$
CONCLUSION: $\sim(\sim Q \cdot P)$,

and the derivation of the premise from the conclusion is begun by using an axiom that states $A \supset B$ and $\sim A \vee B$ are equivalent; thus the first step in the derivation is to transform the premise into the following expression:

$$(\sim R \vee \sim P) \cdot (R \vee Q).$$

The subjects run in these experiments do not even know that they are solving problems in symbolic logic. Instead, they are simply given problems and a set of 12 transformation rules (which are actually axioms of symbolic logic). The subject's task is then to transform the symbols in the premise into those in the conclusion by using these rules. (Of course, the terms *premise* and *conclusion* are avoided in the actual experiment; the subject is simply told to change the expression on the left to the one on the right.)

Table 4.1 illustrates the transformation rules and the protocol of a particular subject attempting to solve the problem specified earlier (Newell and Simon 1963*a*, p. 281). This problem is also solved by a computer following the instructions of GPS.

As mentioned earlier, the success with which GPS simulates the above situation is evaluated by comparing the subject's protocol with GPS's trace. The question now arises: How do we evaluate this similarity? There are a variety of criteria according to which this evaluation may be made; there is, however, one generally agreed-on criterion for stating that a simulation is completely successful.

A simulation is a complete success if the subject's protocol and the program's trace are indistinguishable.

TABLE 4.1 Rules Used and the Protocol of a Subject Solving a Problem

R1.	$A \cdot B \to B \cdot A$ $A \lor B \to B \lor A$	R8.	$A \cdot B \to A$ $A \cdot B \to B$ Applies to main expression only
R2.	$A \supset B \to \sim B \supset \sim A$	R9.	$A \to A \lor X$ Applies to main expression only
R3.	$A \cdot A \leftrightarrow A$ $A \lor A \leftrightarrow A$	R10.	$\left.\begin{array}{l}A\\B\end{array}\right\} \to A \cdot B$ A and B are two main expressions
R4.	$A \cdot (B \cdot C) \leftrightarrow (A \cdot B) \cdot C$ $A \lor (B \lor C) \leftrightarrow (A \lor B) \lor C$	R11.	$\left.\begin{array}{l}A\\A \supset B\end{array}\right\} \to B$ A and $A \supset B$ are two main expressions
R5.	$A \lor B \leftrightarrow \sim(\sim A \cdot \sim B)$	R12.	$\left.\begin{array}{l}A \supset B\\B \supset C\end{array}\right\} \to A \supset C$ $A \supset B$ and $B \supset C$ are two main expressions
R6.	$A \supset B \leftrightarrow \sim A \lor B$		
R7.	$A \cdot (B \lor C) \leftrightarrow (A \cdot B) \lor (A \cdot C)$ $A \lor (B \cdot C) \leftrightarrow (A \lor B) \cdot (A \lor C)$		

Example, showing subject's entire course of solution on problem:

1. $(R \supset \sim P) \cdot (\sim R \supset Q)$	$\sim(\sim Q \cdot P)$
2. $(\sim R \lor \sim P) \cdot (R \lor Q)$	Rule 6 applied to left and right of 1
3. $(\sim R \lor \sim P) \cdot (\sim R \supset Q)$	Rule 6 applied to left of 1
4. $R \supset \sim P$	Rule 8 applied to 1
5. $\sim R \lor \sim P$	Rule 6 applied to 4
6. $\sim R \supset Q$	Rule 8 applied to 1
7. $R \lor Q$	Rule 6 applied to 6
8. $(\sim R \lor \sim P) \cdot (R \lor Q)$	Rule 10 applied to 5 and 7
9. $P \supset \sim R$	Rule 2 applied to 4
10. $\sim Q \supset R$	Rule 2 applied to 6
11. $P \supset Q$	Rule 12 applied to 6 and 9
12. $\sim P \lor Q$	Rule 6 applied to 11
13. $\sim(P \cdot \sim Q)$	Rule 5 applied to 12
14. $\sim(\sim Q \cdot P)$	Rule 1 applied to 13 QED

(The question "distinguished by *whom*?" does arise. But distinguish-ability as a criterion is more explicit than similarity would be, because it is possible to evaluate distinguishability by simply asking a doubter to separate protocols and traces successfully.) The traces of the GPS are impressively similar to the subject's protocol; we venture no judgment of whether they are indistinguishable.

The example of computer simulation presented here concerns problem solving of a rather specialized sort. Computer simulation of problem solving —and other processes—is not intrinsically linked to any particular content area. For example, researchers have worked on simulation of such divergent processes as writing a fugue (Reitman 1965) and investigating an airplane crash (Braunstein 1965).

Before concluding this section, it should be pointed out that the term *simulation* is often used in contexts in which the researcher is not interested in discovering whether his program is a reasonable model of some process but rather in which he accepts his program as an acceptable model and wishes to discover how the process will behave. For example, he may have a program that he believes simulates a certain method of missile production; he then has a computer execute the model, not to discover whether the model is reasonable, but rather to discover whether the method of production will be more or less efficient and costly than other methods. Although such simulation is quite common in other fields, it is relatively rare in psychology.

This section on simulation has been short, perhaps much shorter than warranted by the importance of the work. The reader wishing to pursue simulation further is referred to the chapter by Newell and Simon in the *Handbook of Mathematical Psychology* (1963*b*), which—in contrast to many of the other chapters in this handbook—is written in a manner that can readily be understood by the uninitiated. Other elementary expositions of simulation can be found in Reitman's book *Cognition and Thought* (1965) or in Hunt, Marin, and Stone's book *Experiments in Induction* (1966). Also, an extensive collection of articles has been compiled by Feigenbaum and Feldman (1963).

DECISION

part **II**

chapter 5

INDIVIDUAL
DECISION
MAKING

5.1 INTRODUCTION

The normal course of our lives can be viewed as a series of decisions in which we choose among the various job offers, insurance policies, and evening entertainments that we encounter. Some decisions are easy and painless; others are difficult and troublesome. What makes decisions difficult is the existence of doubt, conflict, or uncertainty.

The uncertainty may stem from incomplete knowledge about the world, as when the outcomes of the decision depend on some future state or event. The uncertainty may also stem from lack of knowledge about oneself, as when one is not sure which of several possible outcomes would be most satisfying. The difficulty in deciding whether or not to carry an umbrella, for instance, results from uncertainty about the weather. The difficulty in deciding which color car to buy, on the other hand, results from uncertainty as to which color would be most pleasing.

This chapter deals with two types of decision problems: decisions with incomplete knowledge and decisions with unsure preferences. Both types of decision problems are accompanied by uncertainty. In the former type, however, the uncertainty concerns the future state of the world, whereas in the latter it concerns the decision maker's own state of mind.

These two paradigms do not exhaust the wide variety of decisions faced by individuals, nor does the discussion cover the range of problems that have been tackled successfully by students in the field. The purpose of this chapter is not to describe the current state of the art but rather to introduce the reader to some of the basic concepts of psychological decision theory.

Decision theory is the study of how decisions are or ought to be made. Thus it has two faces: descriptive and normative. Descriptive decision theory attempts to describe and explain how actual choices are made. It is concerned with the study of variables that determine choice behavior in various contexts. As such, it is a proper branch of psychology. Normative decision theory is concerned with optimal rather than actual choices. Its main function is to prescribe which decision should be made, given the goals of the decision maker and the information available to him. Its results have a prescriptive nature. They assert that if an individual wishes to maximize his expected gain, for example, then he should follow a specified course of action. As such, normative decision theory is a purely deductive discipline.

Despite their different natures, descriptive and normative theories are deeply interrelated in most applications. In the first place there are a variety of situations, such as most economic investments, in which people try very hard to behave optimally. Moreover, when faced with obvious errors of judgment or calculation people often admit them and reverse their choices. Hence, there is an inevitable normative component in any adequate descriptive theory that reflects people's desire to do the best they can. Second, in most interesting decision problems, optimality is not easily defined. The main goal of a company, for example, may be to maximize its profit, yet its reputation and the morale of its employees are also important for their own sake and are often incommensurable with monetary considerations. In such instances a descriptive analysis of the goals is a prerequisite for the application of the normative analysis. Thus, although descriptive and normative analyses differ markedly in goals and orientations, most of their interesting applications contain both normative and descriptive aspects.

This chapter deals exclusively with the static analysis of individual decision making. A comprehensive analysis of the various decision problems, with an emphasis on their mathematical structure, can be found in Luce and Raiffa's *Games and Decisions* (1957). An illuminating discussion of the applications of normative decision theory to managerial and economic decisions can be found in Raiffa (1968). Fishburn's book (1964) also discusses the applications of decision theory from a normative viewpoint. For review of the literature, from a psychological standpoint, the reader is referred to

Edwards (1954c, 1961) and to the more recent surveys by Luce and Suppes (1965) and Becker and McClintock (1967). Some of the pertinent literature has been collected in a volume of readings edited by Edwards and Tversky (1967).

5.2 DECISION WITH INCOMPLETE KNOWLEDGE: THEORIES OF RISKY CHOICE

Decisions with incomplete knowledge, where one does not know for sure which state of the world will, in fact, obtain, are typically represented in the form of a payoff matrix. A payoff matrix is simply a rectangular array whose rows, denoted $a_1, \ldots, a_i, \ldots, a_n$, correspond to the alternatives that are available to the decision maker and whose columns, denoted $s_1, \ldots, s_j, \ldots, s_m$, correspond to the possible states of nature. The entries of the payoff matrix are the outcomes, or the consequences, resulting from a selection of a given row and column. Thus the o_{ij} entry of the matrix represents the outcome obtained when the individual chooses alternative a_i and nature, so to speak, chooses state s_j.

To illustrate, imagine an individual deciding whether or not to carry an umbrella to work. Naturally, the decision would depend on the relative discomfort of getting wet as opposed to the inconvenience of carrying an umbrella. Another major consideration would be the relative likelihoods of the two relevant states of nature, rain and no rain. The choice situation can thus be summarized by the payoff matrix displayed in Fig. 5.1.

It must be pointed out, however, that the representation of an actual decision problem by a payoff matrix is an abstraction in several respects. In the first place the alternative courses of action and the relevant states of the world cannot always be clearly delineated. This does not mean that it is impossible to reconstruct an appropriate representation in these cases but only that a clearly formulated representation may be difficult to obtain. Moreover, this representation is clearly not unique. There are many ways of

	States of nature	
	s_1 — Rain	s_2 — No rain
a_1 — Carry the umbrella	o_{11} — Stay dry carrying the umbrella	o_{12} — Stay dry carrying the umbrella
a_2 — Do not carry the umbrella	o_{21} — Get wet without carrying the umbrella	o_{22} — Stay dry without carrying the umbrella

Alternatives

Fig. 5.1

structuring or representing a decision problem in a payoff matrix form. The art of finding the "right way" of structuring a decision problem contributes a great deal to its successful solution. An appropriate representation of a decision problem in a payoff matrix form, therefore, is the result of an adequate formulation rather than a substitute for one. It is nevertheless a useful analytic tool.

The representation of decisions with incomplete knowledge by payoff matrices suggests distinguishing among three states of knowledge or forms of information under which such decisions are made: certainty, ignorance, and risk.

In decision making under certainty, the decision maker knows exactly which outcome results from each choice. After the choice is made, this known outcome obtains with certainty regardless of nature's choice. This occurs when all the consequences in each row of the payoff matrix are identical, or, equivalently, when the obtained state of the world is known for sure. The choices between roast beef and steak for dinner, or between a trip to Florida or to California are examples of decision making under certainty. Because no random or chance process is involved, such choices are also referred to as riskless.

It is important to realize that this notion of certainty depends vitally on the definition, or the level of analysis, of the consequences. If receiving a particular dinner in a restaurant is regarded as a consequence, then the choice between entrees is a riskless one, because one certainly gets the dinner one orders. Yet, if enjoyment of the meal is viewed as the proper consequence, the choice is no longer riskless, because there is a great deal of uncertainty associated with the outcomes that depends on the quality of the restaurant and the competence of the chef and that might not be completely known in advance. Similarly, enjoyment of a trip depends on the weather in California and in Florida, which is not at all certain. What seems to be a decision under certainty relative to one level of analysis, therefore, may turn into a decision under uncertainty on further analysis of the consequences. For a penetrating analysis of this issue, see Savage (1954, pp. 82–91).

If decision making under certainty is one extreme case in which one knows exactly which state of the world will obtain, then decision making under ignorance[1] is the other extreme in which one knows exactly nothing (or better yet, nothing exactly) about which state of the world will obtain. A decision whether to carry an umbrella, in the absence of any information whatsoever about the likelihoods of the weather conditions, is an example of decision under ignorance. Decision problems of this kind are rare because in most situations one has some information about the likelihood of the relevant states of nature. In fact, some of the approaches to decision under ignorance

---

[1]Decisions under ignorance are commonly referred to as decisions under uncertainty. Because the latter term is also used in a broader sense, however, the former term is preferred.

attempt to reduce them to decisions under risk where the relevant information about the states of the world is utilized in the analysis.

In decision making under risk, it is assumed that the individual can evaluate the likelihoods of the various states of nature. More specifically, his beliefs about the likelihoods of the relevant states can be expressed by some (possibly subjective) probability distribution. Risky choices are essentially gambles whose outcomes are determined jointly by the choice of the individual and the result of some specified random process. The decision maker cannot know, therefore, which state of the world will obtain, but he knows (approximately, at least) the probabilities of occurrences of the various states. In some instances, such as in gambles based on unbiased dice, the objective probabilities are known exactly. In other gambles, such as business investments or insurance policies, only rough subjective estimates of the probabilities are available.

The main part of this section is devoted to the major theory of decision making with incomplete knowledge: the expected utility theory. In the next three subsections the basic model is introduced, the axiomatic structure is discussed, and some empirical tests of the theory are described. Finally, alternative theories that are not based on the expectation principle are studied in the subsequent two subsections.

The Expected Utility Principle

The study of decision making under risk dates back to the 18th century when French noblemen asked their court mathematicians to advise them how to gamble. Although utility theory has changed a great deal since those days, its basic problem remains essentially unchanged. To illustrate, imagine being offered a simple two-outcome gamble at a fixed cost c, where you may win either $\$x$ or nothing depending on a toss of a fair coin. For which values of x would you accept the bet? If you reject the offer, no money changes hands. If you accept it, you receive either $x - c$ (your win minus the price you paid) if a head occurs, or $-c$ (the price you paid) if a tail occurs. The situation is summarized by the payoff matrix displayed in Fig. 5.2. Given a fixed price,

States

	Head	Tail
Accept	$x - c$	$-c$
Reject	0	0

Alternatives

Fig. 5.2

the problem is to formulate a decision rule that would determine the values of x for which the gamble would (or should) be accepted.

One simple decision rule is to compute the expected value of each alternative and to choose the one with the higher expected value. The expected value of an alternative or a gamble is the sum of its outcomes, each weighted by its probability of occurrence. More formally, the expected value of a gamble, with outcomes $x_1, \ldots, x_n$ obtained with probabilities $p_1, \ldots, p_n$, respectively, equals $\sum_{i=1}^{n} p_i x_i$. (For further discussion of the expected value notion, see the appendix.)

The expected value of rejecting the offered gamble, denoted $EV(R)$, is clearly zero because $EV(R) = (\frac{1}{2})0 + (\frac{1}{2})0 = 0$. The expected value of accepting the gamble, denote $EV(A)$, is given by the equation $EV(A) = \frac{1}{2}(x-c) + \frac{1}{2}(-c) = (x/2) - c$. Thus $EV(A) > EV(R)$ whenever $x/2 > c$. According to the expected value principle, therefore, one should accept the offered bet if and only if the cost (c) is less than one half the prize (x). The expected value of a bet can be interpreted as the average outcome resulting from playing it an indefinite (or very large) number of times. Thus, if the gamble is played a very large number of times, one can practically assure himself of an average gain of $(x/2) - c$. We speak of gambles as being favorable, unfavorable, or fair, according to whether their expected values are positive, negative, or zero.

If one follows the expected value rule, therefore, one should accept all favorable bets and reject all unfavorable bets. This is not, however, what people actually do, nor is it what they feel they ought to do. In the first place people gamble by accepting bets whose expected values are negative. For otherwise gambling casinos would be out of business and they are not. Second, people buy insurance and in so doing they are paying the insurance company in order to get rid of an unfavorable gamble. Many people pay a monthly fire insurance premium, for example, to avoid the relatively small chance of losing the value of their property as a consequence of fire. In most cases, however, the price paid for the insurance is higher than the expected value of the undesirable gamble. Otherwise, insurance companies would be out of business and they are not. Moreover, people feel that buying insurance (and in some cases even gambling) is a rational form of behavior that can be defended on normative grounds. Hence, the expected value model is inadequate on both descriptive and normative accounts. In particular, it implies that one should be indifferent with respect to all fair bets. Hence, one should not object to tossing a fair coin to decide whether he wins or loses $1,000, for example. Most reasonable people would probably reject the gamble, however, because the potential gain of $1,000 does not quite compensate for the potential loss of $1,000.

Similar difficulties, arising from a gambling puzzle known as the St. Petersburg paradox, led Daniel Bernoulli, as early as 1738, to formulate the expected utility principle. The expected utility of a gamble, with outcomes $x_1, \ldots, x_n$ obtained with probabilities $p_1, \ldots, p_n$, respectively, equals $\sum_{i=1}^{n} p_i u(x_i)$, where $u(x_i)$ is the utility of the ith outcome. The expected utility principle asserts that the gamble with the highest expected utility is to be chosen. The decision rule proposed by Bernoulli, therefore, is also based on the expectation principle, but it replaces the objective scale of value by a subjective scale of utility. The introduction of a subjective scale results in a more general and plausible model that seems to resolve the difficulties arising from the expected value model. (More than 100 years later, the Bernoullian notion of a subjective scale became the cornerstone of quantitative psychophysics founded by G. T. Fechner.)

The advantages of expected utility theory over expected value theory are numerous. In the first place it allows individuals to have different utilities for money and hence different preferences among gambles. This is essential for any interesting descriptive or normative theory, as individuals' preferences are not (and for this matter need not be) independent of their attitude toward risk. Second, it has been assumed that the more money one has, the less he values each additional increment, or, equivalently, that the utility of any additional dollar diminishes with an increase in capital. These considerations, as well as the insurance phenomena, have led to the decreasing marginal utility hypothesis according to which the utility function is concave, or negatively accelerated. (The similarity to Weber's law is not accidental. In fact, the logarithmic utility function proposed by Bernoulli was the one put forth by Fechner as the form of the general psychophysical law.)

To demonstrate the explanatory power of the expected utility principle, let us suppose, for illustrative purposes, that the utility for money has the following form:

$$u(x) = \begin{cases} \sqrt{x} & \text{if } x \geq 0 \\ -(x^2) & \text{if } x \leq 0. \end{cases}$$

Thus the subjective value of gain grows as the square root of the actual value, whereas the (negative) subjective value of loss grows as the square of the actual value. The graph of the function is portrayed in Fig. 5.3. Although the choice of this particular utility function is arbitrary, it was proposed as early as the 18th century as a prototype for Everyman's utility function, and Stevens (1959) has defended it on the basis of some experimental evidence. If we examine the proposed utility function, it is easy to see that it is strictly concave for any two points that are not in the $[-1, 1]$ interval. That is, a straight line connecting the utilities of any two points (outside that interval) lies entirely below the curve. Stated algebraically,

$$pu(x_1) + (1-p)u(x_2) < u[px_1 + (1-p)x_2]$$

for all x_1, x_2 outside the $[-1, 1]$ interval and for any $0 < p < 1$.

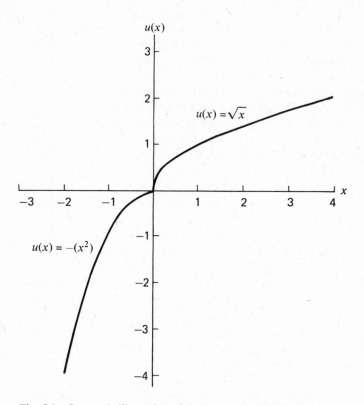

Fig. 5.3 Geometric illustration of the proposed utility function.

The left side of the above inequality, however, is the expected utility of a gamble where one receives x_1 with probability p and x_2 with probability $1-p$. Its right side is the utility of the expected (monetary) value of the same gamble. The above inequality asserts that, given a concave utility function and the expectation principle, one should always prefer receiving a given sum of money over taking any gamble whose expected value equals that sum. Thus the decreasing marginal utility hypothesis, embodied in the concavity of the utility function, can account for the common risk-averse tendency to reject fair bets and to buy insurance policies.

For concreteness, consider an individual who wishes to insure his $3,000 car against theft. Suppose insurance costs $30 a year and that there is 1 chance in 1,000 that the car would be stolen during this time. If he insures his car, he will lose $30 a year, irrespective of whether the car is stolen, as the insurance company will reimburse him in case of theft. If he does not insure his car, he will lose $3,000 if his car is stolen and nothing otherwise. This situation is summarized in the payoff matrix displayed in Fig. 5.4. It is easy to see that the expected value of buying insurance, denoted

EV(B), is less than the expected value of not buying insurance, denoted EV(NB), because EV(B) = -30 whereas EV(NB) = $.001(-3,000)+.999(0)$ = -3. If monetary values, however, are replaced by utilities according to the proposed utility function, the following computation shows that the expected utility of buying insurance, denoted EU(B), is greater than the expected utility of not buying insurance, denoted EU(NB). For: EU(B) = $u(-30)$ = $-(30^2)$ = -900, whereas EU(NB) = $.001$ $u(-3,000)+.999$ $u(0)$ = $-.001$ $(3,000^2)+.999(0)$ = $-9,000$. Thus, although EV(NB) exceeds EV(B), EU(B) exceeds EU(NB). The expected utility principle, in conjunction with a concave utility function, therefore, can account for the purchase of insurance despite its smaller expected value.

The utility function suggested can explain not only the rejection of favorable gambles but also the acceptance of some unfavorable ones. Consider, for example, a simple dice game where you pay \$.50 as a participation fee and you have one chance out of six to win \$2.75. It is not difficult to see that this gamble, denoted G, has a negative expected value, yet its expected utility is positive. To verify this assertion note that

$$\text{EV}(G) = \tfrac{1}{6}(2.25)+\tfrac{5}{6}(-.50) = \tfrac{9}{24}-\tfrac{10}{24} = -\tfrac{1}{24} < 0,$$

whereas

$$\text{EU}(G) = \tfrac{1}{6}u(2.25)+\tfrac{5}{6}u(-.50) = \tfrac{1}{6}(1.50)+\tfrac{5}{6}(-.25) = \tfrac{6}{24}-\tfrac{5}{24} = \tfrac{1}{24} > 0.$$

Hence, by an appropriate choice of a utility function, the purchase of insurance, as well as gambling behavior, can be rationalized. Indeed, a similar rationalization has been proposed by Friedman and Savage (1948).

It is important to realize that we have not shown that people insure their property or gamble on horses in order to maximize some utility function.

States of the world

	Car stolen ($p = .001$)	Car is not stolen ($p = .999$)
Buy insurance	-30	-30
Do not buy insurance	-3000	0

Alternatives

Fig. 5.4

All we have shown is that although these phenomena are incompatible with the expected value principle, they can be accounted for, if an appropriate utility function is introduced.

The utility analysis is not limited to monetary outcomes and it can also be applied to gambles whose consequences are nonmonetary such as the enjoyment of a play, a loss in an election, or a satisfaction from an accomplishment. In fact, the general notion that people act to maximize their utility has formed the basis for the economist's concept of Economic Man, which originated with Jeremy Bentham and James Mill. The expected utility principle combines this general utility maximization notion with the assumption that the utility of a gamble equals the expected utility of its outcomes. If the available gambles, therefore, are to be played over and over again, then the gamble with the highest expected utility would yield the highest utility in the long run. In spite of the intuitive appeal of this rationale, the application of the expected utility principle to essentially unique choice situations requires an independent justification. Modern utility theory provides such a justification in the form of an axiomatic foundation of the expected utility principle.

Modern Utility Theory

Modern utility theory was first developed by von Neumann and Morgenstern as an appendix to their famous *Theory of Games and Economic Behavior* (1947). The theory consists of a set of axioms about preferences among gambles. The basic result of the theory is summarized by a theorem stating that if an individual's preferences satisfy the specified axioms then his behavior can be described, or rationalized, as the maximization of his expected utility. Because the axioms can be regarded as maxims of rational behavior, they provide a normative justification for the expected utility principle. Although several axiomatizations of utility theory have been developed in the last two decades, we present the original formulation of von Neumann and Morgenstern with a few inessential modifications.

The axioms are formulated in terms of a preference-or-indifference relation, denoted $\succsim$, defined on a set of outcomes, denoted A. Later, this set is enriched to include gambles, or probability mixtures, of the form (x, p, y), where outcome x is obtained with probability p and outcome y is obtained with probability $1-p$. Given the primitives $\succsim$ and A, the following axioms are assumed to hold for all outcomes x, y, z in A and for all probabilities p, q that are different from zero or 1.

A1
(x, p, y) is in A.

A2
$\succsim$ is a weak ordering of A, where $\succ$ denotes strict preference and $\sim$ denotes indifference.

A3
$[(x, p, y), q, y] \sim (x, pq, y)$.

A4
If $x \sim y$, then $(x, p, z) \sim (y, p, z)$.

A5
If $x \succ y$, then $x \succ (x, p, y) \succ y$.

A6
If $x \succ y \succ z$, then there exists a probability p such that $y \sim (x, p, z)$.

It is important to realize that utility theory was developed as a prescriptive theory, justified on the basis of normative considerations alone. The close interrelationships between normative and descriptive considerations, however, suggest that utility theory may also be used as a psychological theory of decision making under risk. In discussing the axioms, therefore, we examine them from both normative and descriptive viewpoints.

The first axiom is what is technically called a closure property. It asserts that if x and y are available alternatives, so are all the gambles of the form (x, p, y) that can be formed with x and y as outcomes. Because gambles are defined in terms of their outcomes and their probabilities, it is assumed implicitly that $(x, p, y) = (y, 1-p, x)$. The second axiom requires the observed preference-or-indifference relation to be reflexive, connective, and transitive. That is, for all gambles x, y, z the following conditions are satisfied:

1. Reflexivity: $x \succsim x$.
2. Connectivity: Either $x \succsim y$ or $y \succsim x$ or both.
3. Transitivity: $x \succsim y$ and $y \succsim z$ imply $x \succsim z$.

A detailed discussion of these properties is given in the appendix. Reflexivity is empirically trivial because any gamble is obviously equivalent to itself. Connectivity is also innocuous because any two gambles can be compared with respect to preference. Although transitivity might be violated in certain contexts, it is, nevertheless, a very compelling principle. It is certainly imperative on normative grounds, and it is a plausible descriptive hypothesis.

Axiom 3 is a reducibility condition. It requires that the gamble (x, pq, y), in which x is obtained with probability pq and y with probability $1-pq$, be equivalent, with respect to the preference order, to the compound gamble $[(x, p, y), q, y]$, in which (x, p, y) is obtained with probability q and y with probability $1-q$. Compound gambles differ from simple ones in that their outcomes are themselves gambles rather than pure outcomes, such as monetary values that can be won or lost. Note that the final outcomes of both the simple and the compound gambles are x and y. Furthermore, the probabilities with which x and y are obtained are the same in both gambles.

This follows from the fact that the probability of obtaining x in the compound gambles is the probability of obtaining (x, p, y) in the first stage (i.e., q) multiplied by the probability of obtaining x in the second stage (i.e., p), which equals pq. (Assuming that the probabilities of the two stages are independent.) Consequently, the probability of obtaining y in the compound gamble is $1 - pq$, and hence the two gambles eventually yield the same outcomes with the same probabilities. Thus axiom 3 asserts, in effect, that the preferences depend only on the final outcomes and their probabilities and not on the process by which they are obtained. Normatively, it makes perfect sense to suppose that the choices are invariant with respect to rearrangements of the gambling procedure, as long as the outcomes and their probabilities remain unchanged. If, on the other hand, people have aversions or attractions associated with the actual gambling process, they may not be indifferent between the compound and the corresponding simple gamble.

In general, the psychological interpretation of the axioms raises intricate problems. If all gambles are presented to the individual in terms of their final outcomes and their associated probabilities, then A3 is trivially substantiated. If the gambles are displayed in terms of their immediate rather than final outcomes, the relationship between the compound and the simple gambles may very well escape the subject and A3 can be easily violated. Moreover, two gambles that are formally identical may elicit different responses from the subject because of differences in display, context, and other situational variables. An individual may reject a bet offered to him by a friend, for example, though he may gladly accept a formally identical bet in a gambling casino. The interpretation of utility theory as a behavioral model, therefore, has to be supplemented by a psychological theory that accounts for situational variables that affect risky choices. In the absence of such a theory, the applicability of utility theory is limited to specific contexts and its explanatory power is substantially reduced.

The fourth axiom is a substitutability condition. It states that if x and y are equivalent, then they are substitutable for each other in any gamble, in the sense that $(x, p, z) \sim (y, p, z)$ for any p and z. This axiom excludes the possibility of interacting outcomes in the sense that the probability mixture of x and z can be preferred to the probability mixture of y and z, although x and y, taken alone, are equivalent.

The fifth axiom asserts that if x is preferred to y, then it must be preferred to any probability mixture of x and y, which, in turn, must be preferred to y. It is certainly not objectionable for monetary outcomes. An alleged counterexample to this axiom is Russian roulette; players of this game apparently prefer a probability mixture of living and dying over either one of them alone. For otherwise, one can easily either stay alive or kill oneself, without ever playing the game. A more careful analysis reveals, however, that this situation, perverse as it may be, is not incompatible with axiom 5. The actual outcomes involved in playing Russian roulette are (1) staying alive after playing the game, (2) staying alive without playing the game, and (3) dying in the course of playing the game. In choosing to play Russian roulette, therefore, one prefers a probability mixture of (1) and (3) over (2), rather than a probability mixture of (1) and (2) over both (1) and (2) as the alleged counterexample suggests. The former preference, however, is not incompatible with A5. This argument also demonstrates the errors that can result from an incomplete analysis of the choice situation or from an inappropriate identification of the outcomes. A careful analysis of the payoff matrix is a prerequisite to any serious application of the theory.

The last axiom embodies a continuity or a solvability property. It asserts that if y is between x and z in the preference order (i.e., $x \succ y \succ z$) then there exists a probability p such that the gamble (x, p, z) is equivalent to y. This axiom excludes the possibility that one alternative is "infinitely better" than another one, in the sense that any probability mixture involving the former is preferable to the latter. For a proposed counterexample, let x be the prospect of receiving one dime, let y be the prospect of receiving one nickel, and let z be the prospect of being shot at sunrise. Because $x \succ y \succ z$, A6 requires that there exists a probability p, such that the gamble (x, p, z) in which one receives a dime with probability p or is shot at sunrise with probability $1 - p$ is equivalent to receiving a nickel for sure. Some people find this result unacceptable. Its counterintuitive flavor, however, stems from an inability to comprehend very small probabilities. Thus in the abstract, people feel that there is no positive probability with which they are willing to risk their life for an extra nickel, yet in actual practice a person would cross a street to buy some product for a nickel less, although by doing so he certainly increases the probability of being killed. Hence, the initial intuitions that tend to reject axiom 6 seem inconsistent with everyday behavior.

Axiom 6 captures the relationships between probabilities and values and the form in which they compensate for each other. This form becomes transparent in the following theorem of von Neumann and Morgenstern.

THEOREM 5.1

If axioms A1–A6 are satisfied, then there exists a real-valued utility function u defined on A, such that

1. $x \succsim y$ if and only if $u(x) \geq u(y)$.
2. $u(x, p, y) = pu(x) + (1 - p)u(y)$.

Furthermore, u is an interval scale, that is, if v is any other function satisfying 1 and 2, then there exists numbers b, and $a > 0$ such that $v(x) = au(x) + b$.

Thus the theorem guarantees that whenever the axioms hold, there exists a utility function that (1) preserves the preference order and (2) satisfies the expectation principle as the utility of a gamble equals the expected utility of its outcomes. Moreover, this utility scale is uniquely determined except for an origin and a unit of measurement. The proof of this theorem is quite difficult and therefore omitted. A simplified version of the result can be found in Luce and Raiffa (1957, pp. 23–31).

The main contribution of modern utility theory to the analysis of decision making under risk is in providing sound justification for the Bernoullian expected utility principle. This justification does not depend on long run considerations, hence it is applicable to unique choice situations. Furthermore, the axiomatic structure highlights those aspects of the theory, which are critical for both normative and descriptive applications.

Some people, however, remained unconvinced by the axioms. One of them, Allais (1953), argued that the theory of utility is too restrictive and hence inadequate. To substantiate the claim he constructed the following example of two hypothetical decision situations each involving two gambles, expressed in units of a million dollars.

Situation 1. Choose between
Gamble 1. $\frac{1}{2}$ with probability 1;
Gamble 2. $2\frac{1}{2}$ with probability .10,
$\quad\quad\quad$ $\frac{1}{2}$ with probability .89,
$\quad\quad\quad$ 0 with probability .01.

Situation 2. Choose between
Gamble 3. $\frac{1}{2}$ with probability .11,
$\quad\quad\quad$ 0 with probability .89;
Gamble 4. $2\frac{1}{2}$ with probability .10,
$\quad\quad\quad$ 0 with probability .90.

Most people prefer gamble 1 to gamble 2, presumably because the small probability of missing the chance of a lifetime to become rich seems very unattractive. At the same time most people prefer gamble 4 to gamble 3, presumably because the large difference between the payoffs dominates the small difference between the chances of winning. However, this seemingly innocent pair of preferences is incompatible with utility theory. To demonstrate this, note that the first preference implies that

$$u(\text{gamble 1}) > u(\text{gamble 2})$$

and hence

$$u(\tfrac{1}{2}) > .10u(2\tfrac{1}{2}) + .89u(\tfrac{1}{2}) + .01u(0)$$

so

$$.11u(\tfrac{1}{2}) > .10u(2\tfrac{1}{2}) + .01u(0).$$

Similarly, the second preference implies that

$$u(\text{gamble 4}) > u(\text{gamble 3})$$

and hence

$$.10u(2\tfrac{1}{2})+.90u(0) > .11u(\tfrac{1}{2})+.89u(0)$$

so

$$.10u(2\tfrac{1}{2})+.01u(0) > .11u(\tfrac{1}{2}),$$

which is clearly inconsistent with the inequality derived from the first preference.

How do people react to such inconsistencies between their intuitions and the theory? Some people, who feel committed to their preferences, would undoubtedly reject the expected utility theory. Or, to use Samuelson's phrase, they prefer to "satisfy their preferences and let the axioms satisfy themselves." Others, who feel committed to the theory, tend to reexamine their preferences in the light of the axioms and to revise their initial choices accordingly. An illuminating introspective discussion of Allais's example, from this viewpoint, has been offered by Savage (1954).

Savage admits that, when first presented with Allais's example, he preferred gamble 1 to gamble 2 and gamble 4 to gamble 3 and that he still feels an intuitive attraction to these choices. Yet, he has adopted another way of looking at the problem. One way in which the gambles can be realized is by a lottery with 100 numbered tickets, one of which is drawn at random to determine the outcome according to the payoff matrix presented in Fig. 5.5.

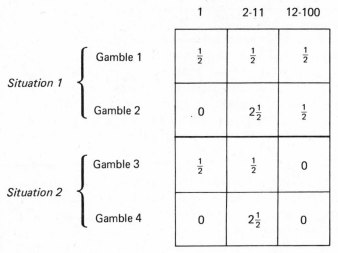

Fig. 5.5

An examination of the payoff matrix reveals that if one of the tickets numbered 12–100 is drawn, it does not matter, in either situation, which gamble is chosen. Hence, one should consider only the possibility that one of the tickets numbered 1–11 will be drawn, in which case the two choice situations are identical. Limiting our attention to tickets 1–11, the problem in both situations is whether a 10:1 chance to win $2\frac{1}{2}$ million is preferred to $\frac{1}{2}$ a million with certainty. If one prefers gamble 1 to gamble 2, therefore, he should also prefer gamble 3 to gamble 4, if he wishes to be consistent. In concluding his discussion Savage (1954) writes:

> It seems to me that in reversing my preference between gamble 3 and 4 I have corrected an error. There is, of course, an important sense in which preferences, being entirely subjective, cannot be in error; but in a different, more subtle sense they can be. Let me illustrate by a simple example containing no reference to uncertainty. A man buying a car for $2,134.56 is tempted to order it with a radio installed, which will bring the total price to $2,228.41, feeling that the difference is trifling. But, when he reflects that, if he already had the car, he certainly would not spend $93.85 for a radio for it, he realizes that he has made an error (p. 103).

The preceding analysis exemplifies how utility theory can be applied to situations where it seems incompatible with one's intuitions. Here, the theory is viewed as a guideline or a corrective tool for a rational man rather than as an accurate model of his nonreflective choices.

Indeed, MacCrimmon (1967) has presented problems of the kind devised by Allais to upper-middle-level executives in order to study both the descriptive validity and the normative appeal of utility theory. He concluded that his subjects tended to regard most of the deviations from the theory as mistakes and were ready to correct them, if given the opportunity.

Another criticism of expected utility theory revolves around the concept of probability. The theory is formulated in terms of gambles whose numerical probabilities are assumed to be known in advance. Such knowledge, however, is missing in most applications. Can the theory be generalized to situations where no a priori knowledge of (numerical) probabilities is available? The answer is positive, provided some consistency requirements are fulfilled.

Savage (1954) has developed an axiomatic theory leading to simultaneous measurement of utility and subjective probability. We do not wish to present this theory here but we do wish to show how the relation "more probable than" between events can be defined in terms of preferences between gambles. Consider the choice situation, displayed in Fig. 5.6, between two gambles G_1 and G_2 whose outcomes x, y, and z depend on whether E, F, or neither event (denoted $\overline{E \cup F}$) occurs. If neither E nor F occurs, there is no reason to prefer one gamble to another. Thus, assuming x is preferred to y, the only apparent reason for preferring G_1 to G_2 is the fact that E seems more probable than F. Stated formally, E is said to be more probable than F if

Events

	E	F	$\overline{E \cup F}$
G_1	x	y	z
G_2	y	x	z

Gambles

Fig. 5.6

and only if G_1 is preferred to G_2. Clearly, some assumptions are needed to guarantee that the above relation is well defined. Indeed, Savage has further shown that his axioms are sufficient to establish the existence of a uniquely additive subjective probability function s and an interval scale utility function u such that

1. $x \gtrsim y$ if and only if $u(x) \geq u(y)$ and
2. $u(x, E, y) = s(E)u(x) + [1 - s(E)]u(y)$,

where (x, E, y) denotes the gamble where x is obtained if E occurs and y otherwise. Because the probabilities, as well as the outcomes, are viewed as subjective, Savage's theory is called the subjective expected utility model, or the SEU model, for short.

The historical development of expectation models reveals a clear trend toward more general and more subjective decision models. In the expected value model, both probability and value are defined objectively. In the expected utility theory, objective values are replaced by utilities, and in the subjective expected utility model, objective probabilities, in addition, are replaced by subjective ones.

The introduction of subjective quantities generalizes the theory in two major respects. They reflect individual differences in the evaluation of outcomes (utilities) and events (subjective probability). At the same time they do not have to be specified in advance, because they can be derived from choices. The common property shared by all objective and subjective expectation models is that the subjective value of a gamble is a composite function of two basic independent factors: the desirability of its outcomes and the likelihood of its events.

Tests of Utility Theory

In recent years there have been several attempts to test the descriptive validity of the subjective expected utility theory. Although the theory may be applicable to many real world problems (such as the selection of a military strategy, a financial investment, or a job offer), it is very difficult to test the theory in these contexts mostly because of the large number of unknown parameters (utilities and subjective probabilities) and the lack of the appropriate controls. Consequently, students of choice behavior have devised simple experimental paradigms, based on choice between gambles, that enable them to test utility theory under controlled experimental conditions. The price paid for these controls is that the scope of the investigation is necessarily limited to those situations that can be studied in the laboratory. The extrapolation from laboratory experiments to real world behavior is always a risky venture. With this problem in mind we turn now to the discussion of some of the methods used to test the theory and to derive utility and subjective probability scales. More specifically, three such methods are discussed. Reviews of the experimental literature and discussions of the related methodological issues can be found in some of the articles cited in the introduction.

The first experimental study of expected utility theory was conducted at Harvard by Mosteller and Nogee (1951). Their subjects were presented with gambles, constructed from possible hands of poker dice, that they could accept or reject. If a subject rejected the gamble, no money changed hands; if he accepted it, he won x cents if he beat the hand and lost a nickel if he did not. The situation is described in the payoff matrix of Fig. 5.7, where the values are expressed in pennies.

The subjects were shown how to calculate the probabilities of the relevant events and were also given a table with the true odds for all the poker dice hands used in the study. By varying the payoffs, the experimenter finds the value of x for which the subject is indifferent between the two alternatives. After that value is found, its utility may be computed in the following fashion. Because the subject is assumed to be indifferent between the two alternatives, $u(\text{Accept}) = u(\text{Reject})$ and hence, according to expected utility theory,

$$u(0) = pu(-5) + (1-p)u(x),$$

where p denotes the (known) probability of beating the hand. Because

States

	Win the hand	Lose the hand
Accept	x	-5
Reject	0	0

Alternatives

Fig. 5.7

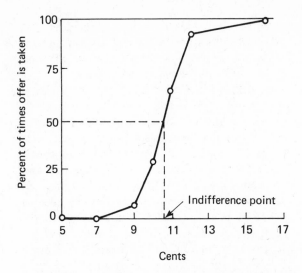

Fig. 5.8 Proportion of times an offered gamble was accepted by one of the subjects in the Mosteller and Nogee experiment.

utility is measured on an interval scale, we can set $u(0) = 0$ and $u(-5) = -1$ to obtain $u(x) = p/(1-p)$.

By varying odds and payoffs, the utility function can be constructed, provided the indifference point can be found. To determine this point, Mosteller and Nogee varied the payoff (i.e., x) systematically and replicated the choices many times over a 4-month period. The proportion of times the subject elected to play each of the gambles was plotted against the corresponding payoff. The point at which the subject accepted the gamble 50 percent of the times was estimated from the graph and taken as the indifference point. An example of such a graph is given in Fig. 5.8. The reader may recall that essentially the same procedure is employed in psychophysics to determine sensation units, or jnd's. Although the proportion of acceptance increased with the payoff, subjects revealed a considerable degree of inconsistency. That is, many gambles were accepted on some replications but rejected on others. This inconsistency is particularly apparent when the graph of Fig. 5.8 is contrasted with the step function (i.e., a function that jumps from 0 to 100 per cent at one point) predicted from any model that does not allow inconsistency.

Fourteen subjects completed the experiment, of whom 9 were Harvard undergraduates and 5 were members of the Massachusetts National Guard. The utility scales derived from the study, in the range between 5 cents and $5.50, were concave (negatively accelerated) for the students and convex (positively accelerated) for the guardsmen. These utility functions were then used to predict, with moderate success, additional choices made by the same subjects involving more complicated gambles.

Although the Mosteller–Nogee study did not provide a very direct test of utility theory, it lent some indirect support to the expected utility principle, and it demonstrated that it is feasible to measure utility experimentally and to predict future behavior on the basis of these measurements.

One criticism of the experiment of Mosteller and Nogee is that their results are also interpretable in terms of subjective probabilities instead of (or in addition to) utilities. The fact that the objective probabilities were known to the subjects does not imply that the subjects actually used these values in their decisions. Davidson, Suppes, and Siegel (1957) conducted a series of studies at Stanford University designed to meet this objection and to measure both utility and subjective probability. Their approach followed an earlier development of Ramsey (1931), which was based on the idea of finding an event whose subjective probability equals one half. Assuming the subjective expected utility model, this event can be used to construct a utility scale, which can then be used to measure the subjective probabilities of other events.

If an event E with subjective probability of one half exists, then its complement $\bar{E}$ also has a subjective probability of one half because, according to the theory, the (subjective) probabilities of complementary events must sum to unity. Consequently, if one regards E and $\bar{E}$ as equiprobable, he should be indifferent between the gamble G_1, where he receives x if E occurs and y otherwise, and the gamble G_2, where he receives y if E occurs and x otherwise. Conversely, if one is indifferent between G_1 and G_2, for all x and y, then his subjective probability for E is equal to that of $\bar{E}$, which must equal one half.

Davidson, Suppes, and Siegel tried several events, but they were forced to reject coin flips and penny matching because their subjects showed systematic preferences for heads over tails, for example. They finally used a six-sided die, with the nonsense syllable ZEJ printed on three of its sides and ZOJ on the other three. This die came reasonably close to satisfying the subjective equiprobability criterion.

After the desired event E is identified, various gambles can be constructed by varying the payoffs, as indicated in Fig. 5.9.

Fig. 5.9

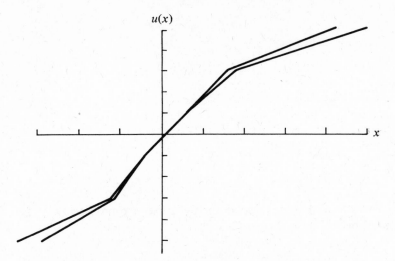

Fig. 5.10 Bounds for the utility curve of subject 9 in the Davidson, Suppes, and Siegel experiment.

If the subject prefers G_1 to G_2, for example, then, according to the subjective expected utility model, there exist utility (u) and subjective probability (s) functions such that

$$s(E)u(x) + s(\bar{E})u(y) \geq s(E)u(z) + s(\bar{E})u(w).$$

But because E was selected so that $s(E) = s(\bar{E})$, the subjective probabilities can be cancelled, and we obtain the inequality

$$u(x) + u(y) \geq u(z) + u(w).$$

By an appropriate selection of payoffs, one can obtain upper and lower bounds on the utility function from the inequalities derived from the choices, provided they are consistent with the model.

Out of the 19 subjects who took part in the study, 15 satisfied the theory and the bounds on their utility scales were determined. Because the bounds were, in general, sufficiently close, they permitted an approximate determination of the shapes of the utility functions, which were nonlinear in most cases. An example of the bounds obtained for one of the subjects is shown in Fig. 5.10.

Suppose a new event F is now introduced into the payoff matrix shown in Fig. 5.11. If the payoffs can be selected so that subjects are indifferent between G_1 and G_2, then according to our theory

$$s(F)u(x) + s(\bar{F})u(y) = s(F)u(z) + s(\bar{F})u(w).$$

States

	F	$\bar{F}$
G_1	x	y
G_2	z	w

Alternatives

Fig. 5.11

Because $s(F)+s(\bar{F}) = 1$, we can solve for the subjective probability of F, which is given by

$$s(F) = \frac{u(w)-u(y)}{u(x)-u(z)+u(w)-u(y)}.$$

Having found the utilities, therefore, by using the special event E, we can now solve for the subjective probabilities of other events as well. Although Davidson, Suppes, and Siegel did not construct subjective probability scales, they applied their procedure to measure the subjective probability of a single event whose objective probability equaled one fourth. The majority of the subjects for whom subjective probability could be calculated tended to underestimate the objective probability.

A more recent attempt to test utility theory and to measure utility and subjective probability simultaneously was conducted by Tversky (1967). Consider a set of gambles of the form (x, p) in which one wins (or loses) \$x if p occurs and receives nothing if p does not occur. Let $M(x, p)$ be the bid, or the minimal selling price of the gamble (x, p). That is, $M(x, p)$ is the smallest amount of money for which one would sell his right to play the gamble. According to utility theory, therefore,

$$u[M(x, p)] = u(x)s(p)+u(0)s(\bar{p}),$$

where u and s are the utility and the subjective probability functions and $\bar{p}$ is the complement of p. Since utility is measured on an interval scale on which the zero point is arbitrary, we can set $u(0) = 0$, and after taking logarithms, we obtain,

$$\log u[M(x, p)] = \log u(x)+\log s(\bar{p}).$$

If both x and p are varied, then the resulting bidding matrix should be additive in the conjoint measurement sense (see Sec. 2.5). That is, the bids can be rescaled monotonically such that the rescaled bid for the gamble (x, p) equals the sum of the scale values of x and p. The additivity of the bidding matrix provides a method for testing the assumption of independence between utility and subjective probability that lies at the heart of utility theory.

To facilitate the measurement process, an additional assumption about the utility function was explored. Suppose utility is a power function of the form $u(x) = x^\theta$ for some $\theta > 0$. Substituting this form in the last equation yields

$$\log [M(x, p)^\theta] = \log x^\theta + \log s(p);$$

thus

$$\log M(x, p) = \log x + \frac{1}{\theta} \log s(p).$$

Hence, if utility is a power function, then the logarithms of the bids should equal the sum of the functions of the gamble's components. Conversely, it is possible to show that if the utility function is monotonic and if the above equation holds for all x and p, then utility must be a power function.

This prediction was tested in an experiment using 11 male inmates in a state prison in Michigan. They were presented with gambles of the form (x, p), where the outcomes varied from a gain of \$1.35 to a loss of that amount, and the events varied in objective probability from .1 to .9. Each subject stated his bid, or his minimum selling price, for every gamble. Each gamble was presented once in each of three sessions. Several gambles, chosen randomly, were played at the end of each session.

Analyses of variance applied to the logarithms of the subjects' bids supported additivity in 41 out of the 44 bidding matrices. The data, therefore, can be accounted for by power utility functions, to the accuracy allowed by their own variability.

The derivation of the utility and the subjective probability scales was based on the observation that for any pair of complementary events p and $\bar{p}$

$$M(x, p)^\theta = x^\theta s(p) \quad \text{and} \quad M(x, \bar{p})^\theta = x^\theta [1 - s(p)].$$

Taking logarithms and solving for θ yields

$$\theta = \frac{\log s(p)}{\log M(x, p) - \log x} = \frac{\log [1 - s(p)]}{\log M(x, \bar{p}) - \log x}.$$

Because the denominators can be calculated from the data, estimates of both θ and $s(p)$ can be obtained. The resulting utility and subjective probability functions for a typical subject are shown in Figs. 5.12 and 5.13.

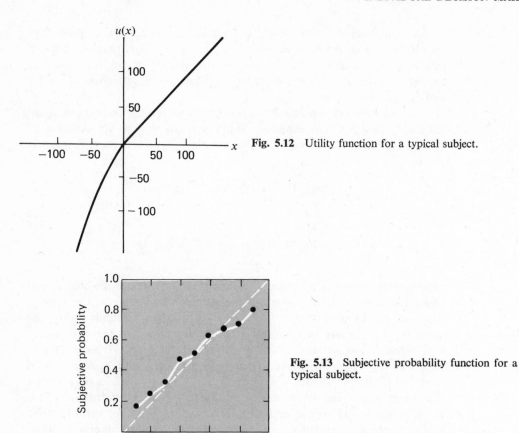

Fig. 5.12 Utility function for a typical subject.

Fig. 5.13 Subjective probability function for a typical subject.

The utility functions tended to be linear for gains and convex for losses. Apparently, the subjects were ready to sell the positive outcome gambles for their expected (monetary) value, but they were willing to pay more than the expected value to get rid of the negative outcome gambles. Such a preference would lead to the purchase of insurance despite an inferior expected monetary value.

Subjective probability scales were linear functions of objective probability for some subjects; most of the subjects, however, overestimated low probabilities and underestimated high ones. This result has also been found in many other studies.

The results obtained in this study have both methodological and substantive implications. From a methodological viewpoint it was shown that the application of additivity analysis to a specified class of gambling experiments yields a simple simultaneous construction of utility and subjective probability scales. From a substantive viewpoint the data support the multiplicative relation between utility and subjective probability embodied in the subjective expected utility principle. Moreover, the results indicate that (within the range of payoffs investigated) the utility of money can be described as a power function of money with different exponents for positive and negative outcomes.

All in all, the three studies reported in this subsection show that the subjective expected utility model provides an adequate account of most of the data obtained in simple gambling experiments. Such findings are of primary interest to the experimental psychologist who is concerned with the question of how people combine various subjective dimensions (e.g., utility and subjective probability) in order to evaluate, or choose among, alternatives. An economist interested in consumer behavior and insurance purchase or a political scientist interested in presidential decisions, for instance, might feel that although utility theory may be applicable to their field of study the experiments thus far performed are too simple and contrived to provide relevant information. It is our hope, nevertheless, that the mathematical and the experimental methods developed in these studies can be extended to the investigation of complex decisions in real world environments.

Special Preference Models

The subjective expected utility model is not the only theory put forth to account for decisions under risk. More than half a century ago, an economist, Irving Fisher (1906), proposed that people base their choices among gambles on the variances of the gambles as well as on the expectations.

The variance of a gamble G, denoted $V(G)$, is given by the formula $V(G) = E(G^2) - E(G)^2$, where G^2 is the gamble obtained from G by squaring its outcomes. In particular, if G has two outcomes x and y obtained with probabilities p and $1-p$, respectively, then its variance equals $p(1-p)(x-y)^2$. The variance is the most common measure of the dispersion of the outcomes, and it seems conceivable that different attitudes toward risk be reflected by preferences for different amounts of variance. Although some types of variance preferences can be accommodated by an appropriate selection of utility functions, Allais (1953) has further argued that, even with the introduction of such utility functions, the expectation principle alone is insufficient to explain risky choices. Allais suggested the investigation of decision models that depend not only on expectation but on other attributes such as variance and skewness as well.

Alternatives to utility theory can be developed by first characterizing each gamble in terms of its objectively defined attributes and then formulating decision rules based on these attributes. Thus, instead of choosing among gambles according to their subjective expected utilities, one can choose among them according to some linear combination of their expectations and variances, for example. The major difficulty with this approach lies in the need to specify in advance the relevant attributes, or dimensions, whose combination accounts for the data. On the other hand, this approach might be a great deal simpler than utility theory in that only a few linear weights, instead of an entire utility function, would be required to explain decisions under risk.

The most general theory of this type is Coombs' ideal point model (1964) and the unfolding method associated with it (see Sec. 3.4). In this model each gamble with monetary outcomes is represented as a probability distribution over the possible outcomes. The gamble obtained by tossing a fair coin 100 times, with heads winning and tails losing, for example, is represented by a binomial distribution with $p = \frac{1}{2}$ and $n = 100$. For any expectation level each individual is assumed to have an ideal distribution, that is, a gamble that he likes best. In choosing among gambles, the individual selects the one that is "closest" to his ideal gamble, in some well-defined sense. Although this model has not been tested in full generality, several studies have demonstrated systematic preferences for some specific aspects of gambles.

In a series of experimental studies, Edwards (1953, 1954a) investigated the existence of specific probability preferences. His subjects chose between two-outcome gambles where the chance events were generated by an eight-hole pinball machine. Edwards found that, for bets with positive expected value, people revealed a strong preference for bets with $\frac{4}{8}$ probability of winning and a definite aversion to bets with $\frac{6}{8}$ probability of winning. For bets with negative expected value, however, people preferred the bet with the lower losing probability. Similar findings were obtained even when the bets differed in their expected value. Because probability and variance were confounded in these studies, Edwards (1954b) conducted another experiment, using the same pinball machine, in which the variance was varied whereas the probability was held constant. The results showed that people exhibit some variance preferences in addition to their probability preferences.

If Coombs' unfolding theory is applied to variance preference, it implies that each individual has an ideal point somewhere along the variance continuum that corresponds to the amount of variance he prefers most. Moreover, his preference for variance decreases monotonically on both sides of the ideal point. Put differently, an individual's preference order, with respect to a given dimension, can be described by a single-peaked preference function over that dimension. (Think of the amount of sugar you prefer in your coffee or of the room temperature you prefer as cases in point).

The reader can easily verify that two-outcome gambles, with constant expectation, are completely specified in terms of their variance and their probability (of receiving the higher payoff, say), which can nevertheless be varied independently. Such gambles provide, therefore, a convenient tool for investigating the nature of both probability and variance preferences and testing unfolding theory. Coombs and Pruitt (1960) conducted an experiment in which 99 undergraduates chose between hypothetical gambles that had zero expectation but that varied in probability and variance independently. The data showed that variance preferences of almost all the subjects were in accord with unfolding theory. About one third of the people preferred high variance, one third low variance, and one third an intermediate amount of variance. As for probability preferences, most subjects satisfied unfolding theory again, but this time the majority of the ideal points lay on one end or another of the probability scale.

Coombs and Pruitt argued that although their findings may be explained by an SEU model, with an arbitrary monotonic utility function, the number of possible preference orderings that are admissible under such a model is considerably larger than the number of orderings admissible under unfolding theory. Hence, the latter model can be regarded as stronger (and more parsimonious) than the former in the sense that it is easier to refute.

The final method of investigating specific preferences in risky choices to be discussed emerges from the theory of achievement motivation (Atkinson 1964). This theory, which stems from the Lewinian–Tolmanian tradition, attempts to explain decisions in situations where a person perceives the outcome of a risky act as contingent (in part) on his own skills. According to the theory, behavior in such situations is determined by the motive to achieve success (M_s), the motive to avoid failure (M_{af}), the incentive values of achieving success and avoiding failure (I_s and I_{af}), and the subjective probability of success (P_s). According to the theory, these five variables are interrelated by the equation

$$T(G) = P_s(M_s I_s) + (1 - P_s)(M_{af} I_{af}),$$

where $T(G)$ is the resultant motivation of act G, or the strength of its response tendency. Note that if we define the utility of success and failure (U_s and U_f) by the expressions

$$U_s = M_s I_s \quad \text{and} \quad U_f = -(M_{af} I_{af}),$$

then $T(G)$ reduces to the subjective expected utility of G. Atkinson, however, makes the critical assumptions that the incentive of success is measured by the complement of the probability of success and that the incentive of avoiding failure is measured by the negative of the probability of success; in symbols, $I_s = 1 - P_s$ and $I_{af} = -P_s$.

These assumptions restrict the applicability of the model to tasks where the reward depends on the difficulty of achieving success and not on the actual payoff attached to it. More specifically, the satisfaction from attaining a goal is a decreasing function of its probability of attainment. The more difficult the target, the greater the satisfaction of achieving it; and the easier the target, the greater the dissatisfaction of failing. This principle stands in direct contradiction to the SEU model, where utilities are assumed to be independent of subjective probabilities.

If we substitute the assumptions about the incentives in the equation for $T(G)$ we obtain

$$T(G) = P_s(1-P_s)(M_s - M_{af}),$$

which is very similar to the variance of a two-outcome gamble. Now, consider a situation in which a person can control the difficulty of his task, or, equivalently, chooses the probability of success. Assuming that the selected difficulty level maximizes $T(G)$, how would it be chosen?

The answer is given by the above equation and it depends on the motive to achieve success and on the motive to avoid failure. If the achievement motive is stronger, then $T(G)$ is maximized if P_s equals one half, but if failure avoidance is greater, then $T(G)$ is maximized if P_s equals zero or one. Hence, the theory predicts that the level of difficulty would be chosen so as to maximize or minimize the variance depending on whether $M_s - M_{af}$ is positive or negative.

This prediction was tested on male college students using a ring-toss game in a study by Atkinson and Litwin (1960). Each subject was given an opportunity to take 10 shots from any distance he chose between 1 and 15 feet from the peg. The experiment was conducted in a realistic game-like atmosphere, where all the subjects stood around to watch each other shoot. The instructions to the subjects were "to see how good you are at this." The motives to achieve success and to avoid failure were measured independently for each subject, using specially devised indices.

The results of the study confirmed the prediction in that significantly more shots were taken from an intermediate distance by men with high need achievement and low fear of failure than by men with low need achievement and high fear of failure. In other words, the former preferred high variance, whereas the latter preferred low variance. Thus Atkinson's model explains variance (or probability) preferences in terms of the needs to achieve success and avoid failure.

As one might expect, the model does not apply to situations where a person recognizes that the outcome is determined by chance alone, regardless of his skills. The distinction between chance and skill, therefore, should not be overlooked. It might be added that in many contexts such as card games, insurance problems, and portfolio selection it is not easy to determine whether luck or skill plays the critical role. A great deal more about the psychology of skill and chance can be found in the books of Cohen (1956, 1960, 1964) and Atkinson (1964). The last book also contains a systematic discussion of the relationship between motivation theory and decision making.

Simplification Principles

All the decision models discussed so far were based on the assumption that the decision maker is capable of evaluating all the available alternatives and examining all the states and the outcomes. In most decisions, however, this assumption is unrealistic. In the first place there are situations where our information concerning the likelihoods of future events is so vague and imprecise that we do not wish to use it in making decisions. Second, the number of alternatives is sometimes so large or the payoff structure so intricate as to make an exhaustive evaluation practically unfeasible. In such cases different approaches to decision theory, based on some simplification scheme, are called for.

One approach attempts to bypass likelihood considerations altogether by developing models for decisions under conditions of ignorance. Another approach attempts to reduce the complexity of the problem to manageable proportions by replacing the maximization principle by a weaker "satisficing" condition. These two approaches are now discussed in turn.

Criteria for decisions under ignorance. Although decisions under ignorance are, admittedly, rare, because some information about likelihoods is almost always available, there are circumstances where we have practically no confidence in the validity of our information. Thus we may be willing to ignore it (momentarily, at least) and to consider decision criteria that do not depend on likelihood considerations. Several such criteria have been proposed (see Milnor 1954). In discussing the criteria, we assume that the problem is given in a payoff matrix form, with alternatives $a_1, \ldots, a_n$, states $s_1, \ldots, s_m$, and entries v_{ij} reflecting the value, or the utility, of the outcome resulting from the choice of alternative a_i given state s_j.

1. *The maximin criterion*: Consider the lowest value obtained under each of the alternatives and choose an alternative whose lowest value is highest. Put differently, select an alternative that maximizes the minimum payoff. This principle guarantees a value of at least $v' = \max_i \min_j v_{ij}$, no matter what happens, whereas no other decision rule can guarantee a higher minimum. Hence, it is optimal if the worst that could happen should always happen, that is, when the state of nature is determined by a hostile opponent. Indeed, the maximin principle plays a central role in the theory of strictly competitive games (see Sec. 7.2). It is a very conservative (or, if you wish, pessimistic) criterion and hence recommendable in those contexts where extreme caution is desired. In contrast to this conservative approach, our next principle is quite extravagant.

2. *The maximax criterion*: Choose an alternative whose highest value is maximal. This principle is optimal if the best that could happen should always happen, that is, when the state of nature is determined by a benevolent agent. Because things, however, are usually neither as bad as we feared nor as good as we hoped, it might be advisable to weigh the best and the worst. This, in essence, is the next criterion, attributable to Hurwicz (1951).

3. *The pessimism-optimism criterion*: For each alternative a_i let v'_i and v''_i denote its minimum and maximum values, respectively, and let $0 \leq \alpha \leq 1$

be a pessimism-optimism index. For each alternative a_i define its α value as $\alpha v_i' + (1-\alpha)v_i''$ and choose an alternative with the highest α value. Note that this criterion generalizes the earlier criteria. For by setting $\alpha = 1$, we obtain the maximin principle, whereas by setting $\alpha = 0$ we obtain the maximax principle. If an intermediate value of α is selected, a mixture of the two principles is obtained.

4. *Principle of insufficient reason*: A method of reducing ignorance to risk, known as the principle of insufficient reason, is to assign equal subjective probabilities to all states of nature. This criterion, which is attributed to J. Bernoulli, is based on the assumption that if there is no reason to believe that one state is more likely to occur than another, then the states should be judged equally probable. Because the partition into states, however, is largely arbitrary and can be redefined at will, the principle of insufficient reason leads to solutions that are also arbitrary.

The final criterion, proposed by Savage (1951), is closely related to the maximin notion, yet it is based on the "regret matrix" rather than on the original payoff matrix.

5. *The minimax regret criterion*: For each state s_j let v_j denote the highest value attainable under that state. That is, $v_j = \max_i v_{ij}$. To each payoff matrix, associate a regret matrix with entries $r_{ij} = v_j - v_{ij}$. Thus each entry of the regret matrix is a measure of the difference between the payoff that is actually obtained and the payoff that could have been obtained if the true state of nature had been known in advance. To each alternative assign its maximal regret value and select an alternative whose maximal regret is minimal. Thus the minimax regret criterion is similar to the maximin cri-

	States			Decision criterion and the alternative selected by it
	S_1	S_2	S_3	
a_1	5	5	5	Maximin
a_2	10	0	0	Maximax
a_3	9	2	2	$\alpha = \frac{1}{2}$
a_4	8	0	8	Equiprobability
a_5	6	1	4	Minimax regret

Alternatives

Fig. 5.14

terion in that it concentrates on the worst possible case, but the worst is defined by the maximal regret rather than by the minimum value.

To illustrate the differences among the criteria, consider the payoff matrix in Fig. 5.14 where each of the five criteria leads to a different choice. The reader is invited to verify this assertion. Although most, or at least some, of the criteria seem plausible on first sight, they all lead to serious difficulties on closer investigation. In fact, it seems that a precise formulation of the problem of decision making under ignorance is not easy to come by. A good critical discussion of these issues can be found in Chapter 13 of *Games and Decisions* by Luce and Raiffa (1957).

The satisficing principle. The other approach to the simplification problem was developed primarily by Simon (1957, p. 241):

> Broadly stated, the task is to replace the global rationality of economic man with a kind of rational behavior that is compatible with the access to information and the computational capabilities that are actually possessed by organisms, including man, in the kind of environments in which such organisms exist.

Simon argues that the classical conception of rationality that is based on unlimited memory and computational capacity should be replaced by a more realistic form of rationality, limited by one's ability to process information. In many real world decision problems, the amount of information that should be processed and evaluated is so vast that expected utility maximization is practically impossible. (A choice of a strategy in a chess game is a case in point.)

The essential simplification built into Simon's model can be described as the replacement of the maximization principle by a satisficing principle. According to this principle, the outcomes are first classified as "satisfactory" or "unsatisfactory" with respect to each of the relevant attributes, and the first alternative that satisfies one's level of aspiration along each attribute is selected. In evaluating investment plans, for example, one may select the first plan that provides satisfactory profit as well as adequate security. What is considered to be a satisfactory profit may change with time and experience as one increases or decreases his aspiration level.

This model is simpler than the utility maximization model in several important respects. It bypasses the problems of evaluating the utility of each outcome and of comparing incommensurable attributes. It does not call for an exploration of all the available alternatives and it requires only a very limited computational capacity.

Yet the model makes sense only in those situations where the process of searching the alternatives or evaluating the outcomes is either unfeasible or costly. Otherwise, why should we stop the search when we find a satisfactory alternative instead of looking for a better one? Such situations are, to be sure, quite common as the cost associated with the evaluation process may be expressed in units of money, time, or aggravation. Although such cost can, in principle, be incorporated within a general utility maximization model, the complexity of the resulting model may render it practically unworkable.

Because, according to Simon's view, each complex decision problem is reformulated by the individual, the model must characterize the subjective process of defining the problem. To do so, a theory describing the cognitive processes involved in the reformulation of a decision problem is required. This requirement has resulted in a shift in emphasis from motivation to cognition as the psychological basis of a theory of choice.

In the late 1950's, Simon and his colleagues[2] began to develop the general problem solver, a computer model of human thinking and problem solving that can be applied to a wide variety of intellectual problems. This model has been described in Chapter 4. To recapitulate, the model has three essential components: (1) a memory containing lists of the relevant objects together with their pertinent attributes; (2) a set of search and selection procedures that are capable of searching, selecting, and regrouping the items stored in memory; and (3) a set of rules that guide the problem-solving process. Like most other computer programs, the lists are processed sequentially and recursively.

The general problem solver has been quite successful in simulating human behavior in simple learning tasks as well as in some complex decision problems. In one of the more interesting applications, Clarkson (1962) employed the general problem solver to investigate the decision process of investment trust officers in a middle-size bank. He first collected a large number of protocols, or verbalized reflections of the subjects who were asked to "think aloud" and to comment on their past decisions. On the basis of these protocols the trust investment process was divided into three parts: (1) the analysis and selection of a list of stocks suitable for current investment, (2) the formulation of an investment policy, and (3) the selection of a portfolio. Each part, in turn, was further subdivided and analyzed and the entire process was described as a list-processing computer program.

To test the descriptive validity of his model, Clarkson performed a simulation experiment. Four accounts were selected and the relevant items of information such as the sum of money available for investment and the basic characteristics of the beneficiaries were fed into the computer model. The actual portfolios selected by the trust officer were then compared to those predicted by the model. A typical comparison of this type is shown in Table 5.1.

The correspondence between the actual and the simulated portfolios is impressive even after considering all the methodological reservations.

---

[2]Newell, Shaw, and Simon (1958).

TABLE 5.1 SIMULATION OF ACCOUNT 1, 1/8/60

Growth Account

Funds Available for Investment: $22,000

Program selected:		Trust officer selected:	
60	General American Transportation	30	Corning Glass
50	Dow Chemical	50	Dow Chemical
10	IBM	10	IBM
60	Merck and Company	50	Merck and Company
45	Owens Corning Fiberglass	45	Owens Corning Fiberglass

Moreover, the ability of the model to simulate complex decisions in such a rich environment is quite promising. Although a great deal more data are needed to evaluate the overall contribution of this approach to the study of choice, it demonstrates the potential efficacy of simplification principles and the essential interrelations between cognitive and decision processes.

Revision of Subjective Probabilities

Suppose you believe, before the opening of the basketball season, that the odds in favor of the Boston Celtics' winning the NBA Championship are 2:1. How would you change this estimate after finding out that the Celtics have won (or lost) their first four games? In this final subsection we discuss the problem of how people revise their subjective probabilities in the light of new information. This problem constitutes a part of (what may be termed) the predecisional process rather than of the decision process itself. Because the perception and the revision of subjective probabilities, however, are closely tied to decision making under risk, they are discussed in this section after some of the relevant mathematics is reviewed.

As shown in the appendix, the conditional probability of the event A given the event B is defined by the formula

$$p(A|B) = \frac{p(A \cap B)}{p(B)} \quad \text{provided} \quad p(B) \neq 0.$$

Consequently,

$$p(A \cap B) = p(B \cap A) = p(A|B)p(B)$$

and

$$p(B|A) = \frac{p(B \cap A)}{p(A)} = \frac{p(A|B)p(B)}{p(A)} \quad \text{provided} \quad p(A) \neq 0.$$

This equation is referred to as *Bayes's theorem* or *Bayes's rule* after the Reverend Thomas Bayes. His formula, which is an immediate consequence of the definition of conditional probability, provides us with a mathematically valid procedure for revising probabilities. Thus if A denotes the event that the Celtics will win the NBA Championship and B denotes the event that the Celtics will lose their first four games, then the revised probability $p(B|A)$ that the Celtics will win the championship given that they have lost their first four games can be computed via Bayes's formula, provided $p(A|B)$ and $p(B)$ are known.

Do people revise subjective probabilities in accordance with Bayes's rule? Ward Edwards and his associates at the University of Michigan have investigated this question in great detail. In a typical experiment the subject is presented with two book bags each of which contains 100 poker chips. One of the bags, however, contains 70 red and 30 blue poker chips, whereas the other bag contains 70 blue and 30 red poker chips. One of the book bags is selected at random and the question is which book bag was chosen.

In the absence of any additional information, all that can be said is that the (prior) probability that the predominantly red book bag was chosen is one half. To obtain additional information, one can sample poker chips from the selected book bag and observe their color. Indeed, in most experiments of this type (see Edwards 1968) poker chips are sampled from the book bag randomly one at a time with replacement, and the subject is asked to estimate (after each sample) the probability that the selected book bag is the predominantly red one.

For concreteness, suppose our subject has sampled 12 poker chips, of which 8 were red and 4 were blue. This outcome is certainly evidence in favor of the hypothesis that the selected book bag is the predominantly red one. How strong is this evidence, or what is the probability of this hypothesis given the observed sample? To calculate this value, let H_R and H_B denote the events (or the hypotheses) that the selected book bag is predominantly red and predominantly blue, respectively, and let D denote the event (or the datum) that the observed sample contains 8 red and 4 blue poker chips, respectively. If we let $\Omega(H_R, H_B)$ be the ratio of $p(H_R|D)$ to $p(H_B|D)$, then by application of Bayes's rule

$$\Omega(H_R, H_B) = \frac{p(H_R|D)}{p(H_B|D)} = \frac{p(D|H_R)p(H_R)}{p(D|H_B)p(H_B)} = \frac{p(D|H_R)}{p(D|H_B)},$$

because the denominators in Bayes's formula cancel and $p(H_R) = p(H_B) = 1/2$ by our assumption. Furthermore, because the sampling process is random and independent, it can readily be shown (using elementary probability theory) that

$$\Omega(H_R, H_B) = \frac{.3^4 \times .7^8}{.3^8 \times .7^4} = \left(\frac{.7}{.3}\right)^4 = 29.6.$$

Hence

$$p(H_R|D) = \frac{\Omega(H_R, H_B)}{1+\Omega(H_R, H_B)} = .97.$$

This value seems surprisingly high to both naive and sophisticated subjects. Most people when faced with this problem produce estimates around .75 and find it difficult to believe that a sample of 8 red and 4 blue poker chips provides such overwhelming evidence in favor of H_R. Essentially the same phenomenon has emerged in several experiments: People are conservative probability estimators in the sense that their estimates are considerably less extreme than those calculated from Bayes's rule. The discrepancy between the estimates of a typical subject and the Bayesian estimates are depicted in Fig. 5.15. The horizontal axis is the difference between the number of red and blue poker chips in the observed sample, denoted $r-b$, and the vertical axis is log $\Omega(H_R, H_B)$. The systematic bias of the subject is evinced by the fact that his estimates fall considerably below the Bayesian estimates. In discussing the theoretical and practical implications of these findings, Edwards, Lindman, and Phillips (1965, pp. 303–19) write:

> Men are incapable of extracting all of the certainty from information that Bayes's theorem indicates is in that information. To put it another way, men are conservative information processors. . . . Whatever the merits or demerits of a built-in tendency to conservatism in information processing in daily life, such a tendency is clearly a hindrance to human effectiveness in information-processing systems. . . . Consequently, the finding of human conservatism raises some problems for the design of man-machine systems intended to perform information processing in a more or less optimal way.

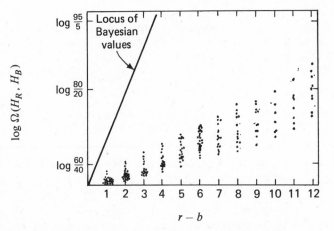

Fig. 5.15 Probability estimates of a subject compared with Bayesian estimates.

Inconsistency is one of the basic characteristics of individual choice behavior. When faced with the same alternatives, under seemingly identical conditions, people do not always make the same choice. Although the lack of consistent preferences may be attributable to factors such as learning, saturation, or changes in taste over time, inconsistencies exist even when the effects of such factors appear negligible. One is led, therefore, to the hypothesis that the observed inconsistency is a consequence of an underlying random process.

The randomness may reflect uncontrolled momentary fluctuations such as attention shifts, or it may correspond to a choice mechanism that is inherently probabilistic. Be that as it may, the most natural way of coping with inconsistent preferences is by replacing the deterministic notion of preference by a probabilistic one. Instead of considering the (absolute) preference of x over y, one may consider the probability of choosing x over y, denoted $p(x, y)$. This probability can be estimated from the relative frequency with which x is chosen over y, and it is commonly viewed as a measure of the degree to which x is preferred over y. If an individual strongly prefers x to y, one would expect $p(x, y)$ to be close to unity and hence $p(y, x)$ close to zero. If, on the other hand, the individual is indifferent between x and y, one would expect $p(x, y)$ to be close to one half. Note that essentially the same principle has been employed in defining indifference points in the study of Mosteller and Nogee (see Fig. 5.8). The deterministic notion of preference is viewed, in this framework, as a special case where all pairwise choice probabilities are either zero, one, or one half.

One of the first to recognize the probabilistic nature of choice behavior was Louis Leon Thurstone. In discussing the process of evaluation and judgment, he wrote:

> An observer is not consistent in his comparative judgments from one occasion to the next. He gives different comparative judgments on successive occasions about the same pair of stimuli. Hence we conclude that the discriminal process corresponding to a given stimulus is not fixed. It fluctuates (1927, p. 271).

To explain the fluctuations in the psychological evaluations of objects, Thurstone introduced the law of comparative judgment, which is described in Sec. 3.3 at some length. The essence of this model is the representation of stimuli as distributions, or random variables, that reflect the momentary fluctuations of their perceived values. The probability of choosing one alternative over another is the probability that the first random variable exceeds the second. Various sets of alternative assumptions about the form and the interrelations among the distributions were proposed by Thurstone. In the simplest case, called Case V, all the distributions are independent and normal with equal variance. The means of the distributions can be easily calculated, in this case, from the observed choice probabilities. The law of comparative judgment is closely related to signal detectability theory (see Chapter 6).

The Thurstonian model was successfully applied to the study of preferences among foods, potential birthday gifts, and other riskless options. Despite Thurstone's emphasis that the model applies "fundamentally to the judgments of a single observer," most of its applications are based on group data. Consequently, it is not easy to evaluate the validity of the law as a descriptive model of individual choice behavior. Nevertheless, Thurstone's contribution to the measurement and the analysis of choice can hardly be exaggerated.

Probabilistic decision theories may be divided into two types: constant utility models and random utility models. Constant utility models assume that each alternative has a constant or fixed utility value and that the probability of choosing one alternative over another is a function of the distance between their utilities. These models are closely related to psychophysical theories in which the probability of judging one object as heavier than another, for instance, is assumed expressable as a monotonic function of the difference between their scale values. The decision problem is viewed as a discrimination problem where the individual is trying to determine which alternative would be more satisfying. The greater the distance between the utilities, the easier the discrimination.

Random utility models assume that the decision makers always chooses the alternative that has the highest utility, but the utilities themselves are random variables rather than constants. The actual choice mechanism, therefore, is purely deterministic, but the utility of each alternative varies from moment to moment.

The two types of probabilistic choice models differ in the locus of the random component. In the constant utility models the randomness is attributable to the decision rule, whereas in the random utility model the randomness is attributable to the utilities. Despite this conceptual difference, some (but not all) models can be viewed either as constant or as random utility models. Signal detectability theory and case V of Thurstone's model are examples.

In the following subsections three probabilistic theories are discussed in turn: Luce's constant utility model, Coombs' random utility model, and Tversky's additive difference model.

A Constant Utility Model (Luce)

In a monograph entitled "Individual Choice Behavior," Luce (1959) presents a probabilistic theory of choice. Luce accepts the basic assumption that choice behavior is governed by a random process, but instead of making additional assumptions about the form of the value distribution (which are typically hard to justify) he assumes that choice probabilities satisfy a simple, but powerful, axiom that serves as a cornerstone of the model.

Suppose that all choice probabilities are neither zero nor one, and let T be a finite set of alternatives, and R be any subset of T. Luce's choice axiom asserts that the probability of choosing an element x of R, from the entire set T, $p(x; T)$, equals the probability that the selected alternative will be in the subset R, $p(R; T)$, multiplied by the probability of choosing x from R, $p(x; R)$. In symbols,

$$p(x; T) = p(x ; R)p(R; T) \quad \text{for} \quad R \subset T.$$

The axiom states that the probability of selecting roast beef (x) from a menu (T), for example, equals the probability of selecting roast beef from the meat entrees (R) times the probability of choosing a meat entree. Put differently, the probability of choosing x from R equals the conditional probability of choosing x from T given that the choice is restricted to R. If $p(x, y) = 0$ for some x, y in T, it is further assumed that x can be deleted from any choice set containing y without affecting the choice probabilities. By repeated applications of this assumption, the problem can be reduced to the imperfect discrimination case where all probabilities differ from zero or one. For simplicity's sake, only this case is discussed in the chapter.

A primary criticism of the axiom is that it does not appear to hold in situations where the choice is divided in some manner into two or more intermediate stages. A modification of an example attributed to Debreu (1960) illustrates this difficulty. Consider an individual who is about to order a meal and who is indifferent between seafood entrees and meat entrees as well as between steak and roast beef. This innocent preference pattern, however, violates the choice axiom. Imagine a menu with three entrees: x, lobster; y, steak; and z, roast beef; let T be the entire menu and R be the first two entrees, i.e., x and y. Because the individual is indifferent between seafood and meat, $p(x; T) = 1/2$; but according to the choice axiom, $p(x; T) = p(x; R)p(R; T) = (1/2)(3/4) = 3/8$.[3]

The example suggests that if a choice set with three elements, x, y, and z contains two elements, say y and z, that are quite similar or even identical, for all practical purposes, then the probability of choosing x over y is very close to the probability of selecting x from the entire set. This hypothesis, which is clearly incompatible with the choice axiom, was supported in a study of choices among gambles conducted by Becker, DeGroot, and Marschak (1963b). The difficulty is not unique to Luce's theory, as it is shared by most probabilistic choice models. As a consequence, one may either concentrate on relatively simple, or homogeneous, alternatives, where the so-called similarity effect is negligible, or attempt to construct more elaborate

---

[3]Because $p(R; T) = 1 - p(z; T) = 1 - p(z; S)p(S;T) = 1 - (1/2)(1/2) = 3/4$, where S denotes the subset of meat entrees, and $p(x; R) = p(x, y) = 1/2$ by the assumption of indifference between seafood and meat.

choice models that incorporate the structure of the choice set and the relationships among the alternatives.

Using the choice axiom and the usual laws of probability theory, Luce derives a large number of interesting consequences, some of which will now be presented. Let R be a subset of T, which consists of the alternatives x and y. By the choice axiom

$$p(x; T) = p(x; R)p(R; T) \quad \text{and} \quad p(y; T) = p(y; R)p(R; T).$$

Dividing the first equation by the second yields

$$\frac{p(x; T)}{p(y; T)} = \frac{p(x; R)}{p(y; R)} = \frac{p(x, y)}{p(y, x)},$$

which is commonly called the constant ratio rule. This rule expresses the fact that, under the choice axiom, the ratio of the form $p(x; R)/p(y; R)$ is independent of R. That is, the ratio of the probability of selecting steak for dinner and the probability of selecting roast beef for dinner is the same for all menus containing both entrees. This rule may be regarded as a probabilistic version of the principle of independence from other alternatives. It can be further shown that the constant ratio rule is, in fact, equivalent to the choice axiom.

Next, the relationship between pairwise choices and choices from larger sets is derived. Because the summation over all y of $p(y; T)$ equals 1,

$$p(x; T) = \frac{p(x; T)}{\sum\limits_{y} p(y; T)} = \frac{1}{\sum\limits_{y} [p(y; T)/p(x; T)]} = \frac{1}{\sum\limits_{y} [p(y, x)/p(x, y)]},$$

according to the constant ratio rule. Hence, all choice probabilities can be expressed as a simple function of the pairwise choice probabilities that contain all the information. Furthermore, a definite relation among triples of pairwise probabilities can also be derived. It is obvious that

$$\frac{p(x; T)p(y; T)p(z; T)}{p(y; T)p(z; T)p(x; T)} = 1.$$

Hence, by the constant ratio rule

$$\frac{p(x, y)p(y, z)p(z, x)}{p(y, x)p(z, y)p(x, z)} = 1,$$

and substituting $p(z, x) = 1 - p(x, z)$, we obtain

$$p(x, z) = \frac{p(x, y)p(y, z)}{p(x, y)p(y, z) + p(z, y)p(y, x)}.$$

Because the relation among triples of pairwise probabilities is also determined by Case V of the Thurstonian model, it can be used as a basis for comparing the models. The predicted values of $p(x, z)$, from known $p(x, y)$ and $p(y, z)$, under the two models, are given in Table 5.2, which is taken from Luce (1959, p. 56).

TABLE 5.2   PREDICTED CHOICE PROBABILITIES UNDER TWO MODELS

$p(x, z)$ Predicted from Luce's Choice Axiom

		$p(y, z)$			
		.6	.7	.8	.9
	.6	.692	.778	.857	.931
$p(x, y)$	.7		.845	.903	.954
	.8			.941	.973
	.9				.988

$p(x, z)$ Predicted from Case V of Thurstone's Model

		$p(y, z)$			
		.6	.7	.8	.9
	.6	.695	.782	.864	.938
$p(x, y)$	.7		.853	.915	.965
	.8			.954	.983
	.9				.995

Although the two models are based on different assumptions, they predict practically the same values and hence it is quite difficult to choose between them on empirical grounds.

One of the more useful consequences of Luce's model is the existence of a ratio scale of preference. To construct the scale, select an arbitrary element a of T and define the scale value of x, denoted $v(x)$, by

$$v(x) = \frac{p(x, a)}{p(a, x)} = \frac{p(x; T)}{p(a; T)}$$

by the constant ratio rule. It can be easily seen now that

$$\frac{v(x)}{v(y)} = \frac{p(x; T)p(a; T)}{p(a; T)p(y; T)} = \frac{p(x; T)}{p(y; T)} = \frac{p(x, y)}{p(y, x)},$$

and hence

$$p(x; T) = \frac{1}{\sum_y [p(y, x)/p(x, y)]} = \frac{1}{\sum_y [v(y)/v(x)]} = \frac{v(x)}{\sum_y v(y)},$$

in particular, if $T = \{x, y\}$, then $p(x, y) = v(x)/[v(x)+v(y)]$.

Therefore, if the choice axiom is satisfied, then it is possible to scale the alternatives in the above manner. Note, however, that v was defined relative to an arbitrary element (a) of T. Suppose a different element (b) is used to define a new scale v'. Hence,

$$v'(x) = \frac{p(x, b)}{p(b, x)} = \frac{p(x; T)}{p(b; T)} = \frac{p(a; T)}{p(b; T)} \frac{p(x; T)}{p(a; T)} = \frac{p(a; T)}{p(b; T)} v(x) = kv(x),$$

and the scale is unique except for multiplication by a positive constant.

This scaling procedure, called the strict utility model, has also been investigated by many other authors, such as Thurstone (1930), Gulliksen (1953), Bradley and Terry (1952), and Becker, DeGroot, and Marschak (1963a).

Although the choice axiom is directly testable, a large number of observations is needed in order to obtain adequate estimates of choice probabilities. Consequently, most studies combine the choices of several individuals in estimating the probabilities. Unfortunately, the model cannot be easily tested on the basis of group data, because each individual in the group may satisfy the axiom, yet the average probabilities violate it or *vice versa*. This fact is demonstrated in the example given in Table 5.3, which is due to Luce (1959, p. 8). Here, both individuals satisfy the axiom, but the group average does not because $(.50)(.50) = .25 \neq .37$.

TABLE 5.3 COMPARISON OF THE CHOICE AXIOM FOR
INDIVIDUAL AND GROUP DATA

	Individual 1	*Individual* 2	*Group Average*
$p(x; T)$	.72	.02	.37
$p(x; R)$	.80	.20	.50
$p(R; T)$	.90	.10	.50

Thus far probabilities were used to describe uncertain choices among alternatives or outcomes. Yet they may also be used to describe uncertain judgments about likelihood of events. More specifically, let $q(E, F)$ denote the subjective probability that the event E is more likely than F. Luce refers to these values as judgment probabilities. To incorporate them into the theory, suppose an individual has to choose between the gambles $x E y$ and $x F y$, where he receives x if E (or F) occurs and y otherwise. The individual may attempt to decompose his decision into two simpler independent problems. First, which of the outcomes (x or y) is preferred, and second, which event (E or F) is believed to be more likely? Luce (1959, p. 78) assumes that both evaluations, of the outcomes and of the events, are probabilistic in nature and that they are statistically independent of each other. Consequently, the probability of choosing one gamble over another should satisfy the decomposition axiom, which says that

$$p(x\,E\,y,\,x\,F\,y) = p(x,\,y)q(E,\,F) + p(y,\,x)q(F,E).$$

As the following example, which is attributed to Savage (see Luce and Suppes 1965, p. 363), demonstrates, judgments of relative likelihood may not be independent of preferences. Let x and y be two greyhound dogs, E the event that x beats y, and F the event that y beats x in a single race between them. The gambler will receive one of the dogs, depending on which gamble was chosen and on which dog wins the race. In the absence of any information about the dogs, the one that won the race would certainly be preferred. Hence, $p(x\,E\,y,\,x\,F\,y)$ equals one, although both $p(x,\,y)$ and $q(E,\,F)$ equal one half. The application of the decomposition principle must be restricted, therefore, to situations where events and outcomes are logically unrelated.

Assuming that both the choice and the judgment probabilities satisfy the choice axiom and that the decomposition principle is valid, Luce was able to show that the subjective probability scale has at most three levels. In other words, if we put all events having the same likelihood into one equivalence class, then, under the above assumptions, all events can be categorized into not more than three equivalence classes. Because both introspection and indirect evidence indicate that this result is far too restrictive, we are led to believe that, by and large, the decomposition and the choice axioms cannot both be satisfied.

Another surprising consequence of these axioms pertains to the payoff

Fig. 5.16

matrix, given in Fig. 5.16. Assuming $x > y > z > w$, it is evident that if E is an event that always occurs, then G_1 is always preferred to G_2; whereas if E is an event that never occurs, then G_2 is always preferred to G_1. Hence, if the subjective probability of E varies from one to zero, so does the probability of choosing G_1 over G_2. The conjunction of the choice axiom and the decomposition principle implies that the choice probability is an increasing step function of the event probability. The theory does not specify the number of steps, but it predicts that the relation is not continuous. This prediction was tested in a study by Luce and Shipley (1962), using five college students.

On each trial each subject was presented with a payoff matrix of the type displayed in Fig. 5.16. The chance events were generated in the same way as in the study of Mosteller and Nogee (1951) described in Sec. 5.2, and the subjects had complete information about the mechanism that generated the chance events. The outcomes were points that were used to determine the subject's bonus. Six different payoff matrices were used for each subject, with 15 closely spaced events, and 50 observations for each event-payoff condition were made. Matrices 1, 2, and 3 satisfied the conditions needed to derive the step-function prediction, and matrices 4, 5, and 6 did not. The results provide some support for the predicted relationships, although there seem to be no differences between the two types of matrices. The data of one of the subjects is shown in Fig. 5.17.

The study of Luce and Shipley illustrates how nonobvious predictions, derived from axioms, can be tested in the laboratory. Some of the derived predictions are often surprising or unexpected on the basis of naive intuitions alone. The above study also illustrates the difficulty of evaluating the adequacy of a model on the basis of a single experiment. Usually, several interrelated experiments are needed in order to judge the descriptive merit of a theory because the results of any given study are often inconclusive.

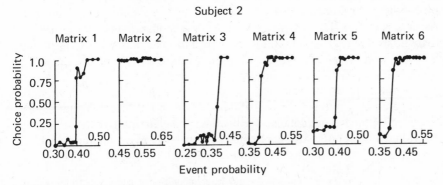

Fig. 5.17 Estimated choice probabilities as a function of event probability for six payoff matrices.

A Random
Utility Model
(Coombs)

The models of Thurstone and Luce, discussed in the previous sections, belong to a more general family of probabilistic models called the strong utility models. In all these models the probability of choosing x over y can be expressed as an increasing function of the difference between their scale values. More formally, a choice model is called a strong utility model if there exists a distribution function F such that

$$p(x, y) = F[u(x) - u(y)] \quad \text{for all probabilities different from 0 or 1.}$$

Equivalently, strong utility models can be defined by the property that

$$p(x, y) \geq p(z, w) \quad \text{if and only if} \quad u(x) - u(y) \geq u(z) - u(w).$$

(In Thurstone's Case V, u is the mean of the corresponding normal distribution, whereas in the case of Luce's model, u corresponds to $\log v$.) The expression on the righthand side of the above equation is equivalent to $u(x) - u(z) \geq u(y) - u(w)$, which in turn is equivalent to $p(x, z) \geq p(y, w)$. The following implication of the model, called the quadruple condition, is thus derived:

$$p(x, y) \geq p(z, w) \quad \text{if and only if} \quad p(x, z) \geq p(y, w).[4]$$

Suppose that $p(x, y)$ and $p(y, z)$ are both greater than one half and that some strong utility model is satisfied. What can be said about $p(x, z)$?

Because $p(x, y) \geq 1/2 = p(z, z)$ and $p(y, z) \geq 1/2 = p(x, x)$, by our assumptions and the fact that $p(w, w) = 1/2$ for any w, we can apply the quadruple condition twice to obtain $p(x, z) \geq p(y, z)$ and $p(y, x) \geq p(z, x)$, or equivalently $p(x, z) \geq p(x, y)$. Hence, under a strong utility model, if $p(x, y) \geq 1/2$ and $p(y, z) \geq 1/2$, then $p(x, z) \geq \max[p(x, y), p(y, z)]$.

This property, called strong (stochastic) transitivity, is the strongest probabilistic version of the transitivity axiom, discussed in Sec. 5.2. Other probabilistic, or stochastic, versions of transitivity have also been explored. Assume $p(x, y) \geq 1/2$ and $p(y, z) \geq 1/2$; then moderate (stochastic) transitivity holds if $p(x, z) \geq \min[p(x, y), p(y, z)]$, and weak (stochastic) transitivity holds if $p(x, z) \geq 1/2$. Obviously, strong transitivity implies moderate transitivity, which, in turn, implies weak transitivity.

Conditions under which strong transitivity holds, or fails to hold, were investigated by Coombs in a probabilistic extension of his unfolding theory (see Sec. 3.4 for further details). In this theory the alternatives as well as the individual's ideal point are represented as distributions, or random variables,

---

[4]In fact, Debreu (1958) showed that the quadruple condition is equivalent to the strong utility model provided the following solvability condition is satisfied: If $p(x, y) > t > p(x, z)$ for some real t, then there exists an alternative w such that $p(x, w) = t$.

along a common underlying dimension. As in the Thurstonian model, the distributions are independent of each other and unimodal. Because both the alternatives and the ideal point are random variables, so is the distance between them. The probability of choosing one alternative over another, therefore, equals the probability that the distance between the alternative and the ideal is less than that between the other alternative and the ideal. Stated more formally, let U_x, U_y, and I denote the random variables associated with the alternatives x, y and the ideal point, respectively; then

$$p(x, y) = p(|U_x - I| \leq |U_y - I|).$$

The selection of the temperature in a room may illustrate the model. Each individual has an ideal temperature level that may, nevertheless, flucutate from moment to moment because of internal factors. Furthermore, the perception or the sensation of a given temperature also exhibits random fluctuations. In comparing two temperature conditions, the individual chooses the one that is closer to his ideal point at the moment of comparison. The choice probabilities are determined by the above equation.

In studying transitivity, we examine, in effect, the relationships within triples of alternatives. Three types of triples of alternatives are distinguished in unfolding theory. To illustrate the distinction, imagine a continuum being folded about the mean ideal point, as shown in Fig. 5.18. A triple (or a pair) of alternatives is unilateral if all the alternatives lie on the same side of the ideal point, and it is bilateral otherwise. The triples (A, B, C) and (D, E, F) in Fig. 5.18 are unilateral, and all others are bilateral. The bilateral triples are further subdivided into split and adjacent triples. A bilateral triple is split if the odd alternative falls between the other two on the folded scale. It is adjacent if the odd alternative is either closer or farther away from the ideal than the other two. The triples (A, E, C) and (D, B, F) in Fig. 5.18 are bilateral and split, whereas all other bilateral triples in the figure are adjacent.

The overlapping areas among the distributions of unilateral triples are, clearly, unaffected by the variability of the ideal. Hence, under fairly general assumptions such as that the distributions are symmetric and with equal variance, strong transitivity should be satisfied. The situation is quite different, however, in the bilateral triples. Here the variability of the ideal point increases the area of overlap (and hence the inconsistency of the preferences) between the distribution of bilateral alternatives but does not affect the unilateral pairs. In bilateral adjacent triples the bilateral pair appears in the premise of the transitivity conditions, whereas in the bilateral split triples it appears in the conclusion. Consequently, strong transitivity is expected to be violated sometimes in the bilateral adjacent triples but never in the bilateral split triples. Weak transitivity should always be satisfied.

These predictions were tested by Coombs (1958) using four students of the University of Amsterdam. Twelve shades of gray varying in brightness

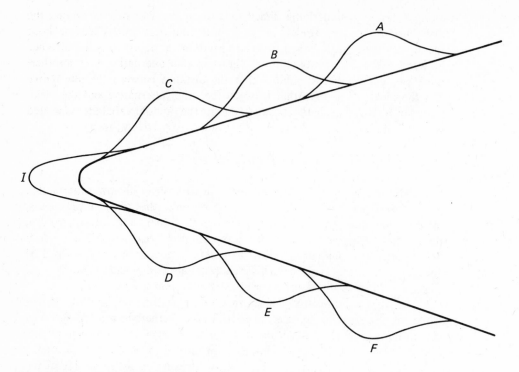

Fig. 5.18 Distributions of stimuli $(A, \ldots, F)$ and an ideal point (I) folded about the mean of the ideal point distribution.

alone were used as stimuli. The subjects were presented with all sets of four stimuli. Within each set they were asked to rank order the stimuli according to how well they represented the subject's notion of an "ideal" gray. Choice probabilities were estimated from the rank order data and then analyzed according to unfolding technique (see Sec. 3.4) to determine the laterality relations. The number of violations of the various transitivity levels in each of the three types of triples is shown in Table 5.4 for each of the subjects.

The experimental data verified the theoretical predictions concerning the violations of strong transitivity. No violations occurred in the bilateral split triples, very few in the unilateral triples, but a substantial number in the bilateral adjacent triples. Weak (but not moderate) transitivity was always satisfied. The predicted effect of laterality was also demonstrated in a study of choice between gambles conducted by Coombs and Pruitt (1960).

The significance of Coombs' study is in demonstrating that choice probabilities cannot be converted into utility differences without considering the relationships among the alternatives and the ideal point. In specifying the laterality conditions under which strong transitivity is satisfied, prob-

TABLE 5.4 NUMBER OF VIOLATIONS OF THE THREE TRANSITIVITY CONDITIONS IN THE THREE TYPES OF TRIPLES

| | | *Transitivity level* | | | |
| | | Strong | Moderate | Weak | *Total Number of Triples* |
Subject	*Triples*				
A	Bilateral adjacent	18	2	0	66
	Unilateral	1	1	0	20
	Bilateral split	0	0	0	34
B	Bilateral adjacent	24	5	0	40
	Unilateral	2	0	0	56
	Bilateral split	0	0	0	24
C	Bilateral adjacent	30	2	0	62
	Unilateral	2	0	0	20
	Bilateral split	0	0	0	38
D	Bilateral adjacent	48	0	0	62
	Unilateral	8	0	0	20
	Bilateral split	0	0	0	38

abilistic unfolding theory contributes to the development of a more complete theory of choice.

Intransitivity and the Evaluation of Multidimensional Alternatives

The transitivity of preferences is probably the simplest and most basic principle of decision theory. The compelling nature of the transitivity principle derives in part from its immediate normative appeal, and in part from the fact that it is a necessary condition for the existence of any order-preserving utility scale (see Chapter 2). To formulate a probabilistic version of transitivity, we first introduce a probabilistic definition of the preference relation. Specifically, we define $x \succsim y$ whenever $p(x, y) \geq 1/2$; that is, x is said to be preferred to y (in a probabilistic sense) whenever x is chosen over y more than 50 percent of the time. Restating the transitivity axiom in terms of this definition yields

$$p(x, y) \geq 1/2 \quad \text{and} \quad p(y, z) \geq 1/2 \quad \text{imply} \quad p(x, z) \geq \tfrac{1}{2}.$$

This condition, which has been called weak stochastic transitivity, or WST, is the most general probabilistic statement of transitivity. Violations of this condition cannot be easily accounted for by inconsistency, or random error, alone.

Despite the almost universal acceptance of transitivity, in either its algebraic or probabilistic version, one can think of several choice situations where transitivity is likely to be violated. The research described in this final subsection explores conditions under which systematic intransitivities can be demonstrated in choices between multidimensional alternatives. For a complete summary of this research, see Tversky (1969).

Consider a simple choice situation in which three alternatives, x, y, and z, vary along two dimensions, I and II, and where their values on these dimensions are given by Table 5.5. For example, the alternatives may be job applicants varying in intelligence (I) and experience (II), where the entries are the candidate's scores on these dimensions. Suppose that the decision maker considers dimension I to be much more important than dimension II but at the same time that he does not regard the scale values as perfectly reliable. An employer, for instance, may regard intelligence as far more important than experience but at the same time be aware that IQ scores are not perfectly reliable.

TABLE 5.5

	Dimensions	
Alternatives	I	II
x	2ϵ	6ϵ
y	3ϵ	4ϵ
z	4ϵ	2ϵ

Consequently, the decision maker may adopt the following rule in choosing between alternatives. If the difference between the alternatives on dimension I is strictly greater than ϵ, choose the alternative with the higher value on dimension I; if the above difference is less than or equal to ϵ, choose the alternative with the higher value on dimension II.

However, when this seemingly reasonable decision rule is applied to Table 5.5, it produces intransitive choices. Because the differences between x and y and between y and z on dimension I are not greater than ϵ, the choices between them are made on the basis of dimension II, yielding $x \succ y$ and $y \succ z$. The difference between x and z on dimension I, however, is greater than ϵ, and hence $z \succ x$, violating transitivity. Thus a decision rule based on a predetermined ordering of the dimensions combined with a threshold, or a semiorder (see Sec. 2.5) produces intransitive choices. To test the applicability of this decision rule, the following set of gambles was constructed.

All gambles were of the form (x, p), where one receives a payoff of $\$x$ if a chance event p occurs and nothing if p does not occur. Each gamble was displayed on a card showing a circle divided into a black and a white sector. The probability of winning corresponded to the relative size of the black sector, and the payoff was printed at the top of each card. The gambles employed in this study are displayed in Table 5.6. Note that, unlike the

TABLE 5.6

Gamble	Probability of Winning	Payoff (in $)	Expected Value
a	7/24	5.00	1.46
b	8/24	4.75	1.58
c	9/24	4.50	1.69
d	10/24	4.25	1.77
e	11/24	4.00	1.83

payoffs, the probabilities were displayed pictorially rather than numerically. Consequently, no exact calculation of expected values was possible. The gambles were constructed so that the expected value increased with probability and decreased with payoff.

Because the display renders the evaluation of payoff differences easier than that of probability differences, it was hypothesized that some subjects would ignore small probability differences and choose between adjacent gambles on the basis of payoffs. (Gambles are called adjacent if they are a step apart along the probability or the payoff dimension.) Because expected value, however, is negatively correlated with payoff, it was further hypothesized that choices between gambles lying far apart in the chain would be made on the basis of expected value, or probability of winning. Such a pattern of preferences must violate transitivity somewhere along the chain from *a* to *e*.

Eight subjects were selected for the experiment on the basis of their behavior in a preliminary study. Each pair of gambles was presented 20 times to each subject in a total of five experimental sessions. On each trial the subject was asked to choose which of the two gambles presented to him he would rather play.

Six out of eight subjects exhibited systematic and significant intransitivities of the predicted type. The data of one subject is displayed in Fig. 5.19, where arrows denote direction of preferences with the associated choice probabilities.

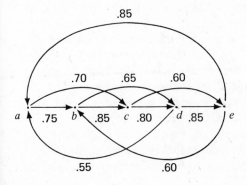

Fig. 5.19 Choice probabilities of one subject.

Figure 5.19 shows that the subject chose between adjacent gambles according to payoffs and between the more extreme gambles according to probability of winning, or expected value, thus violating WST in the predicted manner. Similar intransitivities were demonstrated using college applicants as choice alternatives. It is interesting to note that no subject realized that his preferences were intransitive, and some subjects even denied this possibility emphatically. Nevertheless, the data show that by an appropriate construction of multidimensional alternatives (i.e., alternatives that vary along several relevant dimensions or attributes) consistent and predictable intransitivities can be produced. What are the implications of these findings to psychological theories of choice? In examining the process of choice between multidimensional alternatives, two methods of evaluation have been considered. According to the first method, each (multidimensional) alternative, $x = (x_1, \ldots, x_n)$, is evaluated separately and independently from all other alternatives, and then assigned a number, $u(x)$, reflecting its desirability or subjective value. In choosing between alternatives, x is, then, chosen over y, or $p(x, y) \geq 1/2$, whenever $u(x) \geq u(y)$. Typically, it is further assumed that $u(x) = \sum_{i=1}^{n} u_i(x_i)$; that is, the subjective value of an alternative is expressable as a sum of the subjective values of its components. This is essentially the additive conjoint measurement model discussed in Sec. 2.5.

According to the second evaluation method, the alternatives are compared component-wise. Thus in comparing x and y, for example, each dimension i is evaluated separately across the two alternatives and assigned a (positive or a negative) number $\phi_i(x_i, y_i)$ reflecting the (positive or negative) contribution of the ith dimension to the preference of x over y. These values are then summed over all the relevant dimensions, and x is chosen over y, or $p(x, y) \geq 1/2$, whenever $\sum_{i=1}^{n} \phi_i(x_i, y_i) \geq 0$.

In comparing the former (independent) model with the latter (comparative) model, it is important to note that their applicability is likely to depend on the particular choice situation. The comparative model is expected to be employed whenever it is easier to make component-wise evaluation (e.g., when each of several issues is discussed by several political candidates), whereas the independent model is expected to be employed whenever it is easier to make global evaluations (e.g., when each of several political candidates discusses several issues).

It can readily be seen that the independent model always satisfies WST. For $p(x, y) \geq 1/2$ and $p(y, z) \geq 1/2$ imply $v(x) \geq v(y) \geq v(z)$ and hence $p(x, z) \geq 1/2$. The comparative model, on the other hand, fails to satisfy WST in general. Furthermore, the comparative model generalizes the decision rule underlying the experimental design that led to the intransitivities, because it allows the subject to ignore small differences by letting $\phi_i(x_i, y_i) = 0$ whenever $x_i - y_i \leq \epsilon_i$. The experimental findings, therefore, provide strong support for the comparative over the independent evaluation model. Moreover, in the light of information-processing factors such as the difficulty of the evaluation and the accuracy of the subjective estimate, the transitivity axiom cannot be regarded as an unqualified index of rationality. It is quite possible that in some contexts decisions made via the comparative model would be normatively superior to those made via the independent model despite the fact that the latter is transitive and the former is not. This point illustrates again the role played by descriptive factors, such as information-processing capabilities, in the normative analysis of decision processes.

The main interest in the study of the various probabilistic versions of transitivity (i.e., weak, moderate, and strong) discussed in the last subsections lies not only in the delineation of the conditions under which transitivity is violated but mainly in what the violations reveal about the processes underlying individual choice behavior.

5.4   CONCLUDING COMMENTS

The investigation of individual decision making has yielded a variety of theoretical structures with many potential applications. The empirical studies have shown that the preferences of individuals, under standard experimental conditions, can be explained, or rationalized, by the available models. However, the generality of the models, on the one hand, and the restrictive nature of the experiments, on the other hand, make it very difficult to evaluate the overall adequacy of the various theories. The psychologist's data as well as the layman's intuitions suggest that different decision rules are used in different situations. If this is so, then different models should be applicable in different situations. A complete choice theory, therefore, would have to specify the conditions under which each of the various models is valid. This can be accomplished in several different ways.

One strategy of research is to study one choice model in depth in order to delineate its region of applicability. Another approach is to compare several models under different conditions in order to discover which model is better under which conditions. But regardless of research strategy, the common goal is the characterization of the factors that determine the choice of a particular decision rule. These factors must be incorporated into a more general (or a second-order) theory that would prescribe which model is applicable in which situations. To develop such a general theory both cognitive and perceptual factors have to be taken into account.

Cognitive factors, or more specifically, information-processing variables, determine the capacity and modality of information storage and utilization. Hence they determine how a decision problem is formulated and what methods are used to resolve it. Processing considerations suggest, for example, that as the information load increases (because of an increase in the number of alternatives or in the complexity of the payoff structure) people tend to replace a maximization criterion, requiring an exhaustive examination, by a criterion that is easier to apply.

Perceptual factors refer to the variables that determine the way in which relationships among the alternatives and the entire choice situation are perceived. In the context of decision making under risk, we have seen that people act differently when the risk is perceived as depending on their own skills and not on chance alone. In the study of probabilistic preferences we have seen that the perceived similarity among the alternatives and their relationships to one's ideal point play an important role in controlling choice behavior.

The introduction of cognitive and perceptual factors into decision theory may lead to the construction of more complicated choice models. At the same time such models are likely to provide a more adequate account of human decision processes.

chapter

6

THE
THEORY
OF
SIGNAL
DETECTABILITY

6.1 HISTORICAL BACKGROUND AND ORIGINS

One of the main concerns of psychometrics for 100 years has been the measurement of sensory thresholds—both absolute and difference thresholds. The question asked the subject in the first instance is whether or not a stimulus is present and in the second instance whether or not two stimuli are different or which is greater. The theory of signal detectability (TSD), which first appeared in 1954 (Peterson, Birdsall, and Fox 1954; Van Meter and Middleton 1954), raises serious doubts about the existence of sensory thresholds, suggesting instead response thresholds, and offers the possibility of providing a common framework for much more general problems of perceptual processes and decision making.

The roots of TSD are found in both statistical decision theory and electrical engineering, in the latter case because of concern with the design of sensing devices. As a consequence the theory has much in common with those fields with respect to its language and technology. Although the basic theory originated in an engineering context and was normative in character (concerned with the performance of *ideal* sensing devices), the analogy with human perceptual processes was apparent to Tanner and Swets (1954), who initiated its development and application to human perceptual processes.

What was new in the theory was the explicit distinction between and the *separation* of (1) the observer as a sensor, i.e., his sensitivity, and (2) the observer as a decision maker, i.e., the effect of his values and expectations on his responses. These two aspects are confounded in performance. One doctor may more often prescribe treatment for an allergy than another doctor—he may more often be right but also more often be wrong. Is he a more sensitive detector or is he more willing to say yes? TSD makes it possible to distinguish these two aspects precisely.

Although in its origins TSD was prescriptive (normative) theory for the performance of sensing devices, it can be used as descriptive theory and, under certain conditions, can simultaneously provide a normative standard with which human performance can be compared.

6.2 AN ILLUSTRATIVE EXAMPLE

Although TSD has been vigorously developed in the context of and applied to the detection of auditory and visual signals, the theory is applicable in principle to a much wider area. To emphasize this, the basic concepts of TSD will be illustrated using as an example the detection of brain-damaged individuals on the basis of their performance in finger tapping.

A pamphlet (Reitan 1959) containing the instructions and procedures for administering the neurol-psychological test battery used at the neurol-psychological laboratory, Indiana University Medical Center, reports data that indicate that brain-damaged patients tend to differ from normals in rate of finger tapping. The patient is instructed to rest his arm on the table and then tap his finger as rapidly as he can. Brain-damaged people tend to tap more slowly. The distributions presented in Fig. 6.1 are *adapted* from these data for the convenience of illustrating TSD (the distribution on the right is for the brain-damaged).

TSD is designed for the detection of weak signals against a background of noise, e.g., the quarterback's signals when the stadium is in an uproar.[1] The language and concepts, however, may be applied by analogy to any context in which the sensory input is ambiguous. No theory of this kind is needed for the detection of strong signals that are never confused with the

---

[1]It has been suggested in a term paper by a student (Fred Steinheiser) in an undergraduate mathematical psychology course that TSD could be used to study the existence of ESP. This is the weak signal *par excellence* and the empirical relationships required by TSD could be used to test for the existence of a signal.

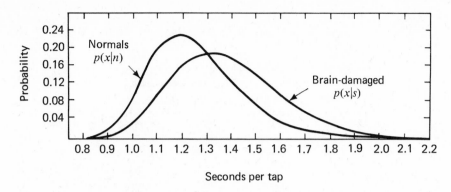

Fig. 6.1 Distribution of finger-tapping time for normal
and for brain-damaged individuals.

background noise. In this example we observe an individual's rate of finger tapping, but this observation, this sensory input, is ambiguous. It is not certain whether the observation signifies that the individual is brain-damaged or normal. Rate of finger tapping is related to brain injury but it is not an unambiguous indicator—it is a weak signal against a background of noise. TSD was constructed for precisely this problem—to specify the best thing to do in such a case—what considerations should enter into the decision and on what basis it should be made.

In the language of TSD we have an observation x and must conclude whether it has been drawn from the distribution for signal against a background of noise or the distribution for noise alone. It is assumed that these distributions are known to the observer and provide him with the probability of the observation x given that the individual is normal or that he is brain-injured; so these are distributions of conditional probabilities, referred to respectively as the noise and signal distributions and designated $p(x|n)$ and $p(x|s)$. Thus the observation $x = 1.20$, we see from Fig. 6.1 and from Table 6.1, has probability .238 if the individual is normal and has probability .163 if the individual is brain-damaged. The first and third columns of Table 6.1 give these conditional probabilities for all values of x.

Clearly, the observation $x = 1.20$ is more likely to have arisen if the individual is normal than if he is brain-damaged. We refer to the ratio of these two conditional probabilities as the likelihood ratio,

$$l(x) = \frac{p(x|s)}{p(x|n)},$$

and the value of $l(x)$ for each x is given in the fifth column of Table 6.1. If $l(x)$ is less than 1, the observation is more likely for the normal population than for the brain-damaged. For example, we see in Table 6.1 that $l(x = 1.20) = .685$. We might be tempted to conclude that it is more likely

TABLE 6.1 PROBABILITY DENSITIES FOR FIG. 6.1 AND THE
RELEVANT TRANSFORMATIONS

	1	2	3	4	5
	Normals		Brain-damaged		
Seconds Per Tap	$p(x\|n)$	Cumulative i.e., $p(y\|n)$	$p(x\|s)$	Cumulative, i.e., $p(y\|s)$	$l(x)$, i.e., $p(x\|s)/p(x\|n)$
.80	.000	1.000	.000	1.000	.000
.90	.014	.986	.002	.998	.143
1.0	.088	.898	.023	.975	.261
1.1	.200	.698	.087	.888	.435
1.2	.238	.460	.163	.725	.685
1.3	.193	.267	.194	.531	1.005
1.4	.125	.142	.176	.355	1.408
1.5	.072	.070	.135	.220	1.875
1.6	.036	.034	.089	.131	2.472
1.7	.018	.016	.052	.079	2.889
1.8	.009	.007	.033	.046	3.667
1.9	.004	.003	.019	.027	4.750
2.0	.002	.001	.011	.016	5.500
2.1	.001	.000	.006	.010	6.000
2.2	.000	.000	.010	.000	∞

this patient is normal. But that conclusion may not be wise as we shall see shortly.

No matter which conclusion we draw, however, we shall sometimes be wrong, and although mistakes are costly, not all mistakes are equally costly. The diagnosis of a brain-damaged person as normal is a different mistake from diagnosing a normal person as brain-damaged. The consequences of these errors could be very different. Similarly, even correct judgments are not necessarily equally valuable, i.e., diagnosing a normal person as normal or a brain-damaged person as brain-damaged. These consequences are referred to as payoffs and are readily displayed in what is called the payoff matrix, illustrated in Fig. 6.2. TSD is a model that takes this payoff matrix into account.

6.3 RESPONSE THRESHOLDS, β

The example in Sec. 6.2 illustrates the fundamental detection problem, also referred to as the yes-no experiment (YN), which we shall now develop more formally. The situation is one in which it is assumed that an observer knows the two conditional probability distributions and the payoff matrix. He is presented with an observation x, and he must decide whether to say yes, a signal is present, or no, it is noise alone. What is the best rule for him to follow in reaching a decision?

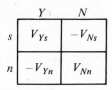

Fig. 6.2 Payoff matrix for *YN* experiment.

There is, of course, no universal answer because it depends on what is meant by *best*, e.g., what criterion variable one wants to maximize, such as expected value. For a wide variety of criteria, TSD provides a common framework and an explicit solution for the decision rule.

The notation used for the payoff matrix in the YN experiment is presented in Fig. 6.2, where *s* or *n* refers to whether a signal or noise alone was presented to the subject and *Y* or *N* refers to whether he responded yes or no. The payoffs are indicated in the cells. V_{Ys} is the value of saying yes when a signal is present, referred to as the value of a *hit*. The *V*'s are to be taken as positive quantities and, as errors are penalized, $-V_{Ns}$ is the cost of saying no when a signal is present. This kind of error is called a *miss* and corresponds to a type II error [acceptance of H_0 (= noise alone) when false] in statistical decision theory (cf. Hays 1963, p. 280). The quantity $-V_{Yn}$ is the cost of saying yes to noise alone. This kind of error is called a *false alarm* and corresponds to a type I error. Finally V_{Nn} is the value of a *correct rejection*, saying no in the presence of noise alone.

Suppose we select expected value as the criterion variable to be maximized. This means that given an observation *x* we shall say yes if the expected value for saying yes is greater than the expected value for saying no. The expression for the expected value of *Y* given the observation *x* is the value of saying yes to signal times the probability that signal was present minus the cost of saying yes to noise times the probability that only noise was present:

$$E(Y|x) = V_{Ys}p(s|x) - V_{Yn}p(n|x).$$

Similarly, the expression for the expected value of *N* given *x* is

$$E(N|x) = V_{Nn}p(n|x) - V_{Ns}p(s|x).$$

The decision rule to maximize expected value requires that the observer say yes if

$$E(Y|x) \geq E(N|x). \tag{6.1}$$

Otherwise he should say no.

Substituting the expressions for the expected values, we have

$$V_{Ys}p(s|x) - Y_{Yn}p(n|x) \geq V_{Nn}p(n|x) - V_{Ns}p(s|x),$$

and rearranging terms, we have

$$\frac{p(s|x)}{p(n|x)} \geq \frac{V_{Nn} + V_{Yn}}{V_{Ys} + V_{Ns}}.$$

(6.2)

Note that the conditional probabilities on the left-hand side in the numerator and denominator, respectively, are the probabilities of signal or noise given the observation x, and are unknown. These, of course, must be distinguished from the conditional probabilities for the observation x given the s or n distribution, which are presumed known, as in Fig. 6.1 and Table 6.1. The relation between these known and these unknown conditional probabilities is expressed by Bayes's rule, which permits us to substitute a relation between known quantities for a relation between unknown quantities. We may arrive at this rule as follows:

From the definition of a conditional probability we may write

$$p(sx) = p(s|x)p(x)$$

or alternatively,

$$p(sx) = p(x|s)p(s).$$

Setting the expressions on the right-hand side of these equations equal to each other and rearranging terms, we have

$$p(s|x) = \frac{p(x|s)p(s)}{p(x)},$$

which is known as Bayes's rule (see also mathematical appendix, Sec. A.9).
    Similarly,

$$p(n|x) = \frac{p(x|n)p(n)}{p(x)},$$

from which we have

$$\frac{p(s|x)}{p(n|x)} = \frac{p(x|s)}{p(n|x)} \frac{p(s)}{p(n)}.$$

(6.3)

The three ratios in Eq. (6.3) are known by the following terms: the ratio $p(s)/p(n)$ is known as the *prior odds*, the ratio next to it we already know as the *likelihood ratio* for the observation x, and the ratio on the left-hand side of the equation gives the *posterior odds*. The posterior odds then, on signal against noise after an observation has been made, are obtained by multiplying the likelihood ratio for the observation times the prior odds.

Substituting (6.3) in (6.2) and rearranging terms, we have

$$\frac{p(x|s)}{p(x|n)} \geq \frac{p(n)}{p(s)} \frac{V_{Nn} + V_{Yn}}{V_{Ys} + V_{Ns}}.$$ (6.4)

Designating the expression on the right as β, we have

$$l(x) \geq \beta.$$

So β is a number that if calculated according to the expression on the right-hand side of Eq. (6.4) will take expectations and values (prior odds and the payoff matrix) into account so as to maximize expected value.

We may summarize the theory up to this point as follows. The observer has an observation x for which he knows or can calculate the likelihood ratio, the left-hand side of Eq. (6.4). He also must know the prior odds of noise alone against signal and he must know the payoff matrix, the right-hand side of Eq. (6.4). He uses these to calculate a quantity called β, which is a cutoff point, a threshold value for the response yes, That is, to maximize his expected value, he should say yes if $l(x)$ is at least as high as β; otherwise he should say no.

An important thing to note about this theory is that the basis for a decision is not the raw sensory input x but a transformation of it to a new *decision axis*, the likelihood ratio. As long as the sensory input is one-dimensional and monotone with the likelihood ratio, there is no essential difference. The difference becomes very important, however, in the more complex case of multidimensional stimuli. Suppose, for example, that the raw sensory input were an r-tuple, i.e., in addition to finger-tapping time several other diagnostic signs were given. The theory requires that the observer be able to associate a likelihood ratio with any such stimulus input and hence the r-dimensional input is transformed into a one-dimensional variable. This is the core of the psychological theory in TSD—that the human observer is conceived of as a likelihood-ratio-type perceiver.

The numerator of the last expression on the right-hand side of Eq. (6.4) is sometimes referred to as the "importance" of noise and the denominator as the importance of signal.

Some examples are instructive in clarifying the relation of the response threshold to expectations and values, i.e., the relation of β to the prior odds and the payoff matrix.

Case 1. Consider first a "base line" case in which the prior odds are even, i.e., signal and noise are equally likely, and the signal and the noise are equally important. Under these conditions $\beta = 1$, and so the observer should say yes to any observation for which

$$\frac{p(x|s)}{p(x|n)} \geq 1.$$

Referring to Fig. 6.1 we see that for any x below 1.30 the ordinate of the n distribution exceeds the ordinate of the s distribution so the likelihood ratio is less than 1. For an x of 1.30 or greater, $l(x)$ is greater than 1 and the observer should say yes. In other words, in this base-line case the observer should respond according to which distribution would more likely give rise to that observation, signal or noise. We shall see that this is not always the best procedure by considering two other cases, one to illustrate the effect of prior odds and the other the effect of the payoff matrix.

Case 2. Suppose that the prior odds were not even, as, for example, if the tapping test were given to a random sample of college students. We would expect instances of brain damage to be quite rare in such a sample, and for purposes of our illustration let us assume that the prior odds are reduced to 1 in 100 and that we left the payoff matrix the same as before. Then $\beta = 99/1$ and so for any observation for which

$$\frac{p(x|s)}{p(x|n)} \geq 99$$

the observer should say yes. We see from Table 6.1 that we would need a finer grid for the categorization of speed of finger tapping to determine that value of x for which $l(x)$ is as large as 99. It is possible, in view of Fig. 6.1, that with a finer grid there would be categories in Table 6.1 with sufficiently large likelihood ratios; if not, then no student would ever be diagnosed as brain-damaged on the basis of finger tapping.

The important point here is that *if the prior odds are unfavorable for the occurrence of the signal, then the evidence needs to be more substantial in order to conclude that the signal is present.* Conversely, if the odds were favorable, as, for example, if other symptoms indicated the odds were 80:20 that the subject had a brain injury, then $\beta = 20/80 = .250$, so any observation for which $l(x) \geq .250$ would lead to a diagnosis of brain injury. In Table 6.1 we see that $l(x)$ exceeds this value for categories in which x is as slow as 1 second/tap.

To see the influence of the payoff matrix on β and the effect of the relative importance of signal and noise, consider the following case.

Case 3. Let the prior odds be even and let the payoff matrix be as shown in Fig. 6.3. Substituting these values in Eq. (6.4), we find that the

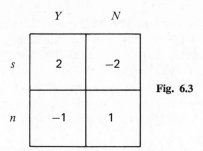

	Y	N
s	2	−2
n	−1	1

Fig. 6.3

observer should say yes if $l(x) \geq \frac{1}{2}$, i.e., according to Table 6.1, $x \geq 1.20$.

This payoff matrix has increased the importance of the signal in the sense that hits are valuable and misses costly compared with false alarms and correct rejections, so one should be more willing to say yes.

One way of seeing the effect of the payoff matrix is by means of Fig. 6.4. Here a hypothetical signal and noise distribution are shown with a vertical line cutting them at x_c, the value of x corresponding to $l(x) = \beta$. The observer says yes for any $x \geq x_c$. The area under the s distribution that is tinted gives the proportion of hits and the similarly tinted area under the n distribution is the proportion of false alarms.

Each of these, of course, has its complement, the proportion of misses and correct rejections, respectively, corresponding to the areas of the appropriate distribution of the left of x_c. A payoff matrix that has increased the importance of the signal, as in this last example, has increased the value of every hit and/or increased the cost of every miss. The effect then is to shift the cutoff defined by x_c to the left corresponding to the lower β because this will increase the proportion of hits and reduce the proportion of misses.

It is evident that if the importance of the signal is decreased relative to noise alone the effect is just the reverse and x_c would shift to the right.

It should now be clear why we speak of response thresholds. β, the critical value of the likelihood ratio, corresponds to a value of x_c and hence

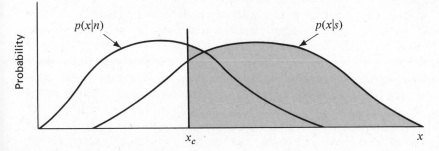

Fig. 6.4 Areas corresponding to proportion of hits and false alarms for a given cutoff point x_c.

is essentially a threshold for saying yes. TSD makes this response threshold a function of expectations (prior odds) and values (the payoff matrix).

Let us summarize certain important points. This theory was developed to guide the design of an ideal sensing device to achieve certain specified goals (such as to maximize expected value) under certain specified conditions (information about signal and noise distributions, the payoff matrix, and prior odds). We have seen that this can be accomplished when the decision axis is a likelihood ratio.

In this illustration the goal was to maximize expected value. There are, of course, alternative goals, such as to maximize percent correct or maximize transmitted information.

It has been shown (Green and Swets 1966, Chapter 3) that for a number of such goals, the optimum decision axis for accomplishing them is the likelihood ratio. The particular value of β that will achieve a particular goal is, of course, not necessarily the same for different goals. The value of β given by Eq. (6.4) achieves the goal of maximizing expected value. If, instead, one wanted to maximize the number of correct decisions, this is equivalent to saying that hits and correct rejections are of equal value and that misses and false alarms are of equal value. Hence the payoff matrix is symmetric and the expression on the right-hand side of Eq. (6.4) is equal to 1, so β is equal to prior odds, as in cases 1 and 2, discussed previously.

The use of the likelihood ratio as the decision axis is especially important when the stimulus input is multidimensional. In this illustrative example the stimulus input was rate of finger tapping, a unidimensional scale. In other cases a stimulus input may be multidimensional as, for example, when other symptoms are simultaneously considered. Each stimulus input x in such a case is a vector with more than one component, a point in a multidimensional space, corresponding to a configuration or pattern of symptoms. TSD requires that to each such point or stimulus input there corresponds a known value for its probability given the normal population (the noise distribution) and given the brain-damaged population (the signal distribution). In this manner multidimensional stimulus inputs are mapped into a one-dimensional decision axis, the likelihood ratio.

It is important to note, also, that to any decision rule based on a value of $l(x)$ there corresponds uniquely a decision rule value on any other decision axis that is strictly monotone with $l(x)$. One reason for the importance of this relation lies in the fact that if the signal distribution and the noise distribution are both normal distributions then the logarithm of the likelihood ratio [which is monotone with $l(x)$] is also normally distributed. In the psychoacoustic laboratory these density distributions can be controlled with proper equipment, so much of the experimental work has been done with normal distributions and known variances (usually equal or nearly equal). This permits the characterization of what is called the *ideal receiver* with which the performance of a human observer can be compared. Before we can discuss this concept, however, we need to know how the behavior of a receiver or observer can be characterized.

6.4 THE ROC CURVE

The performance of any sensory device, human or otherwise, operating on the basis of this theory can be completely described by what is called the *receiver operating characteristic* curve or ROC curve. The receiver says yes whenever the observation x exceeds the critical value x_c. As may be seen in Fig. 6.4, then, the area under the signal distribution above the point x_c is the proportion of times the receiver says yes when a signal is present, i.e., the probability of a hit, and the area under the noise distribution above the same point is the proportion of times the individual says yes when noise alone is present, i.e., the probability of a false alarm. As the areas under these curves to the left of x_c are merely the complements, all the information about the receiver's performance is contained in the hit and false alarm rate.

Let us return to our illustrative example as presented in Table 6.1. We have seen that under appropriate manipulations of the prior odds and the payoff matrix the receiver's critical value of β, and hence x_c, can be changed. The hit rate for various values of x_c is given in Table 6.1 in column 4, these rates being obtained by accumulating the category proportions in column 3 from the bottom of the table. In a similar manner the false alarm rate, presented in column 2, is obtained from column 1.

These values, the hit and the false alarm rate for each possible value of x_c, may be plotted against each other and fall along a curve in the unit square, as shown in Fig. 6.5. This curve is known as the ROC curve. For any fixed set of experimental conditions the theory says there will be a β, corresponding to which will be an x_c, and the observer's hit rate and false alarm rate will be the areas under the signal and noise distributions, respectively, above the point x_c, and the two areas are the coordinates of a point on an ROC curve. Therefore, the performance of a receiver, an individual or otherwise, under a fixed set of conditions, corresponds to a point on an ROC curve.

The diagonal line in this figure is the expected ROC curve if the receiver responded randomly. A point on this diagonal merely reflects a bias for saying yes. Thus, if an observer said yes randomly 80 percent of the time, his hit rate when the signal was actually present would be 80 percent, and his false alarm rate when the signal is not present would also be 80 percent. This diagonal is the limiting ROC curve as the signal distribution approaches the noise distribution. Points below this diagonal would occur only by chance or only if the receiver were deliberately contrary or perverse. Incidentally, it is instructive to note that the very worst a subject could do is to say yes when he should say no and *vice versa* and the resulting ROC

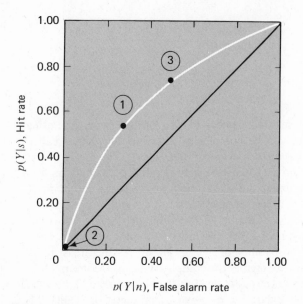

Fig. 6.5 Smoothed ROC curve for the illustrative example:
Cases 1, 2, and 3 are indicated.

curve would be the "complementary" curve on the other side of the diagonal
—the subject could not fall below the curve. Any receiver not inverted or
acting contrarily would generate points above the diagonal.

The curve plotted in Fig. 6.5 is for the illustrative example for which
Fig. 6.1 and Table 6.1 describe the information about the detection situation
available to the receiver. The points marked 1, 2, and 3 refer to cases 1, 2,
and 3 discussed previously in illustrating the effect of prior odds and the
payoff matrix on β. The point $(1, 1)$ would correspond to the hit rate and
false alarm rate if β were sufficiently small so that the observer always said
yes. Such a trigger-happy receiver would never miss, but at the cost of a false
alarm whenever just noise was present. Note that this point $(1, 1)$ is the
right-hand terminus of the ROC curve and corresponds to an x_c that is the
left-hand extreme of the sensory continuum. In other words, as the cutoff x_c
moves from left to right, the corresponding point on the ROC curve moves
from right to left, a frequent source of confusion on first acquaintance with
TSD.

Clearly, as β takes on all possible values a smooth ROC curve will
result and each point on this curve corresponds to a value of β. β is sometimes referred to as the *operating level* of the receiver and may, be given the
following interpretations: It is a likelihood ratio, a threshold for saying yes,
the optimal weighting of hit and false alarm rates for the given conditions,
and the slope of the ROC curve at the point corresponding to the hit and
false alarm rates.

The Measure of Sensitivity, d'

Consider what the resulting ROC curve would be if one were to increase the magnitude of the signal by some constant amount without changing the noise distribution; i.e., in Fig. 6.4 imagine the signal distribution shifted to the right some fixed amount. If the false alarm rate is kept the same as before by leaving x_c where it is in Fig. 6.4, clearly the hit rate will increase as there is more area under the signal distribution to the right of x_c than before. As the hit and false alarm rates are the coordinates of a point on an ROC curve, this point would lie directly above the point before the signal distribution was shifted.

This relation would hold for any value of x_c, so there is a new ROC curve generated lying above the previous one, and indeed there is an entire family of ROC curves corresponding to a signal and a noise distribution characterized by the difference between their means.

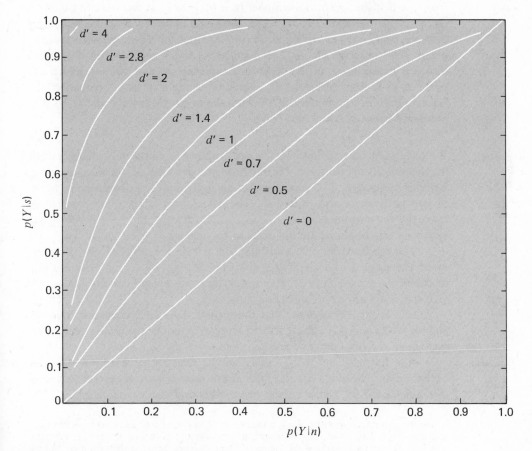

Fig. 6.6 Receiver operating characteristic curves for various values of d'.

It is conventional in TSD to let d' represent this parameter where

$$d' = \frac{\mu_s - \mu_n}{\sigma_n},$$

i.e., the difference between the means divided by the standard deviation of the noise distribution.[2] In Fig. 6.6 a family of such curves is presented. The exact form of the ROC curve is sensitive to the shape of the signal and noise distributions, but the curves may be symmetric under certain conditions, as in Fig. 6.6 for which the underlying signal and noise distributions were normal with equal variance.

Of course, two human observers being tested under identical experimental conditions will not in general behave alike—they would have different hit and false alarm rates. One possible reason is that they differ in sensitivity —for one of the observers the signal distribution may be more distinct from the distribution of noise alone. In other words, if one were to calculate the d' of their respective ROC curves, one such observed d' would be greater than the other—reflecting a greater standardized difference between the two means. This observer's d', d_{obs}, is used as an index of his sensitivity. Note that it is independent of the observer's expectations and utilities, which are reflected in β. This parameter d'_{obs} may be thought of as a "separation" or "discrimination" parameter in that it reflects an observer's ability to discriminate between signal and noise.

Estimation of
β and d'

We have seen that an individual's performance is completely characterized by two empirical measures, the hit rate and the false alarm rate, and that both are necessary. TSD characterizes an individual's performance in terms of two parameters also, β and d'. The calculation of the TSD parameters from the hit and false alarm rate is straightforward and easy if the signal and noise distributions are assumed to be normal.

The observed hit rate and false alarm rate are, respectively, the areas under the signal and noise distributions to the right of x_c (Fig. 6.4). If these distributions are assumed to be normal, then normal probability tables will give the ordinates at x_c and their ratio is β.

If it is further assumed that the distributions have constant variance, and we let Z_n and Z_s be the standard score of x_c under the noise distribution and signal distribution, respectively, then $d' = Z_n - Z_s$.

Alternatively, an ROC curve can be constructed experimentally by obtaining an observer's hit and false alarm rate at each of several values of β, manipulated by means of the prior odds and the payoff matrix. If the

[2] d' as a standardized distance along a latent continuum is almost identical with the basic conception of Thurstone's law of comparative judgment (Chapter 3). In the latter the unit for the standardization is the sigma of the difference between the two distributions rather than the sigma of one of them alone, a distinction with no theoretical implications.

underlying distributions are not assumed to be known, d' cannot be calculated but comparisons can be made between d''s for different observers or the effects of experimental variations on d' can be observed.

Empirical ROC Curves   We illustrate in Fig. 6.7 typical ROC curves with the data of two observers in an experiment reported by Swets (1961). The signal was a pure tone added to a white noise background and the subjects were induced to change

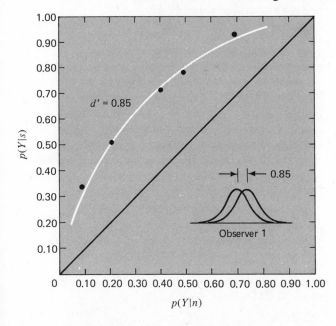

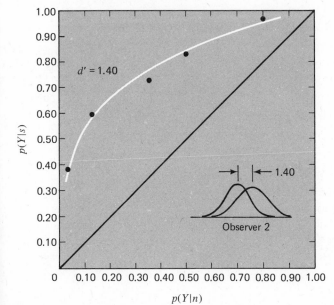

Fig. 6.7 Two theoretical operating characteristic curves with data from a yes-no experiment.

their criterion by experimental variation of prior odds. The values of d' for the best-fitting curve are shown on each graph and the inserts on the lower right show the normal probability distributions underlying the curves. For observer 1 the separation parameter d' is seen to be 0.85 and for observer 2, 1.40, under the convention that the standard deviation of the noise distribution is unity.

Our reason for presenting the empirical curves here is to discuss their distinctive shapes by quoting Swets' discussion (1961, p. 171):

> We may note that the curve fitted to the data of the first observer is symmetrical about the negative diagonal, and that the curve fitted to the data of the second observer is not. Both types of curves are seen frequently; the second curve is especially characteristic of data collected in visual experiments. Theoretically, the curve shown in the graph [for observer 1] will result if the observer knows the signal exactly—that is, if he knows its frequency, amplitude, starting time, duration, and phase. A theoretical curve like the one shown in the graph [for observer 2] results if the observer has inadequate information about frequency and phase, or, as is the case when the signal is a white light, if there is no frequency and phase information. The probability distributions that are shown in the inserts reflect this difference between the operating-characteristic curves.

One might naturally ask just how good can an observer be? What is the maximum possible value of d'? This question cannot in general be answered, but under certain highly controlled experimental conditions and certain assumptions it can be answered; we then have what is called the *ideal receiver*—a mathematical simulation of a physical system designed to behave optimally according to TSD.

6.5   THE IDEAL RECEIVER

At the beginning of this chapter we spoke of TSD as having its roots in statistical decision theory and electrical engineering. Up to this point our discussion has been concerned almost exclusively with the application of statistical decision theory and the concepts of β, d', and the ROC curve, which are very widely applicable and useful. We come now to the other major aspect of TSD, the concept of the ideal receiver, which arose in the design of sensing devices by engineers for detecting auditory signals. This concept also plays a substantial role in the application of TSD to substantive problems of interest to psychologists, particularly problems in the area of sensory and perceptual mechanisms.

A complete understanding of the specification of the ideal receiver requires a deeper level of mathematics and physics than is appropriate for this introductory text. The concept plays such a significant role in much TSD research and literature, however, that it becomes desirable to try to provide the student with even a superficial understanding of the steps involved in its development.

In certain experimental studies of TSD, physical control of the noise and signal distribution is possible. With acoustical stimuli, for example, the noise distribution may be produced approximately by band-limited white Gaussian noise, and for the signal a segment of a pure tone of known voltage, phase, and starting time may be added. Hence, both the noise and signal distributions are normal and have the same variance. The log likelihoods of normal distributions are also normal, and being normal distributions they are completely described by their mean and variance.

Because of the physical nature of these acoustical stimuli, it is possible not only to control the means and variances of these log likelihood distributions but to specify the actual values of these parameters in physical units by applying Shannon's sampling theorem (Grabbe and Woolridge 1958). This theorem states that a continuous wave form with no frequencies above W can be exactly reconstructed if the value of the wave form is known at $2WT$ equally spaced discrete points, where $1/T$ is the lowest frequency.

With band-limited white Gaussian noise, the noise power per unit bandwidth, N_0, is known and the physical energy E of the signal is known. Utilizing Shannon's sampling theorem, these physical properties of the noise and signal are related to the means and variances of the log likelihood distributions for signal and noise. The difference between the means of these distributions is $2E/N_0$, which is also the variance of each of them. The highest value of d', then, that an observer could achieve given these physical characteristics of the acoustical signal and noise is $d'_{opt} = \sqrt{2E/N_0}$, i.e., a function of the signal to noise ratio.

This means that for any prior odds and payoff matrix there is a consequent β that will yield a point on this ROC curve, indexed by d'_{opt}, and the coordinates of this point are the optimum balance of hit and false alarm rate to achieve a specified goal. It should not be necessary to point out that the ideal receiver is not one that makes 100 percent hits and no false alarms but rather one that utilizes all the information available in the most effective manner. Even to a perfect receiver, noise may sometimes sound like a signal.

A concept of ideal receiver has also been constructed for visual signals (Tanner and Jones 1960; Jones 1959) based on the average number of photons in background and signal, target area, duration of signal, and area of and the solid angle at entrance to pupil.

It is important to recognize the role of the concept of the ideal observer in TSD. We note, for example, that the ideal observer does not make any decisions; it merely calculates likelihood ratios. The actual decision is a consequence of other aspects, such as prior odds and payoffs, aspects totally irrelevant to sensory and perceptual mechanisms, and aspects that contaminate efforts to study these mechanisms by the usual psychophysical methods.

Receiver

Ideal   Real

	Ideal	Real
Exactly	C_{11}	C_{12}
Statistically	C_{21}	C_{22}

Signal known

Fig. 6.8 Four-fold classification of psychophysical experiments.

The concept of an ideal receiver is valuable to the psychologist in several respects. It provides a relatively simple model as a first approximation to human performance and it provides a base or standard of comparison. As a model it is a mathematical simulation of human behavior. As human performance does not usually match that of the ideal receiver, what is of interest is not the degree of discrepancy alone but its nature. The manner in which the concept of the ideal receiver can interact with experiments to reveal the parameters of the signal utilized by the observer has been discussed by Tanner and Birdsall (1958) in terms of the four-fold classification given in Fig. 6.8. Four different possible channels are defined, corresponding to the four cells of the figure (where "signal known exactly" means that the frequency, starting time, phase, duration, and amplitude are known).

Suppose, now, an experiment has been performed over channel C_{12} and the parameter d'_{obs} is calculated for that observer. Because the signal is known exactly, d'_{opt} can also be calculated and the efficiency of the receiver, η_r, is defined as follows:

$$\eta_r = \left[\frac{d'_{opt}}{d'_{obs}}\right]^2 .$$

One way of interpreting this index is as follows. If one were to substitute an ideal receiver for the real one, η gives the proportion of the signal energy that would be sufficient for the ideal receiver to perform as well. This is readily seen if we let E_{12} equal the energy of the signal in channel C_{12} and E_{11} be the energy of the signal required in C_{11}; then, from the definition of d',

$$\eta_r = \frac{2E_{11}/N_0}{2E_{12}/N_0} = \frac{E_{11}}{E_{12}} .$$

Now consider channel C_{21}, which, like channel C_{11}, is a mathematical experiment. For example, the signal may be known to the ideal receiver except for phase or except for frequency, such that any phase is equally likely or any frequency within a band is equally likely. For a given energy, E_{21}, performance is calculated, and then the corresponding energy, E_{11}, required for channel C_{11} is calculated and the efficiency index of the transmitter in channel C_{21} is then

$$\eta_t = \frac{E_{11}}{E_{21}}.$$

Suppose $\eta_t = \eta_r$; i.e., we have the same efficiency of performance from an ideal receiver with the signal known only statistically as from our actual observer who knew the signal exactly. Uncertainty in the signal has degraded the performance of the ideal receiver to match the performance of the actual receiver. One might be tempted to say that information that the observer cannot use might as well not be available. The difficulty here is that uncertainty might be introduced into the signal in any of several ways, such as phase or frequency, for example, to degrade the performance of the ideal receiver. How can one test whether the signal has been degraded in exactly those aspects not utilized by the real observer?

Channel C_{22} serves this purpose. The experimenter may degrade the signal in phase, for example, calculate d'_{obs} from the observer's performance, and then η_{tr}, the efficiency index for channel C_{22} against C_{11}. If, then, $\eta_{tr} = \eta_t = \eta_r$, one has verified that phase is an aspect of the signal not utilized by this receiver. And now the line of argument that information not utilized by the receiver might just as well not be there is valid.

The concept of the ideal receiver is useful in other ways, also. One might, for example, study how the ideal receiver would behave under various kinds of experimental manipulation, e.g., mismatching bandwidth (Green, Birdsall, and Tanner 1957), and compare this with human performance.

As is evident, the concept of the ideal receiver is especially useful in studying substantive problems in sensory and perceptual mechanisms and where there is complete physical control of stimulus dimensions.

6.6 IMPLICATIONS FOR SENSORY THRESHOLDS

An alternative to TSD is the classic theory of the threshold, the notion of a lower limit on sensitivity. The idea here is that the observer makes no discriminations below a certain energy level. The probabilistic character of behavior near such energy levels is explained in terms of a fixed cutoff and randomly varying stimulus effects or *vice versa*. We shall consider here two such theories—a high-threshold theory and a low-threshold theory.

We shall also introduce in this section the psychometric function as another way of analyzing detection data (in contrast to the ROC curve) and the forced-choice experimental procedure as another way of collecting it (in contrast to the YN experiment).

High-Threshold Theory

By high-threshold theory is meant a threshold that is rarely exceeded by noise alone—as if, for example, the cutoff value x_c were some three sigma above the mean of the noise distribution—so the probability of noise alone exceeding the threshold is taken to be zero. If an observation x exceeds this threshold, we shall refer to the individual as being in a *detect state*, D, and otherwise not, state $\bar{D}$. In high-threshold theory the individual is assumed to say yes whenever in state D. If the individual is in state $\bar{D}$, he is assumed to guess randomly that a signal is present with probability t, representing a response bias toward saying yes. These conditional probabilities may be compactly presented in matrix form, as in Fig. 6.9.

	Y	N
D	$p(Y\|D) = 1$	$p(N\|D) = 0$
$\bar{D}$	$p(Y\|\bar{D}) = t$	$p(N\|\bar{D}) = 1 - t$

Fig. 6.9 Conditional response probabilities in high-threshold theory.

The sequence of events may be traced one step farther back to the occurrence of the stimulus. If a signal occurred, it may give rise to state D or $\bar{D}$ with probabilities $p(D|s)$ and $1 - p(D|s)$, respectively. These two possible events are displayed as the first two branches of the tree in Fig. 6.10(a). The next branching of the tree leads to the next event, a Y or N, with probabilities as given in the matrix of Fig. 6.9. Similarly, the possible sequences of events if noise occurred are shown in Fig. 6.10(b). Branches with probability zero have been omitted.

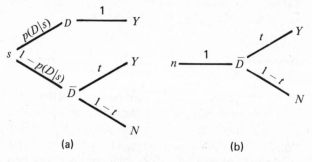

(a)   (b)

Fig. 6.10 Trees of sequences of events from stimulus to response in high-threshold theory.

As successive links in a path are assumed independent, the probability of a path is the product of the probabilities of its several links. Hence expressions for the probability of saying yes to signal and to noise alone fall out readily:

$$p(Y|s) = p(D|s) + t[1 - p(D|s)]$$

$$p(Y|n) = t.$$

Eliminating the parameter t, we have

$$p(Y|s) = p(D|s) + [1 - p(D|s)]p(Y|n) \qquad (6.5)$$

[a linear equation of the form $y = a + (1-a)x$], which is the equation of the ROC curve for high-threshold theory, as shown in Fig. 6.11. At zero false alarm rate the hit rate is $p(D|s)$ and the ROC curve is a straight line from this intercept to the point (1, 1).

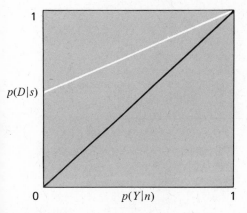

Fig. 6.11 ROC curve for high-threshold theory.

Coombs et al 6.11

An experiment reported by Swets, Tanner, and Birdsall (1961) was designed to test this theory. Using a visual signal of 0.78 foot lamberts and prior odds of 1, they experimentally determined 13 points on each of four observer's ROC curves. Each point is based on a 2-hour experimental session consisting of 200 presentations of noise and 200 of signal, 400 in all. Changes in the operating level β were effected by changes in the payoff matrix, designed to yield β's ranging from .16 to 8.00. The data points of these four subjects are presented in Fig. 6.12. In only one of the observers' data, #1, would the straight-line ROC curve required by high-threshold theory appear to fit the data.

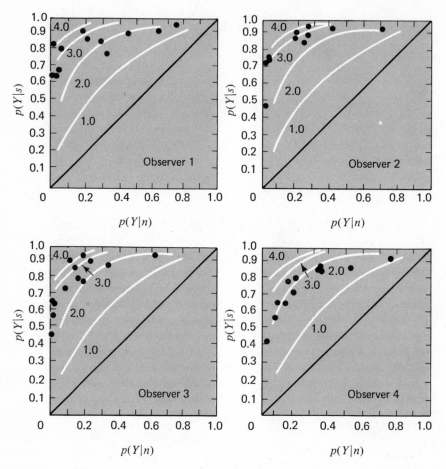

Fig. 6.12 Empirical ROC curves for four observers in a visual signal detection experiment.

The Psychometric Function

Another aspect or way of looking at detection data that proves useful is the psychometric function[3]—a graph of the proportion of yes responses as a function of signal magnitude, ΔI. The typical plot of the psychometric function is an S-shaped curve as illustrated in Fig. 6.13,[4] taken from Swets, Tanner, and Birdsall (1961).

In high-threshold theory the threshold is defined as that signal intensity

[3]This function is to be distinguished from the psychophysical function that is presumed to relate subjective magnitude to physical magnitude as in Fechner's law and the power law (Stevens 1966).
[4]The experiment on which these curves are based involved five values of signal strength (light intensities) including zero, three trained observers run in 16 sessions of 2 hours each, with two different levels of prior odds and a number of payoff matrices that defined values of β from .25 to 3.00. The curves are average curves for the three observers, each curve based on portions of the data selected to be relatively homogeneous in false alarm rate.

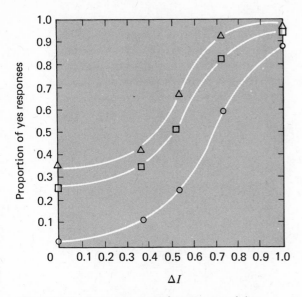

Fig. 6.13 Psychometric curves for uncorrected data.

that would be correctly detected half the time when the false alarm rate is zero. One does not seek to meet such a condition empirically because if the signal does not rise above threshold the observer can only guess so he always gives rise to false alarms. The procedure followed, then, is to correct the psychometric function for guessing in order to obtain the true probability of the signal being above threshold. This corrected probability corresponds to $p(D|s)$, which is given by a rearrangement of Eq. (6.5):

$$p(D|s) = \frac{p(Y|s) - p(Y|n)}{1 - p(Y|n)} . \tag{6.6}$$

According to high-threshold theory, the threshold is invariant after the correction has been made for guessing, i.e., the bias caused by the false alarm rate, so the psychometric functions obtained under different false alarm rates should all be the same after correction for chance success. According to TSD this should not be the case; the observer is continuously sensitive and a change in false alarm rate reflects a change in β, the decision criterion, which cannot be counteracted by a correction for guessing.

In Fig. 6.14 are the psychometric functions for the data in Fig. 6.13, corrected for chance. It is clearly evident that these curves are not super-imposed, that they would not give the same threshold, and that, indeed, the value of ΔI is related to the false alarm rate in the manner predicted by TSD; viz., for a given hit rate as ΔI increases, the false alarm rate must decrease. Indeed, for the three observers in this experiment, the product moment

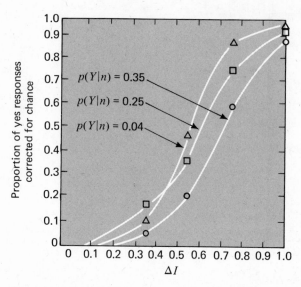

Fig. 6.14 Psychometric curves corrected for chance.

correlations between false alarm rate and the calculated threshold were $-.37$, $-.60$, and $-.81$, which in conjuction are significant beyond the .001 level.

The Forced-Choice Experimental Procedure

The final source of experimental evidence to be presented here comparing high-threshold theory and TSD comes from the forced-choice (FC) experimental procedure. This procedure is the modern version of the classic psychophysical procedure known as the method of constant stimuli and is much favored by experimenters interested in sensory mechanisms and hence wishing to control or eliminate effects of the decision-making variables. There are two varieties of FC procedure, temporal and spatial.

In a temporal FC experiment using auditory stimuli the signal is always present in one of two or more successive intervals of time and the subject is forced to choose the one that in his judgment is most likely to have contained the signal. In the spatial FC procedure the signal, say an added increment of light energy, is present in exactly one of two or more target areas all presented at once.

The subject knows the signal is present and is expected not to generate false alarms except when ΔI is below threshold. The psychometric function, then, may be corrected for guessing by assuming that if there are k alternatives (e.g., temporal intervals) to choose among, $1/k$ is the probability of guessing correctly in the absence of a signal. Inserting this value for $p(Y|n)$ in Eq. (6.6) gives the normalized psychometric function for the forced-choice method with k alternatives.

Parenthetically, the theory underlying this correction for chance success is the same as that found in psychometric theory for correcting scores on multiple-choice examinations. In a true-false exam, for instance, the theory says that if an individual gets an item wrong he must have guessed and we can expect him to get an equal number of items correct by guessing, so the corrected score is the number right minus the number wrong.

Of particular relevance to the comparison of high-threshold theory and TSD is the analysis of second choices in FC experiments. Because the subject knows the signal is present, he is presumed to have taken an observation in each interval and to have reported the signal to be present in that interval with the largest observation. According to high-threshold theory, then, if the observer is incorrect, it means that it is very unlikely any of the remaining observations are above threshold, including the signal. Hence, he should do no better than chance if required to make a second guess after he was wrong the first time. Note that this prediction of chance probability for the second choice is independent of the strength of the signal.

According to TSD, the subject is continuously sensitive so that in, for example, a four-alternative FC experiment, if the highest observation is a sample from the noise distribution, there is a greater than one-third probability that the next highest will be from the signal distribution rather than the noise. This reasoning, of course, may be iterated to third choice and so on. Furthermore, the probability that the second choice will be correct will increase with signal strength.

Data from a second-choice experiment are reported in Fig. 6.15, adapted from Swets, Tanner, and Birdsall (1961). A visual signal was used (0.78 foot lamberts), four observers, and three experimental sessions each of

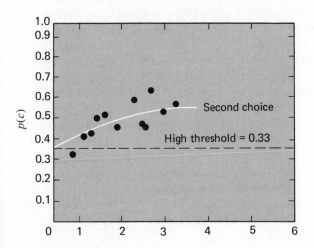

Fig. 6.15 Second-choice data.

150 trials, with the observer reporting a first and second choice. The value of d' differed among subjects and additional variation in d' for two of the subjects was a consequence of not maintaining a constant distance from the target for all three sessions.

The data clearly depart from the chance probability of one third required by high-threshold theory, the overall correct proportion of second choices for all the four subjects combined being .46. Furthermore, the data indicate a relation between d' and the probability of a correct second choice. The curve shown in Fig. 6.15 is the predicted curve if the signal and noise distributions are normal but the signal increment results in an increased variability of the signal distribution given by $\Delta m/\Delta \sigma = 4$.

A somewhat similar experiment has been reported by Eijkman and Vendrik (1963) but on the skin senses of touch and temperature. Here also an analysis of second choices revealed the inadequacy of high-threshold theory in favor of TSD.

It seems clear that high-threshold theory cannot survive this massive attack, presented here in more detail perhaps than necessary. Pursuing the topic to this extent is justified on the grounds that the concept is deeply rooted and persistent on the one hand, and, on the other, the issue has served as a vehicle to introduce the psychometric function, the FC experiment, and the analysis of second-choice data.

High-threshold theory is so named because the threshold is rarely exceeded by noise alone, i.e., presumed located at about $+3\sigma$ in the noise distribution. It seems natural then to consider the possibility of a threshold located well within the noise distribution, say near the mean, and to refer to this as low-threshold theory. Such theory has been considered by Swets, Tanner, and Birdsall (1961) and by Luce (1960, 1963).

It will be recalled that the term *detect state*, D, refers to an observer in the circumstance of an observation being above threshold. Luce proposed that the subject in a D state does not necessarily say yes. If a subject did say yes whenever he is in a detect state, then the probability of a hit would be the same as the probability of his being in a detect state given the signal, and this would be some function of the magnitude of the signal alone. In such a case the hit rate, then, would not be affected by presentation rates and payoffs, which is manifestly not the case.

To provide a heuristic interpretation, we may think of the individual as having a threshold readily exceeded by noise alone and as knowing he is fallible and so sometimes saying no when in a detect state and sometimes saying yes when in the nondetect state; i.e., he responds incorrectly in some random fraction of trials. The effect of the presentation probabilities and payoff matrix is to bias the subject to avoid or to risk false alarms and there is a different ROC curve[5] for these two broad bias categories.

---

[5]Luce calls it an isosensitivity curve.

	D	$\bar{D}$
s	$p(D\|s)$	$1 - p(D\|s)$
n	$p(D\|n)$	$1 - p(D\|n)$

Bias to avoid false alarms

	Y	N
D	t	$1 - t$
$\bar{D}$	0	1

Bias to risk false alarms

	Y	N
D	1	0
$\bar{D}$	u	$1 - u$

Fig. 6.16 Conditional probability matrices in low-threshold theory.

As before, let $p(D|s)$ and $p(D|n)$ be the probability that signal or noise, respectively, gives rise to a detect state D, and let t and u be the probability, respectively, of the observer saying yes when in state D or $\bar{D}$. Therefore we have the conditional probability matrices given in Fig. 6.16. Assume the observer is in one of exactly two bias states, a bias against saying yes (to avoid false alarms) or in favor of saying yes (to risk false alarms). If the observer has the bias to avoid false alarms, then, from the conditional probability matrices of Fig. 6.16 we have the trees shown in Fig. 6.17.

The expressions for the hit and false alarm rate are, then,

$$p(Y|s) = tp(D|s) \tag{6.7}$$

$$p(Y|n) = tp(D|n). \tag{6.8}$$

If the observer has a bias to risk false alarms, we construct the trees shown in Fig. 6.18, from which the expressions for the hit and false alarm rate readily follow:

$$p(Y|s) = p(D|s)+u[1-p(D|s)] \tag{6.9}$$

$$p(Y|n) = p(D|n)+u[1-p(D|n)]. \tag{6.10}$$

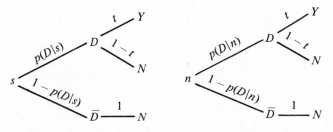

Fig. 6.17 Trees of sequence of events from stimulus to response in low-threshold theory under a bias to avoid false alarms.

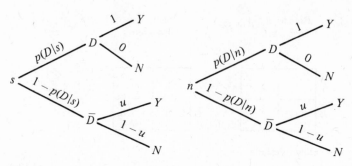

Fig. 6.18 Trees of sequence of events from stimulus to response in low-threshold theory under a bias to risk false alarms.

From Eqs. (6.7) and (6.8), eliminating the parameter t, we have an expression relating the hit and false alarm rate:

$$p(Y|s) = \frac{p(D|s)}{p(D|n)}p(Y|n) \tag{6.11}$$

under the one bias. From Eqs. (6.9) and (6.10) we obtain an expression under the other bias:

$$p(Y|s) = \frac{1-p(D|s)}{1-p(D|n)}p(Y|n) + \frac{p(D|s)-p(D|n)}{1-p(D|n)}. \tag{6.12}$$

Equations (6.11) and (6.12) are the equations of straight lines that intersect at the point $p(D|n)$, $p(D|s)$ and are illustrated in Fig. 6.19. Equation (6.11) is the equation of the lower limb and Eq. (6.12) the upper limb. Try to visualize what happens to this figure as the threshold is raised. Clearly,

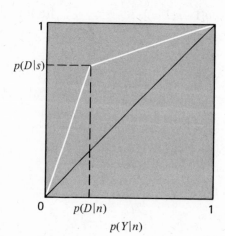

Fig. 6.19 ROC curve for low-threshold theory.

the false alarm rate will diminish $[p(D|n) \rightarrow 0]$, and if the threshold is high enough so that noise alone never gives rise to the D state, we would have only the upper limb of the figure, i.e., high-threshold theory.

This theory of the low threshold assumes the observer works on one of these two limbs depending on his bias, the upper limb being a bias toward saying yes and the lower limb a bias against false alarms.

If we look back again at the data for the four observers in Fig. 6.12, we see that they are not adequate for distinguishing between the two theories, and to date no experiments have substantially discriminated between the ROC curves predicted by TSD and by low-threshold theory. But an experiment reported by Norman (1963) does offer support for the existence of a low differential threshold in hearing.

There is, of course, an infinite range of alternative theories between the single response state of high-threshold theory, the two states of response bias in Luce's theory, and the continuum of response states in TSD. Some of these have been considered and would presumably fit quite well the kind of data currently obtained. Green, for example (Swets 1961), has suggested a two-threshold theory leading to an ROC curve of three linear segments that will surely fit data as well or better than high- or low-threshold theory.

The scientific status of the issue of sensory thresholds versus the continuum of response states in TSD must be said to be still unresolved.

6.7 EXPERIMENTAL INVARIANCE OF d'

One of the reasons for the considerable interest in TSD is its potential generality in the sense of predictability or invariance of parameters over variations in experimental procedures. For example, the ROC curves shown in Fig. 6.12 for four observers in an experiment with visual signals give some indication of the stability of d' as the criterion β was varied. The hit and false alarm rate of each obsever is presented in Table 6.2 for each point (one per day) shown in Fig. 6.12. The third column for each observer contains the estimated d' for each day's observations, assuming the distributions are normal and that the increment to the standard deviation resulting from the signal is one fourth the increment to the mean.

Table 6.3 reports a similar set of data from an auditory experiment (Tanner, Swets, and Green 1956) on two observers. Only one signal level and one noise level were used. The operating level β was varied by setting the a priori probability of a signal at .1, .3, .5, .7, .9. Three hundred observations were taken per day and two days were spent at each operating level.

These data indicate that on the whole the sensitivity measure of the observer is relatively stable over changes in the response criterion.

Of considerable interest are studies indicating the stability of the measure d' over different experimental procedures. In the auditory experi-

TABLE 6.2 HIT RATE, FALSE ALARM RATE, AND d' FOR EACH DAY FOR EACH OF THE FOUR OBSERVERS WHOSE ROC CURVES ARE SHOWN IN FIG. 6.12

	Observer 1			Observer 2			Observer 3			Observer 4		
Day	$p(Y\|n)$	$p(Y\|s)$	d'	$p(Y\|n)$	$p(Y\|s)$	d'	$p(Y\|n)$	$p(Y\|s)$	d'	$p(Y\|n)$	$p(Y\|s)$	d'
1	.32	.77	1.483	.23	.84	2.309	.18	.90	3.231	.18	.77	2.031
2	.50	.88	1.664	.25	.95	2.942	.12	.88	2.096	.35	.83	1.756
3	.65	.91	1.436	.41	.93	2.696	.33	.85	1.996	.49	.87	1.604
4	.78	.96	1.739	.66	.95	1.592	.59	.94	2.173	.74	.93	1.315
5	.05	.63	2.154	.11	.80	2.617	.01	.65	3.001	.17	.71	1.362
6	.06	.79	2.959	.03	.75	3.077	.02	.64	2.656	.12	.64	1.687
7	.20	.85	2.537	.19	.90	.837	.15	.78	2.242	.14	.76	2.171
8	.02	.82	3.853	.02	.73	3.153				.06	.64	2.104
9	.02	.64	2.656	.00	.48	3.802	.00	.45	3.659	.00	.43	3.565
10				.04	.71	2.672	.08	.73	2.383	.05	.56	1.865
11	.19	.89	2.487	.18	.87	2.845	.14	.84	2.762	.34	.84	1.873
12	.29	.84	2.399	.25	.89	2.745	.24	.87	2.555	.34	.86	2.044
13	.03	.64	2.463	.00	.59	4.375	.02	.56	2.293	.04	.43	1.506
Average			2.319			2.743			2.587			1.914

TABLE 6.3 HIT RATE, FALSE ALARM RATE, AND d' FOR EACH DAY'S OBSERVATIONS FOR EACH OF TWO OBSERVERS IN AN AUDITORY SIGNAL DETECTION EXPERIMENT

	Observer 1			Observer 2		
Day	$p(Y\|n)$	$p(Y\|s)$	d'	$p(Y\|n)$	$p(Y\|s)$	d'
1	.05	.47	1.569	.13	.37	0.797
2	.02	.29	1.502	.05	.29	1.090
3	.10	−.58	1.482	.22	.53	.848
4	.16	−.59	1.222	.19	.48	.829
5	.34	−.75	1.094	.46	.82	1.015
6	.37	−.69	0.828	.34	.60	.673
7	−.53	−.83	0.877	−.54	.78	.672
8	.47	−.83	1.029	.50	.79	.807
9	−.74	−.95	1.000	−.59	.88	.948
10	−.86	−.97	0.800	−.79	.96	.943
Average			1.140			.862

ment referred to above, temporal forced-choice data were also obtained using four alternatives and approximately 100 observations for each observer in each of three experimental sessions. The d' estimated for observer 1 in the forced-choice experiment is 1.16 and from the YN experiment, 1.16. For observer 2 the corresponding estimates were 1.03 and .92.

Swets (1959) reports on the stability of estimates of d' based on extensive FC experiments. The signal was a pulsed tone in a background of white noise. Two experiments were run, the first at the University of Michigan with three trained observers under YN, two alternative forced-choice (2AFC), and four alternative forced-choice (4AFC) procedures; four signal energies were used; each subject made 500 observations at each signal energy, observing 2 hours/day. The second experiment was run at Massachusetts Institute of Technology, again with three trained observers, but this time varying the number of alternatives in a forced-choice experiment, using two, three, four, six, and eight alternatives.

The results of the first experiment are presented in Table 6.4.

Varying the number of alternatives in the FC task used in the second experiment had no systematic effect on the estimates of d'. The data are well fitted by curves for d' between 1.50 and 1.70, curves that are within $0.5d'$ of each other, which is no more than the range of experimental error.

An experiment reported by Weintraub and Hake (1962) on visual form discrimination (a square and nearly square rectangle) gave nearly identical values of d' in YN, 3AFC, and 4AFC procedures, even when other rectangles were substituted in some presentations. If the subjects were informed of these extraneous stimuli, their use of the response categories was affected, but not the measures of sensitivity.

Another experimental procedure that appears to be very practical but that can yield experimental results not compatible with those of the YN procedure is the rating scale. Instead of merely reporting the signal present or not, as in the YN experiment, the subject is asked to rate his confidence

TABLE 6.4 Values of d' Obtained by Three Different Procedures (each entry is based on 500 observations)

Signal Level	Observer	YN	2AFC	4AFC
1	1	1.57	1.30	1.23
	2	1.24	1.03	.91
	3	1.48	1.45	1.41
	Mean	1.43	1.26	1.18
2	1	—	—	—
	2	1.40	1.15	1.24
	3	1.64	1.57	1.63
	Mean	1.52	1.36	1.44
3	1	2.05	2.17	1.95
	2	1.51	1.52	1.68
	3	1.90	1.98	2.10
	Mean	1.82	1.89	1.91
4	1	2.47	2.28	2.31
	2	1.83	1.82	1.86
	3	1.98	2.42	2.38
	Mean	2.09	2.17	2.18

that the signal was present. Such ratings may be obtained in any of a variety of forms, a numerical estimate of subjective probability to a verbal categorization of a feeling of confidence.

Pollack and Decker (1958) studied the experimental procedure of ratings on a six-point scale from triple positive to triple negative. The subject rated his confidence that he had correctly received a word that had been mixed with white noise and presented over earphones. They found that requiring the observer to make ratings did not *interfere* with accuracy of reception. In fact the accuracy was better by 3 percent than in a control series that differed only in not requiring a confidence rating.

ROC curves may be constructed from such data, taking advantage of the ordinal properties of the rating scale. A rating scale of k categories can be dichotomized at any of $k-1$ category boundaries. Each of the boundaries is equivalent to a criterion level. The cumulative ratings above a category boundary, conditional on the presence or absence of signal, yield the hit and false alarm rate, respectively, needed for constructing the ROC curve.

If hit and false alarm rates are plotted not as in Fig. 6.7 but on normal graph paper in which normal deviates are linearly spaced, the ROC curves are straight lines if the signal and noise distributions are normal. This is one way, incidentally, of testing the normality assumption. Furthermore, the slope of the straight line is the ratio of the standard deviation of the noise distribution to the standard deviation of the signal distribution. Plotted in normal coordinates Pollack and Decker got linear ROC curves with slopes of 1.

They used three different signal to noise ratios, $s|n$, and found that the different confidence ratings reflected relatively stable proportions of accuracy of reception regardless of the $s|n$ ratio. For example, when a subject used a category "fairly certain" (double plus), his proportion of correct judgments did not vary systematically with the $s|n$ ratio. In other words confidence ratings reflected probability of accuracy, independent of $s|n$ ratio.

Finally, using two, three, and six categories, they made an analysis of the amount of information transmitted (cf. Sec. 10.4) and found that the amount of information transmitted increased moderately with the number of categories of confidence ratings. They constructed the data for two and three categories from the original six categories, however, and this assumes that category boundaries are independent of other boundaries, perhaps a questionable assumption.

Egan, Schulman, and Greenberg (1959) argue that there should be considerable economy in constructing an ROC curve from rating data rather than just YN data. A binary decision requires exactly one criterion, and as a subject is theoretically continuously sensitive, there would be observations that differ substantially from the criterion value. Hence, if a subject is capable of utilizing multiple criteria simultaneously, a multiple category rating scale should provide more information than a binary scale.

In an auditory signal detection experiment they determined the hit and false alarm rate at three operating levels in two different ways: (1) by making 1,440 observations, which the subject rated on a four-point scale in which the category boundaries corresponded to a "strict," "medium," and "lax" criterion, and (2) by making 4,320 observations in a YN experiment, one third of them at each of three criterion levels, corresponding to strict, medium, and lax. Table 6.5 gives the estimates for three subjects' d' and σ_s/σ_n, the reciprocal of the slope of the ROC curve when plotted on normal-normal graph paper.

The subjects were trained observers and it is clear from the data that at least in this case they could adopt the multiple criteria of the rating scale and with considerable economy of effort yield apparently similar parameter values.

This may not be a safe general conclusion because Swets, Tanner, and Birdsall (1961) report a similar comparison in which there appear to be consistent differences. Their's was a visual signal detection experiment comparing the YN procedure with the six-alternative-rating procedure. They found that the rating procedure yielded more stable estimates from 1,200 observations than the YN procedure with 5,000. The ROC curves obtained under the two procedures, however, were not identical. The results for only one of the four observers are reported here (Fig. 6.20) as they all show the same pattern. The ROC curves are plotted in normal coordinates.

The greater variability of the data points from the YN procedure is evident, but more critical is the difference between the ROC curves. The greater slope of the ROC curve (σ_n/σ_s) based on rating data indicates that the signal distribution has more variance under the YN procedure than under the rating procedure. If the slope of the ROC curve is 1, then the greater d' is, the further the ROC curve is from the diagonal. If the slope departs from 1 a problem arises in estimating d' and a solution is proposed by Clarke, Birdsall, and Tanner (1959). In these data, estimates of d' range for the four observers from 2.0 to 3.0 for the YN data and from 1.5 to 2.0 for the rating data.

The authors report in a footnote that this experiment was repeated and

TABLE 6.5 COMPARISON OF ESTIMATES OF d' AND σ_s/σ_n OBTAINED FROM YN AND RATING PROCEDURE

Subject	d'		σ_s/σ_n	
	YN	R	YN	R
1	1.30	1.42	1.03	1.11
2	1.52	1.36	1.06	1.13
3	1.85	1.82	1.36	1.06
Mean	1.56	1.53	1.15	1.10

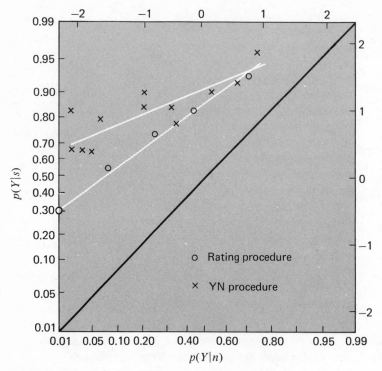

Fig. 6.20 Comparison of the receiver operating characteristic curves obtained from ratings and binary decisions (normal coordinates).

that no reliable or regular differences were found between ROC curves obtained from rating and YN procedures. The replication experiment does not appear to have been reported in detail and there is no corroborated explanation for the differences in results. At present it seems that with visual stimuli the question of the equivalence of ROC curves obtained under the two procedures cannot be definitely answered.

Sorkin (1962) has extended TSD to matching procedures in which the observer's task, after having two presentations of a signal, is to state whether the signals were the same or different. He predicted the probability of an observer saying the same given that the signals were the same by assuming the observer's efficiency is constant between discrimination and matching procedures and using the value of d' estimated in a 2AFC experiment. He got close agreement between the predictions and the actual probabilities in an experiment with five observers.

It is, of course, a very substantial accomplishment for a theory to provide predictability and integration over a wide variety of experimental conditions and procedures. It appears that for a given observer and a given $s|n$ ratio, d' is reasonably constant over variations in β induced by changing the prior odds and the payoff matrix, and, for the most part, over variations in procedures including YN, FC (from two to eight alternatives), ratings of confidence, and matching procedures.

The stability of d' estimates obtained from FC procedures that vary in having from two to eight alternatives has an interesting implication, pointed out by Swets (1959). This stability is predicted by TSD assuming perfect memory. The confirmation of this prediction suggests that the observers can store the temporal sequence and select the largest of eight observations as well as they can when there are only two observations. No decay parameter for memory seems to be required to make the data from 8AFC comparable to that of 2AFC.

6.8   THE HUMAN OBSERVER

In general the human observer performs less well than the ideal receiver. Values of η (cf. Sec. 6.5) reported by Tanner (1956), for example, in an auditory detection experiment ranged for one observer from .045 to .287 and for the other observer from .141 to .750, falling well below $\eta = 1$ for the ideal receiver. Egan, Schulman, and Greenberg (1959) reported an average value of η for their three listeners as .076, which in decibels is -11, and Green (1960) reports that when cues to the nature of the signal are provided the observer's performance may fall only about 3 to 6 decibels below that of the ideal receiver and without aids the observer falls short by 12 to 15 decibels.

The psychometric function for the human observer compared to that of the ideal receiver tends to differ in two respects—it is shifted to the right and its slope increases. Therefore, the human observer has a lower proportion of correct responses for a given signal intensity, particularly for lower signals; this is referred to in the literature as "weak signal suppression."

Swets (1961) discusses three possible interpretations of these discrepancies: noise in the decision process in the form of variability of the response criterion, noise inherent in the human sensory system, and faulty memory. He favors the last interpretation because it accounts for both the shift to the right and the increased slope of the psychometric function. If the observer has faulty memory for the signal, this is equivalent to a signal not being specified exactly but only statistically; i.e., there is some uncertainty about the signal. In the study of channel C_{21} of Fig. 6.8, performance of the ideal receiver falls off in exactly the same manner as that of the human observer—the increased slope is a consequence of the fact that total memory is less important with stronger signals.

In the theory of the ideal receiver the concept of signal uncertainty is expressed in terms of the number of possible signals, represented by M. If $M = 1$, there is only one possible signal and this corresponds to the

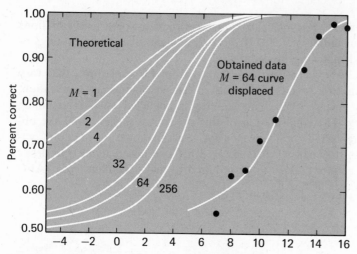

Fig. 6.21 Theoretical psychometric functions for the ideal observer detecting one of M orthogonal signals.

signal known exactly. If the ideal device is deprived of information about any such characteristics of the signal as frequency, phase, starting time, duration, or amplitude, then M increases. The effect on the psychometric function is illustrated in Fig. 6.21, taken from Green (1960). The abscissa is 10 times the logarithm of the ratio of signal energy to noise power density.

In an experimental study of the effect of signal uncertainty on the observer's performance, Green (1961) found that changes in uncertainty of the signal had small effects on the psychometric function and in the same direction as those for the ideal receiver. He suggests that the smallness of the effects could be caused by a high initial uncertainty on the part of the observer about the signal. From Fig. 6.21 it is clear that for low values of M changes in uncertainty have marked effect but from $M = 64$ to $M = 256$, for example, there is relatively little.

On the basis of the slope of the obtained psychometric function, signal uncertainty appears to be in the neighborhood of 100. As there may be uncertainty about several orthogonal characteristics of a signal, their product could yield a substantial signal uncertainty.

The conjecture that uncertainty about the signal reflects faulty memory finds some substantiation in experiments in which aids to memory are provided, as in the "pulsed-carrier" experiment. "In each observation interval we introduced a segment of sine wave whose amplitude was large. This segment matched the signal in frequency, phase, starting time, and duration. It was the observer's task to state whether the signal appeared on top of this pulsed-carrier, or pedestal as J. C. R. Licklider calls it" (Tanner 1961).

The effect on the psychometric function of providing more and more memory aids is to yield functions with progressively flatter slopes. Green

(1960) used a technique that "minimizes practically all uncertainty" and obtained a psychometric function that exactly parallels the $M = 1$, signal-known-exactly case and was displaced about 6 decibels.

Only a small portion of the literature has been surveyed here. For some major references and more advanced treatments, see the following entries in the general bibliography: Green and Swets (1966), Licklider (1959), Luce (1963), and Swets (1964).

There have also been some peripheral developments and applications: Atkinson (1963), Bernbach (1964), Broadbent and Gregory (1963), Creelman (1965), Hack (1963), Mackworth and Taylor (1963), Moore, Linker, and Purcell (1965), Price (1966), and Treisman (1964).

chapter 7

GAME THEORY

7.1 INTRODUCTION

The theory of games is an abstract analysis of conflict of interests among
parties who interact according to rules. As a mathematical system the theory
of games is simply a collection of definitions and theorems and hence is
devoid of empirical meaning. Yet it is probably the most elaborate mathematical theory that has been conceived and developed with an intended
interpretation in the domain of the social sciences. Because game theory
explores the strategies of the interacting parties and determines when and
how their objectives can be attained, it can be viewed as a branch of normative
decision theory (see Sec. 5.1). More specifically, game theory deals with
decision problems whose outcome is determined by the courses of action, or
strategies, taken by each of the parties involved.

This chapter discusses some of the basic concepts of game theory and
presents some aspects of the theory that are of interest to students of the
social sciences. The present treatment is limited to what is technically called

Mr. Column

	C_1	$\cdots$	C_j	$\cdots$	C_n
R_1	O_{11}				O_{1n}
.					
.					
.					
R_i			O_{ij}		
.					
.					
.					
R_m	O_{m1}				O_{mn}

Mr. Row

Fig. 7.1

two-person games in normal form. In such games there are two players, whom we shall call Mr. Row and Mr. Column, or simply R and C. Each player has a set of available strategies denoted $S_R = \{R_1, \ldots, R_m\}$ and $S_C = \{C_1, \ldots, C_n\}$, respectively. The game is played by having each player select one strategy. A pair of chosen strategies (one for each player) determines the outcome of the game. Such games can be described by the payoff matrix displayed in Fig. 7.1. The rows of the matrix represent the strategies of Mr. Row, the columns represent the strategies of Mr. Column, and the cell entries represent the outcomes. More specifically, O_{ij} denotes the outcome that results when Row plays strategy R_i and Column plays strategy C_j. The outcomes may be anything whatsoever. Some examples of outcomes are: Mr. Row is declared winner, Mr. Row pays \$1,000 to Mr. Column, both players take a vacation, etc. Although no restrictions are imposed on the set of outcomes, it is assumed that each player has a preference order with respect to the outcomes and that the order satisfies the axioms of utility theory (see Sec. 5.2) so that it is possible to measure the utility of the outcomes for each player. Hence, as far as game theory is concerned, each outcome O_{ij} can be summarized by a pair of numbers (r_{ij}, c_{ij}) that correspond to the utilities of O_{ij} to players R and C, respectively. Indeed, throughout the chapter we assume that the cell entries in the payoff matrix are the respective utilities of the players. To illustrate, consider a children's game called button-button. In this game R hides a button in his right (R_1) or in his left (R_2) hand, and C guesses whether the button is in the right (C_1) or in the left (C_2) hand. The payoff matrix of the game is shown in Fig. 7.2. Because C wishes to find the button, whereas R wishes he will not, it is assumed that the utilities of the outcomes are such that

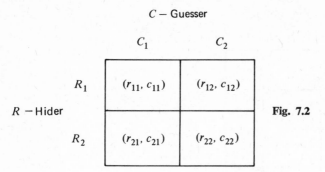

C — Guesser

Fig. 7.2

R —Hider

$$r_{11}, r_{22} < r_{12}, r_{21} \quad \text{but} \quad c_{11}, c_{22} > c_{12}, c_{21}.$$

Those who prefer war stories to children's games can interpret this game as a battle between one commander (R) who has to travel through enemy territory via the northern (R_1) or the southern (R_2) route, and the enemy commander (C) who can place his ambush on the northern (C_1) or the southern (C_2) route. The above inequalities reflect C's will to confront his enemy and R's desire to avoid such a confrontation.

Some readers may object to our static description of a game and argue that most games of interest (e.g., chess, tick-tack-toe, card games) are based on a sequence of alternating moves rather than on a single move of each player. Consequently, they might argue, a game should not be represented by a matrix but rather by a tree diagram that describes the available moves at each stage of the game.

Let us examine the proposed representation for a very simple sequential game. Suppose Mr. Row and Mr. Column are going to play button-button twice. The game starts with R's first choice and ends with C's second choice. The entire course of the game is described as a tree diagram in Fig. 7.3. The nodes represent the choice points of the players and the values at the end of each branch $O_1, \ldots, O_{16}$ represent all the possible outcomes of the game. (To complete the description, we also have to specify what each player knows about his opponent's moves in the course of the game.) When a game is characterized by such a tree diagram, it is said to be represented in an *extensive form*.

Although most games are more naturally described in an extensive form, the analysis of games in that form is very difficult. Hence, it is useful to represent games in a normal (or in a matrix) form, but in order to do so, any complicated sequence of moves must be considered a strategy. For instance, if we wish to represent the above game in a matrix form, we must include strategies such as play 1 on the first move and 2 on the second move if you have won on the first play, and otherwise play 1 on both moves. A strategy in a game such as chess, or tick-tack-toe, described in normal form,

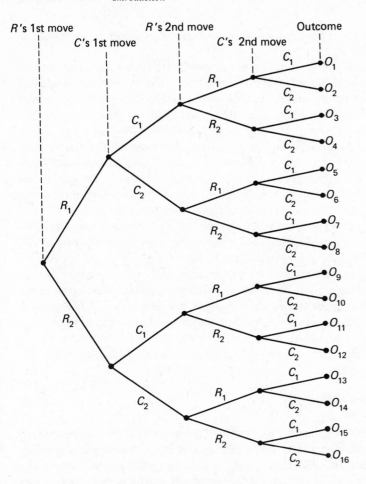

R's 1st move C's 1st move R's 2nd move C's 2nd move Outcome

Fig. 7.3 Tree diagram of the button-button game played twice.

is a detailed program specifying which move to take at any stage given any possible move of the opponent. After the players have selected their strategies, the game is completely determined, and the strategies selected by the players can be fed into a computer to determine the winner. Indeed, the normal representation of a game suppresses its sequential character, and the game is reduced to a single choice of a strategy.

This chapter investigates two classes of games in normal form: strictly competitive games and partly competitive games. Strictly competitive games are games where the interests of the players are diametrically opposed. In such games one player's gain is his opponent's loss. Partly competitive games are games where the interests of the players are partly opposed and partly coincide. The partly competitive games discussed in this chapter allow the players to negotiate their differences. Another type of partly competitive game, called the prisoner's dilemma, where negotiation is excluded, is discussed in Sec. 8.2.

This chapter does not provide a systematic review of game theory, not even within the limited domain selected; nor does it survey the empirical applications of the theory to the behavioral sciences. Fortunately, several good introductory volumes to game theory are available. The epoch-making book of von Neumann and Morgenstern (1944) titled *The Theory of Games and Economic Behavior* is the first general statement of the theory; the nonmathematician may find it difficult. Luce and Raiffa's *Games and Decisions* (1957) is an excellent exposition of game theory, directed toward social scientists, which discusses its applications to the study of conflict. Rapoport's *Two-Person Game Theory* (1966) is a clear, elementary exposition of two-person game theory, whereas Williams' book *The Compleat Strategyst* (1954) is an entirely nonmathematical, but very clever, exposition of some of the ideas embodied in the theory of games. An interesting conceptual application of some game-theoretical notions to the area of political strategy can be found in Schelling's book *The Strategy of Conflict* (1960). The experimental research based on game-theoretical paradigms has been reviewed by Rapoport and Orwant (1962), a volume of reading on game theory directed toward the social sciences was edited by Shubik (1964), and a bibliography of the empirical literature was compiled by McClintock and Messick (1966).

7.2 STRICTLY COMPETITIVE GAMES

Strictly competitive games are games where the interests of the two players are strictly opposed. Hence, the utility of player R is the negative of the utility of player C for all outcomes, i.e., $r_{ij} = -c_{ij}$ for all i and j. Because the sum of the two entries in each cell of the payoff matrix is zero, such games are also called *zero-sum* games. The analysis of zero-sum games has played a central role in the development of the theory of games.

The assumption of strict opposition is quite restrictive and should be interpreted with some care. Many games appear strictly competitive because the loss of one player is the gain of the other player. Such games, however, are not necessarily strictly competitive because the numerical utility of one player need not equal the negative utility of his opponent. This will be the case, for instance, if both players have concave utility functions for money. Despite these limitations, zero-sum games are of great interest partly because they have led to the development of a simple and powerful mathematical theory and partly because they represent in an abstract form the idea of pure, or complete, competition between opponents. Consequently, the analysis of strictly competitive games captures some of the essential strategic features of many real world conflicts of interests that are not, strictly speaking, zero-sum games.

**Games with a
Saddle Point**

To introduce the basic concepts of the theory of zero-sum games, consider the following card game between Mr. Row and Mr. Column (adopted from Kemeny, Snell, and Thompson 1966). Mr. Row is given a hand consisting of a red 5 and a black 5, and Mr. Column is given a hand consisting of a black 5 and a red 3. To play the game, both players simultaneously expose one of their cards. If the cards match in color, R pays C the difference between the numbers on the cards; if the cards do not match in color, C pays R the difference between the numbers on the cards. Let us further suppose that each player wishes only to maximize his gain, so that the game is indeed a strictly competitive one. The payoff matrix of the game is given in Fig. 7.4, where the entries represent payoffs of player R. Because the game is strictly competitive, the payoffs of player C are simply the negative payoffs of R, and hence they can be omitted from the figure.

Which of the cards should each player play? Player R should certainly play 5 black, because no matter which card C plays, R can do no better than to play 5 black. In this case we say that the strategy 5 black *dominates* the strategy 5 red for player R. That is, under no condition can R improve his position by selecting the dominated strategy. Because no reasonable player would play a dominated strategy, it is also called *inadmissible*. The choice for player C is not so easy because neither of his strategies dominates the other. Thus, if R plays 5 black, C should play 5 black, but if R plays 5 red, C should play 3 red. Remember that because the entries are R's payoffs, C wishes to minimize the value of the outcome.

On second thought, C realizes that because R will play 5 black, he should also play 5 black. Furthermore, this strategy guarantees C that he will not lose, an outcome that cannot be guaranteed by his other strategy. In this case we say that the strategies 5 black of both players are in *equilibrium*. That is, it is not advantageous to either player to change his strategy as long as his opponent does not change his strategy. The outcome 0 resulting from these equilibrium strategies is called the *saddle point* of the game: It is the minimum of its row and the maximum of its column. Note that the outcome

Player C

	5 black	3 red
5 black	0	2
5 red	0	−2

Player R (label at left, rows: 5 black, 5 red)

Fig. 7.4

resulting from the choice of 5 red and 5 black is not a saddle point, although it has the same numerical value.

For a better understanding of these concepts, let us consider an example of a slightly more complicated game—a war game between the Row army and the Column army. Suppose the Row army is about to attack a strategic position that is defended by the Column army. The Row commander has three strategies: He can attack from the right, from the center, or from the left. Similarly, the Column commander can concentrate his defensive efforts to the right, to the center, or to the left. The result of the battle, however, also depends on some additional unforeseen factors. Consequently, each outcome in the payoff matrix (Fig. 7.5) is the probability that the Row army will win the battle, given the strategies selected by the two commanders. It is assumed that the battle must end with the victory of one of the armies, and hence the game is strictly competitive because each side wishes to maximize his chances of winning, or, equivalently, to minimize the chances of his opponent winning. Which strategy should each commander follow?

Because each commander does not know which strategy would be selected by his opponent, there seems to be no easy way for choosing a strategy. In particular, for any choice of C there is a different best strategy for R, and for different strategies of R there are different best strategies for C.

In the absence of a better idea, the players may adopt a conservative viewpoint and attempt to evaluate their strategies in terms of their worst outcomes. Player R notes that by playing his right strategy he may get a value as low as .2, because $\min_c$ (right) = .2. The expression $\min_c$ (right) is simply the minimal value in the row labeled "right," which is obtained by scanning over the columns. In the same fashion R notes that $\min_c$ (front) = .1 and that $\min_c$ (left) = .4. In this case R may be tempted to select the left strategy because it yields the highest among the lowest outcomes. Thus by

		Column army defends		
		Right	Front	Left
Row army attacks	Right	.2	.9	.8
	Front	.3	.1	.7
	Left	.4	.5	.6

Fig. 7.5

selecting the left strategy R can assure himself a value of at least .4, which cannot be assured by any other strategy. This choice of the Row player is called a *maximin strategy* because it maximizes the value of $\min_c (r)$ for any Row strategy r. (Essentially the same idea is discussed in Sec. 5.2.)

Similarly, player C notes that the worst outcome (from his standpoint) resulting from his right strategy is only .4 because $\max_r (\text{right}) = .4$. The expression $\max_r (\text{right})$ is simply the largest value in the column labeled "right," which is obtained by scanning over the rows. In the same fashion, C notes that $\max_r (\text{front}) = .9$ and that $\max_r (\text{left}) = .8$. In this case C may be tempted to select his right strategy because it yields the lowest among the highest outcomes. Thus by selecting the right strategy C can assure himself a value of at most .4, which cannot be assured by any other strategy. This choice of the Column player is called a *minimax strategy* because it minimizes the value of $\max_r (c)$ for any Column strategy c.

It seems reasonable, therefore, to expect the Row commander to select his left (maximin) strategy and for the Column commander to select his right (minimax) strategy. If the commanders, however, could anticipate each other's strategies, would they not modify their own strategies to take advantage of their opponent's choice? In general, they might very well do so (in which case the minimax and the maximin strategies do not have very much to offer), but in the present game the commanders have no incentive to change their strategies because left is Row's best strategy against Column's right, whereas right is Column's best strategy against Row's left. These two strategies are, then, in equilibrium because it is not advantageous to either player to change his strategy as long as his opponent does not change his strategy. The equilibrium property is of great importance as it ensures the stability of the maximin and the minimax strategies. The existence of an equilibrium pair of strategies follows from the fact that the payoff matrix contains a saddle point (with a value .4), i.e., a point that is the minimum of its row and the maximum of its column. Moreover, it can be shown that in a zero-sum game a saddle point exists if and only if the maximin and the minimax strategies are in equilibrium.

Games without a Saddle Point

The proposed solution is good as far as it goes, but it does not go very far. Most games do not have a saddle point, and hence no equilibrium strategies can be found. Consider, for example, another war game (Fig. 7.6) between the Row and the Column armies, with two strategies for each side. Each entry represents, again, the probability that the Row army will win the battle, given the strategies selected by the two commanders.

Following the previous analysis, the Row commander is led to select the left strategy, which assures him a .4 probability of success, which cannot be guaranteed by selecting the right strategy. This follows from the fact that $\min_c (\text{left}) = .4 > .2 = \min_c (\text{right})$. Similarly, the Column commander

Column army defends

Right   Left

Row army
attacks

	Right	Left
Right	.2	.6
Left	.8	.4

Fig. 7.6

is led to select the left strategy because $\max_r$ (left) $= .6 < .8 = \max_r$ (right). These maximin and minimax strategies, however, are not in equilibrium because the game does not have a saddle point. Hence, if R expects C to select the left strategy, R should select the right strategy because that will give him the outcome .6. Following R's reasoning, C expects R to select the right strategy and hence C should select the right strategy in order to achieve the outcome .2. By following C's reasoning, R expects C to select the right strategy and hence R should select the left strategy and so on and so forth ad infinitum. The solution offered by the maximin and the minimax strategies can hardly be recommended in this case because the very same reasons that lead C to select a minimax strategy lead R to depart from the maximin strategy, which, in turn, leads C to depart from the minimax strategy, etc. Is there a way out of this circularity?

Game theory offers an ingenious way out of the problem provided we are willing to extend out notion of a strategy. Suppose we allow each player to select not just a single strategy but a probability distribution over the strategies. Thus we allow the Row player, for example, to play his right strategy with probability 1/3 and his left strategy with probability 2/3. In general, a probability distribution over the strategies $R_1, \ldots, R_m$ of player R is a sequence $(p_1, \ldots, p_m)$ of nonnegative numbers satisfying $p_1 + \ldots + p_m = 1$. By choosing a particular probability distribution, the player determines the probability of playing each of the strategies. Such a choice is called a *mixed strategy* because it consists of a probability mixture of the strategies. A strategy that is selected without reference to any probabilistic process is called a *pure strategy*. Any pure strategy, therefore, can be viewed as a mixed strategy in which one strategy is selected with probability one (i.e., with certainty) whereas all the others are selected with probability zero.

The inclusion of mixed strategies in the analysis seems unobjectionable. Because each player is allowed to choose a strategy at will, he can certainly use any chance mechanism (e.g., tossing a coin) to decide which strategy to select. The question is what can be gained by using a mixed strategy? Stated differently, why would a player expect to improve his decision by relying on a chance mechanism?

To answer this question, let us reexamine the last unresolved game. Suppose that player R, being unable to arrive at a satisfactory solution, decides to toss a fair coin and to select the right strategy if heads comes up and the left strategy if tails comes up. Given a particular choice of player C, what is the outcome of R's mixed strategy? The answer to this question is not immediate because we (and for this matter even R himself) do not know in advance which strategy will actually be played. All we know is that there is a probability of one half of playing either strategy. Consequently, only the expected, rather than the actual, outcome can be determined in advance when a mixed strategy is employed.

To evaluate R's mixed strategy, note that if C chooses his right strategy then the expected outcome is $(1/2)(.2)+(1/2)(.8) = .5$, whereas if C chooses his left strategy then the expected outcome is $(1/2)(.6)+(1/2)(.4) = .5$. Hence, regardless of C's choice, R can obtain an expected outcome of .5, which is better, as you recall, than the best outcome (.4) that he can secure by using a pure strategy.

Similarly, suppose player C also decides to use a mixed strategy, playing right with probability 1/4 and left with probability 3/4. To evaluate C's mixed strategy, note that if R plays his right strategy the expected outcome is $(1/4)(.2)+(3/4)(.6) = .5$, whereas if R plays his left strategy the expected outcome is $(1/4)(.8)+(3/4)(.4) = .5$. Hence, regardless of R's choice, C can also obtain an expected outcome of .5, which is better than the best outcome (.6) that he can secure by using a pure strategy. Hence, by using the appropriate mixed strategies both players are able to assure themselves a better expected outcome. Furthermore, the fact that each player can secure an expected outcome that is at least as good as .5 implies that no other strategies (pure or mixed) can assure a more favorable expected outcome to either player. Moreover, it implies that the two mixed strategies must be in equilibrium. That is, the knowledge of the mixed strategy of one's opponent does not make it advantageous to change one's own mixed strategy.

The major result of the theory of games, known as the minimax theorem, asserts that what has been shown to hold in the above example is true in general.

THEOREM 7.1 THE MINIMAX THEOREM

Consider any zero-sum game with players R and C and with respective sets of pure strategies $S_R = \{R_1, \ldots, R_m\}$, $S_C = \{C_1, \ldots, C_n\}$. There exists a number v, called the *value* of the game, and two mixed strategies $(p_1, \ldots, p_m)$ and $(q_1, \ldots, q_n)$ called *optimal* strategies for players R and C, respectively, such that the following three statements are satisfied.

1. By playing his optimal strategy, R can secure an expected outcome of at least v, regardless of the strategy selected by his opponent. Similarly, by playing his optimal strategy, C can secure an expected outcome of at most v, regardless of the strategy selected by his opponent.
2. No other strategy (mixed or pure) can assure either player a more favorable expected outcome; hence the term *optimal* strategy.
3. The two optimal strategies are in equilibrium.

The proof of the minimax theorem, first introduced by von Neumann in 1928, is quite involved and lies beyond the scope of this book. The interested reader is referred to Luce and Raiffa (1957), where several proofs of this theorem are presented. A proof of the theorem for 2×2 games (i.e., games in which each opponent has two pure strategies), including a method for computing the optimal strategies, is sketched later in this section.

The significance of the minimax theorem is in showing that the same type of solution that is attainable, by pure strategies, only in games that have a saddle point, can be attained in any zero-sum game by using mixed strategies. Despite the similarities between the solution of games with a saddle point (using pure strategies) and the solution of games without a saddle point (using mixed strategies), there is an essential difference between them. The difference is that in the former case each player can secure an outcome that is at least as good as the saddle point, whereas in the latter case each player can secure only an *expected* outcome that is at least as good as the value of the game.

Indeed, the solution proposed by the minimax theorem (for games without a saddle point) has been criticized on the grounds that it combines two incongruent decision criteria: that of maximizing the value of the minimal outcome and that of maximizing the expected value of the outcomes. The former decision criterion is a very conservative one since it evaluates strategies only in terms of their worst outcome. The main justification of this criterion, therefore, is its ability to guarantee that the outcome will be at least as good as some predictable value. This property, however, no longer holds after strategies are selected according to their expected, rather than actual, outcomes. Moreover, one may argue that the main appeal of the expectation principle stems from its applicability to repeated plays. In games that are played just once, the expectation principle is much less attractive.

In reply to these criticisms one may argue first that because the outcomes are expressed in utility units and because the measurement of utility has been based on the expectation principle (see Sec. 5.2) the comparability of outcomes and expected outcomes has already been built into the conceptual framework.

Second, the solution proposed by the minimax theorem may not be entirely satisfactory from some viewpoints, but what other possibilities are there? One approach is to adopt the maximin and the minimax strategies, which, as we have already seen, fail to produce a stable solution. Alternatively, one may approach the game as a problem of decision making under risk and attempt to maximize one's expected payoff based on one's estimates of the probabilities of his opponent's choices. How can such estimates be obtained? If one has some information about the strategy to be selected by his opponent, he is certainly well advised to use it in selecting his own strategy. Although such information may be available in some real world games (e.g., poker, war), it is always based on the knowledge of some specific opponent and hence it cannot be incorporated into any general theory of games. In the absence of such specific knowledge and within the constraints of the strategic analysis, it seems very doubtful that the solution proposed by the minimax theorem can be improved in any meaningful way.

Finally, it should be noted that the minimax theorem is not the only rationale for the use of mixed strategies. Another reason for the use of mixed strategies is the attempt to prevent one's opponent from guessing one's moves. Consider, for example, a sequence of plays of the button-button game, described in Sec. 7.1. In this game each player tries to outguess his opponent. Hence, R's best strategy is to hide the button in each hand with probability .5. Similarly, C's best strategy is to guess that the button is hidden in each hand with probability .5. Any departure from a random pattern by one of the players can be capitalized on by his opponent. To determine the actual play, players are advised to use some chance mechanism, e.g., a coin, dice, a roulette wheel, because people seem to be unable to generate proper random sequences.

All the advantages of mixed strategies are based on the assumption that the probabilities alone determine the selected strategy. Thus, if R decides to toss a coin and use his right strategy if heads comes up, for example, then he is not allowed to change his mind afterward. Such tampering clearly violates the assumptions on which the theory of mixed strategies is based.

**The Solution of
2×2 Games**

As already noted, the proof of Theorem 7.1 and the computation of the optimal strategies are quite difficult, even for a game with a moderate-size payoff matrix. Both problems, however, are considerably simpler for 2×2 games. In this subsection we shall present a method for computing the optimal strategies and shall discuss the proof of the minimax theorem in the 2×2 case. Consider the zero-sum game of Fig. 7.7.

If the game has a saddle point, then the minimax theorem is obviously valid, the (pure) maximin and minimax strategies are optimal, and the saddle point outcome is the value of the game. Let us suppose, therefore, that the game does not have a saddle point. The reader is invited to verify the assertion that, in this case, the two entries on one of the diagonals are both larger than the two entries on the other diagonal. That is, a and d are either both larger or both smaller than b and c.

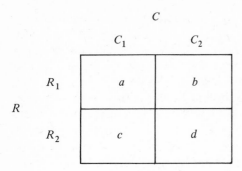

Fig. 7.7

If Theorem 7.1 is valid, then there exists a mixed strategy (p_1, p_2) for player R that assures him an expected outcome of at least v, regardless of C's choice. Consequently,

$$p_1a + p_2c \geq v \quad \text{and} \quad p_1b + p_2d \geq v, \tag{7.1}$$

where the left-hand sides of the first and second inequalities are the expected outcomes of playing the mixed strategy (p_1, p_2) against C_1 and C_2, respectively. Similarly, there exists a mixed strategy (q_1, q_2) for player C that assures him an expected outcome of at most v, regardless of R's choice. Consequently,

$$q_1a + q_2b \leq v \quad \text{and} \quad q_1c + q_2d \leq v, \tag{7.2}$$

where the left-hand sides of the first and second inequalities are the expected outcomes of playing the mixed strategy (q_1, q_2) against R_1 and R_2, respectively. It can be verified, without much difficulty, that if two such mixed strategies (p_1, p_2) and (q_1, q_2) exist then they must be optimal. Hence, all we have to show is that these strategies exist, or equivalently, that inequalities (7.1) and (7.2) have a simultaneous solution. Because equations are easier to solve than inequalities, we may try to find a solution to (7.1) and (7.2) for which the $\geq$ signs are replaced by $=$ signs. If we replace the signs and eliminate v, we can rewrite (7.1) as

$$p_1a + p_2c = p_1b + p_2d \tag{7.3}$$

and (7.2) as

$$q_1a + q_2b = q_1c + q_2d. \tag{7.4}$$

Using the fact that $p_2 = 1 - p_1$ and $q_2 = 1 - q_1$, by the definition of a mixed strategy, we can solve (7.3) and (7.4), obtaining

$$p_1 = \frac{d-c}{a+d-b-c} \qquad (7.5)$$

$$q_1 = \frac{d-b}{a+d-b-c}. \qquad (7.6)$$

Because the game does not have a saddle point, then, by our earlier assertion, a and d must be either both larger or both smaller than b and c. Consequently, both p_1 and q_1 are between zero and one and can thus be qualified as proper probability values. Either p_1 or q_1 may now be used to solve for the value of the game, which is given by

$$v = \frac{ad-bc}{a+d-b-c} \qquad (7.7)$$

Finally, it can be easily verified that the strategies (p_1, p_2) and (q_1, q_2) and the value v, defined by (7.5), (7.6), and (7.7), satisfy (7.1) and (7.2), which reduce to equations upon substitution. The last three equations, therefore, provide simple expressions for computing the optimal strategies and the value of the game for 2×2 games without a saddle point.

Strictly Competitive Experimental Games

The theory of games has been conceived and developed as a normative theory. It attempts to prescribe what rational players should do rather than to describe what typical players actually do. Nevertheless, some of the assumptions that underlie game theory may adequately describe the behavior of individuals in game situations. Indeed, several experiments were conducted in order to compare the strategies proposed by the theory of games to the strategies employed by subjects in playing experimental games.

As an illustrative example we shall discuss one experimental study of strictly competitive games conducted by Kaufman and Becker (1961).

The purpose of the study was to see what strategies are learned and employed in the course of playing several 2×2 zero-sum games. The five games shown in Fig. 7.8 were used in the experiment.

The subject was the row player and the experimenter was the column player. The values in the column labeled OS indicate the optimal (mixed) strategy for the row player. In every game played, the subject was shown the payoff matrix for that game, but, obviously, not the optimal strategy. The subject was told that he is playing against a knowledgeable and hostile opponent whose only goal is to keep the subject's winnings as low as possible. Each subject played each game for 10 trials. On each trial he had to state his strategy by dividing 100 choices between R_1 and R_2, e.g., play R_1 67

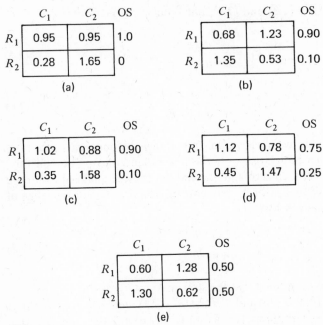

Fig. 7.8

times and R_2 33 times. The subject was further told that his opponent would be informed of his choice and would thereafter select his own strategy. Under these conditions it is clear that the best the row player can do is to play his optimal strategy. The value of all five games was the same, $v = .95$, and the experimenter selected his strategy so that the subject could never do better than v but could do considerably worse. The payoffs were determined by computing the expected outcome resulting from the strategies of the subject and the experimenter. After each trial the subjects recorded the strategies employed and the resulting payoffs.

The results showed that despite the encouraging circumstances the subjects deviated considerably from the optimal strategies prescribed by the theory of strictly competitive games. The deviation from optimality was largest on game (a), where the optimal strategy was pure rather than mixed. In general, the more the optimal strategy deviated from 50:50, the more the player tended to deviate from it. It was also observed that as the experiment progressed the subjects tended to deviate less from the optimal strategy. In discussing the problem of learning an optimal strategy, Kaufman and Becker write:

> Subjects demonstrated the ability to differentiate one of a large number of possible responses (101 strategies). The conditions under which subjects learned in this experiment differed in some ways from previous

experiments on response differentiation.... The subject's task was to pick from a set of rewarded responses that response which was associated with the maximum reward (1961, p. 467).

Naive subjects, clearly, cannot derive the optimal solution from the payoff matrix of the game. They have to learn it through their game-playing experience by attending to their payoffs. The study of experimental games suggests that the problem of learning an optimal strategy is more complicated and less understood than other problems of response differentiation.

7.3 PARTLY COMPETITIVE GAMES

This section is concerned with partly competitive games in which the outcome can be negotiated by the players. Negotiation is a process that takes place before the game and through which the players may come to an agreement about the way they are going to play the game. Naturally the players will enter negotiation only if each of them believes that he can benefit from it. In this section we shall discuss games in which both players can benefit from negotiation and shall explore some formal properties of the negotiated agreements.

Negotiated games must, therefore, be partly competitive games, because if the interests of the players are exactly opposite, they cannot reach a jointly acceptable agreement; whereas if the interests of the players coincide, there is no need to negotiate. Not all partly competitive games, however, need be negotiable. A nonnegotiable partly competitive game, known as the prisoner's dilemma, is described in Sec. 8.2. For a game to be negotiable, the agreement reached by the players must be binding, or otherwise it is of no value. But even if the agreement is binding, there are partly competitive games in which negotiation may be disadvantageous to one of the players. Consider, for example, the following game (adapted from Luce and Raiffa 1957, p. 111) and suppose the outcomes are monetary values (to be won or lost) and that the two players are in a comparable financial state (Fig. 7.9).

	C_1	C_2
R_1	(1, 3)	(3, 1)
R_2	(0, −200)	(2, −300)

Fig. 7.9

Miss Column

	C_1	C_2
R_1	(2, 1)	(−1, −1)
R_2	(−2, −2)	(1, 2)

Mr. Row

Fig. 7.10

It is easily seen that R_1 dominates R_2 and that C_1 dominates C_2 and that, hence, if no negotiation takes place, each player would select his dominant strategy, whereupon the outcome (1, 3) would obtain. If preplay negotiation takes place, however, R can try to talk C into accepting the outcome (3, 1) by threatening to select R_2. By doing so, R causes C a heavy loss at the cost of a slight loss to himself. As a reward for not hurting C, R may force C to choose C_2. If no negotiation occurs, the threat could not be communicated, to the definite advantage of player C.

Negotiation is advantageous to both players in a wide variety of partly competitive games. Furthermore, in many such games preplay agreement is essential in order to attain a reasonably satisfactory outcome for either one of the players. To illustrate, consider a situation where Mr. Row and Miss Column have to choose an evening's entertainment. Suppose Mr. Row wants to go to a hockey game (R_1) rather than to a fashion show (R_2), whereas Miss Column would rather go to the fashion show (C_2) than to the hockey game (C_1). But both prefer spending the evening together to spending it separately. This game, called battle of the sexes (see Luce and Raiffa 1957, pp. 90–94), is represented in the payoff matrix in Fig. 7.10, where the utilities are arbitrary except for their order. To attain the more desired outcomes, the players must coordinate their moves. If no preplay communication is possible, the players may be advised to ignore their partners altogether and to go on their own ways in order to avoid the undesirable outcome resulting from (R_2, C_1), where Mr. Row finds himself alone at the fashion show and Miss Column arrives by herself at the hockey game! O. Henry's short story *Gift of the Magi* is a case in point. Note that both (R_1, C_1) and (R_2, C_2) are in equilibrium but that they do not yield the same payoffs to the two players. A geometric representation of the game is given in Fig. 7.11, where the black points represent the outcomes of the pure strategies and the shaded region represents the outcomes of all available mixed strategies.

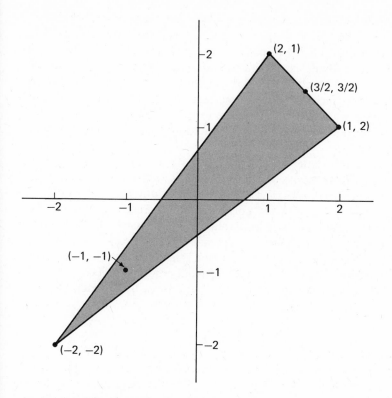

Fig. 7.11 Graphical illustration of the battle of the sexes.

Some parts of the shaded region [e.g., the line segment joining (2, 1) and (1, 2)] can be obtained only through coordinated mixed strategies. That is, a single mixed strategy agreed on by both players. The point (3/2, 3/2), for example, can be attained if both players agree that a fair coin will be tossed and that they will both go to the hockey game or the fashion show depending on whether heads or tails comes up. The outcome (3/2, 3/2), however, cannot be achieved if each player uses an independent mixed strategy. Inspection of Fig. 7.11 suggests that the negotiated outcome must lie on the darkened line joining (2, 1) and (1, 2), because for any available outcome that does not lie on the darkened line, there is an outcome on that line that is preferable to it by both players. This principle is called *Pareto optimality* (after the famous economist who formulated it around the beginning of the twentieth century) and the outcomes that are compatible with this principle are called *admissible*. Examples of admissible and inadmissible strategies were presented in Sec. 7.2.

The difficulty with Pareto optimality is that it does not determine a unique outcome but rather a set of admissible outcomes, among which the players have to select a single outcome. Von Neumann and Morgenstern, the founders of the theory of games, felt that no further restrictions could be imposed on the negotiated outcome within the framework of the theory of games, and that additional constraints would have to stem from psychological considerations (such as the psychology of the players or their bargaining ability) that are not included in the formal strategic analysis. Others, notably J. F. Nash, have attempted to further the formal analysis of the bargaining problem by introducing additional assumptions that lead to a unique negotiated outcome.

To motivate the latter approach, let us have another look at the game described in Fig. 7.11. Because the payoff matrix is symmetric, one may argue that a "fair" solution should yield the same expected payoff to both players and that because (3/2, 3/2) is the only symmetric admissible outcome it is proposed as the (unique) negotiated solution of the game. To justify this solution, note that because there is no possible (formal) reason for favoring one of the players the symmetric solution seems eminently reasonable. Moreover, the point (3/2, 3/2) has the additional property of maximizing the product of the (positive) utilities of the players. Indeed, the latter property characterizes the solution described in the following subsection.

The Bargaining Problem

To state the problem in its general form, consider the plane shown in Fig. 7.11 whose axes are the utilities of the two players. A bargaining problem is described in terms of a set of points S (called the bargaining set) of the form $x = (x_1, x_2)$ in this plane, where each point is a possible outcome whose utilities to players 1 and 2 are x_1 and x_2, respectively. To simplify matters, we assume that the players can always choose not to play, i.e., to maintain their status quo, and that the utility of this state equals zero for both players, i.e., $u(0) = 0$. Hence, the bargaining set must contain the origin (0, 0). Furthermore, the bargaining set is assumed to be bounded, closed and convex. (A set of points is closed if it contains its boundaries and it is convex if any straight line joining two points in the set lies entirely inside the set.)

Both assumptions are quite innocuous. In particular, the convexity of the bargaining set is a consequence of the availability of mixed strategies. For if $x = (x_1, x_2)$ and $y = (y_1, y_2)$ belong to the bargaining set, then the set of all mixed strategies in which x is chosen with probability p and y is chosen with probability $1-p$ generates the entire (straight) line joining x and y. That is, any point along the line corresponds to the expected utilities (for the two players) resulting from selecting the appropriate probability mixture between x and y. [To verify this assertion, note that this line is described by the expression $px+(1-p)y$ for some $0 \le p \le 1$.] Therefore, if mixed strategies are allowed, then the bargaining set S must be convex because it contains the straight line joining any two points in the set.

The task of the players is to select a unique point $z = (z_1, z_2)$ in the bargaining set (yielding utilities of z_1 and z_2 to players 1 and 2, respectively) as their negotiated solution. The problem of arriving at such a negotiated solution has been called the bargaining problem, or, more specifically, the problem of bilateral monopoly. Concrete examples of bilateral monopoly are bargaining between a single buyer and a single seller, trade between two nations, and negotiation between an employer and a labor union.

The solution proposed by Nash (1950) to the abstract bargaining problem attempts to be "fair" in the sense that it reflects only the strategic advantages of the two players. It provides a simple method of determining the solution point, and it is derivable from the following four assumptions.

A1 INVARIANCE WITH RESPECT TO LINEAR TRANSFORMATIONS

If $z = (z_1, z_2)$ is the solution of some bargaining problem, and $z' = (z_1', z_2')$ is the solution of a second bargaining problem obtained from the first one by multiplying the utility scales of players 1 and 2, respectively, by positive constants, k_1, k_2, then $z_1' = k_1 z_1$ and $z_2' = k_2 z_2$.

The rationale behind this assumption is that the utility scales are determined only up to a positive linear transformation (see Secs. 2–3 and 5–2), hence the units of measurement are completely arbitrary, and the solution should be invariant with respect to changes in the units of the utility scales.

A2 PARETO OPTIMALITY

The solution $z = (z_1, z_2)$ must have the following properties:

1. z belongs to the bargaining set.
2. $z_1 \geq 0$; $z_2 \geq 0$.
3. There is no $x = (x_1, x_2)$ different from $z = (z_1, z_2)$ in S such that $x_1 \geq z_1$ and $x_2 \geq z_2$.

The second assumption, which has already been discussed, asserts that the solution must belong to the positive quadrant (i.e., it must be at least as good as the status quo for both players)—and that it lies on the northeastern boundary of the bargaining set.

A3 INDEPENDENCE OF IRRELEVANT ALTERNATIVES

Let R and S be two bargaining sets such that R is included in S, and let z be the solution of S. If z is included in R, then it is the solution of R.

That is, if the solution of the bigger bargaining set (S) is included in the smaller set (R), then it must also be the solution of the smaller set. Stated differently, the elimination of points (other than the solution) from a bargaining set does not change its solution.[1]

A4   SYMMETRY

Suppose the bargaining set S is symmetric, i.e., if (a, b) is in S, then (b, a) is also in S, then the solution $z = (z_1, z_2)$ satisfies $z_1 = z_2$.

Assumption 4 is an egalitarian requirement that excludes any a priori bias favoring one of the players; if the players have identical bargaining positions, they should have the same expected return. The result established by Nash (1950) is summarized by:

THEOREM 7.2

The only solution that satisfies A1, A2, A3, and A4 is the unique (positive) point $z = (z_1, z_2)$ for which $z_1 z_2 \geq x_1 x_2$ for any (positive) point $x = (x_1, x_2)$ in the bargaining set S.

To prove the theorem, consider a bargaining set S and note that because of assumptions 2 and 3 we can consider only those points of S that lie in the positive quadrants, denoted S_0. Select the point $z = (z_1, z_2)$ in S_0 for which the product of the coordinates is maximized, i.e., $z_1 z_2 \geq x_1 x_2$ for any $x = (x_1, x_2)$ in S_0. Because S_0 is closed and bounded, such a point exists, and because S_0 is convex, it is unique. Next, change the units of the axes (i.e., the utility scales) such that the new coordinates of the point (z_1, z_2) are $(1, 1)$ and call the new bargaining set S_1 (see Fig. 7.12). It is readily seen that S_1 is also convex and closed and that for any $y = (y_1, y_2)$ in S_1, $y_1 y_2 \leq 1$; i.e., the product of the coordinates of points of S_1 reaches its maximum at $(1, 1)$. Furthermore, there is no $y = (y_1, y_2)$ in S_1 such that $y_1 + y_2 > 2$. For suppose that such a point exists in S_1; hence, by convexity, so does the line segment joining (y_1, y_2) and $(1, 1)$. Now consider the set R of all points $x = (x_1, x_2)$ satisfying $x_1 x_2 \geq 1$. Clearly, R contains $(1, 1)$ but no other point of S_1. Moreover, the line L joining $(2, 0)$ and $(0, 2)$ is tangent to R at $(1, 1)$. Hence, the line L' joining $(1, 1)$ and any (y_1, y_2) in S_1 satisfying $y_1 + y_2 > 2$ must intersect with R, contrary to our earlier conclusion that $(1, 1)$ is the only point that belongs to both S_1 and R. Consequently, S_1 is included in the triangle with the vertices $(0, 0)$, $(0, 2)$, and $(2, 0)$ denoted S_2. Because S_2 is a symmetric bargaining set, it has the unique solution $(1, 1)$, by assumptions 2 and 4. The point $(1, 1)$, however, also belongs to S_1, which is included in S_2. Hence, by assumption 3, it is the solution of S_1, and by assumption 1, $z = (z_1, z_2)$ is the solution of S_0 and hence of S. Therefore, under Nash's assumptions, the (positive) point $z = (z_1, z_2)$, which satisfies $z_1 z_2 > x_1 x_2$ for all $x = (x_1, x_2)$ in S, is the unique solution to the bargaining problem.

This result is of particular interest because it bypasses the treacherous problem of equating the utilities of the players and because it yields a unique solution that is based only on normative considerations. Like any other normative rule, Nash's solution is not meant to be descriptive; rather it

[1]See Sec. 5.3 for a discussion of this principle in the context of individual decision making.

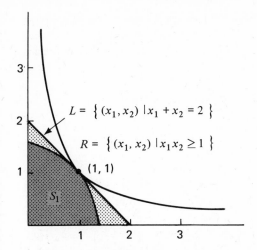

$$L = \left\{ (x_1, x_2) \mid x_1 + x_2 = 2 \right\}$$

$$R = \left\{ (x_1, x_2) \mid x_1 x_2 \geq 1 \right\}$$

(1, 1)

S_1

Fig. 7.12 Geometric illustration for the proof of theorem 7.2.

attempts to reflect what "reasonable" people might accept, in principle, as a "fair" solution to the bargaining problem.

An alternative derivation of the same solution has been presented by Harsanyi (1956), following an earlier development by Zeuthen (1930). Suppose each player makes an offer $x = (x_1, x_2)$ having utilities x_1 and x_2 to players 1 and 2, respectively. Let $x' = (x_1', x_2')$ be the offer made by player 1, and $x'' = (x_1'', x_2'')$ be the offer made by player 2. It is natural to expect that $x_1' \geq x_1''$, and $x_2'' \geq x_2'$, and that both offers are admissible, or Pareto optima. The proposed bargaining model suggests that player 1 concedes to player 2 whenever

$$\frac{x_1' - x_1''}{x_1'} < \frac{x_2'' - x_2'}{x_2''}$$

and player 2 concedes to player 1 whenever the reverse inequality holds. By conceding, a player does not necessarily have to accept his opponent's offer but rather to make another offer. If he wishes not to concede on the next round of the negotiation, his new offer should be more favorable to his opponent. The process terminates when no player has to concede, that is, when the terms on both sides of the above inequality are equal.

To justify the model, one might argue that

$$\frac{x_1' - x_1''}{x_1'} \quad \text{and} \quad \frac{x_2'' - x_2'}{x_2''}$$

can be regarded as measures of the relative losses of concession for players 1 and 2, respectively. The Harsanyi-Zeuthen model asserts, therefore, that the player with the smaller relative loss concedes. Thus player 1 concedes to player 2 if and only if

$$x_2''(x_1' - x_1'') = x_2''x_1' - x_2''x_1'' < x_1'x_2'' - x_1'x_2' = x_1'(x_2'' - x_2'),$$

which holds if and only if

$$x_1''x_2'' > x_1'x_2'.$$

Hence, a player concedes whenever the product of the coordinates of his offer is smaller than that of his opponent. On every round of the negotiation, therefore, the product is increased and the process leads eventually to the maximization of the product, i.e., to the solution proposed by Nash. Thus we have seen that the multiplicative solution to the bargaining problem is derivable from two different rationales: one, developed by Nash, in terms of the nature of the negotiated agreement; and one, developed by Harsanyi and Zeuthen, in terms of the sequential character of the bargaining process.

Bargaining Experiments

To find out how people behave in simple bargaining situations, a psychologist, Sidney Siegel, and an economist, Lawrence Fouraker, have conducted an interesting series of bargaining experiments, summarized in the two monographs by Siegel and Fouraker (1960) and Fouraker and Siegel (1963). These investigators have studied many pairs of subjects in which one was a buyer and the other was a seller of some unspecified commodity. (The pairing of the subjects and the assignment of the roles was done randomly.) The subjects (players) were told that there is only one buyer and one seller, so they must reach a contract. To reach a contract, both seller and buyer had to agree on both the quantity to be sold and the price at which it would be sold. The subjects were equipped with tables showing the profits of both players given any agreement concerning price and quantity, and they were encouraged to maximize their profit because it constitutes their earning in the experiment.

Each player sat in an isolated booth and the negotiation took place by exchanging slips of paper, each containing a proposed price and quantity. The players were further told that they should reach an agreement within an hour. Using this experimental setting, Siegel and Fouraker studied the influence of variables such as level of aspiration and amount of information on the negotiated agreement. One study of particular interest may serve to illustrate the approach.

In this experiment the two players had different amounts of information: complete and incomplete. The player with the complete information knew the profits of both players under any possible contract. The player

TABLE 7.1 Contracts Negotiated by Bargaining Pairs Under Complete-Incomplete Information

| | | Profits, $ | | |
Quantity	Price, $	Buyer	Seller	Joint Payoff
8	1.20	7.44*	3.20	10.64
10	1.30	7.40	3.00*	10.70
9	1.35	6.75*	4.05	10.80
8	1.40	5.84	4.80*	10.64
9	1.40	6.30	4.50*	10.80
8	1.50	5.04*	5.60	10.64
9	1.50	5.40	5.40*	10.80
9	1.50	5.40*	5.40	10.80
9	1.50	5.40	5.40*	10.80
9	1.50	5.40*	5.40	10.80
10	1.55	5.20	5.50*	10.70
10	1.60	4.70*	6.00	10.70
10	1.60	4.70*	6.00	10.70
10	1.60	4.70*	6.00	10.70
9	1.70	3.60	7.20*	10.80

*Asterisks identify the bargainers having complete information.

with the incomplete information knew only his own profit. Furthermore, the former knew that the information of the latter was incomplete, whereas no such knowledge was available to the latter. To achieve the Pareto optima in this study, nine units of the commodity had to be sold, because in that case the joint payoff of the players is maximized, regardless of the way it is divided. The results of the study are presented in Table 7.1. The data show that all contracts were within one unit of the Pareto optima. The profit, however, was not divided in the same fashion in all 15 pairs. The buyer was favored in 5 pairs, the seller was favored in 6 pairs, and 4 pairs were tied. Because the utilities of the participants were not scaled, no direct test of Nash's model is possible. Nevertheless, if the utilities are approximately linear with money (which is not an untenable assumption in the range considered), then Nash's theory demands an equal share of the maximal joint profit to both players.

A further inspection of Table 7.1 reveals that players with incomplete information did better than players with complete information in 7 out of the 11 untied pairs. Although the effect is not statistically significant, it suggests the seemingly counterintuitive hypothesis, discussed by Shelling (1960), that lack of information may be strategically advantageous. In describing the results, Siegel and Fouraker write:

> The bargainer with complete information knew that there was at most only $10.80 in the situation for both subjects. This tended to induce a level of aspiration of $5.40 in him. His rival, not knowing of this constraint, might maintain a substantially higher level of aspiration until near the end of the negotiations (1960, p. 87).

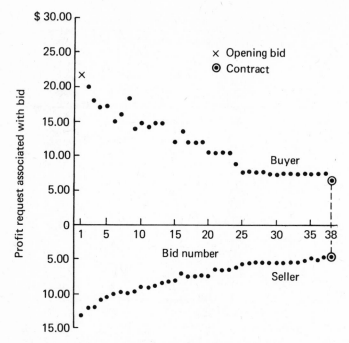

Fig. 7.13 Bargaining pattern of a pair in experimental session 2.

A typical pattern of bids in this study is shown in Fig. 7.13, where the seller had complete information. As can be seen from the graph, the seller, after maintaining a "fair" request of $5.40 for 9 trials (25–34), finally gave in and settled for $4.50. Siegel and Fouraker comment that:

> Such concessions would be very unlikely if the completely informed bargainer did not know that his rival was negotiating in a state of less than complete knowledge. . . . Perhaps it is easier to give in to unknowing greed than to greed committed with full knowledge (1960, pp. 88–90).

Although much more data are needed to evaluate such hypotheses, and the applicability of laboratory experiments to the marketplace should be examined with caution, the bargaining studies of Siegel and Fouraker are an important step toward the experimental analysis of economic behavior.

7.4 CONCLUDING COMMENTS

The contribution of game theory to the social sciences has many faces. First, it has provided the social scientists with an elaborate conceptual framework that can be employed to describe and explain conflict of interests. Furthermore, the abstract nature of the theory renders it applicable to a wide variety of social, economic, and political conflicts that are not commonly regarded as games.

Second, the theory of games prescribes how the participants of the game should act if they wish to maximize some specified goals. The prescriptions of game theory are based on the assumption of infallible rationality, which is certainly inappropriate as a description of people's actual behavior. Nevertheless, it provides a normative base line with which the observed behavior can be compared. In this respect the rational model of game theory plays the same role in the analysis of conflict behavior as does the ideal observer model in the analysis of signal detection (see Chapter 6).

Finally, the investigation of games of strategy has isolated a variety of game types and has provided the social scientist with several paradigms for the study of competition and cooperation. These paradigms, which can be studied in the laboratory, are viewed as abstractions of real conflict in that they summarize the essential features of the conflict in question. Indeed, the investigation of experimental games has been based on the belief that they provide a fruitful paradigm for the study of interpersonal conflict.

LEARNING
AND
INFORMATION
THEORY

---

part III

chapter

8

SEQUENTIAL PROCESSES

8.1 BASIC CONCEPTS

The observation that psychological processes occur in time is trite. The belief that it is fruitful to study the temporal characteristics of these processes is, however, far from trite; it serves as a basis for much productive research in psychology.

This belief is not new. Consider, for example, investigations of the shape of the *learning curve* in situations in which a single response is continuously rewarded. This curve is simply the pictorial representation of the proportion of animals making the rewarded response on any given trial—clearly a temporal characteristic of the learning process.[1] Some psychologists have studied the shape of the learning curve as a problem of interest in its own right, whereas others have studied it in hopes of answering questions

[1] The definition of *learning* as "change in the probability of a response" illustrates the degree to which the investigation of learning is identified with the investigation of its temporal characteristics.

about the nature of learning—such as whether it is insightful or gradual. (Still others have attempted to reduce questions about the nature of learning to questions about the shape of the learning curve.) The point to be made here is that for whatever reason a psychologist studies a learning curve he has made a choice to study a temporal characteristic of learning. Although the reader familiar with learning studies may take it for granted that such studies are concerned with temporal change, he should remember that there are many interesting psychological phenomena whose temporal characteristics are not generally investigated—such as perceptual defense and field dependence. Yet these processes also occur in time.

Another area in which there is great concern with temporal change is social psychology. Consider, for example, the social psychologist who is investigating the effects of upward and downward social mobility. Such mobility is defined in terms of a sequence of social statuses or occupations. Or consider the social psychologist investigating interpersonal interaction. He observes a temporal sequence of social events—person A makes a social gesture toward person B, B returns a gesture to A, and so on.

The investigations of temporal change to be discussed in this chapter all share a common framework; the process studied is conceptualized as being in one of a number of *states* at a given *moment*. For example, a T-maze learning problem may be studied by observing whether a rat turns right or left on a given trial. Here, the behavior of the rat is classified as "right-turning" or "left-turning" behavior, and time is represented as a sequence of trials; thus the rat's behavior is studied by specifying which of two *states* he is in (a right-turning or a left-turning state) at a given *moment* (trial number).

The conceptualization of psychological processes as being in one of a restricted number of states and of time as consisting of a series of moments is limited in that it leads the investigator to ignore many aspects of his data. For example, if the T-maze learning problem is investigated in this framework, the rat's total behavior on a given trial—twitching, preening, vicarious trial and error, etc.—is summarized simply as right turning or left turning. Moreover, the actual time taken to complete a trial is ignored, because the moment of time is by definition the trial itself.

This framework, despite its limitations, has proved useful. It will, then, be presented here in a precise manner.

Consider a process that is in one of a set of states $S = \{S_1, S_2, \ldots, S_m\}$ at each moment in time $\{X_1, X_2, \ldots, X_n, \ldots\}$. The temporal characteristics of this process may be studied by investigating what state it is in at each moment in time. Statements about the temporal characteristics will be of the form "it is in state i at moment n," which will be symbolized

$$X_n = S_i.$$

A complete specification of the temporal characteristics *in this frame-*

work would consist of a statement of what state the process was in at moment 1, what state it was in at moment 2, and so on. That is, a complete specification of its temporal characteristics would consist of a statement of the form

$$X_1 = S_i, \quad X_2 = S_k, \quad X_3 = S_j, \ldots,$$

which may be written more simply as

$$S_i, S_k, S_j, \ldots,$$

where it is understood that the first member of S in the sequence refers to the state the process is in at moment 1, the second member refers to the state the process is in at moment 2, and so on. Thus the study of the temporal characteristics in the present framework is really a study of sequences of states—hence the term *sequential processes* in the title of this chapter. To make sense psychologically, we speak of a process as being "in" a state at a given "moment." Mathematically, however, the problem is one of investigating sequences of states (and a "state"—mathematically viewed—is nothing more than an element of a finite set).

Suppose, for example, we were investigating learning over a sequence of trials, and suppose further that we believed this learning to take place as a result of the animal's insight on a single trial. If we investigated the temporal characteristics of this learning in the present framework, we would conceive of the animal as being in one of two states on each trial:

S_1 The preinsight state
S_2 The postinsight state

The process would then be studied as a sequence of S_1's and S_2's. Note that if our supposition about the insightful nature of the learning is correct this sequence would consist of a string of S_1's followed by a string of S_2's—because after the animal passes from the preinsight state to the postinsight state, he remains in the postinsight state. That is,

$$X_i = S_1 \quad \text{for} \quad i < k,$$

where k is the trial on which insight occurs, and

$$X_i = S_2 \quad \text{for} \quad i \geq k.$$

The assumption that the animal learns by insight can be checked by determining whether the conceptualization of the process as a string of S_1's followed by a string of S_2's fits the data. To make this determination, we would probably assume (as most psychologists postulating learning by insight have assumed) that the animal's probability of making a correct (i.e., rewarded) response when he is in state S_1 is at some chance level and that his probability of making the correct response when he is in state S_2 is 1. Our conceptualization would then imply that the animal's behavior should consist of a string of trials on which he is correct at a chance level followed by a string of trials on which he is always correct. If the animal's behavior fits this pattern, it is consistent with our conceptualization.

For example, one necessary condition for the behavior to fit this pattern is that the probability of a correct response prior to the last incorrect response is at a constant level. By making an incorrect response, the animal indicates he is in state S_1 rather than state S_2; therefore, at all times prior to an incorrect response, he must also have been in state S_1, according to our conceptualization; thus he must be making correct responses at a chance level. In particular, his probability of making a correct response prior to his *last* incorrect response must remain at a chance level. If it does not, we must either postulate a third state or suppose that S_1 and S_2 may alternate in some manner.

As mentioned previously, it is also possible to conceptualize social interactions as sequences of states. Leary (1957) has developed a system of coding interpersonal behavior based on two bipolar dimensions: friendliness versus hostility and dominance versus submission. In its simplest form this coding system classifies each interpersonal act as belonging in one of four states: friendly-dominant (e.g., outgoing), friendly-submissive (e.g., receptive), hostile-dominant (e.g., attacking), or hostile-submissive (e.g., whining). Consider, now, two people interacting. If we use the simplest form of the Leary coding system, we may describe the interaction between two people as consisting of sequences of the following eight states:

S_1 Person 1 is friendly-dominant.

S_2 Person 1 is friendly-submissive.

S_3 Person 1 is hostile-dominant.

S_4 Person 1 is hostile-submissive.

S_5 Person 2 is friendly-dominant.

S_6 Person 2 is friendly-submissive.

S_7 Person 2 is hostile-dominant.

S_8 Person 2 is hostile-submissive.

The interaction between these two people at any given moment may then be described by asserting that $X_n = S_i$, i.e., by specifying which state the interaction is "in" at a given moment n. Alternatively, the entire interaction between the two people may be described by a string of S_i's—the sequence of states the interaction passes through from its initiation to its conclusion.

Note that, as pointed out earlier, the proposed description is impoverished: first in that the actual "flow" of interaction must be segmented into a series of "acts" and second in that each act, no matter how complex, must be assigned one of eight descriptions. Nevertheless, as will be demonstrated later in this chapter, the proposed framework for studying interaction will prove useful.

The complete sequence of social states constitutes the raw data for the psychologist studying interaction in the manner described above. The psychologist does not, however, content himself with a complete explication of such raw data but rather computes *statistics* descriptive of the data. For example, he may compute the proportion of friendly (dominant or submissive) acts in a given interaction sequence, or he may compute the proportion of times a hostile act of person 1 is followed by a friendly act of person 2, and so on. By computing such descriptive statistics, the psychologist is describing his raw data in much the same manner he may describe data consisting of a distribution of numbers by computing the distribution's mean, variance, skewness, and so on.

(In what follows, *moments* will be referred to as *trials*. Although the word *trial* is less descriptively accurate than *moment* in many contexts, it is much more common in the literature and thus it will be used here.)

The basic statistic descriptive of sequential processes is the proportion of times state S_i occurs on the nth trial given that a sequence of states s has occurred on the previous j trials; this sequence s may be of any length. (If, for example, the sequence is of length zero—that is, if no states whatsoever are specified as constituting s—then the proportion of times S_i follows it on trial n is simply equal to the proportion of times S_i occurs on trial n.) Statements about this basic statistic are of the form

$$\hat{p}(X_n = S_i | X_{n-1} \ldots X_{n-j} = s) = a,$$

meaning that a is the proportion of times the sequence s on the j trials preceding trial n is followed by state S_i on trial n.

Although the actual sequence of states yields proportions, the investigator studying such sequences will often speak in terms of *probabilities*. This conceptual jump from proportion to probability should be familiar to the reader. Data yield only proportions, but the investigator is often interested in the probabilities that give rise to the proportions; for example, the investigator wishing to check that the probability a given coin falls heads is .50 will toss the coin a number of times and observe the proportion of heads; this proportion will not precisely equal .50, but it will enable the investigator to evaluate the hypothesis that the probability is .50. Similarly, the proportions

$$\hat{p}(X_n = S_i | X_{n-1} \ldots X_{n-j} = s)$$

will allow the investigator to evaluate the proposition that the probability
of S_i on trial n following s is a certain number. The proposition that the
probability of S_i on trial n following s on the previous j trials is a will be
symbolized as

$$p(X_n = S_i | X_{n-1} \ldots X_{n-j} = s) = a.$$

More importantly, however, the investigator may wish to evaluate
certain hypotheses about *properties* of these probabilities. This evaluation is
important because *types* of sequential processes are defined in terms of such
properties. Important properties that these probabilities may have—and the
types of processes they define—are given below.

It may be that for all X_n and S_i

$$p(X_n = S_i | X_{n-1} \ldots X_{n-j} = s) = p(X_n = S_i);$$

that is, the probability of a state S_i on trial n following any sequence s is a
constant independent of the sequence s. If a sequential process has this
property, it is termed an *independent process*. For example, the process of
tossing a fair coin (S_1 = heads, S_2 = tails) is generally regarded as an
independent process; the fact that any particular sequence of heads or tails
occurs prior to the nth flip does not alter the fact that the probability of
a head on the nth flip is .50 (i.e., is a constant independent of that sequence).[2]

It may occur that for all S_i, X_n, X_m, and all s with nonzero probability

$$p(X_n = S_i | X_{n-1} \ldots X_{n-j} = s) = p(X_m = S_i | X_{m-1} \ldots X_{m-j} = s);$$

that is, the probability that S_i follows a given sequence s is independent
of the trial numbers on which s occurs. If a sequential process has this
property, it is termed a *stationary process*. Suppose, for example, that we
asked a person who believed in the gambler's fallacy to predict the outcome
of a series of coin tosses, and suppose further that our believer predicted
according to the rule that the coin will probably fall heads if and only if
a majority of the last seven tosses were tails. Our believer's predictions
would be characterized as a stationary process, because his predictions are
dependent on a sequence whose trial numbers are irrelevant.

A process that is both independent and stationary is, naturally enough,
termed a *stationary independent process*. To be both stationary and independent, the process must have the property that the probability of a given
state is independent both of the trial number and the preceding states. That is,

$$p(X_n = S_i | X_{n-1} \ldots X_{n-j} = s) = p(S_i).$$

---

[2]Belief to the contrary—for example, the belief that heads is more likely to follow a sequence
consisting mainly of tails—is the well-known *gambler's fallacy*.

The example given of an independent process was also stationary. The probability that a fair coin falls heads is simply .50—independent of the trial number and of previous outcomes.

Consider, now, any sequence of states s on trials X_{n-j} through X_{n-1} and label the state occurring on trial X_{n-1} as S_j. It may occur that for all such sequences and for all S_i and X_n

$$p(X_n = S_i | X_{n-1} \ldots X_{n-j} = s) = p(X_n = S_i | X_{n-1} = S_j);$$

that is, the probability that S_i occurs on trial n following any sequence of states s is independent of all states in that sequence except the one that occurs on trial $n-1$. If a sequential process has this property, it is termed a *Markov process* (alternatively, it is sometimes referred to as *Markovian*).

One common way of characterizing Markov processes is to state that they are *path-independent*. This characterization means that the "path" (i.e., sequence of states) preceding state S_j on trial $n-1$ has no influence on the probability the process will move to state S_i on trial n. The only important consideration is the state the process is in on trial $n-1$.

Consider a process that is *both* stationary *and* Markovian. Such a process is termed a *Markov chain*. Technically, a Markov chain may be defined as follows. Consider any sequence of states s and label the last state in that sequence S_j. It may occur that for all such sequences and all X_n, X_m, and S_i

$$p(X_n = S_i | X_{n-1} \ldots X_{n-j} = s) = p(X_m = S_i | X_{m-1} = S_j);$$

that is, the probability that S_i occurs following any sequence of states s is independent of all states in s except the last and is independent of the trial numbers on which these states occur. If a sequential process has this property, it is termed a *Markov chain*.

To understand the distinction between Markov chains and Markov processes that are not Markov chains, consider the following all-or-none models of a hypothetical concept identification experiment; in this experiment the subject is required to sort objects into two piles; he is told there is a rule for sorting the objects correctly, and he is to discover that rule; on each trial, he places an object presented to him on one of the piles, he states his hypothesis about the sorting rule, and he is told whether or not his hypothesis is correct.

Model 1. The subject is in one of two states on each trial: S_1 is the state in which the subject guesses an incorrect hypothesis and is told he is incorrect; S_2 is the state in which he guesses the correct hypothesis and is told he is correct. After the subject is in S_2, he never returns to S_1 (technically, S_2 is termed an *absorbing* state). There are m hypotheses the subject may state (the subject "has a pool of m hypotheses"). If the subject states an incorrect hypothesis, he returns this hypothesis to his pool and samples another hypothesis at random. Thus, if he is in state S_1 on a given trial, his probability of moving to S_2 on the subsequent trial is $1/m$, for there are always m hypotheses in the pool from which he samples hypotheses, one of which is correct.

Model 2. Model 2 is also based on the assumption that the subject is in one of the same two states: Again, let S_1 be the state in which the subject guesses an incorrect hypothesis and is told he is incorrect, and let S_2 be the state in which he guesses the correct hypothesis and is told he is correct; again, S_2 is an absorbing state and the subject has a pool of m hypotheses. According to this model, however, if the subject guesses an incorrect hypothesis, he discards it—never to consider it again—and on the subsequent trial samples another hypothesis from those remaining in his pool. Thus, if he is in state S_1 on trial $n-1$, his probability of moving to S_2 on trial n is $1/[m-(n-1)] = 1/(m-n+1)$, for he has discarded $n-1$ hypotheses prior to trial n and $m-(n-1)$ therefore remain, one of which is correct.

Clearly, both models are Markovian; in each the probability a subject is in a given state on trial n is simply a function of the state he is in on trial $n-1$. Both maintain that $p(X_n = S_2 | X_{n-1} = S_2) = 1$. The former postulates that $p(X_n = S_2 | X_{n-1} = S_1) = 1/m$, whereas the latter postulates that $p(X_n = S_2 | X_{n-1} = S_1) = 1/(m-n+1)$. Thus the former is seen to be a Markov chain, because the probability of moving from S_1 on trial $n-1$ to S_2 on trial n is independent of the trial number (as is the probability of staying in S_2 on trial n following S_2 on trial $n-1$). Model 2, however, is not a Markov chain model, because the probability of moving from S_1 on trial $n-1$ to S_2 on trial n *is not* independent of the trial number. (Note that the probability of staying in S_2 is *not* similarly dependent on trial number, but *all* probabilities must be stationary if a Markov process is to be a Markov chain.)

A Markov process may sometimes be described by what is termed a *transition matrix*. The rows and columns of such a matrix refer to the states of the process, and each cell entry refers to the probability that the process passes from the row state on trial $n-1$ to the column state on trial n; these probabilities are termed *transition probabilities*. The transition matrices describing models 1 and 2 are given below.

$$
\text{Model 1:} \quad \begin{array}{c} \\ S_1 \\ S_2 \end{array} \begin{array}{cc} S_1 & S_2 \\ \left[\begin{array}{cc} (m-1)/m & 1/m \\ 0 & 1 \end{array} \right]. \end{array}
$$

$$
\text{Model 2:} \quad \begin{array}{c} \\ S_1 \\ S_2 \end{array} \begin{array}{cc} S_1 & S_2 \\ \left[\begin{array}{cc} (m-n)/(m-n+1) & 1/(m-n+1) \\ 0 & 1 \end{array} \right]. \end{array}
$$

In both matrices

$$S_1 = \text{presolution state}$$

$$S_2 = \text{postsolution state.}$$

The general form of any transition matrix is as follows:

$$
\begin{array}{c}
\begin{array}{cccc} S_1 & S_2 & \cdots & S_m \end{array} \\
\begin{array}{c} S_1 \\ S_2 \\ \vdots \\ S_m \end{array}
\left[
\begin{array}{cccc}
p(X_n = S_1 | X_{n-1} = S_1) & p(X_n = S_2 | X_{n-1} = S_1) & \cdots & p(X_n = S_m | X_{n-1} = S_1) \\
p(X_n = S_1 | X_{n-1} = S_2) & \cdots & & \\
& & & \\
p(X_n = S_1 | X_{n-1} = S_m) & \cdots & &
\end{array}
\right].
\end{array}
$$

A Markov process is a Markov chain if and only if it is possible to specify a single transition matrix whose entries are independent of trial number. The transition matrix describes practically everything there is to know about a Markov process, because the probability the process will be in a given state following a sequence of states is dependent wholly on the last state in that sequence. Thus the transition probabilities yield the probability that the process will pass from any sequence of states whatsoever to a given state.

But the transition matrix does not yield a complete characterization of all Markov processes. To understand what information the transition matrix does not yield, consider the following hypothetical transition matrix.

$$
\begin{array}{c}
\begin{array}{cccc} S_1 & S_2 & S_3 & S_4 \end{array} \\
\begin{array}{c} S_1 \\ S_2 \\ S_3 \\ S_4 \end{array}
\left[
\begin{array}{cccc}
p_{11} & p_{12} & 0 & 0 \\
p_{21} & p_{22} & 0 & 0 \\
0 & 0 & p_{33} & p_{34} \\
0 & 0 & p_{43} & p_{44}
\end{array}
\right].
\end{array}
$$

This Markov process will be exclusively in the states S_1 or S_2 if it starts in one of these states or in the states S_3 or S_4 if it begins in one of these. Thus, to have a full characterization of the process, one must know the probabilities with which the process starts in each of the given states; these probabilities are termed *initial probabilities*, or *initial state probabilities*. Although some Markov processes cannot be characterized completely without including initial state probabilities, other Markov processes can be characterized completely by their transition matrices. (For a more thorough discussion of the characteristics of Markov processes, see Feller 1957.)

All-or-none learning models frequently characterize learning as a two-state Markov chain. The learner's response is assumed to be determined entirely by whether he is in a presolution or a postsolution state (sometimes termed *unconditioned* and *conditioned* states); moreover, the probability of moving from the presolution to the postsolution state on any particular trial is assumed to be a constant. Thus the process is postulated to be a Markov chain. [See Bower and Trabasso (1964a) for a more complete discussion of all-or-none models.]

By stating the idea of all-or-none learning explicitly as a Markov chain process, the psychologist can make inferences about what his data should look like. For example, the subjects' average trial of last error yields one indication of what the probability is of passing from the presolution to the postsolution state on any trial. The average number of errors yields another indication. These indications should match.

Particular emphasis has been placed on the fact that if learning is a Markov chain process an error should be a *recurrent event*. By stating that an error is a *recurrent event*, we mean that the probability of any particular pattern of responses following an error is independent of the trial on which the error occurs.[3] The reason for expecting errors to be recurrent events is as follows. The subject's response is entirely determined by which of the two states he is in; the trial number, the length of time he has spent in that state, etc., are irrelevant. By making an error, the subject indicates he is in the presolution state. His probability of staying in that state for the following $m-1$ trials and then moving to the solution state on the mth trial is completely independent of the number of preceding trials he has spent in that state; otherwise, the process would not be a Markov chain. Thus the probability of any particular response pattern following an error is independent of how many trials preceded the error, i.e., is independent of the trial number on which the error occurs.

The question of whether an error is a recurrent event may be answered empirically by observing the pattern of responses after each error (see Sec. 9.3). Restle (1965) has reviewed a number of studies in which errors were found to be recurrent events. In the same paper Restle proposes that the definition of what constitutes all-or-none learning be expanded to include any learning in which an error is a recurrent event (p. 313: "The essential characteristic of all-or-none data is that errors are recurrent events"). Restle shows that there are other models besides Markov chain models that predict that errors are recurrent events.

One way of characterizing the two-state Markov chain model of learning is by asserting that the subject who makes an error is in exactly the same position he was in at the beginning of the experiment; he is in the presolution state, and the fact he is in that state tells us everything we need to know about him to predict his responses. (The assertion that the subject who makes an error is in the same position he was in at the beginning of the experiment could have been used in justifying the expectation that errors should be recurrent events.) Suppose now that the experimenter has been

---

[3]For a more precise definition of *recurrent event*, see Restle (1965, p. 314).

reinforcing response *A*. If the subject who makes an error is in the same position he was in at the beginning of the experiment, he should do just as well at learning response *B* if the experimenter now begins reinforcing *B* as he would have done had the experimenter been reinforcing *B* from the beginning. Moreover, consider a second subject who has been reinforced for making response *B* and who makes an error on the same trial the first subject does. The second subject, because he is also in the same position he was in at the beginning of the experiment, should do no better at learning response *B* than should the first subject (who, remember, was previously reinforced for response *A*).

Bower and Trabasso (1964*b*) have tested these implications of the model in a series of ingenious experiments in which they employ an *alternating reversal shift* procedure. This procedure may be illustrated as follows. Suppose the experimenter is asking subjects to sort playing cards into two piles and that the experimenter is reinforcing the subject for putting red cards on the left pile and black cards on the right pile. The second time the subject makes an error, the experimenter tells him he was correct and now reinforces him for putting red cards on the *right* pile and black cards on the *left* pile. If the subject makes two more errors, he is again told he is correct after he makes the second error, and the reinforcement rule is reversed back to its original form. And so on. If the two-state Markov chain model is correct, subjects learning under this procedure should do just as well as subjects who have been continuously reinforced for one assignment. Bower and Trabasso conducted experiments in concept identification in which this prediction was verified.

It should be noted that the Bower and Trabasso results are consistent with models other than the one they tested, for the result does not imply that the transition probability from the presolution to postsolution state may not vary as a function of trial number. In particular, their results are consistent with a model that assumes the subject discards incorrect hypotheses and that the probability of moving from the presolution to postsolution state therefore increases as the number of trials increases. The results are also consistent with a model that assumes the subject remembers his last response and chooses only hypotheses consistent with whether that response was reinforced or not (see Trabasso and Bower 1966).

8.2 SEQUENTIAL PLAYS OF THE PRISONER'S DILEMMA GAME

In this section, one use of the Markov chain model in empirical research is illustrated. The research described involves repeated plays of the prisoners' dilemma game, and some differences between the way men play and women play.

Games were discussed in Chapter 7, in which brief mention was made of the particular type of game called the *prisoner's dilemma* game; here, the structure of this game will be described at some length; this structure could be described briefly in terms of some of the concepts introduced in Chapter 7, but it is described here without assuming the reader has read that chapter, in order to make the present chapter self-contained.

The game is based on the following situation. Two men rob a bank. They are apprehended by the local district attorney, who knows they have committed the robbery but who does not have sufficient evidence to convict them. The district attorney puts his two prisoners in separate rooms and makes an identical proposition to each. If either prisoner confesses and the other does not, the one who confesses will go free for supplying state's evidence and the other will be sent to jail for 10 years. If they both confess, they will both go to jail for 5 years. If neither confesses, they will both go to jail for a single year on some minor charge such as carrying a concealed weapon. The district attorney informs each prisoner that he has made this same proposition to the other, and he then leaves them in their separate rooms to think.

Each prisoner, being rational, decides to figure out his best course of action for each course of action the other prisoner might take. If the other prisoner confesses, it is clearly better to confess than not to confess, because confession in this circumstance means going to jail for 5 years instead of 10. If the other prisoner does not confess, it is again clearly better to confess than not to confess, because confession in this circumstance means going free rather than going to jail for a year. Thus no matter what the other prisoner does, confession is a better course of action than nonconfession.

The result of such reasoning is that both prisoners confess and go to jail for 5 years. Yet they would both clearly prefer the outcome in which neither confesses and they go to jail only for 1 year. Hence, the dilemma. Rationality dictates that they both adopt a course of action that leads to an outcome that is mutually undesirable.

The dilemma is illustrated in the *game matrix* in Fig. 8.1; the rows of this matrix specify the courses of action open to the first prisoner (technically

		Second prisoner	
		Does not confess	Confesses
First prisoner	Does not confess	1, 1	10, 0
	Confesses	0, 10	5, 5

Fig. 8.1 A prisoner's dilemma game.

termed his *strategies*); the columns specify the strategies available to the second prisoner; any combination of strategies determines an *outcome*, which corresponds to a cell of the matrix; the first entry in each cell indicates the outcome's payoff to the first prisoner (these payoffs are usually specified in terms of *utilities*, but in the present case they are specified in terms of the number of years of lost liberty); the second cell entry indicates the payoff (similarly specified) for the second prisoner. The prisoner's dilemma game may thus be regarded as a special case of the class of partly competitive games discussed in Chapter 7.

The dilemma occurs because the second row *dominates* the first for the first prisoner and the second column dominates the first for the second prisoner. That is, within every column the second row provides a more desirable outcome for the first prisoner; similarly, within every row the second column provides a more desirable outcome for the second prisoner. Rationality therefore dictates that the first prisoner choose the strategy described by the second row and that the second prisoner choose the strategy described by the second column. Collectively, however, both prisoners would prefer the outcome described in row 1 column 1 to that described in row 2 column 2.

In general, a prisoner's dilemma game is one in which (1) each player has a strategy that dominates all others and (2) the outcome that occurs because each player chooses his dominant strategy is less preferred by *all* players than is some other outcome. [For an alternative definition of prisoner's dilemma games, see Rapoport and Chammah (1965*b*, p. 831). Their definition takes account of the possibility that players may redistribute utilities among themselves after the outcome occurs—a possibility that lies beyond the scope of the present chapter.]

Certain armaments races may also be viewed as prisoner's dilemma games. Both sides would prefer disarmament to the armaments race, yet each side may reason as follows: Suppose the other side arms; then I am better off arming than disarming because an armaments race is clearly preferable to being dominated by the other side; if, on the other hand, the other side disarms, I am still better off arming than disarming, because dominating the other side is preferable to general disarmament. Hence, rationality dictates that I arm.

Such an armaments race is illustrated in the game matrix in Fig. 8.2. Even though this matrix does not have numbers in the cells, it is evident that it illustrates a prisoner's dilemma game *so long as each side prefers domination to general disarmament and prefers the armaments race to being dominated.*

Now consider the following hypothetical experiment. Two college students are brought in a room and told they are to play a game in which each must choose one of two strategies—a *cooperative* strategy or a *defecting* strategy. If they both choose the cooperative strategy, they both obtain a

Side B

	Disarm	Arm
Disarm	General disarmament	Side *B* dominates
Arm	Side *A* dominates	Arms race

Side A

Fig. 8.2 The arms race as a prisoner's dilemma.

quarter; if they both choose defecting strategies, they both lose a quarter; if one chooses the cooperative strategy and the other chooses the defecting strategy, the one who chooses the cooperative strategy loses a dollar to the one who chooses the defecting strategy. This game is presented in the game matrix in Fig. 8.3 in which *C* and *D* refer, respectively, to cooperative and defecting strategies. Brief examination of this matrix reveals that it is a prisoner's dilemma game.

Consider, moreover, that these college students must play this game repeatedly and that they are not permitted to communicate verbally with each other. It is clearly to their mutual disadvantage for both to choose strategy *D* continuously, because each time they do they lose a quarter to the experimenter; conversely, it would be clearly to their mutual advantage for both to choose strategy *C* continuously. Yet rationality dictates the choice of strategy *D*.

If we were to play subjects in this situation, we could study how it is they attempt to extricate themselves from their dilemma. Our study might then yield information about social communication and cooperation. Specifically, we might ask questions such as:

1. Is one method of playing more likely than another to lead to an escape from the dilemma?
2. Is one type of subject more likely than another to escape from the dilemma?
3. Is one type of subject more likely than another to play the cooperative strategy?

Player 2

	C	*D*
C	+0.25, +0.25	−1.00, +1.00
D	+1.00, −1.00	−0.25, −0.25

Player 1

Fig. 8.3 The student's dilemma.

4. What effects do the actual payoffs have on the probability of cooperation and of escape from the dilemma?

5. What sorts of past experiences with the other player will increase or decrease the probability of cooperating or escaping from the dilemma?

These questions, and a number of others, have been asked by many investigators. One investigator who has been particularly active in studying successive plays of prisoner's dilemma games is Anatol Rapoport (Rapoport and Chammah 1965*a*). In the remainder of this section we shall describe a study concerning sex differences in repeated playing, a study conducted by Rapoport and his colleague Albert Chammah (Rapoport and Chammah 1965*b*).

Rapoport and Chammah investigated repeated plays of a number of prisoner's dilemma games. These games differed from the hypothetical game presented above in that the payoffs were generally in the order of 1 to 50 mills rather than 25 cents to $1.00 (a mill is one tenth of a cent). Their subjects played the games 300 times in succession.

Because Rapoport and Chammah were interested in sex differences, they asked three types of student pairs to play their games: pairs consisting of two males (henceforth referred to as MM pairs), pairs consisting of two females (WW pairs), and pairs consisting of one male and one female (WM pairs). Rapoport and Chammah ran 70 pairs of each type.

One striking finding was that the males tended to be much more cooperative overall than the females; this finding is summarized in Table 8.1,

TABLE 8.1 PROPORTION OF COOPERATIVE AND DEFECTING STRATEGIES OF DIFFERENT TYPES OF PAIRS

	$\hat{p}(CC)$	$\hat{p}(CD)$	$\hat{p}(DC)$	$\hat{p}(DD)$	$\hat{p}(C)$
MM	.51	.08	.09	.32	.59
WM	.40	.10	.10	.41	.49
WW	.23	.11	.11	.55	.34

adapted from Rapoport and Chammah's article (1965*b*, p. 835). *CC* refers to choices in which both pair members chose the cooperative choice, *CD* refers to choices in which the (arbitrarily labeled) first pair member chose the cooperative strategy whereas the second chose the defecting strategy, and so on. The entries in the table refer to the proportion of each such type of choice made by each pair; also included is the overall proportion of cooperative responses, $\hat{p}(C)$.

A possible explanation for this finding is that men simply have a greater unconditional tendency to cooperate than do women. If so, this tendency should appear from the beginning of the experiment. It does not. To quote Rapoport and Chammah (1965*b*, pp. 835–36):

> Let us therefore examine the evidence against the hypothesis that men and women differ in their inherent (i.e. unconditional) propensity to cooperate. We compare the fraction of the population which choose C on the first play, that is, $C(1)$. It turns out to be the same in the MM and in the WW populations namely, 53%. Likewise the fraction choosing cooperatively on the second play $C(2)$ turns out to be nearly equal. Turning to the initial fraction of individuals choosing cooperatively in mixed pairs, we find that these fractions are higher than in pairs of the same sex (63%) but again the fractions of men and women choosing cooperatively are equal. This near equality persists also on the second play. There is thus some evidence that both men and women are more prone to choose cooperatively when playing against the opposite sex, but there is no evidence that men are more likely to choose cooperatively than are women from the very beginning. Whatever differences we observe in the performances of men and women must be attributed to the effects of *interaction during the course of play* (italics added).

Thus, to understand the sex differences in the overall result, it is necessary to look at the sequential characteristics of the play and see how these characteristics differ for men and women. Rapoport and Chammah examine many of these characteristics, only a few of which will be reported here.

Without assuming that the repeated playing is a Markov chain process, we may still examine the propensity to cooperate on trial n as a function of the outcome on trial $n-1$. These propensities are given by the following probabilities.

$p(C_n|C_{n-1}, C'_{n-1})$: The probability an individual makes a cooperative choice on trial n given both he and his opponent made a cooperative choice on trial $n-1$

$p(C_n|C_{n-1}, D'_{n-1})$: The probability an individual makes a cooperative choice on trial n given he made a cooperative choice on trial $n-1$ and his opponent made a defecting choice

$p(C_n|D_{n-1}, C'_{n-1})$: The probability an individual makes a cooperative choice on trial n given he made a defecting choice on trial $n-1$ and his opponent made a cooperative choice

$p(C_n|D_{n-1}, D'_{n-1})$: The probability an individual makes a cooperative choice on trial n given both he and his opponent made a defecting choice on trial $n-1$

Rapoport and Chammah estimated these probabilities by collapsing across all subjects and all trials within a given type of pair. Their estimates are given in Fig. 8.4.

The largest difference between the three types of pairs is found in the proportions $\hat{p}(C_n|C_{n-1}, C'_{n-1})$ and $\hat{p}(C_n|D_{n-1}, C'_{n-1})$. *The subjects in the MM*

	$\hat{p}(C_n|C_{n-1}, C'_{n-1})$	$\hat{p}(C_n|C_{n-1}, D'_{n-1})$	$\hat{p}(C_n|D_{n-1}, C'_{n-1})$	$\hat{p}(C_n|D_{n-1}, D'_{n-1})$
MM	0.85	0.40	0.38	0.20
WM	0.79	0.42	0.31	0.22
WW	0.75	0.37	0.26	0.15

Fig. 8.4 Estimated probability of choosing the cooperative strategy conditioned on the preceding choices.

pairs had the greatest propensity to cooperate on trial n given their opponent had cooperated on trial n−1, the subjects in the WW pairs had the least propensity to cooperate on trial n given their opponent had cooperated on trial n−1, and the subjects in the WM pairs were intermediate. Rapoport and Chammah conjecture that this greater tendency on the part of men to follow one's opponent's cooperation with cooperation may account for men's greater overall cooperativeness. They write (1965*b*, p. 836), "We therefore conjecture that the men's higher cooperative response frequencies stem from their greater tendency to give tit for tat in situations of this sort."

Unfortunately, the hypothesis that men simply have a greater propensity for reciprocity (i.e., "tit for tat") implies that the values of $\hat{p}(C_n|C_{n-1}, D'_{n-1})$ and $\hat{p}(C_n|D_{n-1}, D'_{n-1})$ should be *less* for men than for women. The data contradict this implication. It is true, however, that (1965*b*, p. 836) "whereas men, playing men, are more inclined to respond cooperatively to the other's cooperative choice than to retaliate against the other's defecting move . . . the reverse is true of women playing women." (Thus the tit for tat hypothesis alone does not explain men's greater cooperativeness, but does so in conjunction with the fact that men have a greater propensity to play tit for tat when cooperation is involved and women when defection is involved.)

Rapoport and Chammah do not present transition matrices showing the transition probabilities of going from one outcome on trial $n-1$ to another on trial n (e.g., the probability of moving from CC to DD). It is, however, possible to estimate these transition probabilities from the data presented. The estimation presented here is based on the assumption that the choices of strategies of the two players are independent of each other *except* for their mutual dependence on the prior outcome. Thus it is assumed that the probability of a CC outcome following a CC outcome is equal to the probability the first player chooses C following CC multiplied by the probability the second player chooses C following CC, i.e., $p(C_n|C_{n-1}, C'_{n-1}) \times p(C_n|C_{n-1}, C'_{n-1})$. The probability of a CD outcome following a CC outcome is assumed to be equal to the probability the first player chooses C following CC multiplied by the probability the second player chooses D following CC, i.e., $p(C_n|C_{n-1}, C'_{n-1})p(D_n|C_{n-1}, C'_{n-1})$. And so on. As before, these probabilities are assumed to be independent of trial number.

The estimated transition matrices based on these assumptions are presented separately for the three groups in Table 8.2. At the far right of each matrix the proportion of cooperative responses following a cooperative response on the part of one's opponent, symbolized $\hat{p}(C_n|C'_{n-1})$, is also presented—separately for each outcome of the preceding trial.

TABLE 8.2 TRIAL-TO-TRIAL TRANSITION PROBABILITIES BETWEEN OUTCOMES

	CC	CD	DC	DD	$\hat{p}(C_n|C'_{n-1})$
Estimated Transition Matrix for MM					
CC	.72	.13	.13	.02	.85
CD	.15	.25	.23	.37	.38
DC	.15	.23	.25	.37	.38
DD	.04	.16	.16	.64	—
Estimated Transition Matrix for WM					
CC	.62	.17	.17	.04	.79
CD	.13	.29	.18	.40	.31
DC	.13	.18	.29	.40	.31
DD	.05	.17	.17	.61	—
Estimated Transition Matrix for WW					
CC	.56	.19	.19	.06	.75
CD	.10	.27	.16	.47	.26
DC	.10	.16	.27	.47	.26
DD	.02	.13	.13	.72	—

Note that for *every* outcome involving cooperation on the part of at least one pair member the estimated probability that the opponent will follow such cooperation with cooperation of his own—$\hat{p}(C_n|C'_{n-1})$—is greatest in the MM pairs, next greatest in the WM pairs, and smallest in the WW pairs. Again, the overall cooperativeness of men seems to be caused by men's greater tendency to follow the other's cooperation with cooperation of one's own.

The analysis of the sequential characteristics of repeated plays led to insight about sex differences. In this analysis repeated playing was treated *as if* it were a Markov chain. It was noted at the beginning of the treatment, however, that there was no assumption that the process *actually* is a Markov chain; certainly it is not. For example, Rapoport and Chammah report a tendency to "lock in" on *CC* or *DD* outcomes—a tendency that clearly indicates the outcome is dependent on outcomes prior to the one immediately preceding, since a single *CC* or *DD* outcome may not result in the lock in. One principle to be learned from the above analysis, then, is that we may profitably treat a process as if it were a Markov chain—we may profitably estimate transition probabilities pooling across trials—without believing the process strictly conforms to the definition of a Markov chain.

8.3 INTERACTION SEQUENCES OF HYPERAGGRESSIVE AND NORMAL BOYS

In this section a second use of the Markov chain model in empirical research is illustrated. The research described involves the social interactions of hyperaggressive boys and how these interactions differ from those of normal boys.

Raush (1965) reports a naturalistic investigation of the relationship (p. 489) "between the antecedent social acts of one child and the subsequent acts of another" found in two groups of boys. The first group consisted of six hyperaggressive boys observed in a residential treatment center (a hospital ward with a milieu treatment program); they were observed in two stages of treatment; the first observation period was after six months of treatment and the second after two years; during the first observation period, they ranged from 9 to 11 years of age and during the second from 10.5 to 12.5. The second group consisted of six normal boys observed in the same setting; they were matched with the hyperaggressive boys with respect to socioeconomic background, and they were the same age the hyperaggressive boys were during the second observation period.

The method of observation is described by Raush as follows (1965, pp. 489, 490):

> Each child, plus those with whom he interacted, was observed twice, systematically over six situations—breakfasts, other mealtimes, structured games, unstructured group activities, group instructional situations, and snack periods just before bedtimes. . . . The technique [of observation] is simply to record each interaction coding in the natural order in which it occurs, and to include in each code a notation of who does what to whom—A hits B, B hits A, A runs away, B shouts an insult at A, etc.

These observations were then coded according to the Leary interpersonal behavior circle (Leary 1957) (the rudiments of this coding system have been presented earlier in this chapter). Here, our interest will be restricted to whether the act is friendly or unfriendly and to whether hyperaggressive and normal boys differ in their reactions to friendly and unfriendly acts.

They do. Raush summarizes their differences as follows (1965, p. 493):

> The hyperaggressive and the normal boys respond rather *similarly* to unfriendly antecedent acts, with 80% and 77% unfriendly responses. Data for the early patient group, studied after 6 months of residential treatment, could not be submitted to an exactly comparable information analysis, but they were consistent in that this latter group responded to unfriendly acts with 75% unfriendly responses. *Where the groups differed was in their responses to friendly antecedent acts.* Among the normals, the friendly acts of one child were followed by unfriendly behavior on the part of the recipient in 8% of instances; the group later in treatment reacted to friendly acts in an

unfriendly fashion in 19% of instances; and for the early patient group, this value is 45%. It is not clear to what extent the effects are due to differences in personality and pathology, or to differences in group formation, or, in the case of the earlier group, to age differences. *It does, however, seem of clinical and practical significance that the groups differed not in their response to hostile gestures, but rather to friendly ones* (italics added).

Without assuming the interaction process is necessarily a Markov chain, we may express Raush's findings in terms of a transition matrix displaying the estimated probabilities with which a friendly or unfriendly act on the part of one child leads to a friendly or unfriendly act on the part of another. Let S_1 be the state in which boy 1 acts friendly, S_2 the state in which boy 1 acts unfriendly, S_3 the state in which boy 2 acts friendly, and S_4 the state in which boy 2 acts unfriendly. The resulting transition matrix would have the following form:

$$
\begin{array}{c}
S_1 \\ S_2 \\ S_3 \\ S_4
\end{array}
\begin{array}{c}
\begin{array}{cccc} S_1 & S_2 & S_3 & S_4 \end{array} \\
\begin{bmatrix}
0 & 0 & p_1 & p_2 \\
0 & 0 & p_3 & p_4 \\
p_1 & p_2 & 0 & 0 \\
p_3 & p_4 & 0 & 0
\end{bmatrix}
\end{array} .
$$

The zeros indicate that there is no transition from one action of a given boy to another action by that same boy. The fact that the probability in cell (1, 3) is the same as the probability in cell (3, 1), (1, 4) the same as (3, 2), and so on indicates that no distinction is drawn between boy 1 and boy 2; we simply estimate the probability of friendliness leading to friendliness, etc.

Because only four entries in the transition matrix yield nonredundant information, the matrix may be presented in abbreviated form as follows:

$$
\begin{array}{c}
F \\ U
\end{array}
\begin{array}{c}
\begin{array}{cc} F & U \end{array} \\
\begin{bmatrix}
p_1 & p_2 \\
p_3 & p_4
\end{bmatrix}
\end{array} .
$$

Here p_1 is the estimated probability that a friendly act leads to a friendly act, p_2 the estimated probability that a friendly act leads to an unfriendly act, etc. Raush's finding may then be summarized in the three abbreviated transition matrices in Table 8.3.

Again, it was not necessary to assume that the process conforms strictly to the definition of a Markov chain in order to estimate transition probabilities. Suppose, however, it does conform. As pointed out earlier in this chapter, the transition matrix together with the initial probabilities yield a complete characterization of a Markov chain. In particular, it is possible to compute the probability that the process is in any given state on any given trial.

Raush tested the hypothesis that the interaction process actually is a Markov chain. From the initial probabilities and the transition matrices,

TABLE 8.3 ESTIMATED TRANSITION PROBABILITIES BETWEEN FRIENDLY AND UNFRIENDLY ACTS

	Normal Children		Hyperaggressive Children After 6 Months of Treatment		After 2 Years of Treatment	
	F	U	F	U	F	U
F	.92	.08	.55	.45	.81	.19
U	.23	.77	.25	.75	.20	.80

he computed—separately for each group—the probability of friendliness on each "trial" (i.e., interaction number). These probabilities may then be compared to the actual probabilities of friendliness.

The way in which these probabilities are computed will be illustrated by examining the hyperaggressive boys after six months of treatment. For ease of exposition F_n will refer to friendliness at the nth act and U_n to unfriendliness. Then, simple, compound, and conditional probabilities may be represented as follows: $p(F_n)$ will refer to the probability that the nth act is friendly, $p(F_n$ and $U_{n-1})$ to the probability that the nth act is friendly and the n-1st act unfriendly, $p(F_n|F_{n-1})$ to the probability the nth act is friendly given the $n-$1st act is friendly, and so on. This notation is simpler than the notation introduced earlier in that in place of the statement $X_n = F$ we write F_n. Such simplification is convenient whenever the number of states is small enough that they may be clearly differentiated without the use of subscripts.

Among the hyperaggressive boys, $p(F_1) = .70$ and $p(U_1) = 1 - p(F_1) = .30$. These initial state probabilities together with the transition matrix may now be used to infer a value for $p(F_2)$. From the axioms of probability theory,

$$p(F_2) = p(F_2 \text{ and } F_1) + p(F_2 \text{ and } U_1) \tag{8.1}$$

$$= p(F_2|F_1)p(F_1) + p(F_2|U_1)p(U_1). \tag{8.2}$$

If the process is a Markov chain, $p(F_2|F_1)$ and $p(F_2|U_1)$ are simply the constant transition probabilities given in the transition matrix (i.e., constant across trials). For the hyperaggressive boys these values are estimated as .55 and .25, respectively. Substituting these values along with the values for $p(F_1)$ and $p(U_1)$ in Eq. (8.2) we obtain

$$p(F_2) = .55 \times .70 + .25 \times .30 = .46.$$

Similarly,

$$p(U_2) = p(U_2|F_1)p(F_1) + p(U_2|U_1)p(U_1) \tag{8.3}$$

$$= .45 \times .70 + .75 \times .30 = .54.$$

These values are most easily obtained by matrix multiplication (Appendix, Sec. A.6). By Eqs. (8.2) and (8.3)

$$[p(F_1) \quad p(U_1)] \begin{bmatrix} p(F_2|F_1) & p(U_2|F_1) \\ p(F_2|U_1) & p(U_2|U_1) \end{bmatrix} = [p(F_2) \quad p(U_2)].$$

Substituting numerical values, we obtain

$$[.70 \quad .30] \begin{bmatrix} .55 & .45 \\ .25 & .75 \end{bmatrix} = [.46 \quad .54].$$

Having thus obtained values for $p(F_2)$ under the Markov chain assumption, we repeat the same steps to obtain the values for $p(F_3)$, and so on. This procedure is based simply on the axioms of probability theory and the Markov chain assumption. The axioms in their most general form yield Eqs. (8.4) and (8.5), or the equivalent matrix, Eq. (8.6):

$$p(F_n) = p(F_n|F_{n-1})p(F_{n-1}) + p(F_n|U_{n-1})p(U_{n-1}) \qquad (8.4)$$

$$p(U_n) = p(U_n|F_{n-1})p(F_{n-1}) + p(U_n|U_{n-1})p(U_{n-1}) \qquad (8.5)$$

$$[p(F_{n-1}) \quad p(U_{n-1})] \begin{bmatrix} p(F_n|F_{n-1}) & p(U_n|F_{n-1}) \\ p(F_n|U_{n-1}) & p(U_n|U_{n-1}) \end{bmatrix} = [p(F_n) \quad p(U_n)]. \quad (8.6)$$

The Markov chain assumption states that the values of the conditional probabilities—$p(F_n|F_{n-1})$, $p(F_n|U_{n-1})$, and so on—do not vary as a function of n. Thus we simply use the overall relative frequencies across all trials to estimate these values.[4]

The percentage of friendly acts predicted from the Markov chain model is shown by the dotted line in Fig. 8.5; the solid line presents the observed frequency of friendly acts. Figure 8.6 presents the same data for the hyper-aggressive boys after two years of treatment, and Fig. 8.7 presents the same data for the normal boys. (These figures are taken from Raush 1965, pp. 495–496.)

Raush summarized the data presented in the figures as follows (1965, p. 496):

> The obtained data for the early patients tended to show a higher proportion of hostile actions than theoretically expected; the later group showed proportions close to, or perhaps slightly less than expected; the control children deviated from expectations in a direction clearly opposite that of the early patients. . . . For the control group, then, there is the suggestion of a corrective factor inhibiting the expected course of increase in hostility.

---

[4]For reasons not entirely clear to the present authors, Raush actually used only the first two acts in estimating these probabilities, not the entire set of acts.

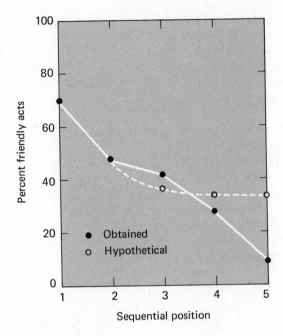

Fig. 8.5 Peer interactions of hyperaggressive boys early in treatment.

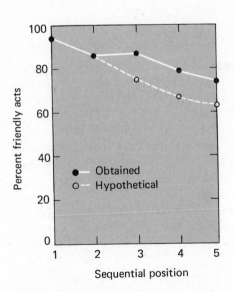

Fig. 8.7 Peer interactions of normal socially adjusted U.S. boys.

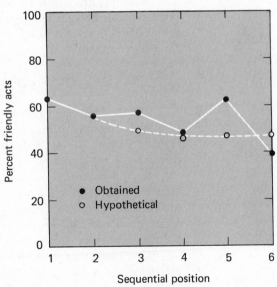

Fig. 8.6 Peer interactions of hyperaggressive boys later in treatment.

Thus Raush rejected the hypothesis that the interaction sequences are Markov chains. The normal boys had a sort of "saving grace" that resulted in fewer unfriendly acts than predicted from the Markov chain model; in contrast, the hyperaggressive boys at the beginning of treatment had a sort of "hostility buildup" that resulted in more unfriendly acts than predicted from the Markov chain model; the hyperaggressive boys after two years of treatment are intermediate.

One characteristic of Fig. 8.5 that may be noted in passing is that the predicted probability of friendliness at the fourth act is equal to the predicted probability of friendliness at the fifth act; that is, $p(F_4) = p(F_5)$. It may immediately be concluded that the predicted probability of friendliness at any time later will also equal that value. An intuitive justification for this conclusion is that because $p(F_6)$ is derived from $p(F_5)$ in the same manner that $p(F_5)$ is derived from $p(F_4)$ the former derivation will not result in a change of probability whenever the latter does not, and so on. A less intuitive justification may be obtained by letting $n = 6$ in Eq. (8.4). Then,

$$p(F_6) = p(F|F)p(F_5) + p(F|U)p(U_5)$$

$$= p(F|F)p(F_5) + p(F|U)[1 - p(F_5)]. \qquad (8.7)$$

The subscripts are omitted from the conditional probabilities because the predictions are being made according to a Markov chain model. Now, because $p(F_5) = p(F_4)$, we may substitute $p(F_4)$ for $p(F_5)$ on the right-hand side of Eq. (8.7) to obtain

$$p(F_6) = p(F|F)p(F_4) + p(F|U)[1 - p(F_4)]. \qquad (8.8)$$

But the right-hand side of Eq. (8.8) equals $p(F_5)$; hence, $p(F_6) = p(F_5)$. In a similar manner, it may be demonstrated that $p(F_7) = p(F_5)$, and so on. [The more rigorously inclined reader may wish to prove that if $p(F_{n-1}) = p(F_5)$ then $p(F_n) = p(F_5)$ and thereby demonstrate our conclusion by induction.]

Such a probability is said to be *stable* or to *stabilize*. If all the probabilities of the states in a Markov chain have stabilized, the chain itself is said to be in a *stable state*, or *steady state*. There are certain necessary and sufficient conditions concerning whether or not Markov chains will reach a steady state, but they lie beyond the scope of this book.

One point that may be made here, however, is that it is possible to determine the stable value a probability will have *if* it stabilizes. Consider the example. From Eq. (8.4) it follows that $p(F_n)$ will equal $p(F_{n-1})$ if and only if

$$p(F_n) = p(F|F)p(F_n) + p(F|U)[1 - p(F_n)]$$

or

$$p(F_n) = \frac{p(F|U)}{1 - p(F|F) + p(F|U)}. \qquad (8.9)$$

Again, the subscripts on the conditional probabilities have been omitted because the process being considered is a Markov chain. In our example

$$p(F_n) = \frac{.25}{1 - .55 + .25} = .36.$$

Consider, now, any m-state Markov chain. By similar manipulation it is possible to determine what the values of the state probabilities will be *if* the chain stabilizes. All that must be done is to perform the multiplication indicated in matrix Eq. (8.10):

$$[p(X_n = S_1) \quad p(X_n = S_2) \quad \ldots \quad p(X_n = S_m)] \begin{bmatrix} \text{the} \\ \text{transition} \\ \text{matrix} \end{bmatrix}$$

$$= [p(X_n = S_1) \quad p(X_n = S_2) \quad \ldots \quad p(X_n = S_m)]. \quad (8.10)$$

What is sought is the m probabilities: $p(X_n = S_1), p(X_n = S_2) \ldots p(X_n = S_m)$. When the transition probabilities are known, the multiplication in (8.10) results in m simultaneous equations all involving these m unknowns.

8.4 DISCUSSION

The Rapoport and Chammah (1965*b*) investigation and the Raush (1965) investigation illustrate two quite different ways in which a Markov chain analysis may yield valuable information. In the Rapoport and Chammah investigation, estimation of transition probabilities helped clarify why men are more cooperative overall than women; these estimates were computed and studied despite the fact the process under investigation was clearly not a Markov chain. In the Raush investigation, estimates of transition probabilities also helped to explain the difference between two groups. In addition, however, the question of whether the process actually was a Markov chain was asked, and the conclusion that it was not led to greater insight into the process studied. Thus it is possible to gain information both by *fitting* data to the Markov chain model and also by *testing* how well the data are fit. This distinction between fitting and testing a model also occurs in the context of scaling theory (see Chapter 3). The point here is that both uses of the Markov chain model may prove fruitful.

chapter *9*

MATHEMATICAL LEARNING THEORY

9.1 EARLY MATHEMATICAL LEARNING THEORY

Mathematical learning theory is one of the most vigorous segments of general mathematical psychology and, aside from psychophysics, probably has the largest literature. According to Gulliksen (1934), the earliest mathematical model of learning appeared in 1907; this model was the forerunner of a model type based on the assumptions that acquisition takes place at a constant rate but that forgetting is proportional to amount learned. These assumptions imply that rate of learning is proportional to the amount still to be learned; i.e., the learning curve (the cumulative error curve as a function of the number of trials) will be negatively accelerated. The fact that most learning curves based on pooled data are negatively accelerated was offered as support for this model. This model is also found in many areas of activity outside psychology; e.g., it may describe the bank balance of an individual with a constant income who spends at a rate proportional to the amount in the balance.

The most popular alternative model of the time, though perhaps the word *popular* is an exaggeration, assumed that learning took place at a rate proportional to the amount already learned but that forgetting was proportional to the square of the amount learned. Another way of putting it is that the rate of learning was assumed proportional to the product of the amount already learned and the amount still to be learned. The shape of the learning curve implied is positively accelerated at first and then negatively accelerated; i.e., it is S-shaped. This model is also found in many areas of activity outside psychology; e.g., it may describe an epidemic that spreads faster the more sick people there are to spread it but that is slowed by the diminishing number of healthy people. In general, the process is autocatalytic, one that stimulates itself and consumes its resources.

Beyond providing an empirical equation that gave a good fit to one gross feature of learning data, the learning curve, these models have contributed nothing to the advancement of learning theory. The first paper to attempt to provide a serious rationale for the learning curve was that of Thurstone in 1930. He considered the two principal variables in learning to be practice and attainment, the former represented by trials or time and the latter by the probability that the act will be successful.

He assumed that the probability of an act on any trial being successful is equal to the proportion of successful acts in the total repertoire of acts made up of the successful plus unsuccessful acts available on that trial. The probability of an error was the complement. He then introduced the law of effect in precise terms: He assumed that there is a probability k that if an act is successful it will be retained and, with the same probability, that if unsuccessful it will be eliminated.

Gulliksen (1934) generalized Thurstone's model by providing a separate parameter for success and failure, i.e., the effects of reward and punishment. He first provided somewhat different interpretations for the probabilities of success and failure by interpreting the probability of success as the relative strength of the association between the correct response and the stimulus rather than the proportion of successful acts in the repertoire as Thurstone did.

The law of effect, then, was introduced by assuming that the effect of reward was to increase the strength of this association. Correspondingly, the effect of punishment was to weaken the strength of the association of the wrong response with the stimulus situation, and the parameters representing these "stamping in" and "stamping out" effects were not necessarily equal.

It can be shown that Gulliksen's assumptions lead to the following equation for the learning curve:

$$U = \alpha\left(1 - \frac{\beta}{w+\beta}\right)^{\gamma}, \tag{9.1}$$

where U and w are the variables and α, β, and γ are parameters in the model with the following interpretations:

U ≡ cumulative errors

w ≡ number of trials

α ≡ the ratio of the initial strength of the incorrect association to the effect of punishment

β ≡ the ratio of the initial strength of the correct association to the effect of reward

γ ≡ the ratio of the effect of punishment to the effect of reward.

The theory has three parameters, α, β, and γ, in Eq. (9.1), in which α might be thought of as the handicap for eliminating errors or the "strength of the incorrect association" measured in "punishment units," β is the strength of the correct association measured in "reward units," and γ reflects the relative strength of punishment and reward.

Gulliksen reports the results of an experiment with seven rats learning a discrimination problem using a Lashley jumping apparatus. Each rat's learning curve was fitted almost perfectly by Eq. (9.1). Of interest then, are the values of the parameters, particularly γ, which ranged from 1.0 for two of the rats to infinity for one of them. According to the interpretation in the theory, then, for all rats the effect of punishment was at least as great as the effect of reward, and one rat learned only from his errors.

From the point of view of the role of mathematical models in an empirical science, it is of interest to note that if $\gamma = 1$ in Eq. (9.1) the expression reduces to Thurstone's model. Therefore, in spite of the quite different interpretation of the parameters, the mathematical expressions are the same and reveal once more that the theory is not a necessary condition for the formal model.[1] Different theories may lead to the same model. Mathematical systems may be looked on as portable theories.

It will be well to keep this thought in mind as we proceed now with the modern approach in mathematical learning theory. Models that have been developed with some particular notion of the psychological processes underlying a set of experimental data may recur as a consequence of quite different notions of the underlying processes.

The modern point of view in mathematical learning theory begins about 1950 and extends considerably the probabilistic approach to behavior theory that Thurstone introduced 20 years earlier. One may identify two concurrent and related paths of development, operator models and state models. The first class of models permits the stages of learning to be infinite in number, whereas only a finite number of stages are possible in the latter class. The first path was initiated by the stochastic learning theory of Robert Bush and Frederick

---

[1]Usually we do not draw a distinction between the terms *theory* and *model*, but sometimes it is useful to distinguish between the purely formal structure (the model) and the interpretation it is given in the real world context (the theory). The reason for this distinction, as indicated here and as we shall see in further examples, is that the same formal structure may arise from quite different conceptualizations.

Mosteller (1951, 1955) and the second path by stimulus sampling theory initiated by William K. Estes in 1950.

The two developments formulate the probabilistic nature of the learning process in the same way. The process is conceived of as a sequence of discrete trials. Each trial consists of the presentation of a stimulus situation to which the subject responds by selecting one from a set of alternative responses in accordance with an associated set of probabilities; the response is followed by an outcome, which may induce changes in the probability values before the next trial. Therefore, in brief, the learning process is analyzed into a sequence of discrete trials, each of which consists of a stimulus, response, outcome, and resultant probability flow. All models are concerned with describing this flow of probability from trial to trial and the resulting sequence of distributions, and so, of course, how they do this and why they do it the way they do constitute their similarities and differences.

We shall provide, in the next two sections, an introduction to each of these two paths in turn. We shall include some of the more elementary mathematical techniques and results, the underlying theory (if any) that motivates particular models, and some of the interrelations.

9.2 OPERATOR MODELS

The Notion of an Operator

We shall begin with a naively "simple" experimental situation and construct a model for it in order to introduce the notion of an *operator*. Then we shall reconsider this example more carefully and see what kinds of (very important) assumptions we could have made to lead us to this model.

Consider the experimental situation in which a rat learns to turn to the right in a single-unit T-maze. On the first trial it is not unreasonable to assume that he has a probability of 1/2 of turning to the right, i.e., $p_1 = .50$. Suppose this particular rat turns right and is rewarded. We might expect his probability of turning right next time, p_2, to be greater than .50, perhaps as high as .70.

Suppose on the next trial the rat turns left and the outcome is negative, i.e., no reward or even some punishment. We would expect the probability of this animal turning right on the third trial, p_3, to be greater than p_2, perhaps .85.

Now suppose on the third trial he turns right and is rewarded again. When this happened on the first trial the probability of turning right increased from .5 to .7, an increment of .2, but clearly it cannot increase the same amount again. How shall we describe the effect of turning right and being rewarded on the probability of turning right?

A constant increment, as we have seen, offers difficulties. An alternative, and simple ones are explored first, is that the increment in probability is a constant proportion or fraction of the amount of change that is still possible.

There are other more considered reasons, which we shall present very shortly, why this simple alternative should be explored. So let us assume that the effect of turning right and being rewarded on the nth trial results in an increment to p_n that is proportional to the amount to be learned, $1 - p_n$, say $a(1 - p_n)$. In this case the probability on the $n + 1$st trial is

$$p_{n+1} = p_n + a(1 - p_n)$$

$$= (1 - a)p_n + a; \qquad (9.2)$$

i.e., the probability on the nth trial is operated on by this linear transformation and becomes the probability on the next trial. Hence, this expression is called a *linear operator* and would be applied on any trial in which the animal turned right and was rewarded.

What happens to p when the animal turns left and is punished? Should the same operator apply? Probably not. So let us designate the first operator Q_1, with corresponding subscripts on the parameters, and the second operator Q_2, and we would have

$$Q_2 p_n = (1 - a_2)p_n + a_2, \qquad (9.3)$$

where the parameter a_2 represents the portion of $(1 - p_n)$ that is added to p_n as a result of turning left and being punished.

Given the animal's sequence of experiences through the first n trials, then, one could calculate the probability of his turning right on the $n + 1$st trial and, indeed, a great variety of statistical characteristics of the data. Then with a number of "equivalent" rats to begin with, one could hope to collect an adequate enough body of data to examine the fit of the model.

The preceding gives us an introductory conception of what a stochastic model looks like and what an operator is, so we turn now to the theory of stochastic models in general.

Experimental Events and Model Events

It will be recalled that on each trial the subject chooses a response and the experimenter an outcome, a pairing that is called an *experimental event*. Can the subject make the same response on different trials? Can the same outcome occur? An animal probably never turns right in a maze exactly the same way twice, and the outcome, in the sense of its impact, is probably never the same twice.

But the construction of theory, and, indeed, the very existence of behavioral science, requires that the answers to the above questions be yes—otherwise each event is a unique event. This gives rise to the notion of an equivalence class of experimental events—any two experimental events are in the same equivalence class if they exhibit certain interesting invariances that lead to the same operator being applied. The application of an operator is an event in the model called a *model event*.

This process of constructing an equivalence class of experimental events to which there corresponds a model event is a creative step in theory construction on the part of the modeler and is not to be taken casually. An illustration may help to clarify this point. Consider a subject guessing which of two lights, the right or the left, will come on in a sequence of such trials. Here a trial consists of the warning stimulus to signify the onset of the trial, the response of the subject, and the outcome.

Like the rat in the T-maze, the subject may start initially with no bias toward predicting the right light, i.e., $p_1 = .50$. One would expect, however, that if the right light comes on, an operator might apply that would increase the probability of predicting the right light. And, of course, another operator would apply whenever the left light came on, an operator that would *decrease* the probability of predicting the right light.

If the right light comes on with probability equal to π_1 and the left light otherwise, this is called a probability learning experiment. The important consideration for us at this point is that the distinct *experimental events*—(predict left, right light on) and (predict right, right light on)—are being treated as members of the same *model event*; i.e., the subject's response would be regarded as irrelevant in this learning process; only the experimenter's choice of outcome determines the operator that applies.

The experimenter may make such an assumption, construct the model, and be able to compare it against data with a model in which the subject's response is not considered irrelevant. Thus the forming of an equivalence class of experimental events to correspond to a model event has theoretical significance.

We now come to two principles that, if they are assumed to hold, lead to the linear operator family of models by Bush and Mosteller. These principles are known as the combining-classes condition and the independence-of-path assumption.

Combining-classes Condition

The combining-classes condition is a form of the "independence from other alternatives" axiom that plays so important a role in choice theory (see, for example, the constant ratio rule, Sec. 5.3; see also Sec. 7.3). In brief, it asserts that the definition of the response alternatives is arbitrary, i.e., the partitioning into discrete alternatives is not unique. Suppose, for example, a subject is in a probability learning experiment with three lights: red, white, and blue. Suppose on some trial the red light comes on and there is a change in the probabilities of the response alternatives. This condition says that it does not matter if the experimenter decides there are two alternatives, red and not red, before he calculates the probabilities for the next trial, or after. That is, the probability of the response "not red" on trial $n+1$ is the same whether we calculate the probability of the response "blue" and of "white" separately for trial $n+1$ and add these together or whether we add them together first and calculate the effect on "not red" of the complementary operator to "red."

Heuristically, the idea is that the effect of the event on the probability of the response "red" is not dependent on the *distribution* of probability over the other responses.

Independence-of-path Assumption

The independence-of-path assumption says that the probability of any response on the next trial is dependent only on its probability on the preceding trial and the event that occurred. This means that the history prior to the last trial is entirely embodied in the probabilities of the responses on that trial. If, for example, two animals have the same probability for a given response, it doesn't matter if their detailed histories are different. Any differences in content and length of their respective sequences are irrelevant.

Another way of interpreting the meaning of this assumption is that there are no delayed effects of an event. The effect of the occurrence of an event on a trial is manifested immediately and completely in the probabilities for the next trial.

A brief review of the combining-classes condition and its implication when taken in conjuction with the independence-of-path assumption is given by Bush (1960). A major consequence is that the operators must be of the form

$$Qp = \alpha p + a, \tag{9.4}$$

i.e., a linear operator. The operator shown in Eq. (9.2) is a special case in which $\alpha = 1 - a$.

This brings us to the matter of admissible values of the parameters and the various forms in which the linear operator may be written.

Form of the Linear Operator

For some purposes it is sometimes useful to write the linear operator in a different form than the *slope-intercept* form shown in Eq. (9.4). For example, we may substitute for α the expression $1 - a - b$ and we would still have a linear equation with two unknowns. Substituting in Eq. (9.4) and expanding, we may write

$$Qp = p + a(1 - p) - bp, \tag{9.5}$$

which is known as the *gain-loss form*. We see from this form that the new value of p is equal to the old value plus an increment proportional to how far p is from the value 1 and a decrement proportional to p itself. In the context in which p is the probability of a correct response and represents the degree to which it has been learned, and the operator reflects a positively reinforcing event, the gain when this operator is applied is proportional to the amount to be learned and the loss (forgetting) is proportional to how much was already learned.

A very useful form of the linear operator is known as the *fixed-point* form. Again we introduce a new parameter, λ, defined as follows:

$$\lambda = \frac{a}{1-\alpha}.$$

Substituting $(1-\alpha)\lambda$ for a in Eq. (9.4), we have

$$Qp = \alpha p + (1-\alpha)\lambda. \qquad (9.6)$$

This form of the linear operator gets its name because when $p = \lambda$ the operator becomes the identity operator; i.e., $Qp = p$. The name *fixed-point* form comes from the fact that λ is a limit point, a fixed value that p approaches when the operator is applied repeatedly. This relation may be shown as follows. If we apply the operator in Eq. (9.6) a second time, we have

$$Q(Qp) = \alpha[\alpha p + (1-\alpha)\lambda] + (1-\alpha)\lambda$$
$$= \alpha^2 p + (1-\alpha^2)\lambda.$$

This result suggests the possibility that if the operator were applied n times we would have the expression

$$Q^n p = \alpha^n p + (1-\alpha^n)\lambda. \qquad (9.7)$$

We know this is true for $n = 1$. Therefore, we assume it is true for any n and see if it is true for $n+1$. If so, we have proved Eq. (9.7) to be true for any integral value of n by induction. Proceeding in this manner, we have

$$Q(Q^n p) = \alpha[\alpha^n p + (1-\alpha^n)\lambda] + (1-\alpha)\lambda.$$

Expanding,

$$Q(Q^n p) = \alpha^{n+1} p + \lambda(\alpha - \alpha^{n+1} + 1 - \alpha)$$

$$= \alpha^{n+1} p + (1-\alpha^{n+1})\lambda.$$

Therefore, the general expression given by Eq. (9.7) is seen to be correct.

If α is between zero and one, then the limit of α^n as $n \to \infty$ is zero; hence,

$$\lim_{n \to \infty} Q^n p = p_\infty = \lambda. \qquad (9.8)$$

Therefore Qp moves p toward λ asymptotically, meaning that as n increases, the difference between p and λ will become arbitrarily small.

Each of these three forms of the linear operator has two parameters and some of their relations may be readily perceived from Fig. 9.1, in which p_{n+1}

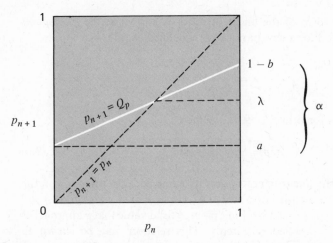

Fig. 9.1 Relations among the parameters of the various forms of the linear operator.

is shown as a function, Qp, of p_n. We see, for example, that α is a learning rate parameter; it is an inverse measure of the *effectiveness* of an event in increasing p.

Inasmuch as the function is constrained to the unit square, i.e., probability must be conserved, there are restrictions on the parameters:

$$0 \leq a, b, \lambda \leq 1; \qquad -a \leq \alpha \leq 1-a.$$

But if α is negative, p oscillates about λ and closes in like a damped pendulum. It is not characteristic of learning phenomena that the probability of a particular response oscillates above and below a particular value before coming to rest but rather that it approaches it from above or below. Hence, in this domain of application of stochastic models it is usually found that $\alpha \geq 0$, which requires that $0 \leq a+b \leq 1$; generally, for most experiments, it is found that estimates of α tend to run above .8.

In many learning experiments the task consists of acquiring a particular response so that the probability of that response approaches unity and the probability of other responses approaches zero. Hence, the most commonly occurring linear operators are of the form

$$Q_1 p = \alpha_1 p$$

$$Q_2 p = \alpha_2 p + (1-\alpha_2).$$

The first is an "extinction" operator which, with repeated application, moves p to zero. The other operator, Q_2, is an "acquisition" operator with the limit point $\lambda_2 = 1$.

Another operator sometimes needed is the identity operator, $Qp = p$, that is, one that leaves p unchanged. This operator is found useful, for example, in a T-maze experiment in which one side is partially reinforced and the other side is never reinforced. If the animal is not reinforced on some trial, it appears that the probability of the correct turn remains unchanged. Interestingly enough, if after acquisition an extinction series is run with no reinforcement on any trial, the probability of the formerly correct turn decreases, which means that the identity operator is no longer applicable. Therefore, during the acquisition phase, the experimental event of no reinforcement corresponds to one model event, the "identity operator," and during the extinction phase the same experimental event corresponds to a different model event, the "extinction operator." This change gives rise to the serious question of the invariance of events. An experimental event corresponds to an event operator in the model, as pointed out earlier, and stochastic models require that this correspondence be invariant.

Types of Events   On any trial n in a learning experiment, each subject makes a response to the stimulus that was present and an event occurs that may change the probability of any given response. It is evident that after a few trials a group of initially homogeneous subjects, in the sense of all having the same probability distribution over the response alternatives, could become differentiated by distinct sequences of events.

For example, with two event operators, Q_1 and Q_2, in two trials there are $2^2 = 4$ possible histories illustrated by the branching diagram of Fig. 9.2. On the left is a single node indicating that all the animals are assumed to have the same p on trial 1. For some animals Q_1 applies as a result of the event on trial 1 and for some animals Q_2 applies. Therefore, on trial 2 we have two nodes, p_{21} and p_{22}, indicating two different values of p and two corresponding subsets of animals.

Again, as a result of trial 2, each of these subsets of animals is par-

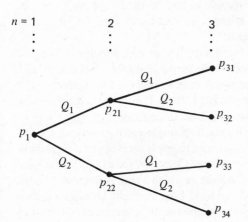

Fig. 9.2   The branching process leading to the distribution of p on each trial.

titioned by the two possible events. Therefore on trial 3 we have four possible distinct values of p corresponding to the four distinct histories represented by the four distinct paths through the branching process to the four distinct termini. Of course, some of these branches may come back together again, indicating that the same value of p may be arrived at by different paths.

With k event operators, after n trials there could be k^n distinct histories and as many different values of p for any one response.

In principle, then, one could calculate from the model the probability of a particular response being made by individuals with a particular history, and then such a theoretical value could be compared with experimental data to test the model.

This tremendous richness of the operator models rapidly exceeds practical experimental limits. With two alternatives and 10 trials, for example, an initially homogeneous group of subjects could be differentiated into 1000 subsets (1,024), each with a different value of p. Although this high degree of differentiation does not necessarily or even usually take place, it is not customary in most cases to work statistically with the small groups of homogeneous subjects characterized by the same history.

As an alternative one may work with the total distribution of p on a given trial and attempt to construct descriptive statistics of this distribution and thereby describe the flow of probability among the response alternatives from trial to trial. Thus, although the model may lead to too fine discrimination of subjects on the basis of histories, statistics such as the average probability of a particular response may be calculated from the model and these statistics can be compared with data. Most of the mathematics of the operator models, and, indeed, many other models, is concerned with statistical problems, such as estimation of parameters, the descriptive statistics of the trial to trial distribution of response probabilities, and testing goodness of fit.

In attempting to construct descriptive statistics of the distribution of probabilities on a given trial, it becomes apparent that experimental events may be classified into three types corresponding to their relation to model events: experimenter-controlled events, subject-controlled events, and experimenter-subject-controlled events.

In the first type, the experimenter-controlled events, which model event applies on a given trial is determined solely by the *outcome* on that trial and is independent of the subject's response. A case in point is the model for the probability learning experiment mentioned earlier. This type of model event is mathematically the most tractable and best understood but suitable only for certain specially contrived experiments. The single-event model is a special case in which the same model event is assumed to apply on every trial regardless of the response of the subject or the outcome. Consider, for example, a single-unit T-maze with reward always on the right in which a trial is terminated only after an animal successfully reached the food box. It might be assumed that turning left followed by turning right was equivalent in the model to turning

Outcome

		Reinforcement on right $\equiv O_1$	Reinforcement on left $\equiv O_2$
Subject's response	Right turn $\equiv A_1$	(A_1, O_1)	(A_1, O_2)
	Left turn $\equiv A_2$	(A_2, O_1)	(A_2, O_2)

Fig. 9.3

right in the first place. If this assumption is made, the same model event, and hence a single operator, is applied on every trial.

Not unexpectedly now, a subject-controlled experiment is one in which model events are determined solely by the *responses* of the subjects and are independent of the outcome. A case in point would be a single-unit T-maze with rewards on both the right and the left sides on every trial. If the model events were an operator for turning right and being rewarded and another for turning left and being rewarded, clearly which operator is to be applied is determined by the subject's response. If there were reward always on one side and punishment always on the other and two corresponding operators, the subject's response would again always determine which operator is to be applied.

Finally, then, we have the type of experiments called experimenter-subject-controlled; in this type knowledge of both the subject's response and the outcome is required to decide which model event occurred and hence which operator applies. In a T-maze, for example, with reward sometimes on the right and sometimes on the left, on any particular trial any of four experimental events might occur, as shown in Fig. 9.3. If different model events are associated with these different experimental events, then clearly which operator applies depends on both the experimenter and the subject.

The Expected Operator

As mentioned earlier, much of the work with operator models involves the search for descriptive statistics such as the mean and variance on trial n of the distribution of p values for a particular response.

A very simple example of this kind of work is the estimation of the mean p value in an experimenter-controlled sequence of events. Consider the following experiment: a single-unit T-maze with reward on the right with probability π and on the left with probability $1 - \pi$. Suppose the model assumes that the effect of turning one way and receiving no reward is the same as the effect of turning the other way and being rewarded. This assumption might be appropriate if we contrived an experiment in which an individual, when he makes the wrong response, knows the other response would have been correct and there is no differential response effect.

In this case we would have two operators Q_1 and Q_2, where Q_1 is applied if the experimental event (A_1, O_1) or (A_2, O_1) occurs [in which O_1 is food on the right (no food on the left)] and Q_2 is applied if (A_1, O_2) or (A_2, O_2) occurs [in which O_2 is food on the left (no food on the right)]. The operators in slope-intercept form are

$$Q_1 p = \alpha_1 p + a_1$$

$$Q_2 p = \alpha_2 p + a_2.$$

Regardless of what the subject does, the first operator would apply with probability π and the second operator with probability $1 - \pi$. That is, on the first trial, we would expect a proportion p_1 of the animals to turn right and $1 - p_1$ to turn left—and a fraction π of those who turned right would find food and the same fraction of those who turned left would not find food.

The operator Q_1, then, may be expected to apply to a fraction π of the animals,

$$\pi = \pi p_1 + \pi(1 - p_1);$$

and the operator Q_2 would apply to the remainder, $1 - \pi$.

Designating the average value of p_n as $\bar{p}_n$, we have, for the average of p_2,

$$\bar{p}_2 = \pi(Q_1 p_1) + (1 - \pi)(Q_2 p_1)$$

$$= \pi(\alpha_1 p_1 + a_1) + (1 - \pi)(\alpha_2 p_1 + a_2)$$

$$= [\pi \alpha_1 + (1 - \pi)\alpha_2]p_1 + [\pi a_1 + (1 - \pi)a_2]$$

$$\bar{p}_2 = \bar{\alpha} p_1 + \bar{a}.$$

We see that the average value of p on the second trial can be obtained by applying a linear operator to p_1, the parameters of which are a weighted average of those of the simple linear operators.

It is easy to show by mathematical induction that

$$\bar{p}_n = \bar{\alpha} \bar{p}_{n-1} + \bar{a},$$

and we have for this experiment what is called the *expected operator*:

$$Q\bar{p} = \bar{\alpha}\bar{p} + \bar{a}. \tag{9.9}$$

This expected operator gives the expected proportion of animals to turn right on each trial (assuming all animals have the same parameters) and one might ask: When learning is complete what proportion of the animals will be turning right?

It will be recalled that the asymptotic value of an operator applied repeatedly is the parameter λ in the fixed-point form of the operator. As the expected operator is itself a linear operator here, then

$$\bar{\lambda} = \frac{\bar{a}}{1-\bar{\alpha}}$$

and would equal $\bar{p}_\infty$ [see Eq. (9.8)]. Hence,

$$\bar{\lambda} = \frac{\pi a_1 + (1-\pi)a_2}{1 - \pi\alpha_1 - (1-\pi)\alpha_2}$$

If the reward were the same whether it occurred on the right or on the left, we might be willing to assume that the learning parameters α_1 and α_2 were equal:

$$\alpha_1 = \alpha_2 = \alpha;$$

so $\bar{\lambda}$ may be written

$$\bar{\lambda} = \frac{\pi a_1}{1-\alpha} + \frac{(1-\pi)a_2}{1-\alpha}$$

$$= \pi\lambda_1 + (1-\pi)\lambda_2.$$

But λ_1 and λ_2 are themselves the limit points of their respective operators and it is not unreasonable to assume that if Q_1 were repeatedly applied the animals would all eventually learn to turn right; i.e., $\lambda_1 = 1$. Similarly, if only Q_2 were repeatedly applied, the animals would all learn to turn left, and so the probability of turning right would go to zero; i.e., $\lambda_2 = 0$.

Substituting, we have the result

$$\bar{\lambda} = \pi, \tag{9.10}$$

which says that in this experimental situation the asymptotic proportion of a group of subjects making a particular response would equal the probability of that response being reinforced.

This result was first obtained by Estes and Straughan (1954), and the phenomenon, when it occurs, has come to be known as "probability matching" behavior. For about a decade there was a considerable flurry of research on probability matching, some of which is discussed in a later section.

In an essentially similar manner expressions can be derived for the second moment, and hence the variance, of the p values generated by the model in this experimenter-controlled sequence of events.

For models with subject-controlled and experimenter-subject-controlled events, only recursive formulas for the moments of the distribution of p values have been obtained. These are expressions that are functions of the previous trial; for example, the first moment (the mean) on trial n depends on the first and the second moment on trial $n-1$; but the second moment on trial $n-1$ depends on the first, second, and third moments on trial $n-2$; and so on. This complicated set of equations has not been solved and has limited usefulness except for certain special applications.

Good use has been made of the computer in such cases by simulating the model by what is called Monte Carlo methods. A set of hypothetical subjects called stat-rats are "run" in the experiment according to the model. This generates the model's data for which descriptive statistics of interest may be calculated and compared with those calculated on data from real subjects. This procedure of using a computer to derive the consequences of a model is coming into wide use, as it permits comparisons to be made that may not otherwise be possible.

Nonlinear Operator Models

Until relatively recently the conception that learning consists of the building up of an associative bond between stimulus and response was almost unrivaled. The fundamental variable in this conception is that of response strength. Behavioral manifestations such as probability of response, latency of response, and amplitude of response are all viewed as functions of this more fundamental variable, response strength, measured on a different scale.

A recent formalization of this conception is Luce's β model. This model is based on his response strength scale, which itself is derived from his choice axiom. The choice axiom and the scaling theory are discussed in Sec. 5.3.

It will be recalled that the linear operator family of models, frequently called the α models, is a consequence of the assumption of path independence and the combining-classes condition. The combining-classes condition requires that the effect of an event on a response probability be independent of the probability distribution over the responses.

Luce retains the independence-of-path assumption but has a different invariance condition on the response probabilities. His basic scaling assumption (equivalent to the choice axiom) is that the *ratio* of the probabilities of two responses be independent of the other responses in the set; this assumption is also known as the constant ratio rule (Clarke 1957).

As seen in Sec. 5.3, this assumption implies a scale of response strength, the v scale, related to the probability of choice by the expression

$$p(A_i) = \frac{v(A_i)}{\sum\limits_{j} v(A_j)} \tag{9.11}$$

where $v(A_i)$ is the strength of the response A_i. That is, if the constant ratio rule is satisfied, then there exists a set of numbers that may be associated with the alternatives as their scale values, having the property that the probability of choosing any alternative out of the set is equal to the scale value of that alternative divided by the sum of the scale values of all the alternatives.

In contrast to the Bush–Mosteller model in which the effect of an event was to change the probability of a response directly by application of a linear operator to p, the assumption that Luce makes is that the effect of an event is to operate *directly* on the response strength and hence *indirectly* on the response probability.

What should be the nature of the transformation on the response strength as a result of an event? Luce showed that as a consequence of two conditions the only admissible transformation is multiplication by a constant.

The two conditions that lead to this conclusion are that (1) the transformation must be independent of the unit of measurement for response strength, the latter being measured on a ratio scale not an absolute scale, and (2) the scale of response strength is unbounded—there is no limit to the strength of an associative bond.

The only transformation on response strength that satisfies these two conditions is multiplication by a constant, and, of course, it must be a positive constant as response strength cannot be negative. We may note, furthermore, that response strength cannot be moved to zero or become infinite from some positive value by such a transformation, and so the probability of a response can never be zero or one.

Luce assumes path independence as in the Bush–Mosteller model, and this means that for a particular response alternative, which operator applies depends only on the event on that trial and not on the previous sequence of events or on the trial number or on the response strength. The transformation on the strength of a particular response, then, may be represented as follows:

$$v_{i,n} = a_k v_{i,n-1}, \tag{9.12}$$

where the subscripts indicate the event (k), the response (i), and the trial (n) and a_k is a positive constant.

Suppose, for example, there are just two responses with strengths v_1 and v_2 on the $n-1$st trial with response probabilities p and q, respectively, and event k occurs. Then,

$$v_{1,n} = a_k v_{1,n-1}$$

$$v_{2,n} = b_k v_{2,n-1}.$$

The effect of the event on the response probability p, then, may be written as follows:

From Eq. (9.11) we have on the n—1st trial

$$p_{n-1} = \frac{v_{1,\,n-1}}{v_{1,\,n-1}+v_{2,\,n-1}} \qquad (9.13)$$

and on the nth trial

$$p_n = \frac{v_{1,\,n}}{v_{1,\,n}+v_{2,\,n}} = \frac{a_k v_{1,\,n-1}}{a_k v_{1,\,n-1}+b_k v_{2,\,n-1}}. \qquad (9.14)$$

Dividing the numerator and denominator by $b_k v_{2,\,n-1}$ and letting $a_k/b_k = \beta_k$ and $v_{1,\,n-1}/v_{2,\,n-1} = v_{n-1}$, we may rewrite Eqs. (9.13) and (9.14) in the form

$$p_{n-1} = \frac{v_{n-1}}{1+v_{n-1}}$$

$$p_n = \frac{\beta_k v_{n-1}}{1+\beta_k v_{n-1}}. \qquad (9.15)$$

Eliminating v_{n-1} in these two equations by solving each for v_{n-1}, setting the resulting two equations equal, and solving for p_n give us the nonlinear[2] operator of what is called the β model:

$$p_n = Q_k p_{n-1} = \frac{\beta_k p_{n-1}}{q_{n-1}+\beta_k p_{n-1}} \qquad (9.16)$$

where $q_{n-1} = 1-p_{n-1}$.

We see, of course, that if the strength of a response is ever zero or if $\beta = 1$ there is no learning.

To see what the limit points of this operator are, we first arrive at an expression for Q^n analogous to Eq. (9.7) and then carry it to the limit, as in Eq. (9.8).

From Eq. (9.15) we may write for the probability of response 1 on trial 2

$$p_2 = \frac{\beta v_1}{1+\beta v_1}$$

---

[2]Although the operator is clearly nonlinear as applied to the response probability p, it may readily be seen to be a linear operator applied to the ratio $p/(1-p)$. In Eq. (9.16) divide p_n by q_n and you have the new operator

$$\frac{p_n}{q_n} = \beta \frac{p_{n-1}}{q_{n-1}} = \beta v_{n-1}.$$

(we have dropped the subscript on β for clarity), and for the next trial

$$p_3 = \frac{\beta v_2}{1+\beta v_2},$$

where

$$v_2 = \frac{v_{1,2}}{v_{2,2}} = \frac{av_{1,1}}{bv_{1,1}} = \beta v_1,$$

and substituting βv_1 for v_2, we have

$$p_3 = \frac{\beta(\beta v_1)}{1+\beta(\beta v_1)} = \frac{\beta^2 v_1}{1+\beta^2 v_1}.$$

It can readily be proved by mathematical induction that, in general, after n successive trials in which this same operator has applied,

$$p_n = \frac{\beta^n v_1}{1+\beta^n v_1} = \frac{v_1}{(1/\beta^n)+v_1},$$

and we see that the limit as n approaches infinity is

$$\lim_{n\to\infty} Q^n p = \begin{cases} 0 & \text{if } \beta < 1 \\ 1 & \text{if } \beta > 1, \end{cases}$$

i.e., it has only extreme limit points in contrast to operators in the linear model which, as we saw, may have limit points other than zero or one.

Another nonlinear operator model, investigated by Audley and Jonckhere (1956), is known as the urn model because of the physical analogy they employ in setting up the equations for the process. They consider an urn with red and black balls in it, a single ball is drawn, and the number of red or black balls in the urn is changed accordingly.

The number of each kind of ball corresponds to the respective strength of the two responses; drawing a red or black ball corresponds, respectively, to a correct rewarded response and an incorrect unrewarded response. The change in the composition of the urn reflects the effect of reinforcement or nonreinforcement.

In two further papers Audley shows how latencies of response as well as probabilities may be described (1958) and emphasizes the applicability of the theory to the description of the performance of a single subject by reporting an experiment with one rat (1957)!

Both the urn model and the β model are strength models in the sense that the effect of reinforcement is directly on the strength of a response and hence indirectly on the probability of the reponse that reflects relative strength.

As Restle (1959) has pointed out, both these models are special cases of a basic assumption of linearity of effect on response strength, $v_{n+1} = av_n + b$, where v_n is the strength of a response on the nth trial. In the β model b is zero and in the urn model $a = 1$.

It is probably obvious that growth of response strength will be more rapid in the β model, which grows like compound interest, than in the urn model, which grows by a constant increment, and that in both models the strength of a response may increase without bound. Luce (1959, p. 96–99) has shown that his response strength model, with some different assumptions, can give rise to the linear operator of Bush and Mosteller, which he calls the α model. To achieve this, he assumes in the first place that the effect of each reinforcing event may be expressed by a linear transformation on the response strengths. Then, to get linearity of change in the probabilities at the same time, he further assumes that the effect of each event on the total response strength is multiplication by some constant factor. This multiplying factor is the sum of the multiplying factors applied to each response strength. Each operator, then, induces a characteristic proportional change in each response strength and a characteristic proportional change in the total response strength.

These assumptions yield the linear operator model for the effect of a reinforcing event on the response probabilities. Therefore, in brief, the linear operator model can be obtained from Luce's choice axiom by assuming, in addition, that the effect of a reinforcing event is to change each response strength by a multiplying factor and, also, to change the total response strength by some constant multiple. In the special case in which the latter constant multiple is 1, the total response strength is a constant, and the effect of a reinforcing event is to redistribute this total.

Audley and Jonckhere also derive the linear operator as a special case of the urn model in which the total number of balls is a constant; i.e., increasing the number of red balls decreases the number of black balls by the same amount.

It is worthwhile noting that the same formal model, in this case the linear operator model, may arise as a consequence of quite different arguments from quite different conceptions: (1) the independence-of-path assumption and the combining-classes condition used by Bush and Mosteller; (2) proportional change assumption for the several response strengths and their total sum in the context of Luce's choice axiom; and (3) a fixed number of balls in the urn model of Audley and Jonckhere.

It should be clear that if some particular conception of an underlying process is unacceptable, it may be possible to find a more palatable one that can lead to the same formal model. Rejection of a conceptualization does not require rejection of the model, and, of course, successful performance by the model does not require acceptance of the conception from which it was derived.

Commutativity of Operators

An interesting feature of the β model is that the operators commute. This means that for any sequence of events response probabilities do not depend on the order in which the events occurred but only on the number of times each one occurred. If on the first three trials for one animal the sequence of events was such that the operators were applied in the order $Q_1 Q_2 Q_1$ and for another animal the sequence was $Q_2 Q_1 Q_1$, then, if they started with the same response probabilities, they ended with the same probabilities.

That this property holds for the β model may be seen from Eq. (9.14) or, more readily, from footnote 2; the effect of a sequence of events on response strength is given by multiplying the corresponding values of β and it does not matter in what order the values are multiplied.

The psychological significance of commutativity of operators is in the implication that events cannot be forgotten. It makes no difference to the probability of a response, i.e., its strength, if, for example, a particular event occurs at the beginning or at the end of a long sequence of other events.

This property of commutativity does not hold in general for the linear operator model, except under the special condition that all operators have the same limit point, λ, or if one of them is the identity operator. Aside from its psychological implications, commutativity is a mathematically simplifying property.

As Sternberg (1963) points out, it is interesting to note that the linear operator model and the β model are the modern versions of the two principal types of early empirical learning equations discussed by Gulliksen: the linear model leading to a negatively accelerated learning curve and the β model leading to a logistic function that is S-shaped.

An Experimental Comparison of the Linear and Nonlinear Operator Models

It appears not to be difficult for one of these models (linear and nonlinear operator) to yield a reasonably close fit to the data of any suitably designed experiment; thus a more common strategy is to compare the fit of two or more models to many aspects of the same data. Indeed, the point is put very well by R. R. Bush: "we shouldn't 'test' goodness-of-fit, we should 'measure' it. And the measures used are most valuable when two or more theories are being compared" (1963, p. 432). And further on he states that "the evaluation of scientific models and theories is not a simple acceptance-rejection problem. We do not 'test' for goodness-of-fit and then either throw the model away or send it to the Bureau of Standards" (p. 462).

Rather, what is done is to seek out the features of one model that result in fitting certain aspects of the data better than another model and then by an inductive inferential process take advantage of these insights in revising the theory. There is no known logic for inductive inference; the role of creativity in science is still secure.

The most difficult of all tasks faced by a model is to predict performance in one experimental situation having estimated the parameters of the model in a previous related experiment. This type of comparison is a study of what is called parameter invariance, and the experiment discussed here is to be taken as illustrative rather than conclusive. This experiment, reported by Curt Fey (1961), compares the Bush–Mosteller linear operator model, referred to as the α model, with the nonlinear β model in a study of parameter invariance.

  Fifty rats were used in the experiment; the apparatus was a single-unit T-maze. The first part of the experiment consisted of running the rats for 30 days, one trial per day, with reward always on the right. For the second part of the experiment the rats were divided randomly into two groups: one group was always rewarded thereafter on the left side (100:0 group) and the other group was rewarded 75 percent of the time on the left and 25 percent of the time on the right in a random sequence (75:25 group). This second part of the experiment lasted 35 days.

  The models and their parameters were defined as shown in Fig. 9.4. Note that in addition to the initial probability, p_1, each model has two parameters: the linear model has parameters α_1 and α_2 associated with reward and nonreward, respectively, and the nonlinear model has parameters β_1 and β_2 serving the same two purposes.

  The parameters were estimated from the data of the 100:0 group in the second part of the experiment and model values were calculated for various

Experimental event		Operators for p_{n+1}	
Response	Outcome	α Model	β Model
Right turn	Reward	$\alpha_1 p_n + (1 - \alpha_1)$	$\dfrac{\beta_1 p_n}{\beta_1 p_n + 1 - p_n}$
Right turn	Nonreward	$\alpha_2 p_n$	$\dfrac{p_n}{p_n + \beta_2(1 - p_n)}$
Left turn	Reward	$\alpha_1 p_n$	$\dfrac{p_n}{p_n + \beta_1(1 - p_n)}$
Left turn	Nonreward	$\alpha_2 p_n + 1 - \alpha_2$	$\dfrac{\beta_2 p_n}{\beta_2 p_n + 1 - p_n}$

Fig. 9.4 Operators of the α and β models for Curt Fey's experiment.

statistics expected for the 75:25 group, which could then be compared with the corresponding statistics from the actual data. A more detailed account of the procedure is as follows.

In the case of the α model the initial probability p was taken to be 1. The parameters α_1 and α_2 were estimated by deriving analytical expressions for the expected number of trials before the first success and the expected total number of errors. These expressions were then equated to the corresponding observed means and the unknown parameters could then be solved for. The estimates were $\alpha_1 = .858$ and $\alpha_2 = .955$; reward was more effective than nonreward.

Initial estimates of the β model parameters were obtained by similar methods but these estimates were modified by means of a Monte Carlo exploration until the learning curve generated by the model was "similar" to that for the data on the 100:0 group and the total number of errors generated by the model matched the corresponding data statistic. The estimates were

TABLE 9.1 Matching of the Models to the 100:0 Group

	Means			Standard Errors		
		Predicted by			Predicted by	
Statistic	*Observed*	α *Model*	β *Model*	*Observed*	α *Model*	β *Model*
Number of S's	25	100	500			
Number of trials	35	35	35			
Total number of errors*‡	12.28	12.28	12.39	.76	.00	.012
Trial of last error	23.16	22.10	26.45	1.00	.25	.038
Trial of first success†	6.88	6.87	6.59	.48	.00	.024
Number of RR sequences	7.48	7.32	7.01	.56	.00	.014
RL	4.76	4.85	5.32	.28	.09	.016
LR	3.80	3.85	4.41	.28	.10	.014
LL	17.96	17.98	17.26	.80	.22	.024
Number of L runs of:						
Length 1	2.00	1.81	1.86	.20	.10	.012
2	.56	.81	.87	.08	.03	.014
3	.44	.51	.57	.08	.03	.006
4	.32	.37	.38	.04	.04	.006
5	.08	.28	.30	.04	.02	.001
Number of R runs of:						
Length 1	2.60	2.70	3.12	.24	.00	.014
2	.80	.81	.83	.16	.00	.008
3	.40	.40	.36	.08	.00	.006
4	.24	.27	.28	.04	.00	.008
5	.20	.20	.20	.04	.00	.004
Total number of R runs	4.80	4.96	5.38	.28	.00	.018

Note: Standard error of the mean was computed from range approximation.
*Used to estimate α_1.
†Used to estimate α_2.
‡Used with shape of learning curve to estimate β_1 and β_2 simultaneously.

TABLE 9.2 TESTING PARAMETER INVARIANCE: FIT OF THE MODELS TO THE 75:25 GROUP

Statistic	Means			Standard Errors		
		Predicted by			Predicted by	
	Observed	α Model	β Model	Observed	α Model	β Model
Number of animals	25	100	200			
Total number of errors	15.92	19.21	19.43	1.04	.22	.03
Trial of last error	27.32	32.71	33.59	1.04	.21	.045
Trial of first success	7.52	7.19	7.56	.64	.16	.07
Number of RR sequences	10.24	11.85	11.81	.88	.25	.045
RL	5.44	7.09	7.33	.28	.10	.035
LR	4.68	6.37	6.75	.32	.09	.035
LL	13.64	8.69	8.11	1.12	.24	.08
Number of L runs of:						
Length 1	2.48	3.63	3.55	.20	.10	.045
2	1.16	1.62	1.68	.20	.05	.03
3	.40	.77	1.09	.08	.03	.02
4	.24	.41	.52	.04	.02	.015
5	.16	.23	.21	.04	.02	.01
Number of R runs of:						
Length 1	2.88	3.52	3.70	.20	.10	.035
2	1.16	1.50	1.63	.12	.05	.03
3	.48	.66	.79	.12	.04	.015
4	.36	.54	.47	.08	.03	.02
5	.20	.38	.29	.08	.02	.01
Total number of R runs	5.68	7.36	7.62	.32	.09	.035

Note: The model parameters were estimated from the 100:0 group. Standard errors were computed from range approximation.

$p_1 = .97$, $\beta_1 = .952$, and $\beta_2 = .647$, implying that nonreward was more effective than reward.[3]

The adequacy of the fit of the models to the data of the 100:0 group, on which the estimations of the parameters are based, is indicated in Table 9.1. The test of parameter invariance of the models is indicated by the adequacy of the fit to the data of the 75:25 group, presented in Table 9.2. Unfortunately, the absence of a quantitative expression for the overall adequacy of the fit of the models prevents their being compared in a simple way. Fey says that the apparent superiority of the α over the β model is not real because the method of estimating the parameters for the α model was superior to the Monte Carlo procedure for estimating the parameters of the β model; he concludes that both models fit the data about equally well.[4]

[3]It will be recalled that $\beta = 1$ implies no learning. For $\beta < 1$, the limit point is zero, and the smaller β, the faster the limit is approached. Therefore, the conclusion in the β model is that nonreward was more effective, and in the α model that reward was more effective. We see that the answer to the question of whether reward is more effective than nonreward is model-bound.

[4]It also appears that the two models fit each other better than either fits the data.

Of course, it is unreasonable to require that all parameters remain unchanged from one experimental situation to another; rather one requires that the model specify how the parameters are to be modified given the parameters of the experimental situation. It is clear from trial of last error, Table 9.2, that the stat-rats of the models learn more slowly, and it is also evident that the number of runs of various lengths are discrepant from the data.

Fey remarks that the discrepancy in learning rate could be handled by specifying how the parameters change in going from a continuous reinforcement to a partial reinforcement schedule but that no small change in the parameters would increase the fit to the "runs" data.

Of course, the requirement that the parameters of a model remain unchanged over experimental situations can be modified to specify how the parameters are to change with changes in the experimental conditions. A parameter for a model event ideally reflects constant features of the organism and the stimulus situation, which hopefully remain constant in any one experiment run under constant environmental conditions. That such parameters should remain unchanged when the experimental conditions are modified is perhaps too much to expect.

A distinction should be clearly made between the notion of the invariance of the *parameters* associated with a model event and the constancy, or lack of it, of the event *effects*. The former refers to the invariance of the formal operator associated with the model, whereas the effect of the operator is a change in the magnitude of the response probability p, and this change, Δp, is not a constant but depends on the magnitude of p on that particular trial.

9.3 STATE MODELS

The class of models discussed in the previous section could be called infinite state models in the sense that the probability of a response may take on any of an infinite set of values. The second class of models, discussed in this section, could be called finite state models in the analogous sense that a response probability may take on only a finite number of distinct values, corresponding to the finite number of states to which the learning process is confined. This distinction in itself is of no particular theoretical significance, but what is important is the underlying conception of the learning process that brings this distinction about.

The theory is a sophisticated development of stimulus-reponse association theory in the Guthrie (1946) tradition. A mathematically rigorous formulation of the ideas was initiated by Estes (1950), who is also most responsible for the direction taken in its development. The basic theoretical ideas are collectively known as stimulus sampling theory in which *stimulus, response, association,* and *reinforcement* are primitive terms. In the case of the stochastic models discussed in the previous section, stimulus, response, association, and reinforcement were not primitive terms. The concept of reinforcement was used as a convenient term to indicate the application of an operator to the probability of a response; we did not need to be talking about learning at all but could have been talking about the ups and downs of the Dow-Jones index of stock prices.

Stimulus sampling theory treats reinforcement and stimulus-response associations on a "molecular" level, in terms of stimulus elements or components, which are left undefined. Phenomena such as transfer of training and stimulus generalization naturally suggest a notion of common elements in different stimulus situations, an idea undoubtedly attributable to Plato but which has flowered only in the last 15 to 20 years.

Stimulus sampling theory breaks up the learning process into discrete trials just as stochastic learning theory does: A trial consists of the presentation of a stimulus, the selection of a response according to an associated set of probabilities, an outcome (reinforcement), and a flow of probability among the response alternatives. The big psychological difference lies in the following ideas.

Stimuli are conceived of as a set of elements or components, left undefined. Each stimulus element is assumed to be associated with exactly one response. The presence (effectiveness) of a stimulus element on a trial affects the probability of the associated response being selected on that trial. A reinforcing event is one that affects the associations between stimulus components and responses and hence affects the probabilities of the responses for the next trial.

Since Estes' initial formulation of these basic ideas, there has been a considerable proliferation of model types and a vast amount of both theoretical and experimental literature. The half-life of most of this literature is exceedingly short. In the 1966 volume of the *Journal of Mathematical Psychology*, for example, there are 11 papers pertaining to mathematical learning theory and 5 of them make no reference to papers published before 1960. Such statistics attest to the vigor and rapidity of development in this area, but they also testify to the difficulty of treating this area in an introductory text on mathematical psychology.

We shall try to provide an overall view of the variety of models within the area, an indication of what has motivated them, a feeling for the trends and directions that seem apparent even in their short history, and some familiarity with the mathematical form and elementary problems of some of the models.

Organization of Models

In surveying the variety of stimulus sampling theory models, one observes two principal aspects in terms of which the models may be conveniently classified and related for our purposes. One of these aspects is the number of elements a stimulus is assumed to be composed of. This number may be specified in the model to be precisely one or two elements, for example, or

Sampling scheme						
Sample size greater than 1		Sample size = 1				
Sample size random	Sample size fixed		1	Small element models		Number of stimulus components
1-element model			1	Small element models		
2-element model			2	Small element models		
Linear model	Component models	Pattern models	$\cdots N \cdots$ — 8	N-element models		

Fig. 9.5 Organization of models.

some unknown but relatively large number N. Models assuming only 1 or 2 stimulus components are sometimes called small-element models and the others are called N-element models.

The other aspect of the models convenient for classification purposes is the sampling scheme. On each trial a sample of the stimulus elements is effective. The samples drawn on successive trials may consist of exactly one element or more than one element. If the sampling scheme calls for a sample size of more than one element, then the samples may be required to be of fixed sample size s, with all elements having equal probability s/N of being sampled; or the size of samples may be assumed to be a random variable. In Fig. 9.5 these aspects of the models have been portrayed showing the classification of the models that results.

We should hasten to point out that there are many more ways in which these models may differ, for example, by introducing "trial-dependent" sampling schemes or "adaptive" sampling schemes (e.g., Restle 1955), but these complications are not necessary for an elementary survey. Some of the other ways in which learning models differ, including the stochastic learning models of the previous section, are discussed in a survey and classification of learning models by Restle (1959).

It should be emphasized that stimulus sampling theory is not a particular model to be accepted or rejected on the basis of some experimental test but rather a way of life in model building. It provides a framework or basic conception for stimulus-response theory that is rich in the number and variety of specific models that can be generated.

Our discussion of these models will follow chronological history as closely as possible to reveal more clearly the motivation underlying new developments and the fashion trends that appear. In capsule form the history begins with Estes' conception of what are called the component models, which turn out to predict successfully some of the results of experimental paradigms for probability learning and stimulus generalization. But the component models were not effective in handling some other aspects of these kinds of experiments or in handling other experimental paradigms, such as that for discrimination learning. He then introduced the conception of the pattern model that is also successful in accounting for certain aspects of these experimental paradigms, including some aspects not accounted for satisfactorily by the component models. The development of mixed models involving both pattern and component conceptions is a natural development and is being explored.

A quite important development was the mathematical and experimental exploration of the one-element model. The one-element model was developed in part because of several striking psychological implications it possessed and in part because of mathematical difficulties with more complex models. In certain very simple paired associate and concept identification experiments the one-element model has accounted for the data with remarkable accuracy. However, when these experiments have anything more than a very simple structure, the one-element model rapidly becomes inadequate to account for the observed learning. Some success has been achieved in more complex situations with two-element models, but they also make predictions that are not borne out in certain experiments.

These results have led to the introduction of additional psychological processes and more complex structure in the models and indeed a whole new way of thinking. The underlying conceptions of stimulus sampling theory seem to have given way to the formulation of the learning process in terms of a finite number of hypothetical psychological states such as long-term and short-term memory storage and transitions between these states induced by reinforcement. The language of learning theory is now information processing language with the use of encoding, storage, and retrieval processes making the influence of the computer apparent; the role it is playing is increasingly large.

This exceedingly abbreviated history ignores much and is correspondingly inadequate; it serves primarily to provide a quick overview and rough historical structure for what will be covered in more detail in the remainder of the chapter.

We shall first discuss component models, then pattern models, and finally small-element models.

Component Models

We can illustrate some of the basic concepts of the component models with a formulation for a simple conditioning experiment. Let us represent the conditioned stimulus as a set of N elements of which a subset C_n are in a conditioned state on the nth trial and $\bar{C}_n$ are unconditioned, where $N = C_n + \bar{C}_n$. C_1 may equal the null set; that is, we may start out with no elements conditioned.

We may conceive of the conditioning process in the following manner. On trial n a sample of stimulus elements are effectively present (sampled). The unconditioned stimulus occurs and serves as a reinforcing event that conditions the stimulus elements sampled on that trial to the unconditioned response. The sample of stimulus elements are then "thrown back" and another sample is taken on the next trial, conditioned, returned, etc.

This way of conceptualizing the conditioning process is not entirely strange but leaves many matters unclear, which is equivalent to saying that this literary description of the process actually describes a host of possibilities. When we put this literary description in mathematical form, some of the choice points at which assumptions are made are clearly revealed. And, of course, the consequences and the empirical implications of the assumptions may be more easily and confidently derived.

As an example of one possible formulation of this process, consider the following [this formulation is in the spirit of Estes' original formulation of statistical learning theory (1950)]:

Let $s \equiv$ the fixed sample size
$C_{s,\,n} \equiv$ the number of conditioned elements in the sample on the nth trial
$N \equiv$ the total number of stimulus elements available in the learning situation
$C_n \equiv$ the total number of conditioned elements available on trial n
$p(A_1|s) \equiv$ the probability of the conditioned response A_1 being emitted given the sample of size s

We make the assumption that the probability of the A_1 response on the nth trial is equal to the proportion of elements conditioned to A_1 present in the sample, i.e.,

$$p_n(A_1|s) = \frac{C_{s,\,n}}{s}. \qquad (9.17)$$

Let us make the further assumption that this proportion is a constant and is equal to the proportion of conditioned elements available on trial n, i.e.

$$\frac{C_{s,\,n}}{s} = \frac{C_n}{N} = p_n. \qquad (9.18)$$

Let us make one further assumption, that as a result of the reinforcing event the unconditioned elements in the sample become conditioned with probability 1 so there is an increment in the number of conditioned elements on the next trial. The increment is equal to the number of elements in the sample not already conditioned, so we may write this increment as follows:

$$C_{n+1} - C_n = s - C_{s,\,n}$$

$$C_{n+1} - C_n = s\left(1 - \frac{C_{s,\,n}}{s}\right). \tag{9.19}$$

Dividing by N and rearranging terms, we have

$$\frac{C_{n+1}}{N} = \frac{C_n}{N} + \frac{s}{N}\left(1 - \frac{C_{s,\,n}}{s}\right).$$

We note that the assumptions in Eqs. (9.17) and (9.18) permit us to substitute probabilities for most of the above terms except the term s/N. But this term represents the proportionate size of the sample of stimulus components, and we shall represent this proportion by a parameter,

$$\theta = \frac{s}{N}.$$

Hence we may now write the above expression as follows:

$$p_{n+1} = p_n + \theta(1 - p_n)$$

or

$$p_{n+1} = (1 - \theta)p_n + \theta. \tag{9.20}$$

It is well to note the similarity of this equation to Eq. (9.6), the linear operator in fixed-point form. In this case our p_n is an expected value, so Eq. (9.20) is an expected operator that is linear on the mean proportion, but individual subjects will differ in detail. We may also note that this expected operator is a special case of Eq. (9.6) in that the fixed point λ is 1, which means that the average proportion of conditioned elements will eventually be 1 and hence that all subjects will ultimately be perfectly conditioned.

One simple empirical implication of this model is the equation for the learning curve. What is desired here is an expression for p_n as a function of the parameters p_1 and θ. Then having estimated these parameters from the data or some portion of it, the entire learning curve follows.

We may write p_2 in terms of p_1 as follows:

$$p_2 = (1-\theta)p_1 + \theta,$$

and we may write p_3 in terms of p_2 and hence p_1:

$$p_3 = (1-\theta)p_2 + \theta = (1-\theta)^2 p_1 + \theta(1-\theta) + \theta = (1-\theta)^2 p_1 + [1-(1-\theta)^2].$$

If we continued this process, it would appear to be a good guess that the following equation gives p_n in each instance in terms of p_1:

$$p_n = (1-\theta)^{n-1} p_1 + [1-(1-\theta)^{n-1}]. \tag{9.21}$$

Having conjectured such an expression, we could then proceed to see if it held true for trial $n+1$, just as was done in proving Eq. (9.7) by mathematical induction. Such induction would prove Eq. (9.21) to be correct.

A more convenient form than Eq. (9.21) may be obtained by merely rearranging terms, as follows:

$$p_n = 1 - (1-p_1)(1-\theta)^{n-1}. \tag{9.22}$$

This equation yields the familiar negatively accelerated exponential growth curve habitually obtained in appropriately designed conditioning experiments.

It is of interest to note parenthetically here that according to this model *learning*, in the sense of an association being established, occurs in an all-or-none manner. Each stimulus element is associated with exactly one response. As a result of the reinforcing event a new association replaces the existing one or no change in the existing association occurs. This conception is in contrast to that of Thurstone and Gulliksen, described earlier, in which the *association* was built up gradually. Yet in spite of this all-or-none assumption of an association, the predicted group learning curve reflects a gradual growth.

The basic conception of stimulus sampling theory may be detected in the writings of Lashley, Hull, Guthrie, and probably others. What Estes has done is to show the way to make these conceptions unambiguous and permit rigorous derivation of empirical implications. One of the desirable consequences is the readily available interpretations for the parameters.

For example, the sample size s might capture the notion of stimulus intensity—the more intense the stimulus, the greater the number of stimulus elements effective on any one trial.[5] Another way of putting it is that $\theta = s/N$ is a learning rate parameter and represents the proportion of elements sampled on any trial.

[5]An interpretation that, experiments indicate, is misleading.

As another example consider an experimental context in which it would be intuitively reasonable to expect some aspects of a stimulus to be more salient or vivid or apparent than others. This expectation leads naturally in the formalization to a parameter θ_i (the probability of an element i being effective on any trial) not being the same for all stimulus components. In this manner Estes and Burke (1953) captured the idea of stimulus variability in that the size of the samples would not be a constant, nor would the samples be homogeneous in terms of components or aspects of the stimulus. If N is large, they showed that if the average value of θ_i were taken as the sampling probability of all elements the approximation would have negligible error. So this component model is one in which the sampling probability θ is fixed for each element, in contrast to the first one we discussed in which sample size s is fixed.

The fact that the expected operator for the component model [Eq. (9.20)] is a linear operator [Eq. (9.6)] was pointed out, and, indeed, in the special case of the component model in which $N = \infty$ and the sample size is large the linear model and the component model are identical stochastic, mathematical processes.

Experimental study of component models. Most of the research on the component models of stimulus sampling theory has involved a single stimulus situation in which there are two or more competing responses each of which may be reinforced part of the time. This paradigm was first designed by Humphreys (1939) as a verbal analogue to a conditioning experiment.

Grant, Hake and Hornseth (1951) were the first to observe a phenomenon in this experimental situation, which is variously called probability matching, probability learning, or probability tracking [a phenomenon mentioned earlier in this chapter with reference to Eq. (9.10)]. This phenomenon stimulated a great deal of research during the next 10 years—in part because it is a phenomenon that can be predicted by the component models[6] and in part because it is a phenomenon contrary to the predictions of one of the most prevalent theories of decision making, a theory based on the idea that man is "rational" and therefore would always make the most frequently rewarded response.

The experimental literature on probability learning has been reviewed, at least in part, several times (Estes 1962, 1964; Tune 1964; Sternberg 1963; Erickson 1966), so we shall mention only a few points of interest. The empirical scope of a law such as probability matching has not been determined; that is to say, although one can design an experiment in which probability matching is almost certain to occur, it is not clear exactly what characterizes such an experiment. Issues such as trying to define the empirical scope of probability

---

[6]The derivation of this prediction proceeds in identical fashion to the derivation of Eq. (9.10) and may be found in Estes and Straughan (1954).

matching lead to classification systems for experiments, such as contingent versus noncontingent, determinate versus nondeterminate, etc.[7]

Although the exact degree of admissible variety of empirical stituations within which probability matching occurs is not known, a great deal of experimental effort has been directed at probability matching and a considerable amount has been learned. Because a violation of any one of the following conditions has been the presumed reason for a failure to obtain probability matching, it would seem that some of the conditions an experiment must meet are these: It must be noncontingent (complete feedback); it must involve only two alternatives with only one reinforcer and one nonreinforcer; the instructions must lead the subject to try to be correct on *every* trial and not imply that the sequence is random; and the analysis should not go beyond the first few hundred trials. Group averages appear to be better than individual performances, and the phenomenon appears more characteristic of some species than of others (Behrend and Bitterman 1961).

There are many other aspects of the data in addition to the asymptotic performance that can be and are used to test the theory, as, for example, the sequential properties of the behavior, discussed in some detail by Anderson (1964, pp. 129–144). It is clear that the component model would imply a positive recency effect in that a reinforced response would have a tendency to be repeated because the effect of a reinforcement is an increase in the probability of that response. Jarvik (1951) reports very clear evidence of a negative recency effect, in an experiment, incidentally, in which probability matching was obtained.

The negative recency effect is the phenomenon of an increasing probability of predicting a nonoccurring event. For example, in predicting a sequence of coin tossings a negative recency effect would be exhibited if the number of subjects predicting tails on a given trial increased monotonically with the length of the preceding sequence of heads. This negative recency effect is also commonly known as the gambler's fallacy. More recent evidence (Cole 1965; Edwards 1961; Lindman and Edwards 1961) throws some doubt on the validity of the negative recency findings. It appears that negative recency, when it occurs, is confined mainly to the early trials.

There are other sequential properties of the data for which the theory is unable to account; these sequential properties typically, but not necessarily, involve specially designed experiments with sequential dependencies. An

[7]The contingent-noncontingent dichotomy reflects whether the probabilities of reinforcing events are contingent on the subject's response or not. If after a subject responds he is merely told whether he was right or wrong, for example, this reinforcement is usually interpreted as contingent, in contrast to reinforcement telling him what the correct response was regardless of his response, i.e., noncontingent reinforcement. This dichotomy corresponds to the Bush–Mosteller classification of reinforcement sequences as experimenter-subject-controlled versus experimenter-controlled. The dichotomy of determinate versus nondeterminate reinforcement refers to whether or not the response that was reinforced on each trial can be specified.

alternating sequence, for example, or any sequence with a repetitive mixed pattern could not be learned under this theory except by possibly restructuring the experimental environment and redefining the classes of experimental events. The model also does not account for the fact that subjects respond appropriately when the probability of an event is made conditional on the preceding event (Anderson 1960).

It now appears that the phenomenon of probability learning is a higher-level mental process than path independence allows (Rose and Vitz 1966; Restle 1961, Chap. 6). Restle has proposed a theory of patterns in guessing in which the subject responds on the basis of matching the current sequence of events with his memory of similar sequences earlier. This approach has proved very promising in some preliminary and limited comparisons with stimulus sampling theory.

Pattern Models The component models do not seem adequate for discrimination learning in that, as Restle (1959, p. 418) and Estes (1959, p. 33) point out, subjects may eventually learn to discriminate perfectly even though there is substantial overlap among samples, as evidenced by transfer between them earlier in the learning process. Also, failure of the component models to account for the fine structure of the data in probability learning has led to the study of alternative assumptions. Particular attention has been given to the sampling process, and a fruitful direction that has been taken is to assume each response is associated not with an element per se but with the entire pattern of elements effective on a trial, so that each sample is a distinct entity or gestalt and is associated with exactly one response. On any one trial, then, the sample of elements that are effective is equivalent to sampling exactly one of these patterns, and the response to which it is connected occurs with probability 1.

Clearly this sampling assumption can be regarded as a special case of the component model in which N is the number of samples or patterns in the population (and may be unrestricted in size) and $s = 1$. For this reason the model is called the N-element pattern model and the sampling scheme is described in Fig. 9.5 as having sample size equal to 1. Because the distinction between the sampling scheme of a pattern model and that of a component model is important, let us rephrase it. A pattern model on one level of analysis (pattern level) requires two different samples to be either identical or completely disjoint, because each sample is a single element. On another level of analysis (component level), two samples may have elements in common.

The pattern models differ from the component models in the conditioning axiom also. In the component models the elements effective on any one trial become conditioned to the response reinforced on that trial (or remain conditioned to it). In the pattern models the single element that is sampled switches its connection to the reinforced response with probability c, which need not be equal to 1.

In the simple probability learning situation with two responses and their corresponding reinforcing events, which occur with probability π and $1-\pi$, the derivation of the empirical implications of the model is quite lengthy, though not difficult. Some of this derivation is contained in Atkinson, Bower, and Crothers (1965, Chap. 8) and more generally in Estes (1959, Chap. 1) so we shall only outline it and discuss the principal results.

The first step is the derivation of the trial to trial transition probabilities between conditioning states. On any given trial some of the patterns are already conditioned to one of the responses and the remainder to the other response. One pattern is sampled, and after the reinforcing event occurs, the number of patterns conditioned to each response is either increased by 1, remains the same, or is decreased by 1.[8]

This process is a Markov chain (see Sec. 8.1) with a finite number of states, as N is finite, and, furthermore, from one trial to the next the process can only remain in its current state or move to an adjacent state (a process called a random walk). It is this property that makes these models so mathematically tractable. With a matrix of transition probabilities that is constant, the asymptotic probability distribution over the various states may be obtained recursively in terms of one of them. The important result here, omitting all the detail of the derivation, is that the ratio of the *transition* probabilities between any two adjacent states is the ratio of their *asymptotic* probabilities. That is, if q_j is the asymptotic probability that exactly j elements are conditioned to response A_1 and if $q_{j,\,j+1}$ is the transition probability from state j to state $j+1$ elements conditioned to A_1, then

$$\frac{q_j}{q_{j+1}} = \frac{q_{j+1,\,j}}{q_{j,\,j+1}}, \tag{9.23}$$

which is known as the ratio rule.

What this rule says is that the ratio of the asymptotic probabilities that exactly j or exactly $j+1$ elements are conditioned to response A_1 is the same as the ratio of two other probabilities, which are trial to trial transition probabilities. The last two probabilities are the probability of going from state $j+1$ to j elements conditioned to A_1 and the probability of going from j to $j+1$ elements conditioned to A_1.

In the simple noncontingent case the trial to trial transition probabilities are a function of the conditioning parameter c, but this factor cancels out in Eq. (9.23), and so the asymptotic state probabilities are independent of the conditioning parameter. This independence is what one would expect because c reflects the rate of learning, or how fast the asymptote is approached, and should not affect the asymptotic values themselves.

---

[8]We note in this formulation that learning can take place only when the subject makes an incorrect response. The pattern effective on a given trial evokes the response to which it is conditioned. If that response is correct, the reinforcement does not affect the conditioning, but if that response is incorrect, the reinforcement may change the conditioning.

Another important feature of the ratio rule is that the ratio of the transition probabilities on the right-hand side of Eq. (9.23) is the ratio of two appropriately chosen neighboring terms in the binomial expansion of $[\pi + (1 - \pi)]^N$, which means that the asymptotic state probabilities are binomially distributed.

From this point the derivation of the mean learning curve and its asymptotic response probabilities and many other statistics of the learning process may be calculated, all of which may be used in estimating parameters and in testing goodness of fit.

The asymptotic response probabilities for the pattern model are referred to by Estes (1957) as a general matching law:

> The general matching law requires no restriction whatever on the schedule of reinforcement. It applies whenever the organism's behavior in a recurring stimulus situation can be described in terms of two (or more) mutually exclusive response classes, one of which is reinforced on each trial. The gist of the law is that, beginning at any point in a learning series, the cumulative proportions of a given response and corresponding reinforcement event tend to equality. In other words, the organism keeps accurate books and in the long run pays out an average of exactly one response per reinforcement (Estes 1957, p. 612).

Suppes and Atkinson (1960, p. 196) report an experiment in which the probability of reinforcing the A_1 response was $\pi = .60$ and the observed mean A_1 response probability for 30 subjects over the last 100 trials (out of a total of 240) was .596. They also derived from the pattern model some predictions of sequential statistics, e.g., the limiting probability of an A_1 response conditional on the occurrence of both an A_1 response and the E_2 reinforcing event on the previous trial. The χ^2 testing the deviations of the observed from predicted sequential probabilities was satisfyingly small.

The pattern model lends itself well to the explanation of how a subject can learn to discriminate perfectly stimuli that have common elements, including the special case of part-whole discrimination. But in this strength lies its weakness. By treating each stimulus as a unique pattern ($s = 1$) it does not lend itself to generalization or transfer between stimuli, processes for which common elements would seem such a natural underlying conception.

This problem was attacked by Restle (1955a, b), who developed his ideas independently of the concepts of stimulus sampling theory. In his terminology the stimulus components are *cues* associated with the reinforcing events, cues to which the subject can learn to make a differential response. He anticipates the pattern model[9] when he says "while cues are thought of as stimulus elements, these elements need not be of the nature of 'points of color' or

[9]Estes' first mention of the pattern model was in 1957 (Estes 1957) in the context of clinicians diagnosing on the basis of patterns of symptoms rather than symptoms as separate independent components. Estes' motivation for the pattern model was also to account for discrimination learning.

'elementary tones.' If a subject can learn a consistent response to a certain configuration despite changes in its constituents, then the configuration is by definition a cue separate from its constituents" (Restle 1955*a*, p. 18). For example, the vowel in a CVC nonsense syllable might be the relevant cue for learning in a paired associate task.

In Restle's early formulation he divides cues into "relevant" and "irrelevant" according to whether they can be used by the subject to predict reward. Relevant cues become conditioned to the response and irrelevant ones become adapted. The course of discrimination learning, then, is described in terms of these two concurrent processes of conditioning and adaptation.

Estes (1959) introduces the notion of a *partially relevant* cue for those whose correlation with the reinforcing event is intermediate between zero and one.

Modified pattern models having some of the properties of component models are called *mixed models* and are being applied to discrimination problems with stimulus overlap. The ordinary component model predicts the transfer effects that occur early in learning but not the perfect discrimination that is finally achieved. The simple pattern model does just the opposite. The mixed model, then, is an expected development in which discrimination learning involves two processes, discrimination in terms of patterns and transfer or generalization in terms of their constituent components (Estes and Hopkins 1961; Friedman and Gelfand 1964).

Some experimental study of this model has been reported (Friedman 1966) in which, for example, the stimulus components *a* and *b* were each conditioned to different responses and the compound (pattern) *ab* was conditioned to a third response. Transfer during acquisition was observed from components to pattern and *vice versa*. The fit of a mixed model was good qualitatively but consistently deviant quantitatively.

Although experimental applications of mixed models appear promising, there is much theoretical development and experimental testing still to be done on the interrelations of the conditioning of patterns and components. Much of the strength of stimulus sampling theory lies in the capability it provides for the precise formulation of alternative assumptions and their consequences for suitably designed experiments, and hence the theory leads to a program of relatively efficient and meaningful experimental studies.

We come finally to an area of recently high activity in mathematical learning theory, the area of small-element models.

Small-element Models

Small-element models constitute the limiting cases of stimulus sampling theory with respect to the number of stimulus components—assumed here to be only one or two. The special case of $N = 1$ was introduced by Estes in 1959 and first studied intensively by Bower (1961, 1962) with very favorable results and then by Suppes and Ginsberg (1963) and Atkinson and Crothers (1964) with less favorable results.

Estes' somewhat casual introduction of the model was in the context of the probability learning experimental paradigm. Bower's initial intensive application was to the problem of paired associate learning. It is in the context of this experimental paradigm and related ones (involving transfer and generalization rather than probability learning) that most of the recent development has taken place in mathematical learning theory. As this work comes at the beginning of a new trend in mathematical learning theory, we shall review its main features.

In Bower's experiment there were 10 items, each consisting of a pair of consonant letters, and a subject was to learn to associate the correct integer, either 1 or 2, with each. For 5 of the items the integer 1 was correct, and for the other 5 the integer 2 was correct. A trial consisted of presenting the item to the subject who responded with 1 or 2 and of then informing him of the correct response. The deck of 10 cards containing the stimuli was shuffled each time and the procedure continued until the subject made two consecutive errorless passes through the deck.

Those trials in which the same item was presented constitute an item sequence so each subject's protocol consists of 10 item sequences, interleafed. Bower ran 29 subjects, so assuming that all subjects were essentially equivalent and that all items were alike (equally difficult), the data provide 290 item sequences. Each item sequence consists of a series of zeroes and ones, indicating correct anticipations and errors, respectively, on the part of the subject.[10]

The statistical features of these item sequences are courted by the model. The structure of the model is simple and most of the mathematical work involves generating expressions for these statistical features out of the structure, using some of these to estimate parameters by fitting some relevant parts of the data, and then comparing additional statistics computed from the data with their values as predicted by the model.

The structure of Bower's one-element model is based on the following axioms:

REPRESENTATION AND SAMPLING AXIOM

Each item is represented by a single stimulus element that is sampled on every trial.

CONDITIONING AXIOM

The element is in one of two conditioning states, C or $\bar{C}$ (conditioned or not conditioned to the correct response); on any reinforced trial, if

---

[10]A one is usually used in a paired associate learning experiment to indicate an error because the total number of errors hopefully tends to a limit regardless of the number of trials. With more than two alternative responses this representation in terms of one or zero would not distinguish between kinds of errors, and such experimental records could not be used to test some of the later models, which distinguish between errors.

the element is in state $\bar{C}$, it has probability c, independent of past events, of moving to state C.

RESPONSE AXIOM

The probability of a correct response is either 1 or g given that the conditioned state is C or $\bar{C}$, respectively (g is a guessing parameter and in Bower's experiment, with two equally likely responses, is set a priori equal to one half).

Note the all-or-none feature of the learning process that has been assumed here: The subject is assumed to have learned (perfectly) the paired associate (i.e., it has become conditioned and the probability of a correct response is 1) or he knows nothing and is just guessing.

These axioms give rise to a representation of the learning process as a Markov chain (see Sec. 8.1), with the following structure:

$$
\begin{array}{c}
\qquad\qquad trial\ n+1 \\
\begin{array}{cc|cc c}
 & & C & \bar{C} & Pr\ \text{(cor)} \\
\hline
trial\ n & C & 1 & 0 & \begin{bmatrix} 1 \\ g \end{bmatrix} \\
 & \bar{C} & c & 1-c &
\end{array}
\end{array} \qquad (9.24)
$$

The matrix on the left is the matrix of transition probabilities between states from trial to trial and the matrix on the right is a probability vector for correct response over the conditioning states on trial n. For example, if on trial n the item is in state C, it will, on all subsequent trials, stay in state C and the individual will respond correctly. If the item is in state $\bar{C}$, (1) it will become conditioned, i.e., move to state C for the next trial, with probability c, or otherwise remain unconditioned and (2) the probability of the individual responding correctly is g.

The Markov chain described by Eq. (9.24) is an absorbing Markov chain. An absorbing Markov chain has at least one absorbing state and it can be reached from any state (not necessarily in one trial). We note that state C is absorbing because it cannot be left and it can be reached from state $\bar{C}$.

To obtain an expression for the learning curve, we want the probability of a correct response on each trial, $p(A_n = 0)$. But the probability of a correct response depends on whether the item is conditioned or not, so we may write the expression

$$
p(A_n = 0) = p(A_n = 0|C_n)p(C_n) + p(A_n = 0|\bar{C}_n)p(\bar{C}_n). \qquad (9.25)
$$

The probability of a correct response given the state of conditioning is the probability vector on the right-hand side of Eq. (9.24) so all we need is

$p(C_n)$ and the $p(\bar{C}_n)$. Because the chain is absorbing, an item can be unconditioned on trial n only if it has survived the previous $n-1$ trials in an unconditioned state. As the trial to trial transition probability for remaining unconditioned is $1-c$, we have

$$p(\bar{C}_n) = (1-c)^{n-1},$$

and hence

$$p(C_n) = 1-p(\bar{C}_n) = 1-(1-c)^{n-1}.$$

Making the appropriate term by term substitutions in Eq. (9.25), we have

$$p(A_n = 0) = (1)[1-(1-c)^{n-1}]+(g)(1-c)^{n-1},$$

which simplifies to

$$p(A_n = 0) = 1-(1-g)(1-c)^{n-1}, \tag{9.26}$$

the typical gradual negatively accelerated learning curve.

There are two points of interest about Eq. (9.26) to be noted; one is that, aside from the interpretation of the parameters, Eq. (9.26) is indistinguishable from Eq. (9.22), which was derived from the component model; and second, we note that, in spite of a basic conception of learning as an all-or-none process, the mean learning curve (with its averaging effect) is gradual and would obscure the existence of such a process.

Once again we see that quite different conceptual sources can lead to the same particular predictions, which is the reason that confirmation of a prediction does not imply acceptance of a theory, and it is also one of the reasons it is desirable to seek contrasting predictions that can be tested on the same data. Such comparisons are helpful in making modifications in a model.

The mathematical tractability of the one-element model is reflected in the ease with which the parameter c may be estimated. An expression for estimating c may be derived as follows.

Let T be the total number of errors on an item. Then the expected total number of errors on an item is the probability of making an error on each trial summed over trials. An error can be made only on a given trial, however, if the individual is in an unconditioned state on that trial and guesses incorrectly. These considerations give rise to an infinite series that is the sum over trials of the probability of making an error on each trial. Thus we have

$$1-g = \text{probability of making an error on the first trial as the individual is in state } \bar{C} \text{ to begin with and he must guess incorrectly}$$

$(1-c)(1-g) =$ probability of making an error on the second trial; it is the product of the probability that the individual must not have been conditioned on the first trial, $(1-c)$, times the probability that he guesses wrong on the second trial, $(1-g)$

$(1-c)^2(1-g) =$ probability of making an error on the third trial; it is the product of the probability that he has not been conditioned on the first two trials, $(1-c)^2$, times the probability that he guesses wrong on the third trial, $(1-g)$

Clearly, then,

$$E(T) = (1-g)+(1-c)(1-g)+(1-c)^2(1-g)+ \ldots +(1-c)^{n-1}(1-g)+ \ldots ,$$

which is a geometric series of the form

$$\sum_{i=0}^{\infty} a^i x$$

where

$$a = 1-c$$

$$x = 1-g$$

$$i = n-1.$$

From elementary algebra the sum of this series is known to be

$$\sum_{i=0}^{\infty} a^i x = \frac{x}{1-a}.$$

Hence, we may write

$$E(T) = \frac{1-g}{1-(1-c)} = \frac{1-g}{c}.$$

The average number of errors on an item, $\tilde{T}$, may be calculated from the data and provides an unbiased estimate of $E(T)$ provided the subjects were run to a stiff criterion of learning. If the guessing parameter is known (in Bower's experiment it was equal to one half), the above expression may then be used to estimate c:

$$\tilde{T} = \frac{1/2}{c} \quad \text{or} \quad c = \frac{1}{2\tilde{T}}.$$

This simple example should not mislead one to believe that the estimation of parameters is always, indeed it is rarely, so simple (see, for example, Bush 1963). Estimation and evaluation are issues of some substance in their own right and call for a substantial understanding of mathematical statistics, as does much of mathematical psychology.

There are many contrasting predictions, not all independent, that can be derived for the incremental process underlying Eq. (9.22) and the all-or-none process underlying Eq. (9.26); Bower (1961) considers 20 of them of which 18 comparisons on his data favor the one-element model.

One of the most striking of these comparisons concerns the number of errors to be expected following an error. In the Markov chain model an error is a *recurrent event* (see Sec. 8.1), which is to say that any trial on which an error occurs may be numbered $n = 0$ and the next trial $n = 1$, etc.; i.e., the occurrence of an error reveals the initial state still obtains; there is no cumulative effect of past trials (learning is all-or-none). So the probability of an error following an error should be constant and independent of n.

In the incremental model the strength of an association is built up steadily with the number of preceding reinforced trials, so the probability of an error following an error should be a decreasing function of n—in fact, in the case of the linear model, a curve complementary to the learning curve, Eq. (9.26).

In Fig. 9.6 we present the curves predicted by the two theories and the data from Bower's experiment.

Further experiments, however, have failed to sustain this striking result. Atkinson and Crothers (1964), for example, in comparing a number of different models on the results of eight experiments, found in six of the experiments that the probability of an error clearly decreased as n increased. The prediction of the incremental model, however, was even more disparate from the data. Atkinson and Crothers suggest that the disparity between their results and those of Bower might have been caused by the fact that he had two response alternatives whereas their experiments had three or four.

What they had in mind is left unstated, but the difference in the number of alternatives might account for the disparity in results in the following way. With only two response alternatives, elimination of an incorrect response is tantamount to "conditioning" of the correct one. With more than two alternatives, elimination of incorrect responses in the course of learning decreases the probability of an error following an error. But the one-element model does not recognize the elimination of incorrect responses. A possible modification of the model, then, is to introduce an error elimination feature, which is just what has been done (see Millward 1964).

Even earlier, Suppes and Ginsberg (1963) pointed out a fundamental property of any simple all-or-none conditioning model: The probability of an error on any trial *before* the last error remains a constant, so there should be

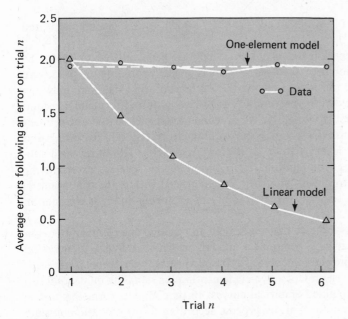

Fig. 9.6 Predictions of linear model and one-element model compared with data.

no evidence of learning if only the data before the last error are analyzed. They called this property *stationarity* and it means, for example, that over any block of n trials prior to conditioning the distribution of the number of correct responses made by the subjects is given by the binomial $(p+q)^n$, where p is the guessing parameter estimated from the data.

For example, at the end of the second trial some subjects can be expected to have made no errors, some to have made exactly one error, and some to have been wrong on both trials. The probability of making no errors is the probability of guessing correctly twice in a row, p^2. The probability of exactly one error is the probability of guessing correctly on the first trial and wrong on the second, pq, or being wrong on the first and right on the second, qp, so, together, $2pq$. The probability of exactly two errors is the probability of guessing incorrectly twice in a row, q^2. These, clearly, are the terms in the expansion of the binomial $(p+q)^2$. This relation may be shown to hold for all values of n.

Suppes and Ginsberg tested 10 different experimental sets of data for this property, constructing Vincent-type learning curves for those trials prior to the last error. In this type of learning curve the proportion of correct responses is plotted against percentiles of trials prior to the last error instead of a fixed-size block of trials. They plotted the learning curve for each quartile of trials before the last error and obtained statistically significant nonstationarity in 6 of the 10 curves, all of which, plus a seventh, appeared concave upward.[11]

Another experimental procedure that has been utilized to study the property of stationarity involves a second guess procedure, a procedure originated for the purpose of testing the assumption that there are only two states of learning. In this procedure a subject is required to make a second guess when his first is wrong. An all-or-none model such as the one-element model would require the second guess accuracy to be constant over trials and at a given chance level. A study of Binford and Gettys (1966) revealed substantial departures from stationarity: Correct second guesses exceeded the predicted chance frequency and their rate increased with n, the trial number. This relation also suggests the desirability of exploring an error elimination feature.

These results indicate that the simple all-or-none one-element model in addition to the large-N component model, which is a linear incremental model, is inadequate and some sort of a compromise between them is suggested. Suppes and Ginsberg present a two-element stimulus sampling model that can account for the obtained empirical curves. In its complete form this model gives rise to a four-state Markov process according to the conditioning state of the two elements, neither, both, or a particular one of them.

If the two elements are not to be distinguished, then the four states collapse to three states, which are simply the number of elements conditioned 0, 1, or 2 and the structure of the model is as follows:

$$
\begin{array}{c}
\textit{trial } n+1 \\[4pt]
\begin{array}{c|ccc|c}
 & C_2 & C_1 & C_0 & Pr\,(\text{cor}) \\
\hline
C_2 & 1 & 0 & 0 & \begin{bmatrix}1\\p\\g\end{bmatrix} \\
C_1 & a & 1-a & 0 & \\
C_0 & 0 & b & 1-b &
\end{array}
\end{array}
\qquad (9.27)
$$

where $0 < g < p < 1$. The paramater g is the initial guessing parameter and p is the guessing parameter when exactly one stimulus element has been conditioned; if $p = 1$ this model clearly reduces to the one-element model. Note that an element is conditioned in an all-or-none manner and that after

---

[11]There are some unresolved statistical problems when averaging over subjects to test stationarity. A slow learner has more trials before his last error so his quartile error scores are larger and possibly more variable than those of the fast learner who has a necessarily constrained variability. Averaging raw error scores over subjects, then, weights the subjects unequally as more variable subjects are weighted proportionately higher. Alternative procedures are to calculate *forward* stationarity or *backward* stationarity. In forward stationarity the number of errors on each trial are counted over only those subjects who have at least one future error. Subjects are dropped when they have made their last error. *Backward* stationarity counts trials backward from the last error, which is assigned trial number zero. The average number of errors, then, is determined for trial $n = -1, -2, \ldots$, etc., dropping subjects when the count has reached the beginning of their sequence.

it has been conditioned it remains conditioned—there is no forgetting, the model does not permit a transition from state (C_1) to state (C_0), and state (C_2) is absorbing.

The model in this form was studied by Theios (1963), who presents a number of its theoretical predictions and a good fit to simple avoidance conditioning data on rats.

This model permits nonstationarity in that the probability of a correct response before the last error will be bounded by g and p and will tend to increase from g to p as a function of n. Atkinson and Crothers (1964) tested the two-element model on eight different sets of experimental paired associate data and found significant discrepancies between the model and the data for five of them.

As these models fail to predict paired associate learning data, they suggest that there may be another psychological process, not represented in the models, influencing the performance, and, in particular, a forgetting process. The existence of such a process is, of course, intuitively acceptable and the idea is captured by permitting a transition from a higher to a lower state of learning.

Because a subject eventually learns, it is reasonable to assume an absorbing state, typically labeled L for long-term memory. But in the course of learning there is empirical evidence of appreciable forgetting over short intervals of time (e.g., Peterson and Peterson 1959), so a short-term memory state S may also be postulated. The initial state is an unconditioned or guessing state, variously labeled G, U, or $\bar{C}$.

With these assumptions we can construct a three-state model that incorporates both an acquisition process and a forgetting process. Each of these processes may be represented by a separate transition matrix, as follows:

$$
\begin{array}{c|ccc}
 & L & S & G \\
\hline
L & 1 & 0 & 0 \\
S & a & 1-a & 0 \\
G & b & 1-b & 0
\end{array}
\qquad
\begin{array}{c|ccc}
 & L & S & G \\
\hline
L & 1 & 0 & 0 \\
S & 0 & 1-f & f \\
G & 0 & 0 & 1
\end{array}
\qquad
\begin{array}{c|ccc}
 & L & S & G \\
\hline
L & 1 & 0 & 0 \\
S & a & (1-a)(1-f) & (1-a)f \\
G & b & (1-b)(1-f) & (1-b)f
\end{array}
\quad (9.28)
$$

$$\quad\quad\quad\quad A \quad\quad\quad\quad\quad\quad\quad\quad\quad B \quad\quad\quad\quad\quad\quad\quad\quad\quad\quad C$$

The matrix A is the "moving ahead" matrix, the matrix B is the "moving backward" matrix, and their product, C, is the trial to trial transition matrix between the three states. This matrix has three parameters, a, b, and f, and the probability of responding correctly in each of these states L, S, G is 1, 1, g, respectively. This model is the general form of the forgetting model in the literature.

Atkinson and Crothers propose a model of this type in which the parameters are reduced to two by assuming $a = b$; they call that model the *LS*-2 model. The assumption of $a = b$ assumes that permanent storage is equally likely whether an item is in short-term storage or whether it is in a guessing state. The structure of the LS-2 model is as follows:

$$
\begin{array}{c|ccc}
 & L & S & \bar{C} \\
\hline
L & 1 & 0 & 0 \\
S & a' & b' & 1-a'-b' \\
\bar{C} & a' & b' & 1-a'b'
\end{array}
\qquad
\begin{array}{c}
Pr\,(\text{cor}) \\[4pt]
\begin{bmatrix} 1 \\ 1 \\ g \end{bmatrix}
\end{array}
. \tag{9.29}
$$

The LS-2 model of Atkinson and Crothers combines learning and forgetting processes, each of which is all or none. This model is a special case of their more general four-state forgetting model, which distinguishes a "forgotten" state F from the initial unlearned state U. This general model has three parameters and is naturally called the LS-3 model. By combining the short-term and the forgotten states into a single state SF and by adjusting the probability of being correct in state SF correspondingly, they derive the following three-state model with three parameters as a particular version of an LS-3 model, with parameters a, c, and f:

$$
\begin{array}{c|ccc}
 & L & SF & U \\
\hline
L & 1 & 0 & 0 \\
SF & a & 1-a & 0 \\
U & a & c-a & 1-c
\end{array}
\qquad
\begin{array}{c}
Pr\,(\text{cor}) \\[4pt]
\begin{bmatrix} 1 \\ 1-f+fg \\ g \end{bmatrix}
\end{array}
. \tag{9.30}
$$

This version assumes that passage into long-term storage occurs with equal probability on any trial regardless of whether the current state is SF or U.

In comparing these models and some others, Atkinson and Crothers found that the LS-2 model was clearly unsatisfactory, but the above version of the LS-3 model [Eq. (9.30)] was one of the best in fitting the data of the eight experiments, showing a significant discrepancy on only two of them. It provided a substantially better fit than the two-element model [Eq. (9.27)], which also has three states and three parameters.

Some of the recent experimental work on short-term memory (e.g., Peterson and Peterson 1959) substantiates the intuitively compelling notion that in the "simple" paired associate learning tasks used in these studies the subject, upon being told the correct association, learns it, in the sense that if he were asked immediately he would be able to give the correct answer with probability 1. With one-trial acquisition of these simple items, he can make errors on later trials only if he forgets.

Further experimental results (e.g., Hellyer 1962) indicate that the probability of forgetting between trials decreases as a function of practice.

This evidence led Bernbach (1965) to the view that *learning* was a *decrease* in the probability of *forgetting*, and he developed a forgetting model in which he assumed that this decrease could be approximated by a step function in which the probability of forgetting took on only two values, δ and zero.

There is also experimental evidence (e.g., Postman 1961) that an incorrect response may proactively inhibit recall of the correct response, as if the *wrong* response had been *learned*. Bernbach captured this idea in his model with the notion of an "error state" E in which the preceding error will be repeated with probability 1.

On this basis Bernbach formulated a four-state absorbing Markov chain with three parameters. The structure of this model is as follows:

$$
\begin{array}{c|cccc|c}
 & L & S & U & E & Pr\,(\text{cor}) \\
\hline
L & 0 & 0 & 0 & 0 & \begin{bmatrix}1\end{bmatrix} \\
S & \theta & (1-\theta)(1-\delta) & (1-\theta)\delta & 0 & 1 \\
U & 0 & [1-\beta(1-g)](1-\delta) & \delta & \beta(1-g)(1-\delta) & g \\
E & 0 & (1-\beta)(1-\delta) & \delta & \beta(1-\delta) & 0
\end{array}, \tag{9.31}
$$

where the parameters have the following interpretation:

- $g \equiv$ probability of guessing correctly in the unconditioned state, $g = 1/r$, where r is the number of response alternatives
- $\beta \equiv$ probability of entering state E given an incorrect response
- $\delta \equiv$ probability of becoming unconditioned (U) from the short-term memory state (S), i.e., probability of forgetting
- $\theta \equiv$ probability of entering long-term memory (L) from short-term memory (S)

One of the interesting features of this model is its prediction that the repeat of an error is more probable than the occurrence of a different error, a prediction that is borne out in the experimental results Bernbach reports.

If β is assumed to be equal to zero, then the E state is eliminated from the model and it takes the following form:

$$
\begin{array}{c|ccc|c}
 & L & S & U & Pr\,(\text{cor}) \\
\hline
L & 1 & 0 & 0 & \begin{bmatrix}1\end{bmatrix} \\
S & \theta & (1-\theta)(1-\delta) & (1-\theta)\delta & 1 \\
U & 0 & 1-\delta & \delta & g
\end{array}. \tag{9.32}
$$

Here we have a two-parameter forgetting model with three states and it becomes mathematically equivalent to the *LS*-2 model [Eq. (9.29)], which means that no experimental data could distinguish between them,[12] as shown by Atkinson and Crothers (1964). So the successes and failures of this

---

[12]This introduces the notion of identifiability in models, on which a most important paper has been written by Greeno and Steiner (1964), discussed below.

forgetting model would be the same as those of the *LS*-2; both of these models predict stationarity, for example.

In another effort to introduce nonstationarity, Atkinson and Crothers (1964; cf. also Calfee and Atkinson 1965) developed the notion that the probability of forgetting an item that was in short-term memory was dependent on the number of unlearned items intervening between two successive presentations of the item. The model otherwise retained the essential structure of the *LS*-2 model. This trial-dependent forgetting (TDF) model could then be written with two or three parameters depending on whether an additional parameter was introduced for forgetting during the intertrial interval.

Because the TDF model has a transition matrix that is dependent on the trial number, derivations of the statistical features of sequences generated by the model are much more difficult. Insofar as fitting data is concerned, the TDF model with three parameters did as well as, but no better than, the *LS*-3 model; with two parameters it did not do as well as the *LS*-2 model.

Other attempts to introduce nonstationarity include the introduction of an error elimination feature in the learning process (Millward 1964). The idea here is that a subject may learn that a particular response is wrong but still not know which is right. In the simplest case of three response alternatives the structure of the model may be formulated as follows:

$$
\begin{array}{c|ccc}
 & C & \bar{E} & U \\
\hline
C & 1 & 0 & 0 \\
\bar{E} & a & 1-a & 0 \\
U & c & (1-c)e & (1-c)(1-e)
\end{array}
\qquad
\begin{array}{c}
Pr\ (\mathrm{cor}) \\
\begin{bmatrix} 1 \\ 1/2 \\ 1/3 \end{bmatrix},
\end{array}
\qquad (9.33)
$$

where $\bar{E}$ is the state in which one wrong response has been eliminated.

This model reduces to the two-element model if $c = 0$, and if only two response alternatives are used in the experiment, it reduces to the one-element model. The model is reported to do well on nonstationarity and on second guess data. As indicated earlier, an all-or-none model would require the second guess accuracy to be chance, whereas the error elimination model would permit the second guess to do better than chance and be increasingly good as n increases.

Although this model has some very good features, it gets unwieldy with more than three response alternatives, and if added to a forgetting model, then, one would need to add the feature of forgetting the error elimination. These complications have led to the neglect of this model in spite of its intuitively compelling nature.

In this section on finite state models the student will have noted that we started the discussion in the context of stimulus sampling theory but have been increasingly utilizing the vocabulary of information processing and Markov chains. One could, of course, formulate these last models in terms of stimulus sampling theory—and, indeed, as we have seen, stimulus sampling theory was their precursor—but most of the current theorists attempt to formulate directly a conception of "what is going on" in terms of transitions among hypothetical states. One of the most recent books on mathematical learning theory (Atkinson, Bower, and Crothers 1965), for example, though developing special cases of stimulus sampling theory throughout the book, relegates stimulus sampling theory, as such, to a single late chapter.

These simple small-element models are now quite well understood, both theoretically and experimentally, for simple experimental paradigms. In general, it would appear that the best data for most of these models are data obtained when the subject submits to the experimental environment in a passive manner and lets the reinforcements "shape" him without his active involvement.

This assumed passivity is one of the differences between the data with which mathematical learning theory is concerned and that with which decision processes theory is concerned. The former data are generated by an essentially "mindless" guessing process that is presumed to be shaped by reinforcement, as in the theories of probability learning and concept formation; the data of decision processes are presumed to involve high-level cognition with a minimum of randomness.

These attempts to describe the differences between the data of decision processes and the data of learning theory caricature them or at least are less accurate now than they once were. Perhaps the contrast between the two areas might be better made in the following terms.

Decision processes theory is largely concerned with preferential choice under steady-state or equilibrium conditions. In other words the theories deal largely with a static process. The conceptualization behind mathematical learning theory is that of a dynamic process. The former is concerned with the effect of the current state on choice behavior and the latter with the effect of choice on the current state. In still other terms the former may be regarded as the study of motivation and the cognitive nature of choice; the latter is the study of learning and the adaptive nature of choice. The recognition that behavior is both cognitive and adaptive is evident in recent developments in both fields. There are, for example, the current application of Bayesian statistical theory to decision making (see Sec. 5.2 and Edwards, Lindman, and Phillips 1965), which incorporates the effect of new information on the decision variables, and the recent development by Bower (1966) of a multi-component theory of memory trace that recognizes the deeper cognitive nature of the learning process. These examples are evidence of diffusion into common problems and possibly even common data.

A possible point of view is that the more complex cognitive processes are composed of the more elementary shaping processes as components. Restle is an active proponent of this "cognitive" point of view. He regards more complex cognitive learning as multistage learning involving more than one step.

The subject faced with a task involving learning the cues to the correct response, as in concept formation, discrimination learning, and maze learning, has a set of hypotheses or habits that Restle calls strategies. On any trial the subject samples from this set of strategies, which may be organized into a hierarchy of concepts, and each stage of learning is accomplished in an all-or-none fashion (Restle 1962, 1964; Polson, Restle, and Polson 1965). One thing not clear in his theory is where this set of strategies comes from, which is the most "cognitive" part of the process.

Of great value to the study of the interaction between theory and data are purely mathematical analyses of general classes of models. The Atkinson–Crothers paper previously referred to is a case in point, and the study by Greeno and Steiner (1964) is another. Greeno and Steiner show that Restle's selection of strategies theory is equivalent to the one-element model in the sense that for appropriate values of their respective parameters each would fit any set of observed sequences equally well.

Many of these theories, if not most, involve hypothetical states or variables that are not always identifiable[13] in an experiment. In the one-element model, for example, on the first trial after the last error it is not known whether that correct response indicates that the subject guessed correctly or whether the item is in the conditioned state.

Greeno and Steiner show that for any such unidentifiable theory an equivalent Markov process can be constructed with identifiable states. They do this for an all-or-none learning process by redefining states into an error state (R, where the symbol signifies a recurrent event) in which an error is certain and two other states, A and S. In both of the last states a correct response is certain, but the instances of state A are those correct responses following the last occurrence of R. Prior to the last occurrence of R there may be a flow back and forth between correct guesses and incorrect responses, and the instances of correct guesses are lumped together and called state S. Clearly, states A, R, and S are identifiable in any learning experiment run to a strict criterion of learning.

If two theories with unidentifiable states are equivalent to the same identifiable theory, then they are themselves equivalent insofar as the data of an experiment are concerned. This statement does not mean that substantive differences between such theories are unimportant, but rather it serves to divert research effort from futile attempts to distinguish between theories with experiments for which the theories are equivalent.

Restle's selection of strategies theory, as pointed out by Greeno and Scandura (1966), is a generalization of the pattern theory of *learning* in that the separate aspects or components of a stimulus may individually as well as

---

[13]A state is identifiable if in each possible sequence of observable events every occurrence of that state can be identified. If all the states specified in a theory are identifiable, then the theory is.

collectively constitute patterns, one of which is sampled on each trial. On the other hand the mixed pattern component model is a more general theory of *transfer* than the selection of strategies theory in that any common elements between patterns will contribute to transfer in the mixed model but not necessarily in the selection of strategies theory.

Greeno and Scandura incorporate the most general form of these theories of learning and transfer into a single theory of all-or-none learning and all-or-none transfer. By the latter concept is meant that if transfer did not occur on just presentation of an item when the appropriate cue was there (having previously been learned as the correct encoding of another item), then subsequent performance on such items would be the same as on control items that have no common elements to permit transfer from previously learned items. They formulate this theory as a four-state Markov chain and report an experiment that substantially supports the theory.

The mathematical complexity of all but the very simplest models now requires that parameter estimation be accomplished by means of computerized search procedures and this is one valuable use of the computer in research. But another role for the computer has developed. As more complex experimental paradigms are studied, it is anticipated that the complexity of the models will increase and the computer will play an increasingly significant role in simulating and developing theory. Evidence of such a trend is contained in the increasing use of an *information processing* approach in theory building, with notions of storage, retrieval, and encoding of stimuli as psychological processes and different storage banks as states of a system (e.g., Simon and Feigenbaum 1964; Gregg and Simon 1967).

Such approaches as stimulus sampling theory and information processing may be looked on as styles in analogizing that are fruitful to the extent that they generate extensive and interrelated experimental explorations. An experiment without a theory is meaningless. A good theory at this stage is one that stimulates and gives meaning to a wide variety of experimental observations. Stimulus sampling theories are a case in point for, as Carterette (1965) expressed it, these theories developed symbiotically with detailed experimental analysis.

These styles in analogizing are much affected, of course, by the available models—be they interpretable physically, as in Thurstone's and Audley's urn models, or biologically or be they completely abstract (i.e., without interpretation). Developing familiarity with a potential model system tends to influence the direction of theory development—a case in point, here, being the influence that the mathematics of Markov chains has had on learning theories (Estes 1962, p. 11).

Another instance of the effect of available models on styles in analogizing may be seen in the effect that the success of mathematical learning theory is having on theorizing in quite different substantive areas; see, for example, Binder's approach to leadership in small groups (Binder, Burton, and

Terebinski 1965), Cohen's approach to conflict and conformity (Cohen 1964), and Roby's study of belief states and the uses of evidence (Roby 1965).

One might detect a similar pattern in the increasing familiarity of computer technology influencing the development of information processing theories of learning. The latter style in theorizing is thrusting itself forward and, in liaison with the computer, may prove as fruitful as stimulus sampling theory has, by reexamining experimental paradigms in a new light and permitting the testing of theory in the finer structure of the data.

chapter 10

INFORMATION THEORY

10.1 INTRODUCTION

This chapter begins with two introductory sentences from well-known books about information theory.

> There is no reason to expect anyone to know what the word *information* means to an information theorist unless he has been told (Raisbeck 1964, p. 2).

> The technical meaning of "information" is not radically different from its everyday meaning; it is merely more precise (Attneave 1959, p. 1).

These quotes are not as contradictory as they may appear to be. Taken together, they mean that the term *information* as used in information theory has a technical meaning—a meaning that cannot be inferred from an examination of the everyday usage of the term and that is not identical to its meaning in everyday usage. But the meaning of the term is not at variance with its everyday meaning.

At the beginning of this chapter the technical meanings of the terms *information, uncertainty*, and *transmission* will be examined. Because these technical meanings are related to everyday meaning, everyday examples will be used to make the development of the technical terms intuitively palpable. These examples should not imply, however, that the technical meanings are primarily an extension of the everyday meanings.

Section 10.2 develops the technical meaning of the terms *information* and *uncertainty*. This section is followed by Sec. 10.3 in which various properties of these terms are examined. Section 10.4 then develops the technical meaning of the term *transmission*. The last five sections (10.5–10.9) concern the application of these concepts to psychology.

10.2   THE CONCEPTS OF INFORMATION AND UNCERTAINTY

As is well known, the *variance* of a distribution of n discrete numbers (x_1, $x_2, \ldots, x_n$) is equal to

$$\frac{\sum_i (x_i - \bar{x})^2}{n}$$

where

$$\bar{x} = \frac{\sum_i x_i}{n}.$$

The technical meaning of the term *variance* consists of this computational formula. Even if we were to supply a verbal definition of the term—e.g., "the average squared deviation about the mean"—the verbal definition would be precisely equivalent to the computational formula. In fact, the technical meaning of any statistic consists of its computational formula.

Information and *uncertainty*, like variance, are statistics. Like the term *variance*, therefore, the terms *information* and *uncertainty* derive precise technical meaning from the formulas used to compute them.

These statistics are used to describe a wide variety of communications systems—telegraph systems, telephone systems, systems of face-to-face verbal contact, and so on. These systems may be quite dissimilar physically. What they all have in common is that some message is delivered from something that may be termed a *message source* to something that may be termed a *receiver*. The statistic *information* is a number that describes how much information is conveyed from source to receiver when a given message is delivered. The assumption on which this quantification is based is that there are probabilities associated with the messages that may be delivered and that the amount of information conveyed by a particular message may be determined from its probability of delivery.

Consider, then, that a message source is to select exactly one message from a set of possible messages:

$$X = \{x_1, x_2, \ldots, x_i, \ldots, x_n\}.$$

Consider, further, that there is a given probability that each message will be selected. That is, there is a set of probabilities:

$$P(X) = \{p(x_1), p(x_2), \ldots, p(x_i), \ldots, p(x_n)\}$$

such that for each i, $p(x_i)$ is the probability that x_i will be selected from X.

The first principle on which the information measure will be based is that the more probable a message, the less information it conveys. If we let $I(x_i)$ refer to the amount of information conveyed by x_i, this principle may be stated as follows:

P1

$$I(x_i) < I(x_k) \quad \text{if and only if} \quad p(x_i) > p(x_k).$$

[It must be remembered that the information conveyed by a message—that is, $I(x_i)$—is a number.]

This principle is in accord with common usage of the term *information*. For example, we may regard the high school graduation speaker as conveying one of a possible set of messages to the graduating class. If he says something trite—that is, if he conveys a highly probable message—we judge he has said very little or nothing. On the other hand, if he delivers a message that is highly improbable in the setting (e.g., "the main determinant of success in life is chance"), then we conclude he has really said something.

Note that according to the principle it is the probability of a message's delivery—and not its content—that determines its information value; content is important only insofar as it affects probability. For example, in the above illustration, it is the unusualness of the message "the main determinant of success in life is chance" that makes it convey a lot of information (not its truthfulness). And it must be emphasized that *the amount of information a message conveys varies from context to context because the probability of delivering that message varies from context to context*. The point of information theory is not to determine the probability of a message's selection but to specify the amount of information given such probabilities.

Now consider a message source that sends two messages, first a message from the set

$$X = \{x_1, x_2, \ldots, x_i, \ldots, x_n\}$$

and then a message from the set

$$Y = \{y_1, y_2, \ldots, y_j, \ldots, y_m\}$$

(these message sets need not be different).

As mentioned at the beginning of this section, it is assumed that the amount of information conveyed by a message is determined by its probability of selection. Thus the amount of information conveyed by a message x_i may be symbolized by $f[p(x_i)]$, indicating that it is some (as yet unknown) function of $p(x_i)$. Similarly, the amount of information conveyed by a message y_j given a message x_i has already been selected is a function of the probability of y_j's selection given x_i has previously been selected. This amount may be symbolized by $f[p(y_j|x_i)]$, where $p(y_j|x_i)$ refers to the probability of y_j's selection given x_i's selection.

The second principle on which the definition of *information* is based may be stated as follows: If the messages x_i and y_j are selected, the amount of information conveyed by both of them should equal the amount conveyed by x_i plus the amount conveyed by y_j given x_i has been selected. Remembering that information is a function of probability, we see this principle is equivalent to

P2
$$I(x_i \text{ and } y_j) = f[p(x_i)] + f[p(y_j|x_i)].$$

But we may also view the selection of x_i and y_j as the selection of a *single* message from the message set formed by the Cartesian product of X and Y. That is, we may view the situation as one in which a single message is sent from the following message set:

$$\begin{bmatrix} (x_1, y_1) & (x_1, y_2) \ldots (x_1, y_j) \ldots (x_1, y_m) \\ (x_2, y_1) & (x_2, y_2) \ldots (x_2, y_j) \ldots (x_2, y_m) \\ \vdots & \vdots \quad\quad \vdots \quad\quad \vdots \\ (x_i, y_1) & (x_i, y_2) \ldots (x_i, y_j) \ldots (x_i, y_m) \\ \vdots & \vdots \quad\quad \vdots \quad\quad \vdots \\ (x_n, y_1) & (x_n, y_2) \ldots (x_n, y_j) \ldots (x_n, y_m) \end{bmatrix}.$$

The information conveyed by the message pair (x_i, y_j) is a function of the probability that pair is selected, that is,

$$I(x_i \text{ and } y_j) = f[p(x_i \text{ and } y_j)].$$

Substituting in P2, we obtain

$$f[p(x_i \text{ and } y_j)] = f[p(x_i)] + f[p(y_j|x_i)].$$

But $p(x_i$ and $y_j) = p(y_j$ and $x_i)$, and by the elementary axioms of probability $p(y_j$ and $x_i) = p(y_j|x_i)p(x_i)$. Thus we conclude that f must satisfy the condition that

$$f[p(y_j|x_i)p(x_i)] = f[p(y_j|x_i)]+f[p(x_i)].$$

For the moment, let $p(y_j|x_i)$ be symbolized by an a and $p(x_i)$ be symbolized by a b. The condition that f must satisfy may then be written as

$$f(ab) = f(a)+f(b).$$

The most common function satisfying this condition is the logarithmic function (because $\log ab = \log a+\log b$). Hence, we shall set $f(a) = k \log a$, where k is some constant. Thus

$$I(x_i) = f[p(x_i)] = k \log p(x_i).$$

The question is what k should be. Returning to P1, we note that as $p(x_i)$ decreases, $I(x_i) = k \log p(x_i)$ should increase and *vice versa*. But because $p(x_i)$ is less than 1, $\log p(x_i)$ becomes *increasingly negative* as $p(x_i)$ decreases. To make $I(x_i) = k \log p(x_i)$ become *increasingly positive* as $p(x_i)$ decreases, we need simply have k be some negative number. We choose -1 for convenience. Our conclusion:

$$I(x_i) = -\log p(x_i).$$

It is possible to prove that $I(x_i) = k \log p(x_i)$ with $k < 0$ is the *only* function satisfying both P1 and P2, but such a proof lies well beyond the scope of this presentation.[1]

To recapitulate:

P1
$$I(x_i) < I(x_k) \quad \text{if and only if} \quad p(x_i) > p(x_k)$$

and

P2
$$I(x_i \text{ and } y_j) = f[p(x_i)]+f[p(y_j|x_i)]$$

together imply

$$I(x_i) = -\log p(x_i).$$

[1]Actually, I must satisfy additional constraints of a technical nature; the reader is referred to Luce (1960, pp. 24–25).

Finally, we consider the *expected information* conveyed by an entire set of messages, $X = \{x_1, x_2, \ldots, x_i, \ldots, x_n\}$. By the definition of *expectation*, the expectation equals the sum of the information in the several possible messages multiplied by their probabilities,

$$= -\sum_{i=1}^{n} p(x_i) \log p(x_i).$$

This expected information is termed the *uncertainty* associated with a message set and is symbolized as $U(X)$. Thus

$$U(X) = -\sum_{i=1}^{n} p(x_i) \log p(x_i).$$

The term *uncertainty* is also in accord with common usage. We are uncertain about which message we shall receive to the degree to which the expected amount of information the message conveys is high, where *information* is an inverse monotonic function of probability.

Note that both *information* and *uncertainty* are numbers; the former is a number describing a message, whereas the latter is a number describing a message set. Thus these are descriptive statistics, and their definitions are given by the formulas according to which they are computed.

The unique determination of these numbers depends on the base of the logarithm chosen. When the logarithm is taken to the base 2, the resulting numbers are referred to as *bits* (the etymology of the term *bits* will be included in Sec. 10.3). The "number of bits of information" conveyed by message x_i equals $-\log_2 p(x_i)$, and the "number of bits of uncertainty" associated with message set X equals

$$U(X) = -\sum_{i=1}^{n} p(x_i) \log_2 p(x_i). \tag{10.1}$$

10.3   PROPERTIES OF UNCERTAINTY

Consider the situation in which all messages from a message set X are equally likely to be delivered. Then, as $p(x_i) = 1/n$,

$$I(x_i) = -\log \frac{1}{n} = \log n$$

and

$$U(X) = -\sum_{i=1}^{n} \frac{1}{n} \log \frac{1}{n} = -\frac{n}{n} \log \frac{1}{n} = \log n.$$

Here, when messages are equally likely, the information conveyed by each and the uncertainty of the set are equivalent.

We could have considered this situation first and then generalized to the situation in which not all messages are equally likely. If we had proceeded in this manner, our first principle would have been that information should increase as n increases. Our second principle would have been that the amount of information conveyed by a message from a set of n equally likely messages and by a message from an independent set of m equally likely messages should be the sum of the information conveyed by the first plus the information conveyed by the second.

Because, however, the two message sets are independent, there will be nm equally likely *pairs* of messages, and hence the amount of information conveyed by a pair should be a function of nm. Letting the information conveyed by a message from a set of n equally likely messages be symbolized by $f(n)$, the second principle would therefore have been equivalent to the statement

$$f(nm) = f(n) + f(m),$$

and our conclusion would again have been that f must be a logarithmic function. The simple function, log n, satisfies the first principle.

Thus log n is the amount of information conveyed by a message from a set of n equally likely messages. Again, this amount is expressed in *bits* when the log is taken to the base 2.

The above argument can then be generalized to message sets in which the messages are not equally likely. To appreciate this generalization, consider a message set $X = \{x_1, x_2, x_3\}$ consisting of messages with probabilities 1/2 (for message x_1's being selected), 1/4 (for message x_2's being selected), and 1/4 (for message x_3's being selected). Let the selection of the message be considered in two steps: First, it is determined that the message is either from the subset $\{x_1\}$ or from the subset $\{x_2, x_3\}$. Because it is equally likely that the message selected is from either of these two subsets, the uncertainty associated with this first step is one bit, ($\log_2 2$). With probability 1/2 the message to be selected is from the subset $\{x_1\}$, in which case no further information needs to be conveyed; the message is, in fact, x_1. With probability 1/2, however, there must be a second step in the selection, and this step conveys one additional bit of information; for with probability 1/2 the second step involves selection of one message from the subset $\{x_2, x_3\}$ of two equally likely messages. Thus one bit of information is conveyed in the first step of the selection, with probability 1/2 no additional information is conveyed in a second step, and with probability 1/2 an additional bit of information is conveyed in a second step. The expected information (*uncertainty*) is therefore $1\frac{1}{2}$ bits. But this result is given by the formula

$$U(X) = -\sum_{i=1}^{n} p(x_i) \log_2 p(x_i)$$

$$= -\tfrac{1}{2} \log_2 \tfrac{1}{2} - \tfrac{1}{4} \log_2 \tfrac{1}{4} - \tfrac{1}{4} \log_2 \tfrac{1}{4}$$

$$= \tfrac{1}{2} + \tfrac{1}{2} + \tfrac{1}{2}$$

$$= 1\tfrac{1}{2}.$$

Part of the motivation for considering sets of equally probable messages comes from the relation of such sets to *codes*. Consider, for example, a code consisting of two symbols (e.g., a dot and a dash, a zero and a one); such a code is termed a *binary* code. Let a *word of length m* be defined as a sequence of m of these symbols. Clearly, there are 2^m possible words of length m in binary code. (The first element in the word may be either of the two symbols in the code, the second may be either of two symbols, and so on.) Now consider the following question: *What is the minimal word length we must use if we wish to convey one of n equally likely messages in a binary code?*

For simplicity, we shall consider only the case where n is some power of 2. The answer to this question lies in finding an m with the property that

$$2^m = n,$$

because there will be 2^m different words of length m, and we want each of these words to refer to one of the n messages.

By taking logarithms of both sides of the above equation, we obtain

$$\log 2^m = \log n$$

or

$$m \log 2 = \log n.$$

If the logarithm is taken to the base 2, the conclusion is that

$$m = \log_2 n$$

(because $\log_2 2 = 1$). But $\log_2 n$ is also the number of bits of information conveyed by a message from the set of messages under consideration and the uncertainty associated with that set. Thus *the minimal length of a word in binary code that can be used to convey one of n equally likely messages from a message set is equal to the number of bits of uncertainty associated with that set.*

(The etymology of the term *bits* is explained by the above conclusion; *bits* is a contraction of "binary digits.")

For example, consider that we are spies at a missile base on a checkerboard (see Fig. 10.1) and that we wish to convey the location of the base by

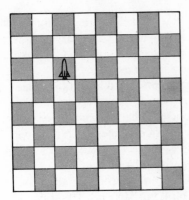

Fig. 10.1   Missile base on the checkerboard.

using a binary code (e.g., dots and dashes). We wish to specify one of the 64 equally likely squares as the location of the base. Because we are in great danger of being caught while we deliver the message, we wish to make it as short as possible. It can immediately be concluded that the message will have to be at least six units long, because $\log_2 64 = 6$. (That is, there are $2^6 = 64$ possible "words" of length six in a binary code.) Following is a code that could be used: Let the first unit indicate whether the base is on the left or right half of the board (a dot indicates the left and a dash the right); let the second unit indicate whether the base is on the top or bottom of the *remaining* squares (a dot indicates the top and a dash the bottom); let the third unit indicate whether the base is on the left or the right of the squares still remaining; and so on. Then, the message used to specify the base illustrated in Fig. 10.1 would be "$. . - - . .$".[2]

Another example of a code that could be used would be as follows: Let the first unit indicate whether the base is the left or the right half of the board (again let a dot indicate left and a dash right); let the second unit indicate whether the base is on the left or right half of the remaining squares, and let the third unit indicate whether the base is on the left or right half of the squares remaining still. (By now, the column has been specified.) Now let the fourth unit indicate whether the base is on the top or the bottom half of that column (again letting a dot indicate top and a dash bottom), and so on. In this code the message specifying the base illustrated in Fig. 10.1 will be "$. - . . - .$".

Note that both of the above codes have a property in common: *Each successive unit eliminates half the remaining possibilities.* In fact, *any* code we could devise that satisfied our condition of being minimal would have that property. For if we consider all possible words, exactly half will begin with a dot (and half with a dash), exactly half will have a dot as a second unit (and half with a dash), exactly half will have a dot as a third unit (and

---

[2]The example of finding a square on a checkerboard does not originate with the present authors. It was first introduced into the literature by Fred Attneave, and our discussion follows his closely (1959, pp. 3–6).

half a dash), and so on. Thus each succeeding unit must eliminate exactly half the remaining possible words that could be formed, and if the binary code is used optimally, each word will refer to a possible message; hence, each succeeding unit must eliminate exactly half the possible messages.

Because the number of bits is related to minimal word length (as established above) and because each unit in such words has the property of eliminating half the possible messages, we conclude that *the number of bits of uncertainty associated with a set of equally likely messages is equal to the number of units necessary to specify a message when each successive unit eliminates half the remaining possible messages.*

Again, we could have defined *bits* in terms of this property, and some authors have, for example, Attneave (1959, p. 4); in fact, his definition of "number of bits of information" follows his discussion of how to locate a square on a checkerboard.

It should also be noted that in the checkerboard example all words were of equal length—six units. Why could not the average word length be decreased by substituting words of lesser length for some of the words of length six? For example, substitute a single dot for the word ". . . . . .". We cannot. For if we did so, a blank space would, in effect, become a third symbol, and the code would no longer be a binary code. That is, if (dot, blank, blank, blank, blank, blank) differed from (dot, dash, dash, dash, dash, dash) and from (dot, dot, dot, dot, dot, dot), the blank would be just as much a symbol in the code as would a dot or a dash. And the condition considered was that the code be binary, i.e., consist of only two symbols.

It is not necessary to restrict ourselves to binary codes to reach the conclusions outlined above. Suppose, for example, we were considering a code with an alphabet of n symbols. It would then be possible to construct n^m words of length m. If we wished to determine the minimal word length needed to deliver one of N equally likely messages, we would solve for m in the equation $n^m = N$. Specifically, $m = \log N/\log n$. Equivalently, $m = \log_n N$ (because by taking logarithms to the base n, the term $\log n$ becomes 1). Then we might conclude that the number of units of uncertainty (termed *nits* or something) associated with a set of N equally likely messages is equal to the minimal length of the word required to deliver one of these messages in our code. Moreover, we would probably note that the maximally efficient codes are those in which each successive symbol reduces the possible messages that are being delivered by a factor of $1/n$. And we would conclude that the number of units of uncertainty associated with a message set of N equally likely messages is equal to the number of units necessary to specify the message when each successive unit reduces the number of remaining possible messages by a factor of n.

Now consider a message set mentioned earlier. In response to the question of what a typical student is doing at 11 o'clock in the evening, a message is delivered from the following set:

x_1: talking, $p(x_1) = \frac{1}{2}$
x_2: consuming, $p(x_2) = \frac{1}{4}$
x_3: neither talking nor consuming, $p(x_3) = \frac{1}{4}$

Suppose we wished to convey one of these messages with a binary code of dots and dashes. Let a single dash convey message x_1, a dot and a dash convey message x_2, and a dot and a dot convey message x_3. With probability 1/2 the word delivering the message will be of length one unit, and with probability 1/2 the word will be of length two units. Thus the *expected length* of the word will be one and one-half units. But one and one-half is the number of bits of uncertainty associated with the message set. Thus just as we found that the length of a word in binary code that conveys one of 2^n equally likely messages is equal to the number of bits of uncertainty associated with that set ($=n$), we find that the expected length of a word that conveys one of a number of messages that are not equally likely is equal to the uncertainty of that set.

Two points must be clarified before a general principle is stated. First, there was the objection to using words of unequal length in the checkerboard example because such use would involve making the blank space a third symbol. The same objection does not apply here, because there is no word beginning with a dash other than the word consisting of a single dash. Hence, there is no distinction between dash blank and dash anything else. Second, it might be asked why we do not let x_2 be represented by a single dot, thereby decreasing the expected word length to one and one-fourth units. If we did make this assignment, we would again be introducing a blank space in the code because dot blank would be different from dot dot.

A left-handed code is one in which no word is the beginning of another word. The code described above is left-handed. So are the codes described for locating the missile base on the checkerboard. (In fact, all codes consisting of words of the same length are left-handed codes.) *It is a provable theorem that if a left-handed binary code is used to specify a message from a message set the expected word length can never be less than the number of bits of uncertainty associated with the message set* (Shannon 1948).

Of course, the expected length can be greater. It can be greater if we assign words to messages in an inefficient manner. For example, suppose we assign a dash to x_3 in the above set, a dot dot to x_2, and a dot dash to x_1. Expected word length would then be one and three-quarters units. Thus, what the theorem states is that the uncertainty of a message set is a *lower bound* on the expected word length.

Codes that depart from maximal efficiency are said to be *redundant*, and the degree of this departure is termed their degree of redundancy. (Later, there will be an exact definition of what is meant by degree of redundancy.)

By now, we have examined five ways by which the concept of the *uncertainty of a message set* could be defined.

1. The *uncertainty* of a message set could be defined as the expected information, where *information* is a number associated with each message that satisfies P1 and P2.
2. The *uncertainty* of a set of equally likely messages could be defined as a number that satisfies the two conditions mentioned that were highly similar to P1 and P2. The concept of *uncertainty* could then be generalized to apply to message sets in which not all messages are equally likely.
3. The *uncertainty*—measured in bits—of a set of equally likely messages could be defined as the minimal length of a word in binary code that can be used to convey one of the messages. The concept of *uncertainty* could then be generalized to apply to message sets in which not all messages are equally likely.
4. The *uncertainty*—measured in bits—of a set of equally likely messages could be defined as the number of units necessary to specify a message when each successive unit eliminates half the remaining possible messages. The concept of *uncertainty* could then be generalized to apply to message sets in which not all messages are equally likely.
5. The *uncertainty*—measured in bits—of a message set could be defined as the lower bound on the expected word length when a left-handed binary code is used to deliver the message.

The point is that all the definitions yield the same result:

$$U(X) = - \sum_{i=1}^{n} p(x_i) \log p(x_i).$$

And this formula yields a unique determination of *number of bits* when the logs are taken to the base 2. As was pointed out at the beginning of this chapter, the precise definition of a statistic resides in its computational formula. Because all definitions yield the same formula, all are equally good.

In organizing this chapter, we chose definition 1 and treated definitions 2–5 as properties. Had we not been interested in developing the reader's intuitive appreciation of the concept, we might best have proceeded by defining *uncertainty* in terms of its computational formula and then treating definitions 1–5 as properties.

One point of caution. All authors (of whom we have knowledge) would agree with our definition of *uncertainty*. Some authors, however, do not treat *information* separately from *uncertainty*, but rather use the two terms interchangeably. (This is particularly true of authors who begin by considering sets of equally likely messages, for in such sets the two quantities are identical.) Of these authors, some use a term such as *surprisal* in places where we have used the term *information*, whereas others do not consider the information content of single messages at all. Usually, however, the author's intent is clear. At some point in his text, he will state whether he means *information* to refer to $-\log p(x_i)$ or $-\sum_{i=1}^{n} p(x_i) \log p(x_i)$.

10.4 TRANSMISSION

Consider a set of messages $X = \{x_1, x_2, \ldots, x_i, \ldots, x_n\}$ and a set $Y = \{y_1, y_2, \ldots, y_j, \ldots, y_m\}$ and their Cartesian product $X \times Y$. Again, let $p(x_i)$ refer to the probability of selecting $x_i \in X$, let $p(y_j)$ refer to the probability of selecting $y_j \in Y$, and let $p(x_i, y_j)$ refer to the probability of selecting $(x_i, y_j) \in X \times Y$.

Suppose x_i is selected; then the information that would be conveyed by y_j were it selected would be

$$-\log p(y_j|x_i).$$

Thus the expected uncertainty of Y given that message x_i is selected from X would be

$$-\sum_{j=1}^{m} p(y_j|x_i) \log p(y_j|x_i).$$

The expected uncertainty of Y given that *some* message from X is selected is therefore

$$-\sum_{i=1}^{n} p(x_i) \sum_{j=1}^{m} p(y_j|x_i) \log p(y_j|x_i).$$

That is, we determine the uncertainty of Y given that x_1 is selected and multiply it by the probability that x_1 is selected; we determine the uncertainty of Y given that x_2 is selected and multiply it by the probability that x_2 is selected; and so on. Then we sum across all possibilities from X.

The expected uncertainty of Y given some message from X will be symbolized $U(Y|X)$. It is termed the *conditional uncertainty of Y given X*. That is,

$$U(Y|X) = -\sum_{i=1}^{n} p(x_i) \sum_{j=1}^{m} p(y_j|x_i) \log p(y_j|x_i). \tag{10.2}$$

The *information transmitted from X to Y* is defined as *the uncertainty of Y minus the conditional uncertainty of Y given X*. Letting information transmitted from X to Y be symbolized by $T(X, Y)$, we have

$$T(X, Y) = U(Y) - U(Y|X).$$

Immediately, it is desirable to prove a theorem about $T(X, Y)$. Let $U(X \times Y)$, written as $U(XY)$, refer to the uncertainty of $X \times Y$—which is

$$U(XY) = -\sum_{i=1}^{n} \sum_{j=1}^{m} p(x_i, y_j) \log p(x_i, y_j) \qquad (10.3)$$

Then:

THEOREM 10.1

$$T(X, Y) = U(X) + U(Y) - U(XY).$$

Proof

Because $T(X, Y) = U(Y) - U(Y|X)$ by definition, it is only necessary to prove that $-U(Y|X) = U(X) - U(XY)$. We begin by considering the computational formula for $-U(Y|X)$, from Eq. (10.2),

$$-U(Y|X) = \sum_{i=1}^{n} p(x_i) \sum_{j=1}^{m} p(y_j|x_i) \log p(y_j|x_i).$$

But by the basic laws of probability $p(y_j|x_i) = p(x_i, y_j)/p(x_i)$. Thus, substituting in the formula for $-U(Y|X)$, we obtain

$$-U(Y|X) = \sum_{i=1}^{n} p(x_i) \sum_{j=1}^{m} \frac{p(x_i, y_j)}{p(x_i)} \log \frac{p(x_i, y_j)}{p(x_i)}.$$

But because $p(x_i)$ after the second summation sign is a constant when summed across j, it may be placed outside the summation sign. Thus

$$-U(Y|X) = \sum_{i=1}^{n} \frac{p(x_i)}{p(x_i)} \sum_{j=1}^{m} p(x_i, y_j) \log \frac{p(x_i, y_j)}{p(x_i)}$$

$$= \sum_{i=1}^{n} \sum_{j=1}^{m} p(x_i, y_j) \log \frac{p(x_i, y_j)}{p(x_i)}.$$

But because $\log [p(x_i, y_j)/p(x_i)] = \log p(x_i, y_j) - \log p(x_i)$, we obtain

$$-U(Y|X) = \sum_{i=1}^{n} \sum_{j=1}^{m} p(x_i, y_j) [\log p(x_i, y_j) - \log p(x_i)]$$

$$= \sum_{i=1}^{n} \sum_{j=1}^{m} p(x_i, y_j) \log p(x_i, y_j) - \sum_{i=1}^{n} \sum_{j=1}^{m} p(x_i, y_j) \log p(x_i).$$

Finally, because

$$\sum_{j=1}^{m} p(x_i, y_j) = p(x_i),$$

we may substitute this equality in the second term of the equation to conclude

$$-U(Y|X) = \sum_{i=1}^{n} \sum_{j=1}^{m} p(x_i, y_j) \log p(x_i, y_j) - \sum_{i=1}^{n} p(x_i) \log p(x_i)$$

$$= -U(XY) + U(X)$$

or

$$U(X) - U(XY),$$

which establishes the theorem.

The first consequence of the theorem is that the amount of information transmitted from X to Y equals the amount transmitted from Y to X; that is, $T(X, Y) = T(Y, X)$ always. This equality is shown by the theorem, because if X is substituted for Y in it and *vice versa* its right-hand side remains unchanged. Thus we speak of the information transmitted *between* X and Y and make no statement about its directionality.

Second, the theorem enables us to identify uncertainty and information transmitted with areas in Venn or Euler diagrams, as in Fig. 10.2.

In Fig. 10.2, the area labeled $T(X, Y)$ is equal to the area labeled $U(X)$ plus the area labeled $U(Y)$ minus the area labeled $U(XY)$—just as $T(X, Y) = U(X) + U(Y) - U(XY)$.

Figure 10.2 also illustrates the fact that $T(X, Y)$ is equal to the maximal

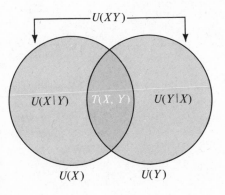

Fig. 10.2 Venn diagram of the relationships between simple uncertainties, conditional uncertainties, and transmission.

amount of uncertainty that could be associated with $X \times Y$ minus the amount that actually is, because the maximal value $U(XY)$ could have is $U(X) + U(Y)$, as shown in the figure. This property—that the amount of information transmitted between two message sets is equal to the maximal possible value of the uncertainty of their Cartesian product minus the actual value—can serve as a basis for defining the amount of information transmitted between several message sets. Such information transmission is generally termed *multivariate constraint*, or simply *constraint*.

That is, the *multivariate constraint* between message sets $X_1, X_2, \ldots, X_s$ is equal to the *maximal value of the uncertainty of their Cartesian product minus the actual value*. Because the maximal value of the uncertainty of their Cartesian product is equal to the sum of their respective uncertainties (see Fig. 10.2), we conclude that the multivariate constraint between message sets $X_1, X_2, \ldots, X_s$ equals

$$\sum_{i=1}^{s} U(X_i) - U(X_1 \times X_2 \times \ldots \times X_s).$$

For an elementary discussion of multivariate constraint, see Attneave (1959); for a more exhaustive discussion, see Garner (1962) and Toda's review (1963) of Garner's book. In this chapter, our discussion is limited to information transmitted between two message sets.

Thus *transmission* measures the constraint between sets of entities that can be conceptualized as message sets. For a discussion of how this measure is related to other measures of constraint, see Garner and McGill (1956).

Information transmission is most easily computed from a *joint probability matrix*. Let the joint probabilities of message pairs from X and Y be represented in a matrix designated $P(X \times Y)$, as in Fig. 10.3.

The sum of the probabilities in row i of this matrix equals $p(x_i)$; that is, as pointed out in the proof of our theorem,

$$P(X \times Y) = \begin{bmatrix} p(x_1, y_1), p(x_1, y_2), \ldots, p(x_1, y_m) \\ p(x_2, y_1) \\ \cdot \\ \cdot \\ \cdot \\ p(x_n, y_1) \qquad \cdot \quad \cdot \quad \cdot \end{bmatrix}$$

Fig. 10.3 Joint probability matrix.

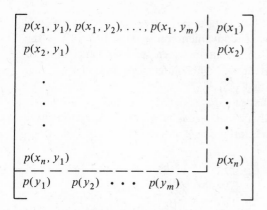

Fig. 10.4 Joint probability matrix with marginal probabilities included.

$$\sum_{j=1}^{m} p(x_i, y_j) = p(x_i).$$

Similarly, the sum of the probabilities in column j equals $p(y_j)$. These sums are termed *marginal probabilities*. The set $P(X \times Y)$ with the marginal probabilities included is presented in Fig. 10.4.

Thus the marginal probabilities formed by summing the rows across columns constitute the set $P(X)$, and the marginal probabilities formed by summing the columns across rows constitute the set $P(Y)$. And it therefore follows that the information transmitted between X and Y—$T(X, Y)$—is equal to the sum of the uncertainties computed from the marginal entries minus the uncertainty computed from the probabilities in the entire matrix.

The *coefficient of constraint of X on Y* is defined as *one minus the conditional uncertainty of Y given X divided by the uncertainty of Y.* Letting this coefficient be symbolized by $C_{Y \cdot X}$,

$$C_{Y \cdot X} = 1 - \frac{U(Y|X)}{U(Y)}$$

$$= \frac{U(Y) - U(Y|X)}{U(Y)}$$

$$= \frac{T(X, Y)}{U(Y)}. \tag{10.4}$$

The coefficient is simply the proportion of the uncertainty associated with a given message set that is transmitted from another set.

Note that $C_{Y \cdot X}$ will not equal $C_{X \cdot Y}$ except when $U(Y) = U(X)$. Nevertheless, the information transmitted from X to Y will always equal the information transmitted from Y to X, as pointed out earlier. In general, the coefficient of constraint is simply a convenient ratio, and $T(X, Y)$ is the variable that tells the *amount* of constraint between sets. Statistical tests of significance, for example, are based on the absolute magnitude of $T(X, Y)$, not its relative magnitude ($C_{X \cdot Y}$ or $C_{Y \cdot X}$).

A closely allied concept is that of *redundancy*, symbolized R.

Redundancy is conventionally defined as *one minus the actual uncertainty of a message set divided by the maximal possible uncertainty*. That is,

$$R(X) = 1 - \frac{\text{actual } U(X)}{\text{maximal } U(X)}.$$

Note that this measure depends on what we consider $U(X)$ to be and what we consider the "maximal $U(X)$" to be. Usually, maximal uncertainty is considered to be that uncertainty that would be associated with X were all messages equally likely, i.e., $\log n$. Thus

$$R(X) = 1 - \frac{U(X)}{\log n}. \tag{10.5}$$

On the other hand, $U(X)$ is not always so easy to determine. This difficulty will be illustrated by example.

The English language is often said to have a high degree of redundancy because each word *in context* has much less uncertainty associated with it than do words considered out of context—and much much less uncertainty associated with it than $\log n$, where n is the number of words in the English language. For example, if I say "shut off the alarm ————," the next word has a high probability of being either *dammit* or *clock*. It has a rather small probability of being *cheese*. And in general if I view the fifth word of sentences as being messages selected from sets of possible messages there is much less uncertainty associated with these sets if I know the first four words than if I do not.

The problem with determining *the* redundancy of English is that the actual uncertainty will vary with the breadth of the context in which the word (message) is considered. If, for example, we consider only the preceding word, *the* uncertainty associated with words is much greater than if we consider the preceding two words or three words. Moreover, if we consider the "complete" context in which a word appears, there is almost no uncertainty at all associated with it. (Delete a single word at random in a book, and you have very little uncertainty concerning what word it is.) Thus we cannot speak of *the* redundancy of English but rather must speak of how redundant English words are *given* certain contexts in which the words appear.

To incorporate the context into the measurement on the redundancy of English, authors have spoken of *orders* of redundancy. First-order English is

English in which each word is considered separately and its probability is determined from (an estimate of) the probability with which it appears in English. Because not all words are equally likely, such English would have a certain degree of redundancy associated with it; this redundancy is the first-order redundancy of English. Second-order English is English in which each word is considered within the context of the preceding word, and the second-order redundancy of English is the redundancy associated with words so considered. Third-order English is English in which each word is considered within the context of the two preceding words, and so on.

It appears to the present authors that it is much simpler to talk about information transmitted from various contexts to words, or to talk about the conditional uncertainty of words given various contexts, than to talk about orders of English. For example, if we were to consider the conditional uncertainty of fifth words given the preceding four, we would simply apply our knowledge that this conditional uncertainty is equal to the uncertainty associated with sequences of five words minus the uncertainty associated with sequences of four words. The relationships involved in this example are illustrated in Fig. 10.5. If, then, we wished to construct ratios, coefficients of constraint, etc., we could easily do so.

An additional example: Suppose we wish to measure how prejudiced (prone to stereotyping) an individual is by noting how redundant (the word is used colloquially) his ascription of personality characteristics is when we know the ethnic origin of the person he is describing. That is, we have a message set X consisting of ethnic origins and a message set Y consisting of personality descriptions. We present our individual with a person of a given origin (i.e., we present him with a message from X), and he picks a personality description (i.e., he picks a message from Y). We wish to argue that the more information transmitted from X to Y, the more prejudiced the individual is. Suppose, however, we attempt to measure his prejudice with a measure of redundancy rather than transmission. According to Eq. (10.5),

$$R(Y) = 1 - \frac{U(Y)}{\log m} = \frac{\log m - U(Y)}{\log m}.$$

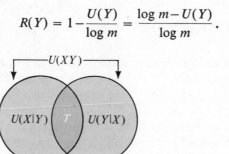

$X \equiv$ sequences of four words
$Y \equiv$ single words
$X \times Y \equiv$ sequences of five words

Fig. 10.5 Venn diagram of information transmitted by words in context.

$R(Y)$ is then a decrease in uncertainty *relative to log m*. But we are now comparing the actual uncertainty to the uncertainty that would describe the individual's responses were he to use each personality characteristic with equal probability. Instead, we would be interested in comparing the actual uncertainty to the uncertainty describing his responses when he does *not* know the ethnic origin of the person he is characterizing. The relative decrease in uncertainty viewed in this manner is precisely the coefficient of constraint of X (the ethnic origin) on Y (the personality characteristics).

Because the coefficient of constraint can describe any constraint described by redundancy, because it can describe more types of constraint, and because it is less ambiguous, it is perhaps a preferable concept. The reader should, however, be thoroughly familiar with the term *redundancy*, because it is widely used.

Finally, the use of the term *redundancy* as defined above may be related to its use in describing codes. It was stated earlier that the degree of redundancy of a code is the degree to which it departs from maximal efficiency. The formula for redundancy, Eq. (10.5), may be used to give a precise measure of this degree of departure. In this equation, $U(X)$ may refer to the uncertainty associated with the message set from which a message is actually selected by the code being considered; maximal $U(X)$ then refers to the uncertainty associated with a message set from which a message *could* be selected *were* the code used with maximal efficiency. If, for example, a binary code with words of length four were used to specify one of eight equally likely messages, the uncertainty associated with the message set from which a message is actually delivered is three bits. This same code *could*, however, be used to specify one of 16 equally likely messages were it used with maximal efficiency, in which case it would be used to select a message from a set that has four bits of uncertainty associated with it. Hence, the degree to which the code as it is actually used departs from maximal efficiency is $1 - 3/4$, or 25 percent. It is 25 percent redundant.

10.5   APPLICATION TO ANALYSIS OF FORM

Many psychologists have been interested in studying the predictability of forms, such as visual shapes, and the psychological impact of that predictability. For example, the entire outline of a circle may be predicted from any of its arcs, as in Fig. 10.6(a); in contrast, the relationship between the parts of the shape presented in Fig. 10.6(b) is not so obvious. And certainly the circle is more easily recalled, "forms a better gestalt," and so on than does the shape in Fig. 10.6(b). We would also find general agreement that one of the main reasons the music of classical composers (e.g., Mozart) has a different (psychological) quality than that of neoromantic composers (e.g., Shosta-

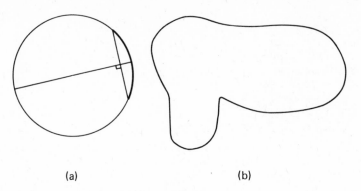

(a)   (b)

Fig. 10.6 A circle and an irregular form.

kovich) is because melodic and harmonic sequences of the former are more predictable than those of the latter.[3]

Shortly after information theory was developed, a number of psychologists independently came up with the idea that its statistics could be used to measure predictability (Attneave 1954; Weinstein and Fitts 1954; Hochberg and McAlister 1953). The basic conception was that the degree of predictability of a form could be measured in terms of uncertainty, that the degree to which some parts of a form could be predicted from others could be measured by conditional uncertainty. The statistic that became most used was redundancy, and for some time there were articles concerning recognition, recall, rated complexity, and discrimination of visual form as a function of *the* redundancy of the form. As pointed out in Sec. 10.4, however, the measurement of redundancy can be somewhat elusive, because it is dependent on how we conceptualize our message set and on what we regard the maximal uncertainty associated with it to be.

Despite the problems with applying the statistics of information theory to the analysis of visual form, some empirical generalizations of interest have been established—at least tentatively. They may be found in Garner's book *Uncertainty and Structure as Psychological Concepts*. Here, discussion will be limited to how it is that information theory measures may be applied to analyze visual form and to the problems that arise in such application. Discussion will center about the visual form known as the *metric figure*, which was developed in the early 1950's by Paul Fitts and his associates at Ohio State (Fitts, Weinstein, Rappaport, Anderson, and Leonard 1956; Weinstein and Fitts 1954).

[3]For a review of the analysis of musical form and the application of information theory to this analysis, see Cohen (1962); oddly enough, at the time Cohen's review was written, analysis was restricted almost exclusively to melodic sequence, whereas harmonic sequence would appear to be much simpler to analyze.

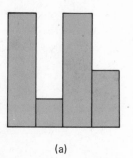
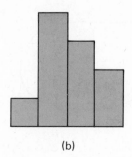

(a)   (b)

Fig. 10.7   Metric figures.

Such metric figures are constructed of columns of varying height. For example, the figures in Fig. 10.7 consist of four columns that vary in height from one to four units.

The measure of uncertainty associated with metric figures is dependent on their construction. For example, the figure in Fig. 10.7(a) was constructed according to the rule that each column could be from one to four units high, with equal probability. The figure in Fig. 10.7(b) was constructed according to the rule that each column must be of a different height—again with the stipulation that all such figures are equally likely to be constructed. Thus there are 4^4, or 256, figures that are constructed with equal likelihood according to the rules governing construction of the first figure and 4!, or 24, figures that are constructed with equal likelihood according to the rules governing construction of the second figure. Thus Fitts and his associates argue that there are $\log_2 256 = 8$ bits of uncertainty associated with figures of the first type and $\log_2 24 = 4.58$ bits of uncertainty associated with figures of the second type. Further, because figures of the first type are not constrained in any way, the uncertainty associated with these figures is considered to be maximal; thus they are regarded as 0 percent redundant, whereas the redundancy of figures of the second type is regarded to be $1 - 4.58/8$, or .53.

Several experiments were conducted in which the subject's task was to pick out a particular metric figure from a display of many metric figures. A typical finding was that the figure was most easily picked out if it was one labeled nonredundant in a display of figures labeled redundant. (Figures were constructed according to many different rules that led to different degrees of redundancy.)

Garner (1962), in commenting on the Ohio State work, argued that those figures labeled redundant were actually nonredundant and *vice versa.* Consider the figures in Fig. 10.7. Garner argues that no matter how the figures were constructed the subject will be presented with an array of only n of some particular type, and hence the actual uncertainty associated with the figures with which he is presented is $\log_2 n$. Now, 256 figures *could* have been constructed according to the rule governing construction of figures of the first type, whereas only 24 could have been constructed according to the rules governing construction of figures of the second type. Hence, Garner argues, the values of maximum uncertainty should be $\log_2 256 = 8$ for figures of the first type and $\log_2 24 = 4.58$ for figures of the second type. It follows that for the figures of the first type the value for redundancy should be $1 - [(\log_2 n)/8]$, which will be greater than $1 - [(\log_2 n)/4.58]$, the value for redundancy of figures of the second type.

It would seem reasonable to ask which analysis, Garner's or Fitts's, is correct. *Redundancy* is a technical term defined by an explicit formula: $1 - [\text{actual } U(X)/\text{maximal } U(X)]$. It would seem, therefore, that there could be little room for controversy about the value of redundancy, except in a situation in which there is disagreement about the probabilities associated with the messages in X; such a situation does not exist in the present controversy, because Fitts and Garner are in agreement about the probabilities with which the figures are presented.

But neither analysis is correct or incorrect. Although the formula is explicit, it does not specify what is meant by actual $U(X)$ or maximal $U(X)$ in any given application. Fitts conceptualizes actual $U(X)$ in terms of the figure construction; Garner conceptualizes actual $U(X)$ in terms of the figure population. Fitts conceptualizes maximal $U(X)$ in terms of the number of figures that could be constructed according to any rule, and Garner in terms of the number that could be constructed according to the rule actually in use.

Evans has proposed that the conceptualization of redundancy be dependent on the task with which the subject is faced (1967, p. 104).

Consider the following two lists:

WA 5–3174	872 3185
WA 5–7393	296 2618
WA 5–8286	513 2366

In which list are the examples more redundant? The answer depends on the purpose involved. If one is going to memorize the lists, the first list is more redundant because a part of each item is surplus; it need not be memorized for each item. But if one is going to discriminate between pairs of items, the second list exhibits greater redundancy because pairs of items in the second list have more elements differing between them.

Thus, when the task is one of recalling metric figures, the measure of redundancy proposed by Fitts *et al.* seems most appropriate; the subject can use the fact that all columns are of a different height to his advantage in such tasks. When, however, the problem is one of discriminating between stimuli, the measure proposed by Garner seems most appropriate; the larger the set of possible stimuli, the more ways in which the stimuli actually chosen can differ from each other. Evans reaches this same conclusion with respect to the difference between the Fitts and Garner measures, although he bases this conclusion on a somewhat elaborate theoretical rationale not presented here.

Attneave also indicates that the definition of redundancy—and other measures—should take account of the subject's reaction to the form. He writes (1959, p. 83), "We should constantly bear in mind, however, that the subject need not perceive objects in accordance with the experimenter's descriptive system." Consider metric figures. It is quite evident that the subject will perceive them in terms of their shape rather than in terms of the rules governing their construction. If, by pure chance, a metric figure of the first type in Fig. 10.7 happens to consist of four columns of equal length, it will then be perceived as a rectangle—a highly redundant figure. It is possible to guard against such aberrations by dealing with populations of figures rather than single figures.

But even then, suppose the subject simply does not perceive the redundancy in the population. It is possible for the subject not to act differently to figures of the first and second type in Fig. 10.7 because *for him* there is no functional difference; they might all appear and function as if they had all been generated without constraint. Or consider the subject who does not notice the fact that all three telephone numbers in the first column of Evans's example begin with WA 5. This redundancy then may not help his recall (although there are numerous experimental demonstrations that people performing various tasks may make use of cues of which they are unaware).

It may appear farfetched to the reader that such obvious structure should not have any effect, but consider the apparent "nonsense" shape in Fig. 10.6. It happens that this shape was generated by a rule that is just as restrictive, determinant, and predictable as the rule governing generation of a circle.[4]

In terms of polar coordinates the formula for generating a circle is

$$r = k \text{ (a constant).}$$

In terms of polar coordinates the formula for generating the shape in Fig. 10.6(b) is[5]

$$r = \sin \theta + \sin 2\theta + \sin 3\theta + 3.$$

The shape of each figure may be generated completely by knowing (1) the location of any point on its perimeter and (2) the angle θ between that point and the origin of the figure.

---

[4]The reader unfamiliar with polar coordinates should accept this assertion at face value and skip the section explaining the rule.
[5]We are indebted to William Chaplin for dreaming up this function and for programming a computer to obtain its actual shape.

Thus Evans proposes that the application of information theory statistics to the analysis of form should depend on the task involved; Attneave indicates that it should depend on the subject's perception of the form; and the above analysis suggests that it should depend on the subject's understanding of the rule generating the form. If we allow such dependence, however, we are not analyzing the form *itself*,[6] and when we use our dependent measures as independent variables, we run a risk of circularity. (If, for example, we define *redundancy* in such a way that it involves aspects of the stimulus most relevant to the task involved, it would be circular to state that the task is facilitated *because* the stimulus is redundant.)

10.6 APPLICATION TO HUMAN PERFORMANCE

The value the statistics *information*, *uncertainty*, and *transmission* have had in describing communications systems has led psychologists to suppose they may have value in describing contingency between stimulus and response. The outside world is conceptualized as a message source that delivers messages (i.e., stimuli) to an organism, and when the organism delivers a message (i.e., his response), this message depends partially on what message has been delivered to him. That is, stimuli are conceptualized as messages and responses are conceptualized as messages. T describes statistical constraint between stimuli and responses. This conceptualization is illustrated in Fig. 10.8.

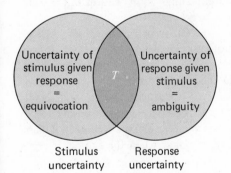

Fig. 10.8 Venn diagram of statistical constraint between stimuli and responses.

The uncertainty of the stimulus given the response is referred to as *equivocation*. (In common language a response that could have been elicited by a number of stimuli is termed an equivocal response.) The uncertainty of the response given the stimulus is termed *ambiguity*. (In common language an ambiguous stimulus is one that may elicit a number of responses.)

This conceptualization may be used to study *any* psychological processes provided (1) it is possible to partition stimulation into a set of discrete stimuli

[6]The question of what constitutes a stimulus may be raised at this point.

each of which has a probability associated with it and (2) it is possible to partition responses into a set of discrete responses each of which has a probability associated with it. It is, then, possible to measure T under a variety of conditions that we think may affect it.

In actual practice, however, this conceptualization has been used mainly to study human performance—situations in which the subject is supposed to make a response designated as "correct" (which could be anything from learning a paired associate to identifying words flashed at extremely brief intervals to accurately following a path in a rotor pursuit task). There are, in psychology, a large number of situations in which no response is correct—situations in which a subject is to make whatever response he deems appropriate rather than to learn a response designated as appropriate by the experimenter. But, with few exceptions, the statistics of information theory have not been used to describe these situations.

Human performance tasks may be classified in terms of *what constitutes error*. If, for example, the subject is to learn a given response to each of several stimuli, any uncertainty associated with the response given the stimulus is error. Tasks in which uncertainty associated with the response given the stimulus is error will be referred to as *ambiguity intolerant tasks*. Conversely, if each stimulus requires one or more distinct responses—that is, if no two stimuli require the same response—any uncertainty about the stimulus given the response is error. Tasks in which uncertainty associated with the stimulus given the response is error will be referred to as *equivocation intolerant tasks*. Finally, if a task is both ambiguity intolerant and equivocation intolerant, it will be referred to as a *pure transmission task*.

Figure 10.9 illustrates these three types of human performance tasks. The distinction between the three types of tasks closely parallels distinctions proposed by Posner (1964); the only difference is that Posner's distinctions have psychological implications, whereas the present distinctions are made in terms of task requirements.

Bush, Galanter, and Luce (1963) have proposed a classification of choice experiments that is highly similar to that presented here. Experiments in which there is a one-one pairing of stimulus and response when the subject is per-

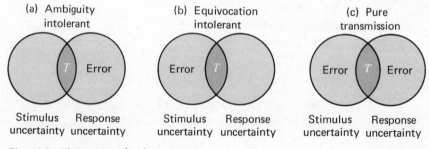

(a) Ambiguity intolerant   (b) Equivocation intolerant   (c) Pure transmission

Stimulus   Response   Stimulus   Response   Stimulus   Response
uncertainty uncertainty   uncertainty uncertainty   uncertainty uncertainty

Fig. 10.9 Three types of tasks.

forming perfectly are termed *complete identification* experiments; such experiments are classified as pure transmission tasks in the present terminology. Experiments in which there is a many-one pairing of stimulus and response are termed *partial identification* experiments; such experiments are classified as ambiguity intolerant tasks in the present terminology. Finally, experiments in which there is a one-many pairing of stimulus and response are termed *optional identification* experiments; such experiments are classified as equivocation intolerant tasks in the present terminology.

Thus far most of the human performance tasks analyzed by use of information theory statistics have been pure transmission tasks; they will be considered first in this chapter.

10.7 PURE TRANSMISSION TASKS

One-One Absolute Judgment

In a one-one absolute judgment task, the subject is to assign a single correct response to each stimulus; moreover, each stimulus requires a separate response. For example, learning to specify the notes in the octave above middle C when they are played on the piano is a one-one absolute judgment task.

Any task that requires a separate response to be associated with each separate stimulus really consists of three problems:

1. The stimuli must be discriminated.
2. The responses must be learned.
3. The associations between stimuli and responses must be established.

Absolute judgment tasks are those in which only the first problem must be solved. The subject is given a set of responses with which he is familiar, and the stimulus-response association is "compatible"; for example, the subject must label 10 tones varying in loudness with the numbers 1 (least loud) to 10 (most loud). Hence, the term *judgment* refers to ability to discriminate stimuli.

Absolute judgment may be described by information theory statistics as follows. Each stimulus is conceptualized as a message from a set of possible messages; hence, there is an uncertainty associated with the stimulus set—which, of course, is a function of the number of stimuli that must be discriminated and the probabilities with which they are presented to the subject. Each response of the subject is conceptualized as a message. Because the responses are emitted with various probabilities, and because the probabilities of various responses are partially contingent on which stimuli are presented, there is uncertainty associated with the subject's responses, and information is transmitted from the stimulus set to the response set. As in all pure transmission tasks, any conditional uncertainty associated with the response given the stimulus is error, as is any conditional uncertainty associated with the stimulus given the response. Thus, if the subject performs perfectly, the uncertainty of the stimulus set equals the uncertainty of the response set equals T.

Subjects do not, however, perform perfectly (if they did, there would be nothing of interest to study). The typical absolute judgment task, then, involves manipulating the stimulus uncertainty and observing how the response uncertainty and T vary as this stimulus uncertainty varies.

As would be expected, T in general increases as the stimulus uncertainty increases. *But if the stimuli vary on a single dimension only, T reaches an asymptotic value at some level of stimulus uncertainty and does not increase thereafter as stimulus uncertainty increases.* The asymptotic value of T depends, among other things, on the sensory dimension on which the stimuli vary. Thus for tones varying in pitch T asymptotes at about 2.5 bits; for tones varying in loudness T asymptotes at about 2.3 bits; for tastes T asymptotes at about 1.9 bits; and for a pointer position on a line T asymptotes at about 3.25 bits. That is, no matter how much we increase the stimulus uncertainty, if the stimuli are restricted to varying on a single dimension, we will obtain no more information transmission between stimulus and responses than the amounts mentioned above. By varying the stimulus uncertainty, we increase error; the increase in potential information transmission caused by the increased stimulus uncertainty is exactly balanced by a decrease in potential transmission caused by error. One of the intriguing aspects of this finding is that—within obvious limits—the spacing of the stimuli on the dimension has little effect on T [but see Alluisi (1957) for some important, though not surprising, qualifications]. It is the *uncertainty* of the stimulus set that is the crucial independent variable.

The typical graph relating stimulus uncertainty to T is given in Fig. 10.10. T increases in a roughly linear manner as stimulus uncertainty increases and then becomes flat at an asymptotic level. This asymptotic value is referred to as T_{max}.

There is some speculation that if stimulus uncertainty is greatly increased, T may ultimately decrease, because of "information overload."

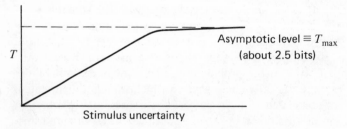

Fig. 10.10 T as a function of stimulus uncertainty.

The evidence concerning one-one absolute judgment of stimuli varying on a single dimension is summarized in a famous article by Miller entitled "The Magical Number Seven Plus or Minus Two" (1956). The number seven in the title refers to the number of stimuli that—*if perfectly discriminated*—would result in the asymptotic amount of information being transmitted. That is, by transmitting about 2.5 bits of information when judging a number of stimuli greater than seven, the subject is transmitting about the same amount of information he would were he judging seven or so stimuli perfectly. Because this amount is roughly constant across sensory modalities, the number seven is roughly constant—hence magical.

Before generalizing from this finding, one must understand the exact nature of the variables involved. T is simply *a* statistic that describes the subject's performance. It is labeled "transmission," but it by no means completely characterizes the subject's performance, not even those aspects of his performance that we would refer to as involving *transmission* in the everyday sense of the term. The fact that T remains constant after a given level of stimulus uncertainty is reached simply means that any increase in $U(X)$ (stimulus uncertainty) is matched by an increase in $U(XY) - U(Y)$ [here, $U(Y)$ refers to the uncertainty of the response], so that $T = U(X) + U(Y) - U(XY) = U(X) - [U(XY) - U(Y)]$ remains constant.

In particular, the *pattern* of the subject's responses to the stimuli is not described by these statistics. (To take an extreme case, if the subject misjudged every stimulus and gave it the same wrong label each time, the amount of information transmitted would be exactly the same as if he judged each stimulus correctly.) The insensitivity of the information theory statistics to pattern of response may be understood by noting that *any permutation of rows and columns of a joint probability matrix does not affect the information theory statistics describing it.* The marginal probabilities remain the same if the rows and columns are permuted; hence, the sum of their uncertainties is unchanged. And the cell probabilities remain unchanged; hence, the uncertainty associated with them remains unchanged. But as pointed out earlier, T is simply equal to the sum of the uncertainties associated with the marginal sets minus the uncertainty associated with the entire matrix. Hence, T remains unchanged.

Clearly, however, many essential aspects of the subject's performance in an absolute judgment task are characterized by his pattern of responses, i.e., by the set $P(X \times Y)$. For example, this pattern tells us whether the subject's errors are near misses or random responses.

It is particularly important, therefore, to think of the magic number seven as a limit on our ability to transmit information only insofar as it is a limit on T. It is entirely possible that we increase our ability to transmit information (in the colloquial sense) when we increase stimulus uncertainty beyond 2.5 bits. For example, the pattern of our errors may be such that we make only small mistakes (near misses), and these may be situations in which such errors are not bad. It might be better to supply a pilot with a finely graded

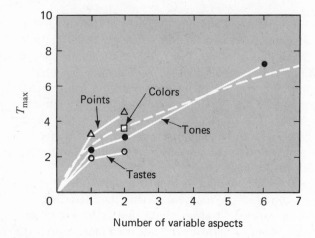

Fig. 10.11 T_{max} as a function of the number of variable aspects.

altimeter and know he will make a number of slight errors in reading it than to supply him with seven plus or minus two grades and know he will read it perfectly (each grade representing several thousand feet).

Now consider the information transmitted in a one-one absolute judgment task when the stimuli vary on more than one dimension. For example, consider stimuli that are points in a square. We know from the previously mentioned experiments that the amount of information transmitted when the subject judges points (counterpositions) on a line asymptotes at about 3.25 bits. Because a square is a space defined by two lines, it might be reasonable to conjecture that the amount of information transmitted when the subject judges points in a square should asymptote at $3.25 + 3.25 = 6.5$ bits. The actual asymptotic value is 4.6 bits. In similar experiments it has been found that the asymptotic value for tones varying in loudness is 2.3 bits, for tones varying in pitch is 2.5 bits, but for tones varying in both pitch and loudness is 3.1 bits (not 4.8). These experiments are summarized by Miller when he states that the addition of independently variable attributes (dimensions) to the stimuli increases maximal transmission but at a decreasing rate. Therefore, if we were to plot T_{max} as a function of number of dimensions, we would obtain a function something like that illustrated in Fig. 10.11 (taken from Miller's article).

One important note: The increase in T_{max} with the number of dimensions does not depend on these dimensions being statistically independent of each other. T_{max} increases as long as the dimensions *can* vary independently.

These results have an important application: If we wish a person to discriminate a given number of stimuli, his performance will be better if we let the stimuli vary on many dimensions than if we let them vary on a single dimension (particularly if there are more than seven stimuli). This application is important in problems such as designing display panels for men operating machines when their operation is dependent on the information coded in these display panels. (For example, the airplane pilot's operation of his airplane is based largely on information coded in the display panel he sees.)

Reaction Time

Psychologists have also studied the *reaction time* of subjects making absolute judgments. Here, again, the subject is supposed to associate one response to each stimulus. The subject's instructions, however, are to respond to each stimulus *as quickly as possible*, and it is the resulting reaction time that is studied.

Consider one-one absolute judgment. The typical reaction time experiment involves relating reaction time to the amount of information the subject is supposed to transmit (which, if he is reacting correctly, will equal the amount of uncertainty in the stimulus and response sets). Because the concern is with reaction time rather than with discovering maximal values for information transmission, the task is usually one in which the subject always responds correctly. He responds, however, with varying latency. In such errorless tasks the amount transmitted is exactly equal to the stimulus uncertainty; thus the experimenter in a typical task speaks of stimulus uncertainty as his independent variable rather than speaking of transmission. The dependent variable is, of course, reaction time.

Here, we shall briefly describe a single experiment. Hyman (1953) presented subjects with a display of lights similar to that illustrated in Fig. 10.12.

The squares in the figure indicate lights that could be flashed. The subject learned a name for each light, and when a given light was flashed, he was to say that name as quickly as possible. As each light flashed, a timer was activated, and a device attached to the subject's throat automatically stopped the timer when he began to speak; thus his reaction time could be recorded with great accuracy. As in all absolute judgment tasks, the problem consisted of discriminating which stimulus was presented, not in learning the responses or learning the pairings between stimuli and responses. The responses

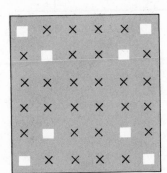

Fig. 10.12 Schematic drawing of Hyman's stimulus display.

were monosyllables starting with the consonant b and ending with the sound of one of the numbers between one and eight (bun, boo, bee, bor, bive, bix, beven, bate). The pairing of the light and the syllable was accomplished through extensive pretraining.

Again, the stimuli may be conceptualized as forming a message set, and the uncertainty of this message set—i.e., the stimulus uncertainty—may be computed from the probabilities with which the stimuli are presented. The purpose of the experiment was to relate the subject's reaction time to this uncertainty.

Hyman conducted three separate experiments. In the first he varied the number of stimuli that could be presented (the number of lights that could be flashed), and all were presented with equal probability. In the second he varied both the number of stimuli and the probabilities with which they were presented. In the third, he varied the number of stimuli and the sequential dependencies between stimuli. (That is, in the third experiment, the probability with which each light would be flashed depended on which light was flashed on the immediately preceding trial; thus the uncertainty associated with the stimulus set was really the conditional uncertainty of the stimulus *given* the preceding stimulus.)

The eight conditions in the second experiment are listed in Table 10.1. Each condition involves greater stimulus uncertainty than the preceding condition. It is *not* the case, however, that each condition involves more stimuli. For example, condition 5 has 1.75 bits of uncertainty associated with four stimuli, whereas condition 4 has 1.39 bits associated with six stimuli. Thus we may plot mean reaction time as a function of stimulus uncertainty and as a function of number of stimuli without having these two variables perfectly confounded.

TABLE 10.1 THE EIGHT CONDITIONS IN HYMAN'S SECOND EXPERIMENT

Condition Number	Number of Lights	Probability of Each Light Being Flashed	Uncertainty in Bits
1	2	$\frac{1}{10}, \frac{9}{10}$	.47
2	2	$\frac{2}{10}, \frac{8}{10}$	.72
3	4	$\frac{1}{16}, \frac{1}{16}, \frac{1}{16}, \frac{13}{16}$	.99
4	6	$\frac{1}{20}, \frac{1}{20}, \frac{1}{20}, \frac{1}{20}, \frac{1}{20}, \frac{15}{20}$	1.39
5	4	$\frac{1}{8}, \frac{1}{8}, \frac{2}{8}, \frac{4}{8}$	1.75
6	6	$\frac{1}{10}, \frac{1}{10}, \frac{1}{10}, \frac{1}{10}, \frac{1}{10}, \frac{5}{10}$	2.16
7	8	$\frac{1}{16}, \frac{1}{16}, \frac{1}{16}, \frac{1}{16}, \frac{1}{16}, \frac{1}{16}, \frac{2}{16}, \frac{8}{16}$	2.38
8	8	$\frac{1}{16}, \frac{1}{16}, \frac{1}{16}, \frac{1}{16}, \frac{2}{16}, \frac{2}{16}, \frac{4}{16}, \frac{4}{16}$	2.75

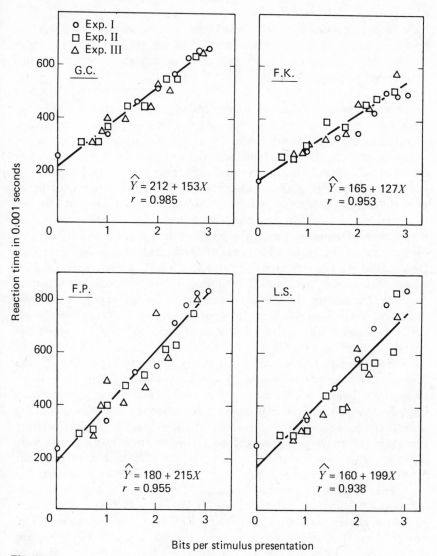

Fig. 10.13

It turns out that the mean reaction time is roughly a linear function of stimulus uncertainty. If stimulus uncertainty increases, mean reaction time increases, even if the number of stimuli decreases. This function is illustrated in Fig. 10.13 (taken from Hyman). Each graph illustrates the performance of a separate subject.

On the other hand, it is not the case that reaction time for each separate stimulus is a function of the amount of information conveyed by that stimulus. In general, the reaction for the stimuli conveying a great deal of information (i.e., the improbable stimuli) is shorter than would be predicted by such a principle, and the reaction time for the stimuli conveying less information (i.e., the more probable ones) is longer. It is the *average* reaction time to the entire *set* of stimuli that varies as a function of the stimulus uncertainty.

Experimentally Induced Error

A pure transmission task closely related to absolute judgment is *identification*. Here, once more, the subject is supposed to give a single response to each single stimulus. And again the difficulty of the task lies not in learning the responses or in pairing the stimuli with the responses but in discriminating the stimuli. The feature that makes an identification task distinctive is that the stimuli used could be perfectly discriminated if they were presented under normal conditions, but they are presented under conditions that interfere with their recognition. For example, printed words that could be clearly read if they were presented to the subject under normal conditions are presented for extremely brief periods of times (using, for example, a tachistoscope). Or a spoken word is presented to a subject on a tape that has a great deal of white noise superimposed on it. The subject's difficulty in making the correct response (i.e., naming the stimulus) lies, then, in discriminating the stimulus under such conditions. Moreover, it is not the uncertainty of the stimulus set per se that limits the subject's ability to respond correctly but rather the interfering conditions that limit his performance.

Here, a single experiment will be briefly described. Miller, Bruner, and Postman (1954) presented strings of eight letters in a tachistoscope. These strings were flashed for extremely brief intervals. These strings approximated English to varying degrees, and this approximation led to a definition of the uncertainty associated with each letter in the string (the more the string approximated English, the less the uncertainty). Thus these experimenters could study the number of letters identified correctly as a function of the exposure time and the uncertainty associated with each letter in the string.

The strings of letters were composed of zero-order, first-order, second-order, and third-order English. Zero-order English is English in which each element is chosen with equal probability. Earlier in this chapter, orders of English were discussed in which *element* referred to words. In the present context *element* refers to letter, so that zero-order English refers to strings of letters each of which is chosen at random with equal probability. Examples of zero-order English strings (taken from Miller, Bruner, and Postman) are EAPMZCEN, YRULPZOG, OZHGPMTJ, and OLEGOMNW.

First-order English strings consist of strings where each letter is chosen with the probability with which it actually appears in English text; letters are *not* chosen at random. Examples of first-order English (again taken from Miller, Bruner, and Postman) are NHGTTEPE, STANVGOP, ZTYEHULP, and EINOAASE.

Second-order strings are those where each letter is chosen with the probability with which it follows the preceding letter in actual English text.

Similarly, third-order strings are those in which each letter is chosen with the probability with which it follows the preceding two letters in actual English text. Examples of third-order English strings are EXPRESPE, RICANING, VERNALIT, and BERKELEY.

Each order of English has a corresponding uncertainty associated with it. For example, each letter in a string of zero-order English has $\log_2 26$ bits of uncertainty associated with it—because all 26 letters are equally likely. Each letter in a first-order English string has somewhat less uncertainty associated with it, because not all letters appear with equal probability in actual English text. Second-order English has even less uncertainty associated with it. Letting X refer to the (message set consisting of) previous letters and letting Y refer to the (message set consisting of) letters generated in a second-order English string, the average uncertainty associated with each of the letters so generated is the conditional uncertainty $U(Y|X)$. $U(Y|X)$ is most easily computed from the formula $U(Y|X) = U(XY) - U(X)$; i.e., the conditional uncertainty is equal to the uncertainty associated with pairs of letters minus the uncertainty associated with single letters.

Miller, Bruner, and Postman found that for any given exposure time the less the approximation to English—i.e., the greater the uncertainty associated with each letter in the string—the fewer the number of letters correctly identified. In fact, for any given exposure time, the number of letters correctly identified multiplied by the uncertainty associated with each letter is roughly constant. This finding holds if the letter is considered to be correctly identified only if the subject places it in the correct position in the string, and also if it is considered correctly identified whenever the subject correctly identifies it as being in the string somewhere, whether or not he states its position correctly. It is *not* the case, however, that the number of correctly identified letters multiplied by their uncertainty is a linear function of exposure time.

The authors conclude that the greater identifiability of the strings more closely approximating English is caused by the redundancy of these strings. Garner (1962), however, has pointed out that the redundancy per se cannot account for the greater accuracy of identification. For suppose we were to make a one-one substitution of the letters in nth order English for each other, e.g., substitute z for a and *vice versa*, y for b and *vice versa*, and so on. Such a substitution would not affect the redundancy of the strings; it would not affect the conditional uncertainty of a letter given the $n-1$ preceding letters. It would change *which* letters followed which, but the uncertainties referring to entire sets of letters would remain unchanged. (Instead of b following a with probability p_1, y would follow z with probability p_1, whereas instead of y following z with probability p_2, b would follow a with probability p_2. And so on.) Surely such a substitution would result in strings that did not approximate English at all and would, therefore, be hard to identify. Thus is it not strictly the uncertainty of the letter strings that determines how many letters may be identified in a given period of time, but it is the familiarity of these strings that determines how many letters may be identified (or perhaps their pronouncibility). And this familiarity is *measured* by the uncertainty. Moreover, these strings must incorporate the actual sequential dependencies of English text if this measurement is to be fruitful. If we set up probabilities indicating which letters would follow which $n-1$ preceding letters, and if these probabilities do not correspond to the actual probabilities of English text, the uncertainty associated with the resulting nth-order non-English would undoubtedly be unrelated to its identifiability.

The sentence

GSRH RH VMTORHS KILHV

contains strings as unfamiliar as those found in zero-order English, despite the fact it was formed from (highly redundant) ordinary English using the substitution rule proposed above. (It is formed from the sentence "this is English prose.")

Memorization

Another pure transmission task is *memorization*. The subject is presented with a stimulus, and his response consists of recalling this stimulus. Any conditional uncertainty about the stimulus with which he was presented given his response is error, and any conditional uncertainty about his response given the stimulus with which he was presented is error.

Short-term memory tasks are those in which the subject is supposed to remember the stimulus for a short period of time. When we describe short-term memory tasks with information theory statistics, we discover no constants, no laws. It is, for example, as easy to repeat correctly eight randomly chosen letters as eight randomly chosen digits—despite the fact that there is $\log_2 26$ bits of uncertainty associated with each letter and only $\log_2 10$ bits of uncertainty associated with each digit. In short-term memory, then, there is no asymptotic value for the amount of information that can be transmitted between the stimulus (the material to be remembered) and the response (the repetition of this material). There is, however, a maximum value on the number of *conceptual units* that may be repeated perfectly. Such conceptual units are termed *chunks*. Miller (1956) states in his summary of experimental material that the number of chunks that can be repeated with perfect accuracy is about eight—whether these chunks are numbers, consonants, words, or whatnots.

There is an important application of the finding that the amount we can remember depends on the number of chunks in the stimulus to be remembered rather than on the number of bits. It is that we can increase the amount of information we remember by choosing chunks that have a great deal of information associated with them. To illustrate, suppose we wish to remember a series of zeros and ones. According to Miller, we could not be expected to remember a series of more than eight or so accurately—*if* what we attempt to remember are the individual zeros and ones. Suppose, however, that we code each sequence of three zeros and ones into a number from one to eight according to binary arithmetic. Now, by remembering eight numbers between one and eight we can reproduce 24 zeros and ones, simply by recoding each digit into its appropriate sequence of zeros and ones. We still remember eight chunks, but we now remember 24 bits of information rather than eight. Using this device, Sidney Smith was able to teach himself to repeat long sequences of zeros and ones. (Smith's work is reported in Miller's article.) And Smith's method could be improved on by someone who was familiar with 64 symbols (e.g., letters of different alphabets). Each pair of numbers from zero to eight could then be remembered as a single symbol (because there are 64 pairs), and then eight symbols would correspond to $8 \times 2 \times 3 = 48$ zeros and ones.

Perhaps the amount of information that can be remembered is limited only by our ability to code that information into eight or so chunks.

Critique

All the tasks described above are pure transmission tasks. In most of these tasks the experimenter has varied stimulus uncertainty and observed transmission, reaction time, and so on. It should be noted, however, that in a pure transmission task stimulus uncertainty equals response uncertainty whenever the subject performs perfectly (and, in fact, both then equal T). Thus we regard any manipulation of stimulus uncertainty equally well as being a manipulation of response uncertainty (or, strictly speaking, a manipulation of *potential* response uncertainty—because the subject who does not perform perfectly will not match the experimenter's increase in stimulus uncertainty with a corresponding increase in his response uncertainty). The following question naturally arises: Is stimulus uncertainty the controlling variable or is response uncertainty?

This question has not been given a definitive answer. Certainly, the tasks so far presented cannot provide an answer to this question, because in all of them stimulus uncertainty and (potential) response uncertainty are perfectly confounded. Perhaps the question does not warrant an answer; the controlling variable need not be *either* stimulus uncertainty *or* response uncertainty.

Some psychologists have, however, conducted experiments in which the stimulus uncertainty and reponse uncertainty can be separated. In particular, Pollack (1959) had subjects listen to spondees on a tape on which white noise was superimposed. (A spondee is a word composed of two long syllables.) Pollack varied the stimulus uncertainty by choosing the spondees from among sets of differing numbers of equally likely elements. He also varied response uncertainty by presenting the subject with sets of differing numbers of spondees from which to choose the one he heard. Thus Pollack varied stimulus uncertainty and response uncertainty independently. He found that subjects' accuracy of recognition was determined more by response uncertainty than by stimulus uncertainty. It should be noted, however, that in all the experimental conditions he studied response uncertainty was less than or equal to stimulus uncertainty.

10.8   AMBIGUITY INTOLERANT TASKS

An ambiguity intolerant task that is not a pure transmission task is one in which any uncertainty concerning the response given the stimulus is error but uncertainty concerning the stimulus given the response is not. For example, a classification task in which many stimuli are classified into the same category is such a task. If the task is performed correctly, it is possible to predict with certainty the category into which each stimulus will be placed; knowing the category in which a stimulus is placed does not, however, allow us to predict with certainty which stimulus it is.

If an ambiguity intolerant task is perfectly performed, there is no conditional uncertainty concerning the response given the stimulus, but there must be some conditional uncertainty concerning the stimulus given the response—or the task is a pure transmission task. Thus Fig. 10.14 represents perfect performance on an ambiguity intolerant task that is not a pure transmission task.

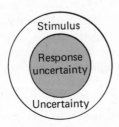

Fig. 10.14   Schematic diagram of an ambiguity intolerant task.

Such tasks have been investigated and discussed primarily by Posner (1964), and we shall follow his discussion closely here.

Posner distinguishes between ambiguity intolerant tasks that involve *filtering* and those that involve *information reduction*. A filtering task is one in which some aspects of the stimulus (or stimuli) are ignored in order to arrive at a correct response, whereas an information reduction task is one in which all aspects of the stimulus (or stimuli) must be considered. Classifying four-digit numbers as odd or even is an example of a filtering task; it is necessary only to attend to the last digit. Adding two four-digit numbers is an example of a reduction task; all digits must be considered.

Filtering is an extremely important process. Consider the following quote from Gerard (1960, p. 1939):

. . . the possible inflow of information is in the millions of bits per second, but the amount that can be handled is only in the tens. Problems of input overload are met everywhere and several devices are used in "defense" as queuing, grouping, and omission. Rats learn a simple discrimination in 10–20 trials while monkeys with richer awareness may require twenty fold more. Men, similarly, having their attention drawn to minute variations in the coloring of marbles, may fail to sort on the basis of major color differences. Repeatedly students have outperformed expert social psychologists in judging group discussions, as secretaries have surpassed psychiatrists in rating interviews, when using given rules for selecting particular information from the total offered. Sophisticated problem solvers often become entrapped in an hypothesis more inextricably than do naive ones; the tree may blot out the woods for anyone. The real skill of the talented thinker is discarding irrelevancies, in going for the jugular of the problem. WHAT IS OMITTED IN PERCEPTION, MEMORY AND REASONING IS OF THE HIGHEST MOMENT.

Consider, now, ambiguity intolerant tasks that do not involve filtering but rather require the subject to attend to the entire input, for example, adding two numbers. Clearly, the difficulty of such tasks is related to the degree to which the subject must transform the input in order to arrive at the correct output. Posner suggests that the degree of transformation may be measured with the statistics of information theory. Specifically, he suggests that the uncertainty of the input and the uncertainty of the output may be compared to arrive at such a measure. He writes (1962, p. 6):

> If, for example, he [a subject] is given 6 numbers randomly selected with replacement from 0 to 9 they represent 19.8 bits, but the sum is a number from 0 to 54, less than 6 bits of information. Yet in losing the specific details of the component numbers making up a sum, the subject has clearly not made an error but rather has accomplished his task.

When Posner discusses *information reduction* in the above quote, he is talking about a psychological process; the subject must *do* something with the stimulus in order to arrive at a response that is less complex. (A single sum is less complex than are the two numbers on which it is based.) What is implied in the above passage, however, is that this information reduction may be *measured* by comparing the uncertainty of the stimulus with the uncertainty of the response. Because the latter is always less in an ambiguity intolerant task, Posner makes this comparison by subtracting the response uncertainty from the stimulus uncertainty; he terms the resulting statistic *information reduction*. Note that it is equivalent to the conditional uncertainty of the stimulus given the response. (In some of his work, Posner does not distinguish between his two uses of the term *information reduction*. In the present volume we shall use the term to refer to the psychological process and refer to the statistic Posner defines as *statistical information reduction*.)

The procedure for measuring statistical information reduction is straightforward. Compute the uncertainty of the stimulus, compute the uncertainty of the response, and subtract. Suppose, for example, a subject is asked to add two numbers randomly chosen with equal probability from the integers one through eight and then classify the result as an A if the sum is above eight and odd or below eight and even and as a B otherwise. There are $\log_2 8$, or three, bits of uncertainty associated with each of the digits and hence six bits of uncertainty associated with the input pair. There is one bit of uncertainty associated with the response (because responses of A and B are equally likely).[7] Hence, the amount of statistical information reduction is six minus one, or five bits. Note that if the subject had been simply asked to add the numbers, his response would have been a number from 2 to 16 (not equally probable); his response uncertainty would have been greater, and hence—because the stimulus uncertainty remains unchanged—the amount of statistical information reduction would have been less. And the addition task is easier than the addition plus classification task!

Posner has conducted a number of experiments to test the general hypothesis that—*other factors held constant*—the greater the amount of statistical information reduction involved in a given task, the greater its difficulty. Here, one of Posner's experiments will be described briefly.

In this experiment subjects were read series of eight numbers from 1 to 64, each number being equally likely; subjects were asked to perform one of five tasks with these numbers. In all tasks the stimulus uncertainty is 48 bits. This figure can be derived in two ways: Because each of eight numbers is equally likely to be any number from 1 to 64, there are 64^8 equally likely possibilities for the set of eight numbers; thus the stimulus uncertainty is $\log_2 64^8 = \log_2 2^{6 \times 8} = \log_2 2^{48} = 48$ bits. Equivalently, because each number is equally likely to be any from 1 to 64, there are $\log_2 64 = 6$ bits of uncertainty associated with each number, hence $8 \times 6 = 48$ bits associated with the entire series of eight. Posner's tasks were as follows:

Task 1: writing down the numbers. No statistical information reduction is involved in this task, because there is as much uncertainty associated with the subject's response as with the stimulus (for the response is supposed to match the stimulus exactly).

Task 2: partial addition. In this task each successive pair of numbers is added. There are approximately 6.9 bits of uncertainty associated with each sum. (To determine the latter uncertainty, figure out the probability of each possible sum from 2 to 128 and then compute the uncertainty of this distribution.) Because there are four such sums, there are 4×6.9 bits of uncertainty associated with the response, or 27.5 bits. Thus the amount of statistical information reduction is $48 - 27.5$, or 20.5 bits.

---

[7]This statement is not exactly true; actually, there are 29 A's and 35 B's. We treat them as equally likely, however, to illustrate the point. And even though they are not exactly equally likely, their uncertainty is just a little less than 1.

Task 3: two-bit classification. In this task the subject classifies each stimulus as high (above 32) or low *and* odd or even. Given equally likely numbers from 1 to 64, each of the four possible classifications (high-odd, high-even, etc.) is equally likely. Hence, there are two bits of response uncertainty associated with each number, or 16 bits in total. It follows there are $48 - 16 = 32$ bits of statistical information reduction in this task.[8]

Task 4: one-bit classification. In this task the subject classifies each stimulus as either an *A* (if it is high and odd *or* low and even) or a *B* (if it is high and even or low and odd). Because these two classifications are equally likely, there is one bit of response uncertainty associated with each classification, and hence eight bits of response uncertainty overall, or 40 bits of statistical information reduction.

Task 5: complete addition. In this task the subject is asked to add all eight numbers. The amount of statistical information reduction involved in this task is 40.3 bits. (The amount of response uncertainty is derived in the same manner as it was in task 2 and then subtracted from 48 to yield the amount of reduction.)

Posner presented each task at one of three speeds: The numbers in the series were presented in four-second intervals, at two-second intervals, and at one-second intervals. The decrease in the percentage of correct responses at each level of statistical information reduction is presented in Fig. 10.15 [taken from Posner (1964)]. Clearly the figure supports the hypothesis that the greater the amount of statistical information reduction, the more difficult the task.

In addition, Posner had subjects rate the difficulty of the tasks. The order of the tasks determined from the mean difficulty ranks corresponded perfectly to the amount of statistical information reduction required by each. The recording task had the lowest mean rank and so on.

Posner has done other experiments showing not only that statistical information reduction of a task can be used as an indicator of task difficulty, but that it also can be used as an indicator of the degree to which the task will interfere with memory of stimulus material immediately preceding the task. The greater the amount of statistical information reduction, the more it interferes with the memory of the stimuli immediately preceding it.

Thus the greater the amount of statistical information reduction involved in a task, the more difficult it is rated to be, the more performance declines with speeding, and the more the task interferes with memory for immediately preceding material. Other cognitive phenomena may—in the future—be studied in terms of the amount of statistical information reduction

---

[8]The subject could make some high versus low classifications on the basis of the first digit only, and he could make all the odd versus even classifications on the basis of the second digit only. Because he must make *both* classifications, however, he must attend to the entire number.

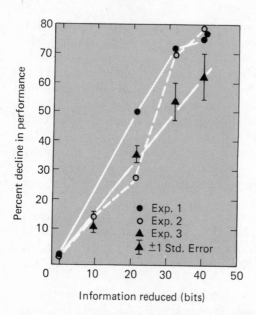

Fig. 10.15 Percentage decline in performance with speeding as a function of the amount of information reduced.

they involve. To quote the late Paul Fitts (1962), "the system of classifying and quantifying 'thinking' in terms of amount of information reduction required, which is the basic theme of Dr. Posner's work, provides important evidence regarding the nature of human thinking, and opens up new avenues to the quantitative study of thinking processes."

Three aspects of Posner's experiments must, however, be noted. First, they all involve manipulating statistical information reduction by holding stimulus uncertainty constant and varying response uncertainty. It is not clear whether statistical information reduction would be a good measure of intellectual difficulty if it were manipulated by holding response uncertainty constant and varying stimulus uncertainty; for example, it might be just as easy to classify numbers from 1 to 128 as A's (high and odd or low and even) or B's as it is to classify numbers from 1 to 64 by the same rule.[9]

Second, statistical information reduction is claimed to be a measure of intellectual difficulty only when all aspects of the stimulus must be examined in order to determine the appropriate response, that is, only when the task involves information reduction (in the psychological sense) as opposed to filtering.

Third, Posner is proposing information reduction as *a* measure of intellectual difficulty, not *the sole* measure of intellectual difficulty. Other

[9]As pointed out by David Cross (personal communication).

factors, such as stimulus-response compatibility, clearly influence the difficulty of an intellectual task (Fitts and Switzer 1962).

10.9 CRITIQUE

Throughout this chapter we have emphasized that the terms *information*, *uncertainty*, and *transmission* are descriptive statistics; *information* describes a single probability, *uncertainty* describes a set of probabilities, and *transmission* describes the constraint between two (or more) sets of probabilities. The reason for our emphasis was that the terms can easily take on excess meaning because of their real world connotations. Such excess meaning is undesirable, because it generates confusion about their essential nature, as descriptive statistics.

One common confusion arising from their connotations is the belief that they should be used as statistics only to describe processes that involve communication, in the real world sense of that term. After all, they are information theory statistics, so we should expect them to be applicable only where some sort of information is being exchanged, processed, or transmitted. But statistics are neither applicable nor inapplicable. It makes no more sense to ask whether the concept of *information transmission* is applicable to a given psychological process than to ask whether the concept of *variance* is applicable. *Information transmission* is a statistic that may be computed whenever there are two or more sets of probabilities available—just as *variance* is a statistic that may be computed whenever a set of numbers is available. Whether these statistics are fruitful and whether their computation helps clarify or obscure the data (or underlying process) is, of course, another problem. The point is that statistics are statistics.

But just as the connotations of these terms may lead to an unnecessary restriction of their use, these same connotations may lead to an inflated idea of what it is they describe. For example, authors will measure the statistical transmission involved in a psychological task and then treat this statistic as if it somehow described the essential aspect of the psychological process they study. It should be clear, however, that the term *transmission* used as an information theory statistic and the term *transmission* used to refer to a psychological process are far from identical. Moreover, the former may not even be a very good measure of the latter. (We have discussed a situation in which we thought it might be misleading; in absolute judgment tasks, because statistical transmission does not take account of the magnitude of the subject's errors, it does not characterize his accuracy as fully as we would wish.)

Thus, when the statistics of information theory are found to be applicable to a particular psychological process—i.e., when measuring variables in terms of these statistics yields consistent and predictable results—it is always legitimate to ask *why*. An attempt to answer this question may yield additional insight into the process.

Consider Posner's work on information reduction. As pointed out earlier, when he talks about subjects combining information and reducing information in order to arrive at a correct response, he is referring to a psychological process. When he measures statistical information reduction in terms of the number of bits of uncertainty about the stimulus given the response, he is referring to a statistic. Why should the statistic yield a good measure of the process he is investigating? Vague appeal to the semantic fact that both process and statistic involve the term *information* provides no answer at all.

Perhaps the question can be answered by a more detailed examination of the nature of the statistic and the nature of the tasks. The statistic measures, in effect, the degree to which the stimulus is unpredictable from the response. The tasks, however, are ones in which the *response* should be perfectly predictable from the *stimulus* because there are correct answers. Hence, the degree to which the stimulus is unpredictable from the response is a good measure of stimulus-response independence when the task is being performed correctly. It is reasonable to hypothesize that the greater the independence between stimulus and response in a structured task, the greater the involvement of the mediating process. It follows that the higher the value of the information reduction statistic, the more the mediating processes are contributing to the production of the response. Hence, the information reduction measure works.

The above analysis of why the measure works is quite compatible with the view of many Gestalt psychologists, who maintain that thinking can be inferred whenever behavior is not stimulus-bound. (And presumably a statistic that yields the degree to which behavior is not stimulus-bound would be a good rough measure of amount of thinking.) The above analysis also suggests that Posner's results may be generalizable to situations in which the unpredictability of the stimulus given the response is measured by some statistic not found in information theory.

MATHEMATICAL
APPENDIX

A.1 INTRODUCTION

The type of mathematics used in mathematical psychology is often not the same as that used in the physical sciences. Specifically, physical sciences tend to make use of the differential and integral calculus, whereas mathematical psychology tends to make use of that sort of mathematics taught in courses on the "foundations" of mathematics.

Unhappily for mathematical psychology, however, courses in foundations of mathematics are usually taught only after differential and integral calculus in college or in the first and second grade (for those children lucky enough to be brought up on the new math). Consequently, most psychologists have not been trained in the type of mathematics mathematical psychology uses.

In hopes of partially compensating for the lack of background we expect on the part of most readers, we are including this mathematical appendix. It introduces the reader to the abstract notions of set, Cartesian product, relation, function, distance, and probability. We view this chapter as a "partial" compensation for ignorance, because we realize that one cannot expect most readers to understand these concepts fully without extensive contact with them—without using them in problems, without thinking about them for long periods of time. But this chapter does provide the essentials necessary to understand these concepts, and the reader may either use it as a "refresher," as a means of obtaining a vague understanding, or as a reference to be used in conjunction with other texts presenting these concepts to non-mathematicians—such as that of Kemeny, Snell, and Thompson (1966). Finally, this chapter attempts to make the book self-contained.

A.2 SETS

A *set* is a collection of entities considered together as a whole. For example, we may consider the set of even numbers, the set of odd numbers between zero and 10, the set of psychologists, the set of schizophrenics, and so on. The particular entities making up these sets are termed the *elements* of these sets; e.g., the numbers $1, 3, 5, 7$, and 9 are the elements of the set of odd numbers between zero and 10.

Sets are not limited to those whose elements are objects or numbers. We may, for example, consider the "set of all pairs of events having the property that the first preceded the second"; an example of an element of this set would be the sinking of the Spanish Armada and the election of John F. Kennedy to the presidency of the United States. We can even consider sets of sets, such as the set of all sets containing a single element.

Sets are characterized in terms of the elements they contain. Thus we may specify a set either by *describing* its elements or by *listing* them. Suppose, for example, we wish to specify the set of all odd numbers between zero and 10. The preceding sentence has described this set; if we wished to use formal notation, we would write $\{x : x$ is an odd number between zero and $10\}$, which could be read as "the set of all entities x such that x is an odd number between zero and ten." On the other hand, we could simply list the elements of this set; if we wished to use formal notation, we would write $\{1, 3, 5, 7, 9\}$.

It should be made clear that the set $\{x : x$ is an odd number between zero and $10\}$ and the set $\{1, 3, 5, 7, 9\}$ are identical; moreover, there is no particular advantage in specifying this set by describing its elements or by listing them.

The relationship between specifying a set by describing its elements and specifying it by listing them is not always so simple. In the first place we may describe a set with an infinite number of elements, for example, the set of even numbers. If we were to specify this set by listing its elements, we would list the first few elements in order and then write three dots—to mean something like "continue this list indefinitely in the same manner." Thus we may specify the set $\{x : x$ is an even number$\}$ as $\{2, 4, 6, 8, \ldots\}$. Of course, it is necessary that the person to whom we are specifying the set has the same idea as we do about how to continue the list.

Sometimes, however, we may describe a set whose elements we cannot list. Consider, for example, the sets of people who could have elected Barry Goldwater president of the United States in 1964 if they had all voted for him; for example, the set consisting of all voters is such a set—because if all voters had voted for Goldwater, he would have won the election. Any set of people controlling a majority of the electoral college vote is such a set. (And there are, in fact, literally billions of such sets.) Now let us consider the *smallest* of these sets.

(Note that this set will consist of a small minority of the voters, for each state that must be won will be won by a single vote and every state lost will be lost unanimously.)

We have just specified a set—the smallest set of voters who could have elected Barry Goldwater president. We cannot, however, list the elements of this set—i.e., the actual voters in it—because we cannot say whether a particular voter is in it or not.

(Actually, our example is oversimplified, because there are a number of such sets; there is no unique smallest set; there will always be many ways of winning a given state by one vote, and hence a number of sets of voters who elect Goldwater by winning some states by one vote and losing the others unanimously.)

In the above example, we *could* have listed the elements of the set (or of the sets), if we had had an indefinite amount of time to figure out every possible combination of voters who could have elected Goldwater and then list the voters in the smallest combination(s). There are circumstances, however, in which we *cannot* list the elements of a set no matter what we do; for example, mathematical learning theorists often specify the "set of stimulus elements" without conceiving of the possibility of listing this set's elements.

Whether its elements are described or listed, however, a set is characterized in terms of its elements. It immediately follows that *two sets are identical if and only if they contain the same elements*. This conclusion—sometimes termed the *principle of set equivalence*—means that if we are to maintain that two sets are equivalent we must convince ourselves that the elements contained in one of the sets, as described or listed, are exactly the same elements contained in the other set, as described or listed. For example, the set $\{1, 3, 5, 7, 9\}$ is equivalent to the set $\{x : x$ is an odd number between zero and 10$\}$, and the set $\{x : x$ is a pair of events having the property that the first preceded the second$\}$ is equivalent to the set $\{x : x$ is a pair of events having the property that the second succeeded the first$\}$.

The principle of set equivalence immediately leads to a consequence that is not so obvious: The set of two-eyed cyclopses is equivalent to the set of hornless unicorns. Both sets contain the same elements—none; hence, they are equivalent. We speak of a set containing no elements as *a* null set; because, however, all null sets are equivalent by the principle of set equivalence, they constitute *the* null set. We do not distinguish between the set of two-eyed cyclopses and the set of hornless unicorns (or, for that matter, between the set of one-eyed cyclopses and the set of one-horned unicorns). All such sets, being equivalent, are *the* null set, which is symbolized ∅.

Because we have defined the null set, we shall now define the converse of the null set. The *universal* set, which we shall symbolize as *U*, is the set containing all elements.

Naturally, "all elements" cannot mean "all conceivable elements of every sort," because there are too many such elements to consider, and some of them will clearly be irrelevant to the sorts of sets we are discussing. By "all," we mean all the elements in the context we are considering. For example, if we were discussing sets of schizophrenics and psychologists, we would probably take "all" to mean "all people" and accordingly define the universal set as the set of all people. If we are discussing sets of even and odd numbers, we would mean the set of all numbers when we refer to the universal set. Roughly speaking, then, the *universal set* is the set of all elements in the universe we are discussing, i.e., in our domain of discourse.

We are now in a position to define the *complement* of a particular set: *The complement of a particular set is the set containing all the elements in the universal set that are not in the particular set considered.* For example, the complement of the set of schizophrenics is the set containing all people who are not schizophrenic; similarly, the complement of the set of even numbers is the set of all numbers that are not even (i.e., the set of odd numbers). Note that by considering only elements in the universal set we have limited ourselves to a particular domain of discourse. We do not define the complement of the set of schizophrenics as the set of *everything* that is not schizophrenic, e.g., chairs, molecules, pairs of events, etc. We do not define the complement of the set of even numbers in such a way that it includes schizophrenics (which, after all, are not even numbers).

Often, the limitation of the elements considered to a particular domain of discourse is implicit, rather than explicit—as is the specification of the universal set. On the other hand, we may be explicit about what types of elements we are considering, i.e., about our universal set. We might begin a discussion, for example, by stating "consider the universe of humans and the set of schizophrenics contained in that universe. . . ."

In summary, we have defined the concept of a set (a collection of entities considered as a whole), the concept of the null set (the set containing no elements), the concept of the universal set (the set containing all elements under discussion), and the concept of the complement of a set (the set containing all the elements in the universal set not contained in the set).

We now consider combinations of sets. In what follows, we shall symbolize sets by uppercase letters $A, B, C, \ldots$, and the elements of sets by lowercase letters x, y, z, ... We shall symbolize the fact that a particular entity x is an element of a set A by writing $x \in A$; we shall symbolize the fact that a particular entity is not an element of A by writing $x \notin A$, or, equivalently, we may write $x \in -A$, meaning x is an element of the complement of A. As mentioned before, we shall symbolize the null set by $\varnothing$ and the universal set by U.

The set of entities that are *both* elements of a set A and elements of a set B are said to be elements of the *intersection* of the sets A and B. For example, if the set A is the set of schizophrenics and the set B is the set of psychologists, then the intersection of A and B is the set of all people who are both schizophrenics and psychologists (that is, the set of schizophrenic psychologists). The intersection of any two sets A and B is symbolized $A \cap B$, and its formal definition is $\{x : x \in A \text{ and } x \in B\}$. (Often, the *and* in the definition is itself symbolized by a figure looking like an upside down V; thus, formally defined, $A \cap B = \{x : x \in A \wedge x \in B\}$.)

Is the intersection of two sets itself a set? Certainly, because it is a well-defined collection of entities. For example, if we consider the intersection of the set of odd numbers and the set of numbers between zero and 10, we are considering the set of odd numbers between zero and 10, a set we have already discussed. (Note that there is nothing to prevent our considering the intersection of a finite set with an infinite set.)

The set of elements that are *either* elements of a set A *or* elements of a set B are said to be elements of the *union* of the sets A and B. For example, if A is the set of schizophrenics and the set B is the set of psychologists, then the union of A and B is the set of all people who are either schizophrenics or psychologists. The union of any two sets A and B is symbolized as $A \cup B$, and its formal definition is $\{x : x \in A \text{ or } x \in B\}$. (Often, the *or* in the definition is itself symbolized by a figure looking like a V; thus, formally defined, $A \cup B = \{x : x \in A \vee x \in B\}$.)

As in the case of intersections, the union of two sets is itself a set, because it is a well-defined collection of elements. For example, if we consider the union of the set of odd numbers between zero and 6 and the set of odd numbers between 6 and 10, we are considering the set of odd numbers between zero and 10 once more.

It is important to note that the definition of *union* does not preclude the possibility that a particular element in the union of two sets is in *both* sets; for example, the union of the set of odd numbers between zero and 6 and the set of odd numbers between 6 and 10 is $\{1, 3, 5, 7, 9\}$—as is the union of the set of odd numbers between zero and 8 and the set of odd numbers between 2 and 10. (In mathematical and logical discussion, the word *or*, or the symbol $\vee$, always means, roughly, "one or the other or both." Technically, we term this the nonexclusive sense of the word *or*.)

It is sometimes helpful to visualize sets as circles or areas on a plane and think of their elements as the points in these areas; such visualizations are

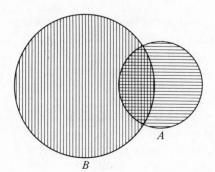

Fig. A.1   Venn diagram of the intersection of two sets.

termed *Venn* diagrams if the areas are circular and *Euler* diagrams if the areas take on many shapes. For example, Fig. A.1 is a Venn diagram. A set A is visualized as the circle with horizontal stripes and a set B as the circle with vertical stripes; $A \cap B$ is then visualized as the area with both horizontal and vertical stripes and $A \cup B$ as the area with either horizontal or vertical stripes.

Having defined the notions of intersection and union, we are now in a position to define many combinations of two sets and their complements; for example, in addition to $A \cap B$, there is

$$A \cap -B = \{x : x \in A \wedge x \notin B\} = \{x : x \in A \wedge x \in -B\},$$

$$-A \cap B = \{x : x \notin A \wedge x \in B\} = \{x : x \in -A \wedge x \in B\},$$

and

$$-A \cap -B = \{x : x \notin A \wedge x \notin B\} = \{x : x \in -A \wedge x \in -B\}.$$

For example, if A is the set of odd numbers between zero and 8 and B is the set of odd numbers between 2 and 10, then $A \cap -B = \{1\}$, $-A \cap B = \{9\}$, and $-A \cap -B = \{x : x$ is a number other than 1, 3, 5, 7, or 9$\}$. Similarly, in addition to $A \cup B$, there is

$$A \cup -B,$$

$$-A \cup B,$$

and

$$-A \cup -B,$$

all defined in an analogous manner. For example, if A is the set of odd numbers between zero and 8 and B is the set of odd numbers between 2 and 10, then $A \cup -B = \{x : x$ is either an odd number between zero and 8 or x is not an odd number between 2 and 10$\} = \{x : x$ is a number other than 9$\}$, and so on.

Note that when A and B are sets defined as above, $A \cup -B = -(-A \cap B)$; that is, the set consisting of the union of A and $-B$ is exactly equivalent to the complement of the set consisting of the intersection of $-A$

and *B*. Specifically, $\{x : x$ is a number other than $9\}$ is the complement of the set $\{9\}$. This fact is an instance of a general principle termed DeMorgan's law.

DeMorgan's Law

$$A \cap B = -(-A \cup -B) \quad \text{and} \quad A \cup B = -(-A \cap -B).$$

Proof of the principle

If an element is in $A \cap B$, it is in *A and B*; thus it cannot be in either $-A$ or $-B$; hence it must be in the complement of $-A \cup -B$; conversely, if it is in the complement of $-A \cup -B$, it is in neither $-A$ nor $-B$; hence it is in both *A* and *B*, i.e., in $A \cap B$. The second part of the principle is proved in exactly the same fashion.

In addition to defining intersections and unions of two sets and their complements, we may define intersections and unions of intersections and unions. Consider, for example, $(A \cap -B) \cup (-A \cap B)$—the set of all elements that are either in the intersection of *A* and $-B$ or in the intersection of $-A$ and *B*. This union of intersections is a perfectly well-defined set of elements, sometimes termed the *symmetric difference* of *A* and *B*. It is illustrated by the shaded area in the Euler diagram pictured in Fig. A.2.

We have thus far defined what is meant by sets and by combinations of sets (intersections and unions). We shall not discuss combinations of more than two sets, because the generalization is straightforward. We shall instead consider some relationships between sets.

A set *A* is termed a *subset* of a set *B* whenever *A* is contained in *B*. For example, if the set *A* is the set of paranoid schizophrenics and the set *B* is the set of schizophrenics, then *A* is a subset of *B*. If *A* is a subset of *B*, we symbolize this fact by writing

$$A \subseteq B.$$

The rigorous statement of this relationship is that $A \subseteq B$ if and only if $x \in A$ implies $x \in B$.

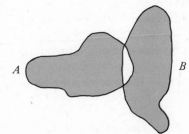

Fig. A.2 Euler diagram of the symmetric difference.

Fig. A.3   Venn diagram of set inclusion.

Note that A and B are equivalent if and only if $A \subseteq B$ *and* $B \subseteq A$.

The relationship $A \subseteq B$ is illustrated in the Venn diagram in Fig. A.3. Note that in Fig. A.3, $A \cap B = A$ and $A \cup B = B$. Is it always true that $A \subseteq B$ if and only if $A \cap B = A$ and $A \cup B = B$? By looking at the definitions of *subset*, *union*, and *intersection*, we can convince ourselves that the answer to this question is yes. The reader may prove for himself that the answer is yes by examining the definitions of subset and set equivalence.

When $A \subseteq B$ and $A \neq B$, A is termed a *proper* subset of B, and this relationship is symbolized as

$$A \subset B.$$

Another relation sets may have is that they are *mutually exclusive*—that is, that they have no elements in common. For example, the set of odd numbers and the set of even numbers are mutually exclusive.

Mutual exclusion is formally defined in terms of the null set, for to say two sets have no elements in common is equivalent to stating that their intersection is the null set. That is, A and B are mutually exclusive if and only if $A \cap B = \varnothing$.

Now having considered relations that sets may have with each other, we may consider *systems* of relationships. The system with which we are most concerned is based on both the notion of subset and the notion of mutual exclusion.

A system of mutually exclusive sets that together form a given set is said to form a *partition* of that set. For example, the subsets of "plants" and "animals" form a partition of the set of "organisms." And the subsets of "species" form a partition of the set of "animals."

A partition is formally defined as follows:

A system of sets $A_1, A_2, \ldots, A_n$ is a partition of a set S if and only if

1. $A_i \cap A_j = \varnothing$ for all $i \neq j$ (that is, every two different sets are mutually exclusive), and
2. $A_1 \cup A_2 \ldots \cup A_n = S$ (that is, the union of all the subsets is equivalent to S).

Often, we refer to these conditions by stating that the sets $A_1, A_2, \ldots, A_n$

are *mutually exclusive and exhaustive*. In addition to stating that such sets form a partition of the set *S*, we often state that *S* is *partitioned into* these subsets.

Consider, for example, the set $S = \{a, b, c, d\}$. The following systems of subsets form partitions of *S*.

1. $\{a\}, \{b\}, \{c\}, \{d\}$,
2. $\{a\}, \{b, c, d\}$,
3. $\{a, b\}, \{c, d\}$, and even
4. $\varnothing, \{a, b, c, d\}$,

as does any system of subsets obtained by rearranging the elements in the above examples. On the other hand, the system of sets

$$\{a, b, d\}, \quad \{c, d\}$$

does not form a partition of *S*, because these subsets are not mutually exclusive.

If, for example, we could classify emotional reactions to frustration into mutually exclusive categories such as rage, depression, fear, etc., this classification would be a partition of the behaviors following frustration—provided, of course, that all such behaviors could be subsumed in one of these categories. On the other hand, classification of American voters into Democrats, Republicans, and liberals does not form a partition, both because a voter may belong to more than one of these subsets (e.g., be a liberal Democrat) and because a voter may belong to none (e.g., be a nonliberal prohibitionist).

Finally, we must consider *subpartitions*, as well as partitions. A subpartition exists whenever one or more subsets of a partition is itself divided into subsets forming a partition.

For example, consider the set $S = \{a, b, c, d\}$ partitioned into the sets $\{a, b\}$ and $\{c, d\}$. Each of these sets, in turn, may be partitioned—the former into the subsets $\{a\}$ and $\{b\}$ and the latter into the subsets $\{c\}$ and $\{d\}$. Such a further partition is naturally called a subpartition.

Given any subpartition, we may illustrate it with a *tree* diagram. Each subset in a partition and subpartition is represented by a point (or node) in such a diagram, and the subsets into which it itself is partitioned are connected to it by lines (or branches). For example, the subpartition we have just described above is illustrated by the tree diagram in Fig. A.4.

A subpartition need not be as symmetric as that presented in Fig. A.4. For example, the set $S = \{a, b, c, d\}$ could be subpartitioned in a manner illustrated in Fig. A.5.

Note that in Figs. A.4 and A.5 we first form a partition of *S* itself and then partition the subsets comprising the original partition. When we partition these subsets, however, we have formed a perfectly good partition of the

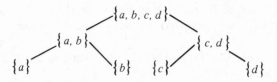

Fig. A.4 Tree diagram of a partition and subpartitions.

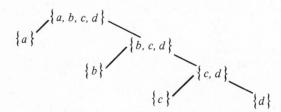

Fig. A.5 Tree diagram of another partition and subpartitions.

original set S. Thus $\{a\}$, $\{b\}$, $\{c\}$, and $\{d\}$ form a partition of S—as do (Fig. A.5) $\{a\}$, $\{b\}$, and $\{c, d\}$.

An example of partition and subpartition in psychology may be found in the attempt to classify major mental illnesses. First, mental illness is partitioned into psychosis (characterized by a lack of contact with reality) and neurosis (characterized by a lack of contact with one's own feelings). Psychosis, in turn, is partitioned into schizophrenias (characterized by constant lack of contact) and manic depressive states (cyclical disorders). Schizophrenia is finally partitioned into simple schizophrenia (characterized by progressive withdrawal from reality), hebephrenic schizophrenia (characterized by silliness), catatonic schizophrenia (characterized by muteness and immobility), and paranoid schizophrenia (characterized by the existence of a delusional system). On the other hand, neurosis is partitioned into real neuroses (in which the individual experiences directly the anxiety caused by his feelings) and psychoneuroses (in which the individual's anxiety is "bound" in symptoms—thought to be "derivatives" of his own feelings). The real neuroses are partitioned into hypochondria, neurasthenia, and organ neuroses, whereas the psychoneuroses are partitioned into hysteria (in which the individual experiences the effect connected with his feelings but does not experience the anxiety or understand the content of these feelings) and obsessive states (in which the individual sometimes knows the content of his feelings but experiences neither the effect nor the anxiety connected with them). This partition is illustrated in the tree diagram presented in Fig. A.6.

When we state that a given type of illness is partitioned into two or more subtypes, we mean, of course, that the set containing all the people suffering from the given type may be partitioned into two or more subsets. A problem with the above partition arises because although (some) authorities on

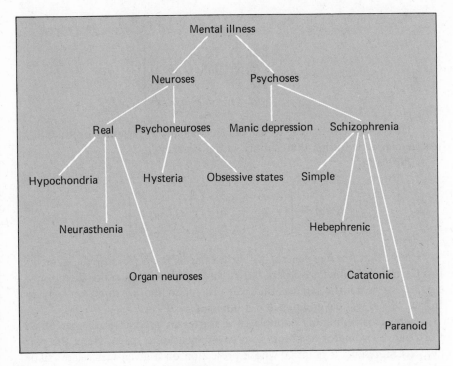

Fig. A.6 Tree diagram of major mental illnesses.

mental illness will agree about how to divide each type of illness into mutually exclusive and exhaustive subsets there is not a great deal of agreement about how a given patient should be classified. Thus we have a situation in which we have defined a relation between sets (a partition) in terms of the set elements, but we cannot decide exactly to which sets these elements belong.

A.3 CARTESIAN PRODUCTS

The *Cartesian product* of two sets A and B is the *set* of all *ordered pairs* of elements x and y such that $x \in A$ and $y \in B$. The Cartesian product is written

$$A \times B$$

and sometimes referred to as "*A* cross *B*." A particular ordered pair contained in a Cartesian product is written (x, y).

The word *set* in the definition was italicized to emphasize that the Cartesian product of two sets is itself a set—a set whose elements are ordered pairs. (It must be kept in mind that it is not the elements of A and B that are elements of $A \times B$ but rather pairs of these elements.)

For example, let the set $A = \{a, b, c, d\}$ and the set $B = \{x, y, z\}$; then

$$A \times B = \begin{bmatrix} (a, x) & (a, y) & (a, z) \\ (b, x) & (b, y) & (b, z) \\ (c, x) & (c, y) & (c, z) \\ (d, x) & (d, y) & (d, z) \end{bmatrix}.$$

(It is often convenient to list the elements of a Cartesian product in a rectangular array rather than simply within brackets.)
Similarly,

$$B \times A = \begin{bmatrix} (x, a) & (x, b) & (x, c) & (x, d) \\ (y, a) & (y, b) & (y, c) & (y, d) \\ (z, a) & (z, b) & (z, c) & (z, d) \end{bmatrix}.$$

Note that $A \times B$ in general is not the same as $B \times A$, because the elements in a Cartesian product are *ordered* pairs, and a pair ordered in one direction— e.g., (d, x)—is not the same as that pair ordered in another direction—(x, d). In fact, $A \times B$ will never equal $B \times A$ unless $A = B$.

The most common example of a Cartesian product is the set of all Cartesian coordinates of points in a two-dimensional space. Here, the pair (x_1, x_2) represents a point X whose projection on a given Cartesian axis is x_1 and whose projection on an axis at right angles to that axis is x_2. Letting R represent the set of real numbers, we see that

$$(x_1, x_2) \in R \times R.$$

Another example of a Cartesian product is the set of all pairs of positive integers. That is, letting $I = \{1, 2, 3 \ldots\}$ be the set of positive integers, we have

$$I \times I = \begin{bmatrix} (1, 1) & (1, 2) & (1, 3) \ldots \\ (2, 1) & (2, 2) & (2, 3) \ldots \\ (3, 1) & (3, 2) & (3, 3) \ldots \\ \vdots & \vdots & \vdots \end{bmatrix}.$$

Finally, let us consider an unusual Cartesian product that we shall discuss later. Let $B = \{b_1, b_2, b_3, \ldots\}$ be the set of all men living or dead who are or were the brothers of someone, and let $P = \{p_1, p_2, p_3, \ldots\}$ be the set of all people living or dead. (Note that $B \subset P$.) We may define

$$B \times P = \begin{bmatrix} (b_1, p_1) & (b_1, p_2) & (b_1, p_3) \ldots \\ (b_2, p_1) & (b_2, p_2) & (b_2, p_3) \ldots \\ (b_3, p_1) & (b_3, p_2) & (b_3, p_3) \ldots \\ \vdots & \vdots & \vdots \end{bmatrix}.$$

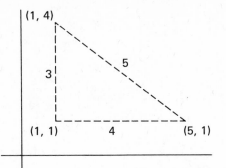

Fig. A.7 Euclidean distance in a two-dimensional space.

We also can have Cartesian products of more than one set. The generalization is straightforward. For example, $A \times B \times C$ is the set of all ordered triples (x, y, z) such that $x \in A$, $y \in B$, and $z \in C$. We term such an ordered triple a *three-tuple* and speak of three-tuples, four-tuples, . . . or n-tuples when we refer to the elements of the Cartesian products of three, four, or n sets.

One of the reasons for an interest in Cartesian products is that it is possible to explicate complex (and important) mathematical relationships in terms of them. Here, we shall briefly demonstrate how a very complex idea—Euclidean distance in two-dimensional space—may be specified in terms of Cartesian products.

Consider the two points in two-dimensional space illustrated in Fig. A.7. The distance between these points is five units—as can be calculated from the Pythagorean theorem. (The reader may recognize that the dotted lines form a three-four-five triangle.)

Now consider the five-tuple, $(1, 4, 5, 1, 5)$, and interpret it as meaning "the distance between the point whose coordinates are given in the first two terms of the five-tuple and the point whose coordinates are given in the third and fourth term of the five-tuple is given by the fifth term in the five-tuple." Other examples of five-tuples that could be similarly interpreted are $(0, 0, 0, 6, 6)$, $(0, 0, 1, 1, \sqrt{2})$, and so on. Some five-tuples that could not be interpreted in the above manner are $(0, 0, 0, 0, \sqrt{7})$, $(1, 4, 5, 1, 3/2)$, and so on.

Now every such five-tuple, whether it could be interpreted as above or not, is an element of $R \times R \times R \times R \times R$, where R refers to the set of real numbers. This Cartesian product contains *all possible* five-tuples. Only certain of these five-tuples satisfy the following relation: The distance between the point whose coordinates are given in the first two terms of the five-tuple and the point whose coordinates are given in the third and fourth term of the five-tuple is given in the fifth term of the five-tuple. Those five-tuples satisfying this relation form a proper subset of the Cartesian product $R \times R \times R \times R \times R$. *Thus, if we wished to explicate what it is we mean by the relation Euclidean distance between points in two-dimensional space, we could do so simply by denoting this subset of $R \times R \times R \times R \times R$.*

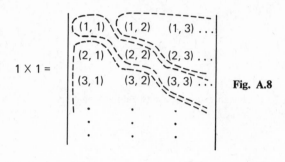

$1 \times 1 =$

Fig. A.8

Just as we could specify sets either by describing their elements or by listing them, we can specify mathematical relations either by describing them or by listing the n-tuples satisfying them. (Of course, this list will usually be infinite.) *These n-tuples will form a subset of a Cartesian product.*

Let us return to simple examples. The Cartesian product of the set of positive integers cross itself has already been mentioned. See Fig. A.8. We may divide (by the dotted lines) the ordered pairs comprising this product into those above the diagonal, those below the diagonal, and those on the diagonal. Those above the diagonal specify the relation "the first element in the pair is smaller than the second," those below the diagonal specify the relation "the first element in the pair is larger than the second," and those on the diagonal specify the relation "the two elements of the pair are equal." Thus (restricting ourselves to positive integers) we have specified the relations "less than," "greater than," and "equals" by denoting three subsets of $I \times I$. Similarly, we may specify the relation "is uncle of" by denoting a subset of the Cartesian product $B \times P$, where B is again the set of all brothers (living or dead) and P is the set of all people (living or dead).

We may now give a rigorous definition of the notion of *relation*. *A relation R is a subset of a Cartesian product.* If a particular ordered pair (x, y) or ordered n-tuple $(x, y, z, \ldots)$ is in the subset, we shall write $(x, y) \in R$ or $(x, y, z, \ldots) \in R$, respectively.

In what follows we shall limit attention to relations consisting of ordered pairs, because the generalization to relations consisting of n-tuples is straightforward. When dealing with ordered pairs only, $(x, y) \in R$ is sometimes written $x R y$.

Following are a number of definitions concerning relations.

The *domain* of a relation R is the set of all elements x for which there exists a y such that $(x, y) \in R$. That is, the domain of R is the set $\{x : \text{there exists some } y \text{ such that } (x, y) \in R\}$.

For example, the set of all uncles is the domain of the relation "is uncle of." Note that the set of all brothers is *not* the domain, because it is not true that every brother is an uncle (that is—in more stilted prose—because it is not true that for each brother there exists someone whose uncle he is). The set of all positive integers is the domain of the relation "less than," when we consider only positive integers, because for any given integer there exists some integer (in fact, an infinite number of integers) that it is less than. The domain of the relation "greater than" (again restricted to positive integers) consists of all integers *except 1*.

The *range* of a relation R is the set of all elements y for which there exists some x such that $(x, y) \in R$. That is, the range of R is the set $\{y :$ there exists some x such that $(x, y) \in R\}$.

For example, the set of all people who have uncles is the range of the relation "is uncle of." The set of all positive integers except 1 is the range of the relation "less than," when we consider only positive integers, and the set of *all* positive integers is the range of the relation "greater than."

Note that the domain of a relation and range of a relation need not have any special relationship; it is not the case that they need be exclusive, or identical—nor does one need to be a subset of the other. It depends on the relation. (Question: Why is the domain of the relation "father of" a subset of the range?)

The *field* of a relation R is the union of its domain and its range.

A relation is *reflexive* if and only if any element in its domain bears that relation to itself. That is, a relation R is reflexive if and only if x in its domain implies $(x, x) \in R$. For example, "equals" is a reflexive relation, as is "greater than or equal to."

On the other hand, "uncle of" is not reflexive; in fact, it is *never* the case that $(x, x) \in R$, where R refers to "uncle of." We term such a relation *irreflexive*. That is, a relation is irreflexive if and only if x in its domain implies $(x, x) \notin R$. For example, "unequal to" is an irreflexive relation, as is "greater than."

Some relations are neither reflexive nor irreflexive. For example, the relation "sums to ten" is neither. It is not reflexive because $(2, 8) \in R$, but $(2, 2) \notin R$. Nor is it irreflexive, because $(5, 5) \in R$. "Hates" is another relation that is neither reflexive nor irreflexive—if we admit the possibility that some people hate themselves and others do not.

A relation R is *symmetric* if and only if $(x, y) \in R$ implies $(y, x) \in R$. For example, "equals" is a symmetric relation, for if x equals y, y equals x.

A relation R is *asymmetric* if and only if $(x, y) \in R$ implies $(y, x) \notin R$. For example, "greater than" is an asymmetric relation, for if x is greater than y, then y is not greater than x.

Here, the words *symmetric* and *asymmetric* have been used in their ordinary sense. We now introduce the notion of *antisymmetry*.

A relation R is antisymmetric if and only if $(x, y) \in R$ and $(y, x) \in R$ together imply $x = y$. For example, the relation "subset of" is antisymmetric, for if A is a subset of B and B is a subset of A, then $A = B$. The relation "greater than or equal to" is also antisymmetric. Interestingly enough, "is the square of" is antisymmetric, for if $(x, y) \in R$—that is, y is the square of x—and $(y, x) \in R$, then $x = y \, (= 1)$.

And, of course, there are relations that are neither symmetric, nor asymmetric, nor antisymmetric.

A relation R is *transitive* if and only if $(x, y) \in R$, and $(y, z) \in R$ together imply $(x, z) \in R$. The most common examples of transitive relations are "greater than," "less than," "is a subset of," and "equals." For if x is (greater than/less than/a subset of/equal to) y, and y is (greater than/less than/a subset of/equal to) z, then x is (greater than/less than/a subset of/equal to) z. Other examples of transitive relations are "is of a higher social class than" and "knows more Spanish vocabulary than."

A relation R is *never transitive* if and only if $(x, y) \in R$ and $(y, z) \in R$ together imply $(x, z) \notin R$. For example, the relation "father of" is never transitive, for if x is the father of y and y is the father of z, then x cannot be the father of z (in fact, he is his grandfather). It would be desirable to be able to term this condition *intransitivity*, but this term through popular usage has come to mean "not transitive" in the sense that it is not *always* the case that $(x, y) \in R$ and $(y, z) \in R$ together imply $(x, z) \in R$.

Again, there are relations that are neither transitive nor never transitive. For example, the relation "brother of" is neither. [Although this relation may at first appear transitive, it is not. For suppose Bill and Bob are brothers; then (Bill, Bob) $\in R$ and (Bob, Bill) $\in R$, but we cannot conclude (Bill, Bill) $\in R$, as would be required by transitivity.]

A relation R is *strongly connected* if and only if for all x, y in its field $(x, y) \in R$ or $(y, x) \in R$. For example, the relation "greater than or equal to" on the field of integers is strongly connected.

A relation R is *weakly connected* if and only if for all x, y in its field $(x, y) \in R$, or $(y, x) \in R$, or $x = y$. For example, "greater than" on the field of positive integers is weakly connected.

Clearly, any relation that is strongly connected is also weakly connected, but the converse is not true.

A relation R is *many-one* if each element of the domain is paired with exactly one element of the range. This notion is formally defined by stating that if an element of the domain is paired with two elements of the range then these elements must be identical. That is, a relation R is many-one if and only if $(x, y) \in R$ and $(x, z) \in R$ together imply $y = z$. For example, let us define a relation on the field of positive and negative integers as follows: $(x, y) \in R$ means $x^2 = y$. This relation is many-one, because there is exactly one y paired with each x. Note, however, that there is more than one x paired with each y; e.g., $(-2, 4) \in R$ and $(2, 4) \in R$. This fact is irrelevant to the question of whether the relation is many-one.

If, however, it is true that each range element is paired with exactly one domain element, the relation is *one-many*. This notion is formally defined by stating that if an element in the range is paired with two elements in the domain then these elements are equal. That is, a relation R is one-many if and only if $(x, y) \in R$ and $(z, y) \in R$ together imply that $x = z$. For example, let

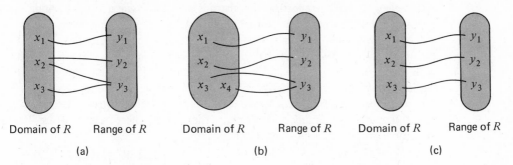

Domain of R Range of R Domain of R Range of R Domain of R Range of R

(a)   (b)   (c)

Fig. A.9 Some types of relations.

us define a relation on the field of positive and negative integers as follows: $(x, y) \in R$ means $x = y^2$. This relation is one-many (and not many-one).

A *one-one* relation is a relation that is both many-one and one-many. For example, let us define a relation on the field of positive and negative integers as follows: $(x, y) \in R$ means $x = 2y$. Any given y value is paired with exactly one x value and *vice versa*.

Note that many-one, one-many, and one-one relations are defined by the nonexistence of certain pairs; many-one relations cannot contain the pairs $(a, b), (a, c)$, where $b \neq c$; one-many relations cannot contain the pairs (a, b), (c, b), where $a \neq c$; and one-one relations cannot contain either type of pair.

Often, we can illustrate relations, and properties of relations, by letting the domain of the relation be represented by one area, by letting the range be represented by another area, and by letting the pairs of elements forming the relation be joined by lines. For example, Fig. A.9(a) illustrates a relation that consists of the pairs $(x_1, y_1), (x_2, y_2), (x_2, y_3)$, and (x_3, y_3); this relation is neither many-one nor one-many. Figure A.9(b) illustrates the relation that consists of the pairs $(x_1, y_1), (x_2, y_2), (x_3, y_3)$, and (x_4, y_3); this is a many-one relation. Figure A.9(c) illustrates a one-one relation that consists of the pairs $(x_1, y_1), (x_2, y_2)$, and (x_3, y_3).

A.4   EQUIVALENCE RELATIONS, ORDER RELATIONS, AND FUNCTIONS

An *equivalence* relation is any relation that is reflexive, symmetric, and transitive. *Equals* is the most well-known equivalence relation, for $x = x$ (reflexivity), $x = y$ implies $y = x$ (symmetry), and $x = y$ and $y = z$ together imply $x = z$ (transitivity). Another common equivalence relation is that defined on a partition. Consider a set S partitioned into subsets $A_1, A_2, \ldots, A_n$. "From the same subset as" is an equivalence relation, because any element x is from the same subset as itself, x and y are from the same subset if and only if y and x are from the same subset, and if x and y are from the same subset and y and z are from the same subset, then x and z are from the same subset. We could even have defined *partition* in terms of this equivalence relation. And, in fact, the subsets forming a partition are often referred to as *equivalence classes*.

An *order* relation is any relation that is transitive. The emphasis in this definition is on the word *any*, because the concept of *order* is often identified with the particular order relations "greater than" or "less than." As pointed out in the definition of transitivity, however, there are many transitive relations, for example, "equals," "is a subset of," "is of a higher social class than," and "knows more Spanish vocabulary than." All these relations are by definition order relations—because they are all transitive.

If $(x, y) \in R$, where R is an order relation, x and y are said to be *ordered by R* (or "with respect to" R).

An order relation is *complete* or *simple* if and only if it is connected. That is, an order relation is complete if and only if it is always possible to state for any x and y in its field that $(x, y) \in R$ or $(y, x) \in R$ (or $x = y$). For example, the relation "greater than" on the field of positive integers is a complete order relation, because for any two integers x and y, x is either greater than y or y is greater than x (or $x = y$).

When an order relation is complete (simple), the elements of its field are said to be *completely* or *simply* ordered by such a relation [because for any set of distinct elements $(x, y) \in R$ or $(y, x) \in R$].

Although order relations literally order pairs of elements, we may think of a complete order as ordering the elements themselves in what is termed a *chain*; for example, the order relation "less than" on the field of positive integers is a complete order, and the integers themselves form a chain: $1 < 2 < 3 < 4. \ldots$ It should be clear that such a chain may be formed if and only if the order relation is complete—for if two elements were not ordered by the relation, they could not be placed in such a chain, or by transitivity they would become ordered.

An order relation that is not complete is termed a *partial* order relation. For example, "is a subset of" is usually a partial order relation, because the field of this relation is often a system of sets that are not always subsets of each other. Consider, for example, the system of sets illustrated in Fig. A.10. A is a subset of both B and C, both B and C are subsets of D, and—as required by transitivity—A is a subset of D. Nevertheless, the order is not complete because B is neither a subset of C, nor C of B.

To give the sets illustrated in Fig. A.10 a concrete interpretation, suppose A is the set of Spanish vocabulary words known by individual a, B the set of Spanish vocabulary words known by individual b, and so on. If we say an individual "knows no more Spanish vocabulary than" another if and only if the first individual does not know any words the other does not know, then the relation "knows no more Spanish vocabulary than" is a partial order relation. a knows no more than b and c, and b and c know no more than d, but it is neither the case that b knows no more than c nor *vice versa*. b and c are *incomparable*.

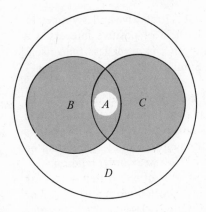

Fig. A.10 Set inclusion as a partial order.

When an order relation is a partial order relation, the elements of its field are said to be *partially ordered* by it.

Another example of a partial order relation is the relation "is of a higher social class than." Although it is easily maintained that a doctor (even a physician) is of a higher social class than a poorly paid high school teacher and a well-paid skilled laborer, and although both these are of a higher social class than an unskilled worker, it could be maintained that the poorly paid high school teacher and the well-paid skilled worker are inherently incomparable with respect to social class. A critic, however, could argue that if we had a rigorous idea of what we meant by social class we could order these people. In response, it could be pointed out that there are many rigorous ideas of order relations that are not complete orders. (Consider, for example, the idea of "subset of.")

The example of social class is illustrated in Fig. A.11; such an illustration is termed a *Hasse* diagram. (Note that the Hasse diagram of a completely ordered set of elements is a straight line.)

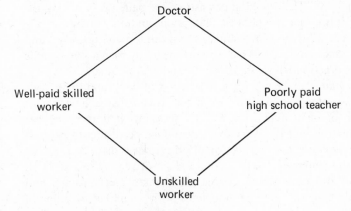

Fig. A.11 Hasse diagram of social class.

An order relation is *strong* if and only if it is irreflexive and asymmetric. For example, the relation "less than" on the field of positive integers is a strong order relation, because a positive integer x is never less than itself, nor can x be less than y and y be less than x. Similarly, "is a proper subset of" is a strong order relation.

An order relation is *weak* if and only if it is reflexive and antisymmetric. For example, the relation "less than or equal to" on the field of positive integers is a weak order relation, because a positive integer x is always less than or equal to itself, and if x is less than or equal to y and y is less than or equal to x, then $x = y$. Similarly, "is a subset of" is a weak order relation.

If R is a strong order relation, $(x, y) \in R$ is often written $x < y$ or $y > x$. If R is a weak order relation, $(x, y) \in R$ is often written as $x \le y$ or $y \ge x$. These symbols most often refer to the relations "less than" (or "greater than") and "less than or equal to" (or "greater than or equal to") on fields of numbers, but they may refer to other strong or weak order relations as well.

The question of whether an order relation is complete or partial and the question of whether it is strong or weak are two independent questions. The first refers to whether the order relation orders all elements in its field, whereas the second refers to properties of the ordering. Unfortunately, however, vocabulary is not uniform; authors will refer to weak order relations as partial order relations, and *vice versa*. One can usually tell from the other remarks of the author the distinction to which he has reference.

A *function* is any many-one relation. As stated previously, a relation R is many-one if and only if $(x, y) \in R$ and $(x, z) \in R$ imply that $y = z$; that is, a relation is many-one (hence a function) if and only if each element in the domain of the relation is paired with exactly one element in the range.

Now strictly speaking, a function is a relation. Often, however, when a function exists with domain X and range Y, we speak loosely of the range as if it itself were a function of the domain; we often state in such a situation that "Y is a function of X." Consider, for example, the function expressed by the equation $y = x^2$. This function consists of the pairs (x, y) having the property $y = x^2$; it is a function because there is one and only one value of y associated with each value of x. We sometimes speak loosely, however, and state that "Y is a function of X." What is really meant by such a statement is that there exists a function whose domain is X and whose range is Y.

Thus, if we state that "behavior is a function of habit and drive," we mean that we have some rule in mind that associates a single behavior with each combination of habit and drive. Strictly speaking, it is the rule that constitutes the function, not the behavior. In contrast, according to psychoanalytic theory, behavior is not "a function of" drive nor is drive "a function of" behavior; by this statement, we mean that a single drive may be associated with a number of different behaviors (via the defense mechanisms), and conversely a single behavior may be associated with a number of different drives (via overdetermination). It is true, however, that according to psychoanalytic theory behavior is supposed to be "a function of" drives *and* defenses —i.e., there is supposed to be a rule that associates each combination of drive and defense with a unique behavior.

Many scientists are primarily interested in functional relations, because if a variable Y is a function of a variable X, we may make a specific prediction about the value of Y when we know the value of X, and this prediction may be checked (and refuted) in the real world.

A *one-one* function is simply a one-one relation, that is, a relation that is both many-one and one-many. For example, the function $x = 2y$ is one-one, whereas the function $x^2 = y$ is not (both these relations have been discussed earlier).

If behavior is a function of habit and drive, then there is one and only one behavior associated with (elicited by) each combination of habit and drive. Such a function is said to be a *function of two variables*. More abstractly, a function is a *function of n variables* if and only if there is a single value in the range of the function associated with each *combination* of the n variables. In other words, the domain of a function of n variables consists of n-tuples.

A.5 DISTANCE

It is assumed the reader is thoroughly familiar with the concrete notion of *distance* between points in space. Here, the notion will be generalized through the use of concepts introduced earlier in this appendix.

Viewed abstractly, distance is simply a number associated with pairs of things called points. Moreover, one and only one number is associated with each pair. Thus *distance* may be explicated in terms of the concept of *function*. Specifically, consider a set X of things called points. Consider, further, that for each pair $(x, y) \in X \times X$ there is associated a unique element of R (the real numbers). This number—let it be symbolized by $d(x, y)$—is termed the *distance between points x and y*. The three-tuples $[x, y, d(x, y)]$ form a subset of the Cartesian product $X \times X \times R$, and the distance between x and y is a function of the two variables X and X, because each combination of variables has a unique real number associated with it. The rule determining which real number it should be is termed a *distance function*.

Not all functions assigning real valued numbers to pairs of points are distance functions. The numbers assigned to the pairs of points must satisfy certain conditions listed below. These conditions are all very familiar properties of the notion of distance considered concretely.

It was stated earlier that the concept of distance to be presented would be a generalization of the concrete notion of distance. What we meant by this statement was that the properties used to define the notion of distance abstractly are all familiar properties of distance considered concretely. The generalization occurs because *any* function that satisfies these properties is termed a *distance function*, and the number assigned by this function—however it may be determined—is termed *distance*.

Specifically, consider the set X and a function assigning a unique number $d(x, y)$ to every pair $(x, y) \in X \times X$. This function will be termed a *distance function* and the number it assigns the *distance between x and y* if and only if $d(x, y)$ satisfies conditions D1 through D4.

D1

$d(x, y) \geq 0$. That is, the distance between any two points is never negative.

D2

$d(x, y) = 0$ if and only if $x = y$. That is, the distance between two identical points is always zero, and the distance between two different points is never zero.

D3

$d(x, y) = d(y, x)$. That is, distance is symmetric; the distance between x and y is the same as the distance between y and x.

D4

$d(x, y) + d(y, z) \geq d(x, z)$. That is, the sum of the distances between any points (x and z) and a third point (y) is always greater than or equal to the distance between these points; this condition is termed the *triangular inequality*; the term stems from the fact that in concrete space the sum of two sides of a triangle is always at least as great as the third side (x, y, and z in the above condition may be thought of as the vertices of a triangle).

Perhaps the simplest type of distance function is that which assigns the number 1 to pairs of distinct elements and the number 0 to pairs of identical elements. That is,

    1. $d(x, y) = 1$ if and only if $x \neq y$.
    2. $d(x, y) = 0$ if and only if $x = y$.

This function is a distance function because it satisfies D1 through D4.

    1. D1 is satisfied because both 1 and 0 are greater than or equal to 0.
    2. D2 is satisfied directly from part (2) of the definition.
    3. D3 is satisfied because x is identical with (different from) y if and only if y is identical with (different from) x.

4. D4 could be violated only if $d(x, y) = 0$, $d(x, z) = 0$, but $d(x, z) = 1$. But if $d(x, y) = 0$ and $d(y, z) = 0$, then by definition $x = y$ and $y = z$. From which we conclude that $x = z$, and therefore $d(x, z)$ must also be 0.

It is readily seen that the definition of distance function specified above may be applicable to *any* set. We simply term the elements of these sets *points* when we discuss the distance between them. There is a particular type of entity, however, to which the concept of distance has particular application; these entities are termed *vectors*.

A *vector* is an entity satisfying certain abstract conditions that need not be discussed here. For our purposes, it is necessary to deal only with *finite dimensional vectors*, and such vectors may be considered as *n-tuples of real numbers*.[1] The numbers forming the *n*-tuples are termed the *components* of the vector. Thus, if we represent finite dimensional vectors by lowercase boldface letters, we can write

$$\mathbf{x} = (x_1, x_2, \ldots, x_n),$$

where each x_i refers to a particular real number. $\mathbf{x}$ is the vector; the x_i's are its components.

n-tuples correspond to points in *Cartesian space*. (It is assumed the reader is familiar with the concept of a Cartesian space, that is, a space with Cartesian coordinates.) This correspondence is as follows: Let $\mathbf{x} = (x_1, x_2, \ldots, x_n)$ be an *n*-tuple. $\mathbf{x}$ may be associated with a point in *n*-dimensional Cartesian space whose projection on the first coordinate is x_1, whose projection on the second coordinate is x_2, and so on. Clearly, this association is one-one; that is, there is only one point in *n*-dimensional Cartesian space associated with each *n*-tuple, and each *n*-tuple is associated with a unique point in this space. Thus, *n*-tuples (i.e., finite dimensional vectors) may be visualized as points in *n*-dimensional space. We say, variously, that such vectors "correspond to" points in space, "may be represented by" points in space, "have a one-one relation to" points in space, and so on; sometimes we even say a finite dimensional vector "*is*" a point in *n*-dimensional space.

For example, the vector $\mathbf{x} = (2, 3)$ is represented in Cartesian space in Fig. A.12.

Distance between finite dimensional vectors is defined in terms of the vectors' components.

The most common distance function is the well-known Euclidean dist-

---

[1]The reader already familiar with the abstract definition of *vector* will note that a finite dimensional vector can always be uniquely represented as a linear combination of basis vectors. The scalars forming this combination, considered in the proper order, therefore form a unique *n*-tuple that completely characterizes the vector.

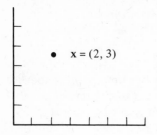

x = (2, 3)

Fig. A.12   Vector as a point.

ance function. Let $\mathbf{x} = (x_1, x_2, \ldots, x_n)$ and $\mathbf{y} = (y_1, y_2, \ldots, y_n)$ be two vectors. Then, the Euclidean distance between them is

$$\left[\sum_{i=1}^{n} (x_i - y_i)^2 \right]^{1/2}.$$

That is, the distance between vectors $\mathbf{x}$ and $\mathbf{y}$ is equal to the square root of the sum of the squared differences between their components. When representing vectors as points in Cartesian space, we state this function as follows: The distance between points $\mathbf{x}$ and $\mathbf{y}$ is equal to the square root of the sum of the squared differences between $\mathbf{x}$'s and $\mathbf{y}$'s projection on each coordinate. This distance function is illustrated in Fig. A.13.

It is possible to define more than one distance function on a given space. Still considering Cartesian space, for example, we can define the distance between two points as equal to the sum of the absolute difference of their components (i.e., the sum of the absolute difference of their projections). That is,

$$d(\mathbf{x}, \mathbf{y}) = \sum_{i=1}^{n} |x_i - y_i|.$$

In the above example

$$d(\mathbf{x}, \mathbf{y}) = |6 - 2| + |6 - 3|$$

$$= 7.$$

The above distance function is often termed the *city-block distance;* in effect, to "get" from $\mathbf{x}$ to $\mathbf{y}$, one must "travel along lines parallel to the coordinates"—much as one must (in some cities) travel along perpendicular roads to get from one place to a place diagonally across from it. In the example in Fig. A.13, one must travel four units along coordinate 1 and three units along coordinate 2.

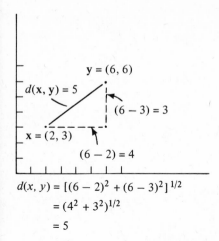

$$d(x, y) = [(6 - 2)^2 + (6 - 3)^2]^{1/2}$$
$$= (4^2 + 3^2)^{1/2}$$
$$= 5$$

Fig. A.13 Euclidean distance function.

Even the following function is a distance function: $d(x, y) = 1/i$, where i is the first component on which x and y differ.

Such a function could be termed a *scan* distance; in effect, we scan the components in a given order until we find two that differ, and the distance we have traveled is equivalent to the inverse of the number of components we have to scan. In the example in Fig. A.13, we scan only the first component— 2 for x and 6 for y—before we find a difference; thus the distance traveled in $1/1 = 1$.

In addition to being defined for pairs of elements from a given set, *distance* may be defined for pairs of sets themselves. (Of course, viewed abstractly, pairs of sets are just pairs of elements of a set of sets.) First, however, it is necessary to define a *measure function*.

A measure function is a function that associates a real number with a set; the number so associated is termed the *measure* of the set. Note the analogy with distance function—which is a function that associates a number with each pair of elements from a set, the number so associated being termed the *distance* between the elements in the set.

The analogy with distance function continues. Just as not any number associated with a pair of elements is a distance, not any number associated with a set is a measure. The number associated with the set must satisfy certain conditions. And just as the conditions a distance function must satisfy are properties of the concrete notion of distance, the conditions that a measure function must satisfy are properties of the concrete notion of number. A measure of a set may never be negative, and the measure of the union of two mutually exclusive sets is equal to the sum of the measures—just as the number of elements in a set is always positive, and the number of elements in two sets having no elements in common is equal to the sum of the number of elements in each.

Specifically, consider a function that assigns to each set A a real number

$m(A)$. This function will be termed a *measure function* and the number $m(A)$ will be termed a *measure* of A if and only if this function satisfies conditions M1 and M2.[2]

M1

$$m(A) \geq 0.$$

M2

If $A \cap B = \varnothing$, then $m(A \cup B) = m(A) + m(B)$.

From M1 and M2 it immediately follows that

M3

$$m(A \cup B) = m(A) + m(B) - m(A \cap B).$$

For $A \cup B$ can be partitioned into A and $B \cap -A$. Because these parts are exclusive, the measure of $A \cup B$ equals the sum of their measures, i.e., $m(A) + m(B \cap -A)$. But $m(B \cap -A)$ can be determined by noting that B itself can be partitioned into disjoint parts $B \cap A$ and $B \cap -A$; thus, $m(B) = m(B \cap A) + m(B \cap -A)$, or $m(B \cap -A) = m(B) - m(B \cap A)$. It follows that $m(A \cup B) = m(A) + m(B) - m(B \cap A)$.

Distance between sets can be defined in terms of measure functions as follows:

$$d(A, B) = m(A \cup B) - m(A \cap B)$$

$$= m(A) + m(B) - 2m(A \cap B)$$

$$= m(A \cap -B) + m(-A \cap B).$$

It is left to the reader to prove that these three expressions are equivalent and that $d(A, B)$ as defined satisfies D1 through D4. [*Hint:* Note that $m(A \cap B) = m(A \cap B \cap C) + m(A \cap B \cap -C)$.]

The notion of distance is important in psychological scaling partly because of its intimate connection with the notion of psychological dissimilarity. Many psychologists have assumed explicitly or implicitly that stimuli and/or organisms may be located in a space and that the degree of similarity between these entities should be a function of distance in this space. For example, Restle (1959, p. 207) writes:

[2]*Measure* and later *probability* are defined here for finite collections of sets. It is also possible, and for many purposes preferable, to define these concepts for countably infinite collections of sets. Applications thus far in psychology, however, do not often involve such collections; we see no point in introducing such collections here.

Basic to many psychological discussions is the concept of similarity, which is used to arrange objects or events. Two things which are quite similar are psychologically close together and two things which are quite dissimilar are psychologically distant.

That psychological dissimilarity is *by definition* a distance is implicit in the work of Shepard (1962), who points out the "rough isomorphism" between the two concepts—specifically, that it can be argued that the concept of psychological dissimilarity satisfies D1 through D4.

A.6 MULTIPLICATION OF VECTORS AND MATRICES

Consider the Euclidean distance between two vectors $\mathbf{x} = (x_1, x_2, \ldots, x_n)$ and $\mathbf{y} = (y_1, y_2, \ldots, y_n)$, each of which is a distance d from the vector $\mathbf{O} = (0, 0, \ldots, 0)$; this $\mathbf{O}$ vector is often referred to as the "origin" of the space.

By definition, the Euclidean distance between $\mathbf{x}$ and $\mathbf{y}$ is equal to

$$\left[\sum_{i=1}^{n} (x_i - y_i)^2 \right]^{1/2},$$

which equals

$$\left[\sum_{i=1}^{n} (x_i^2 - 2x_i y_i + y_i^2) \right]^{1/2},$$

which in turn equals

$$\left[\sum_{i=1}^{n} x_i^2 - 2 \sum_{i=1}^{n} x_i y_i + \sum_{i=1}^{n} y_i^2 \right]^{1/2}.$$

But because the vectors $\mathbf{x}$ and $\mathbf{y}$ are both d units away from the vector $\mathbf{O}$, it follows that $\sum_{i=1}^{n} x_i^2$ and $\sum_{i=1}^{n} y_i^2$ both equal d^2 [because $\sum_{i=1}^{n} x_1^2 = \sum_{i=1}^{n} (x_i - 0)^2$]. Hence, the distance between $\mathbf{x}$ and $\mathbf{y}$ equals

$$\left[d^2 - 2 \sum_{i=1}^{n} x_i y_i + d^2 \right]^{1/2}$$

or

$$\left[2 \left(d^2 - \sum_{i=1}^{n} x_i y_i \right) \right]^{1/2}.$$

In the above expression, d^2 and 2 are both constants; hence, the distance between $\mathbf{x}$ and $\mathbf{y}$ is determined solely by the expression $\sum_{i=1}^{n} x_i y_i$.

This expression is termed the *product* or *dot product* of the vectors $\mathbf{x}$ and $\mathbf{y}$; it is symbolized $\mathbf{x} \cdot \mathbf{y}$. Computing the dot product of two vectors is said to involve *multiplication* of the vectors. For example, if we multiply the vectors (4, 3, 1, 1) and (2, 3, 3, 2), we conclude that their dot product is $4 \cdot 2 + 3 \cdot 3 + 1 \cdot 3 + 1 \cdot 2$, or 22.

The dot product of two vectors equally distant from the origin of a space determines the distance between those vectors. The dot product has many other applications as well. Hence, certain conventions have arisen for dealing with dot products. One of these conventions involves expressing vectors as rows or columns of numbers; specifically when $\mathbf{x} \cdot \mathbf{y}$ is computed, the vector $\mathbf{x}$ is often represented as a row consisting of its components, whereas the vector $\mathbf{y}$ is often represented as a column consisting of its components; thus the multiplication of the vector (4, 3, 1, 1) and the vector (2, 3, 3, 2) may be represented as follows:

$$[4 \ 3 \ 1 \ 1] \begin{bmatrix} 2 \\ 3 \\ 3 \\ 2 \end{bmatrix} = 22.$$

Sometimes a vector [such as (4, 3, 1, 1)] is referred to as a *row vector* when its components are written in a row, whereas a vector such as

$$\begin{bmatrix} 2 \\ 3 \\ 3 \\ 2 \end{bmatrix}$$

is referred to as a *column vector*.

Suppose, now, that we had three vectors $\mathbf{x}_1$, $\mathbf{x}_2$, and $\mathbf{x}_3$ and that we wished to compute the dot product of each of these vectors with the vector $\mathbf{y}$. Specifically, let $\mathbf{x}_1 = (4, 3, 1, 1)$, let $\mathbf{x}_2 = (1, 3, 8, 2)$, and let $\mathbf{x}_3 = (7, 2, 2, 4)$; again let $\mathbf{y} = (2, 3, 3, 2)$; then $\mathbf{x}_1 \cdot \mathbf{y} = 4 \cdot 2 + 3 \cdot 3 + 1 \cdot 3 + 1 \cdot 2 = 22$, $\mathbf{x}_2 \cdot \mathbf{y} = 1 \cdot 2 + 3 \cdot 3 + 8 \cdot 3 + 2 \cdot 2 = 39$, and $\mathbf{x}_3 \cdot \mathbf{y} = 7 \cdot 2 + 2 \cdot 3 + 2 \cdot 3 + 4 \cdot 2 = 34$. Using the same convention explained earlier, we may express these three dot products as follows:

$$\begin{matrix} [4 \ 3 \ 1 \ 1] \\ [1 \ 3 \ 8 \ 2] \\ [7 \ 2 \ 2 \ 4] \end{matrix} \begin{bmatrix} 2 \\ 3 \\ 3 \\ 2 \end{bmatrix} = \begin{matrix} [22] \\ [39] \\ [34]. \end{matrix}$$

A slight change in brackets yields

$$
\begin{bmatrix} 4 & 3 & 1 & 1 \\ 1 & 3 & 8 & 2 \\ 7 & 2 & 2 & 4 \end{bmatrix} \begin{bmatrix} 2 \\ 3 \\ 3 \\ 2 \end{bmatrix} = \begin{bmatrix} 22 \\ 39 \\ 34 \end{bmatrix}.
$$

A rectangular array, such as

$$
\begin{bmatrix} 4 & 3 & 1 & 1 \\ 1 & 3 & 8 & 2 \\ 7 & 2 & 2 & 4 \end{bmatrix},
$$

is termed a *matrix. We multiply a matrix by a vector when each row of the matrix is treated as a vector whose dot product with the column vector is computed.* The result of such multiplication is a set of dot products, the number of such dot products being equal to the number of rows in the matrix; these products are displayed in the form of a column vector. The matrix is said to *premultiply* the original vector; the vector is said to *postmultiply* the matrix.

Now consider a number of vectors $x_1, x_2, \ldots, x_n$ and a number of vectors $y_1, y_2, \ldots, y_n$, all with the same number of components. Suppose we wish to compute the dot product of each combination $x_i \cdot y_j$. We need simply let the x's form the row of a matrix and the y's form the columns of another; then by multiplying all the rows by each of the columns in turn, we will obtain a set of column vectors; these column vectors themselves form a matrix. Hence, two matrices are multiplied together to form a third.

For example, consider again the vectors $x_1 = (4, 3, 1, 1)$, $x_2 = (1, 3, 8, 2)$, and $x_3 = (7, 2, 2, 4)$; consider again the vector $y_1 = (2, 3, 3, 2)$ and in addition the vectors $y_2 = (1, 7, 3, 1)$ and $y_3 = (1, 2, 3, 4)$. Now the dot products of all the x's with all the y's may be represented as follows:

$$
\begin{matrix} [4 \ 3 \ 1 \ 1] \\ [1 \ 3 \ 8 \ 2] \\ [7 \ 2 \ 2 \ 4] \end{matrix} \begin{bmatrix} 2 \\ 3 \\ 3 \\ 2 \end{bmatrix} \begin{bmatrix} 1 \\ 7 \\ 3 \\ 1 \end{bmatrix} \begin{bmatrix} 1 \\ 2 \\ 3 \\ 4 \end{bmatrix} = \begin{matrix} [22] \ [29] \ [17] \\ [39] \ [48] \ [39] \\ [34] \ [31] \ [33]. \end{matrix}
$$

A slight change in brackets yields

$$
\begin{bmatrix} 4 & 3 & 1 & 1 \\ 1 & 3 & 8 & 2 \\ 7 & 2 & 2 & 4 \end{bmatrix} \begin{bmatrix} 2 & 1 & 1 \\ 3 & 7 & 2 \\ 3 & 3 & 3 \\ 2 & 1 & 4 \end{bmatrix} = \begin{bmatrix} 22 & 29 & 17 \\ 39 & 48 & 39 \\ 34 & 31 & 33 \end{bmatrix}.
$$

The two rectangular arrays on the left are matrices, as is the rectangular array on the right. Hence, two matrices have been multiplied together to form a third. In summary, the way in which such multiplication is performed is by regarding each row of the first matrix as a row vector and each column of the second as a column vector; the dot product of the row vectors with each column vector in turn yields a column vector; these column vectors grouped together yield a matrix. This procedure is, quite naturally, termed *matrix multiplication*. The first matrix is said to *premultiply* the second, and the second to *postmultiply* the first.

Matrix multiplication has a great many uses in mathematics, particularly in applied mathematics. One such application arises in Chapter 8 of this book. The reader may note than in order for matrix multiplication to be performed the number of columns in the first matrix must equal the number of rows in the second and that the number of rows in the resulting matrix will equal the number in the first whereas its number of columns will equal the number in the second. (Why?)

A.7   PERMUTATIONS AND COMBINATIONS

A *permutation* of a set of n elements is a simple ordering of those elements. For example, the order of books on a given shelf is a permutation of those books.

Often, we are concerned with the total number of *possible* permutations of n elements; e.g., how many possible ways could a set of books be ordered (left to right) on a shelf? If there were three books—labeled A, B, and C—the total number of possible permutations is as follows: ABC, ACB, BAC, BCA, CAB, and CBA.

In general, if there are n elements, any one of these can be used as the first element in the order; given the first element, any one of the $n-1$ remaining elements can be used as the second; given the first two elements, any one of the remaining $n-2$ may be used as the third, and so on. Thus the total number of possible permutations of n elements is

$$n(n-1)(n-2)\cdots(2)(1) = n!.$$

The symbol $n!$ is read *n-factorial*.

Often, people speak of n-factorial as being the "number of permutations" rather than the "number of possible permutations."

Now suppose there are more books than spaces on the shelf; specifically, there are n books and only three spaces. How many possible arrangements are there?

Clearly, there are $n(n-1)(n-2)$ possible arrangements, for any of n books may be placed in the left-most space, any of the remaining $n-1$ books may be placed in the next space, and any of the remaining $n-2$ books may be placed in the final space. But note that

$$n(n-1)(n-2) = \frac{n(n-1)(n-2)(n-3)(n-4)\cdots(2)(1)}{(n-3)(n-4)\cdots(2)(1)} = \frac{n!}{(n-3)!}.$$

This number of possible arrangements is referred to as the number of permutations of n books taken three at a time.

The general formula, then, for the number of permutations of n elements taken r at a time is $n!/(n-r)!$.

Now suppose that we are not concerned with the order of the books on the shelf but simply with the number of possible sets of three that can be chosen from the n available. The formula $n!/(n-3)!$ counts each possible permutation of the three books chosen as a separate arrangement. Because we wish to count all such permutations as a single arrangement, we must divide the formula by the number of such permutations, which is $3!$.

Thus the number of subsets of three books that can be chosen from a set of n books is $n!/(n-3)!3!$, and the general formula for the number of subsets of r elements that can be chosen from a set of n elements is $n!/(n-r)!r!$. This formula is often abbreviated $\binom{n}{r}$, and we speak of the number of ways of choosing n things r at a time.

Why is it that the number of ways of choosing n things r at a time is equal to the number of ways of choosing n things $n-r$ at a time? This conclusion is obvious from the formulas for $\binom{n}{r}$ and $\binom{n}{n-r}$, but try to give a much simpler explanation. (*Hint:* What is the relationship between choosing something and not choosing something?)

A.8 PROBABILITY OF EVENTS IN DISCRETE SAMPLE SPACES

Suppose a card is drawn at random from an ordinary deck; what is the probability that the card will be a spade? Because there are 52 cards in the deck of which 13 are spades, this probability is 13/52, or 1/4.

If an experiment can result in one of n equally likely and mutually exclusive outcomes and we specify a set of m of these outcomes, the probability that the outcome will be in the set specified is m/n. The m equally likely and mutually exclusive outcomes all together constitute an *event;* the possible outcomes are said to form a *sample space.* Thus we speak of the probability of a particular event E_i given a sample space S, and this probability is written $p(i)$.

Experiment 1. Consider five different cards drawn at random from an ordinary deck. What is the probability that they will all be spades? The sample space S consists of all possible sets of five different cards drawn from a deck of 52 cards, and the event E_i consists of all possible sets of five spades drawn from a population of 13 spades. There are $\binom{52}{5}$ outcomes in S and $\binom{13}{5}$ outcomes in E_i; hence,

$$p(i) = \frac{\binom{13}{5}}{\binom{52}{5}} = \frac{13 \times 12 \times 11 \times 10 \times 9}{52 \times 51 \times 50 \times 49 \times 48},$$

which is approximately .0005.

It must be emphasized that the elements of the sample space are the possible *outcomes* of the experiment (in experiment 1, each set of five different cards is an outcome); the playing cards themselves do not constitute elements.

Experiment 2. Consider five cards drawn at random from a deck in such a way that after each card is drawn it is replaced in the deck and the deck is shuffled. What is the probability that five cards drawn in this manner will all be spades? The sample space is not the same as that of the last experiment; the outcomes constituting it are no longer sets of five *different* cards, but sets of five cards. There are 52^5 such outcomes (the first card may be any of 52, the second any of 52, and so on), of which 13^5 outcomes are all spades (the first may be any of 13 spades, the second any of 13 spades, and so on). Thus $p(i) = 13^5/52^5 = (1/4)^5$, which is approximately .001.

We may determine this probability in another manner. Suppose we note only the suit of the card drawn from the deck and ignore its value. The sample space would then consist of outcomes specifying patterns of five suits; for example, one such pattern would be spade, diamond, spade, heart, club. There are 4^5 equally likely outcomes defined in this manner (the first card may be any of four suits, the second any of four suits, etc.), but only one of these outcomes—spade, spade, spade, spade, spade—defines the event of drawing all spades. Hence, we again conclude the probability of drawing all spades is $1/4^5 = (1/4)^5$.

There is often more than one way to determine a probability when performing such experiments. To do so, however, it is necessary to conceptualize *a* sample space whose elements are mutually exclusive and equally likely outcomes of the experiment, and the event whose probability is desired must be defined as a subset of these outcomes.

Experiment 1 is an example of *sampling without replacement* (after a card is drawn, it is not replaced in the deck), whereas experiment 2 is an example of *sampling with replacement* (each card is replaced). The importance of this distinction lies in the fact that it is possible to sample from the same physical objects yet obtain different sample spaces.

Now suppose a single card is drawn from an ordinary deck. Consider the following question: What is the probability the card is a spade *given* we know it is a black card? To answer this question, we note that there are 26 black cards of which 13 are spades. The desired probability is, therefore, 13/26, or 1/2.

Such a probability is termed a *conditional* probability. Briefly, a *conditional probability* is one in which we are restricted to a given subspace of our original sample space. The numerical value of the conditional probability of an event is equal to the number of outcomes in both the event and the subspace we are considering divided by the number of outcomes in the subspace. In effect, the subspace has become a new sample space. But a subspace of a sample space is, by definition, an event. Thus we speak of *the conditional probability of an event E_i given an event E_j*; this probability is symbolized $p(i|j)$; its numerical value is equal to the number of outcomes common to E_i and E_j divided by the number of outcomes in E_j. Note that the number of outcomes common to E_i and E_j is just that number in E_i when we restrict our attention to those in E_j.

In the first example of conditional probability the event considered was a subset of the event it was conditional upon; i.e., the event consisting of drawing a spade was a subset of the event consisting of drawing a black card. It is not always—or usually—true that when we speak of E_i given E_j we are talking of cases in which $E_i \subseteq E_j$. For example, we might be interested in the probability of drawing a flush given we have drawn all red cards. The outcomes constituting the event "drawing a flush" are not contained in the outcomes constituting "drawing five red cards," because the event of drawing a flush includes outcomes consisting of drawing sets of five spades and five clubs. To determine the conditional probability, however, we restrict our attention to those outcomes common to the two events, i.e., to flushes that are red. There are $2 \times \binom{13}{5}$ such red flushes; there are $\binom{26}{5}$ drawn consisting of five red cards; hence the desired conditional probability is

$$\frac{2 \times \binom{13}{5}}{\binom{26}{5}} = \frac{2 \times \left(\dfrac{13 \times 12 \times 11 \times 10 \times 9}{5 \times 4 \times 3 \times 2 \times 1}\right)}{\left(\dfrac{26 \times 25 \times 24 \times 23 \times 22}{5 \times 4 \times 3 \times 2 \times 1}\right)} = \text{about } .04.$$

Some experiments may be analyzed either in terms of conditional probabilities or in terms of unconditional probabilities. Consider, for example, the experiment mentioned earlier in which five cards are drawn from a deck without replacement; we wish to determine the probability that they are all spades. According to the previous analysis, the probability is

$$\frac{\binom{13}{5}}{\binom{52}{5}} = \frac{13 \times 12 \times 11 \times 10 \times 9}{52 \times 51 \times 50 \times 49 \times 48} \, .$$

Now consider the problem in conditional terms, where the draw of each spade is considered conditional upon the event that all previous draws were spades. The probability that the first card is a spade is 13/52, because there are 52 cards that could be drawn of which 13 are spades. *Given* the first is a spade, what is the probability the second is a spade? There are 13×12 ways of drawing two spades from a deck and 52×51 ways of drawing two cards. Hence, the probability of the event that both cards are spades is $(13 \times 12)/(52 \times 51)$. Dividing this by the probability of the event that the first is a spade (13/52) yields 12/51—which is the probability the second is a spade given the first is a spade. Sensible, because there are 51 cards left in the deck of which (given the first drawn is a spade) 12 are spades. Similarly, the probability the third is a spade given the first two are spades is 11/50. And so on.

It is evident—and here we appeal to the reader's intuition or his past knowledge of probability—that the probability of drawing four spades is equal to the probability the first draw is a spade multiplied by the probability the second is a spade given the first is a spade multiplied by the probability the third is a spade given the first two are spades, etc. This number is

$$\left(\frac{13}{52}\right) \times \left(\frac{12}{51}\right) \times \left(\frac{11}{50}\right) \times \left(\frac{10}{49}\right) \times \left(\frac{9}{48}\right),$$

which is of course equal to

$$\left(\frac{13 \times 12 \times 11 \times 10 \times 9}{52 \times 51 \times 50 \times 49 \times 48}\right).$$

Now we shall consider four properties of the probability of events in sample spaces; these properties will later form the basis of the abstract concept of *probability*—just as four properties of concrete distance formed the basis of the abstract concept of *distance* and two properties of number formed the basis of the abstract concept of *measure*.

P1

$$0 \le p(i) \le 1.$$

This property holds because the number of equally likely outcomes constituting an event will never be more than the number in the sample space (nor less than zero). That is, $0 \le m \le n$; hence, $0 \le m/n \le 1$. But m/n was the definition of $p(i)$.

P2

Letting $p(S)$ refer to the probability of the event equivalent to the sample space, $p(S) = 1$.

This property follows because $p(S) = n/n = 1$.

P3

If $E_i \cap E_j = \varnothing$, then $p(i \text{ or } j) = p(i) + p(j)$.

Here, $p(i \text{ or } j)$ refers to the probability that either event i or event j occurs, that is, the probability that the outcome is in the event $E_i \cup E_j$. The above property holds because if there are m outcomes in E_i and m' in E_j, and if E_i and E_j have no outcomes in common, then there are $m + m'$ outcomes in $E_i \cup E_j$; hence,

$$p(i \text{ or } j) = \frac{m+m'}{n} = \frac{m}{n} + \frac{m'}{n} = p(i) + p(j).$$

Conditions P2 and P3 taken together imply a property that is often regarded as fundamental; here it will be labeled P3'.

P3'

If $E_1, E_2, \ldots, E_i, \ldots, E_n$ form a partition of S, then

$$\sum_{i=1}^{n} p(i) = 1.$$

$\sum_{i=1}^{n} p(i)$ refers, of course, to the sum of the probabilities of each of the events in the partition.

The proof of this property stems from repeated application of P3. Because $E_1 \cap E_2 = \varnothing, p(1 \text{ or } 2) = p(1) + p(2)$. Then, because $(E_1 \cup E_2) \cap E_3 = \varnothing$, $p(1 \text{ or } 2 \text{ or } 3) = p(1 \text{ or } 2) + p(3) = p(1) + p(2) + p(3)$, and so on, until we determine that $p(1 \text{ or } 2 \cdots \text{ or } n) = p(1) + p(2) \cdots + p(n) = \sum_{i=1}^{n} p(i)$. But $p(1 \text{ or } 2 \cdots \text{ or } n) = p(S)$. Hence, by P2, $1 = p(1 \text{ or } 2 \cdots \text{ or } n) = \sum_{i=1}^{n} p(i)$.
Finally,

P4

$$p(i|j) = \frac{p(i \text{ and } j)}{p(j)}.$$

Let m be the number of equally likely outcomes in E_j and let m' be the number common to E_i and E_j (i.e., the number in $E_i \cap E_j$). By definition, $p(i|j) = m'/m = (m'/s)/(m/s) = p(i \text{ and } j)/p(j)$.

A.9 THE GENERAL CONCEPT OF PROBABILITY

Often we speak of the probabilities of events that are not sets of equally likely outcomes in a sample space. For example, we speak of the probability of the event that it will snow in September in Ann Arbor, Michigan, the probability of the event that the New York Yankees will win the American League pennant in a given year, the probability of the event that we avoid a nuclear war, and so on. Some of these probabilities appear to have reference to relative frequencies (the snow in September example), some to fair betting odds (the Yankees example), and some to "rational opinion" (the nuclear war example). In all the examples, however, we have reference to a number between zero and one, and a careful analysis of all justifications for such numbers will reveal that they must satisfy P1 through P4.

It is not the purpose of this appendix to prove that probability defined in terms of relative frequencies, fair betting odds, or rational opinion satisfies P1 through P4, although it can be proved. Rather, we define *probability* in terms of these properties, just as we have earlier defined *distance* and *measure* in terms of such properties.

Specifically, consider a set S of events $\{E_1, E_2, \ldots, E_i, \ldots, E_n\}$ having the property that at least one of these events occurs. Consider a function that assigns a real number $p(i)$ to each event E_i; that function will be termed a *probability function* and the number it assigns a *probability* if and only if $p(i)$ satisfies conditions P1 through P4.[3]

P1
$$0 \le p(i) \le 1.$$

P2
$$p(S) = 1.$$

P3
$$\text{If } E_i \cap E_j = \varnothing, \text{ then } p(i \text{ or } j) = p(i) + p(j).$$

P4
$$p(i|j) = \frac{p(i \text{ and } j)}{p(j)}.$$

[3]See footnote to the definition of measure, p. 376.

The terms $p(S)$, $p(i$ or $j)$, $p(i$ and $j)$, and $p(i|j)$ have exactly the same meaning they had earlier. $E_i \cap E_j$ has a slightly more general meaning; here, $E_i \cap E_j = \varnothing$ means that E_i and E_j are "mutually exclusive" in the sense that if one occurs the other cannot.

And as before, P2 and P3 imply

P3′

If $E_1, E_2, \ldots, E_i, \ldots, E_n$ is a partition of S, then $\sum_{i=1}^{n} p(i) = 1$.

Two events E_i and E_j are *independent* if and only if $p(i$ and $j) = p(i)p(j)$. By P4, however, $p(i$ and $j) = p(i|j)p(j)$; hence, two events are independent if and only if $p(i|j)p(j) = p(i)p(j)$, which [if $p(j) \neq 0$] is true if and only if $p(i|j) = p(i)$. The latter condition may be a more intuitively appealing definition of independence than is the original one. Events E_i and E_j are independent if and only if the probability of E_i given E_j is just exactly equal to the probability of E_i considered alone. And because $p(i$ and $j) = p(j$ and $i)$, E_i and E_j's independence is also equivalent to the condition that $p(j|i) = p(j)$ [here, provided $p(i) \neq 0$].

Consider experiment 1. The probability the first card drawn is a spade is 13/52; the probability the second card is a spade given the first one is a spade is 12/51, for there are 51 cards left in the deck of which 12 are spades. The probability a random draw is a spade, however, is 13/52. It follows that the events "the first card is a spade" and "the second card is a spade" are not independent.

Because $p(i$ and $j) = p(j$ and $i)$, it follows from P4 that $p(i|j)p(j) = p(j|i)p(i)$, or:

BAYES' THEOREM

$$p(i|j) = \frac{p(j|i)p(i)}{p(j)}.$$

$p(i|j)$ is termed the *inverse probability* of $p(j|i)$ and *vice versa*.

One widely used application of Bayes' theorem is that of judging that the probability of a certain hypothesis is true given certain evidence. Letting h_i indicate hypothesis i and e indicate evidence, we see from Bayes' theorem that

$$p(h_i|e) = \frac{p(e|h_i)p(h_i)}{p(e)}.$$

$p(h_i)$ is often termed the a priori probability of h_i, because it is determined prior to examination of the evidence e, and $p(h_i|e)$ is termed the a posteriori probability.

Example: Suppose there are two boxes A and B such that box A contains

80 percent white marbles and 20 percent red, whereas box B contains 40 percent white and 60 percent red. The two boxes are hidden from view, but we are able to sample marbles—with replacement—from one of them. Suppose further that we are not equally likely to sample from either box, but our probability of sampling from A prior to evidence is .2, whereas our probability of sampling from B is .8. We draw four marbles, and they are all white. What is the probability we have sampled from box A?

Let h_1 be the hypothesis that we have sampled from box A and h_2 be the hypothesis we have sampled from box B; let e be the evidence, in this case the fact we have drawn four straight white marbles. $p(h_1) = .2$, and $p(h_2) = .8$, because these two probabilities are independent of evidence, whereas $p(e|h_1) = .8^4$ and $p(e|h_2) = .4^4$. $p(e) = p(e|h_1)p(h_1) + p(e|h_2)p(h_2) = .8^4 \times .2 + .4^4 \times .8$, which is approximately .10.

Thus $p(h_1|e) = p(e|h_1)p(h_1)/p(e) = (.8^4 \times .2)/.1 \cong .8$, whereas $p(h_2|e) \cong p(e|h_2)p(h_2)/p(e) = (.4^4 \times .8)/.1 = .2$. The probability we have drawn the marbles from box A is approximately .8.

As well as being defined for events, hypotheses, etc., probability may be defined on sets that have measures; specifically, $p(A|B) = m(A \cap B)/m(B)$, where m is a measure function. This function satisfies P1 through P4.

Sometimes events have values associated with them. For example, if a coin is tossed for a $1 stake and the individual calling the toss calls heads, the event that the coin falls heads has a value of $+$ $1 for that individual, and the event that the coin falls tails has a value of $-$ $1 for him.

Whenever each event in a set of mutually exclusive events has a value associated with it, we may speak of the *expected value* of the entire set. Briefly, the expected value of a set is equal to the sum of the values of its events weighted by their respective probabilities. In the above example the expected value is equal to the value of the event the coin falls heads ($+$ $1) multiplied by its probability (1/2 if the coin is fair) plus the value of the event the coin falls tails ($-$ $1) multiplied by its probability (1/2). The expected value is zero. (Note that the expected value of this set is not equal to the value of either of its events.)

The concept of *expected value* is developed formally as follows. Consider a set of mutually exclusive events $\{E_1, E_2, \ldots, E_i, \ldots, E_n\}$ that form a partition of a set S. Consider, further, that each event E_i has a value V_i associated with it. The *expected value* of the set, symbolized $E(S)$, is equal to $\sum_{i=1}^{n} V_i p(i)$.

Expected value is sometimes referred to simply as *expectation*, but the latter term is somewhat misleading because we may also define other sorts of expectations. For example, the expectation of the squared value of a set of mutually exclusive events is $\sum_{i=1}^{n} V_i^2 p(i)$, the expectation of the cubed value is $\sum_{i=1}^{n} V_i^3 p(i)$, and so on. These expectations define important characteristics of sets of events having values. For example, the *variance* of a set of such events is equal to the expectation of the squared value minus the squared expectation of the value. That is, formally defined, the variance of a set of mutually exclusive events is equal to $\sum_{i=1}^{n} V_i^2 p(i) - [E(S)]^2$. The variance of S is sometimes symbolized as $V(S)$. It can also be demonstrated that $V(S) = \sum_{i=1}^{n} p(i)[V_i - E(S)]^2$.

The concepts of expected value and variance should be familiar to the reader who has had some training in elementary statistics—training we assume in writing this book. In elementary statistics these concepts are usually applied to distributions of numbers or probability distributions.

Table A.1 summarizes the major concepts and notation introduced in this appendix.

TABLE A.1 SUMMARY OF CONCEPTS, SYMBOLS, AND DEFINITIONS

Concept	Symbol	Definition
Set	A	$\{x : x \in A\}$
Complement	$-A$	$\{x : x \notin A\}$
Intersection	$A \cap B$	$\{x : x \in A \text{ and } x \in B\}$
Union	$A \cup B$	$\{x : x \in A \text{ or } x \in B\}$
Subset	$A \subseteq B$	$x \in A$ implies $x \in B$
Cartesian product	$A \times B$	$\{(x, y) : x \in A \text{ and } y \in B\}$
Relation	R [n.b. $(x, y) \in R$ written $x \, R \, y$]	$R \subseteq X \times Y$, where X is domain and Y is range of R
Order relation		Satisfies transitivity: $x \, R \, y$ and $y \, R \, z$ imply $x \, R \, z$
Function		Satisfies many-one property: $x \, R \, y$ and $x \, R \, z$ imply $y = z$
Distance	$d(X, Y)$	Satisfies D1 through D4: D1 $d(x, y) \geq 0$ D2 $d(x, y) = 0$ if and only if $x = y$ D3 $d(x, y) = d(y, x)$ D4 $d(x, y) + d(y, z) \geq d(x, z)$
Measure	$m(A)$	Satisfies M1 and M2: M1 $m(A) \geq 0$ M2 If $A \cap B = \varnothing$, then $m(A \cup B) = m(A) + m(B)$
Probability	$p(i)$	Satisfies P1 through P4: P1 $0 \leq p(i) \leq 1$ P2 $p(S) = 1$ P3 If $E_i \cap E_j = \varnothing$, then $p(i \text{ or } j) = p(i) + p(j)$ P4 $p(i \vert j) = p(i \text{ and } j)/p(j)$

BIBLIOGRAPHY

Adams, E. W., Fagot, R. F., and Robinson, R. E. A theory of appropriate statistics. Psychometrika, 1965, 30, 99–127.

Allais, M. Le comportement de l'homme rationnel devant le risque: Critique des postulats et axiomes de l'ecole americaine. Econometrica, 1953, 21, 503–46.

Alluisi, E. A. Conditions affecting the amount of information in absolute judgments. Psychological Review, 1957, 64, 97–103.

Anderson, N. H. An evaluation of stimulus sampling theory. In A. W. Melton (ed.), *Categories in human learning*. New York: Academic Press, 1964.

Anderson, N. H. Effect of first-order conditional probability in a two-choice learning situation. Journal of Experimental Psychology, 1960, 59, 73–93.

Arieti, S. *Interpretation of schizophrenia*. New York: Bruner, 1955.

Atkinson, J. W. *An introduction to motivation*. Princeton, N.J. Van Nostrand, 1964.

Atkinson, J. W., and Litwin, G. H. Achievement motive and test anxiety conceived as motive to approach success and motive to avoid failure. Journal of Abnormal and Social Psychology, 1960, 60, 52–63.

Atkinson, R. C. A variable sensitivity theory of signal detection. Psychological Review, 1963, 70, 91–106.

Atkinson, R. C., Bower, G. H., and Crothers, E. J. *An introduction to mathematical learning theory.* New York: Wiley, 1965.

Atkinson, R. C., and Crothers, E. J. A comparison of paired associate learning models having different acquisition and retention axioms. Journal of Mathematical Psychology, 1964, 1, 285–315.

Attneave, F. *Applications of information theory to psychology: A summary of basic concepts, methods, and results.* New York: Holt, Rinehart & Winston, 1959.

Attneave, F. Some informational aspects of visual perception. Psychological Review, 1954, 61, 183–93.

Audley, R. J. The inclusion of response times within a stochastic description of the learning behavior of individual subjects. Psychometrika, 1958, 23, 25–31.

Audley, R. J. A stochastic description of the learning behavior of an individual subject. Quarterly Journal of Experimental Psychology, 1957, 9, 12–20.

Audley, R. J., and Jonckhere, A. R. Stochastic processes and learning behaviour. British Journal of Statistical Psychology, 1956, 9, 87–94.

Bartlett, F. C. *Thinking: An experimental and social study.* New York: Basic Books, 1958.

Bartlett, F. C. *Remembering: A study in experimental and social psychology.* London: Cambridge Univ. Press, 1932.

Beals, R., Krantz, D. H., and Tversky, A. Foundations of multidimensional scaling. Psychological Review, 1968, 75, 127–42.

Beckenbach, E., and Bellman, R. *An introduction to inequalities.* New York: Random House, 1961.

Becker, G. M., DeGroot, M. H., and Marschak, J. Stochastic models of choice behavior. Behavioral Science, 1963, 8, 41–55. (*a*)

Becker, G. M., DeGroot, M. H., and Marschak, J. Probabilities of choices among very similar objects. Behavioral Science, 1963, 8, 306–11. (*b*)

Becker, G. M., and McClintock, C. G. Value: Behavioral decision theory. Annual Review of Psychology, 1967, 18, 239–86.

Behrend, E. R., and Bitterman, M. E. Probability matching in the fish. American Journal of Psychology, 1961, 74, 542–51.

Berge, C. *The theory of graphs and its applications.* New York: Wiley, 1962.

Bernbach, H. A. A forgetting model for paired associate learning. Journal of Mathematical Psychology, 1965, 2, 128–44.

Bernbach, H. A. *Detection theory for recognition memory.* Michigan Mathematical Psychology Program Technical Report No. MMPP 64–4. Ann Arbor: Univ. of Michigan, 1964.

Binder, A., Burton, R. W., and Terebinski, S. J. Leadership in small groups: A mathematical approach. Journal of Experimental Psychology, 1965, 69, 126–34.

Binford, J. R., and Gettys, C. Nonstationarity in paired-associate learning as indicated by a second guess procedure. Journal of Mathematical Psychology, 1964, 1, 190–203.

Bower, G. H. A multicomponent theory of the memory trace. In K. W. Spence, J. T. Spence, and N. H. Anderson (eds.), *The psychology of learning and motivation: Advances in research and theory*, vol. I. New York: Academic Press, 1966.

Bower, G. H. A model for response and training variables in paired-associate learning. Psychological Review, 1962, 69, 34–53.

Bower, G. H. Application of a model to paired-associate learning. Psychometrika, 1961, 26, 255–80.

Bower, G. H., and Trabasso, T. Concept identification. In R. C. Atkinson (ed.), *Studies in mathematical psychology*. Stanford, Calif.: Stanford Univ. Press, 1964, pp. 32–94. (*a*)

Bower, G. H., and Trabasso, T. Reversals prior to solution in concept identification. Journal of Experimental Psychology, 1964, 66, 409–18. (*b*)

Bradley, R. A., and Terry, M. E. Rank analysis of incomplete block designs. I. The method of paired comparisons, Biometrika, 1952, 39, 324–45.

Braunstein, M. Human decision processes. Paper presented at the annual meeting of the Midwestern Psychological Association, Chicago, 1965.

Broadbent, D. E., and Gregory, M. Vigilance considered as a statistical decision. British Journal of Psychology, 1963, 54, 309–23.

Bush, R. R. Estimation and evaluation. In R. D. Luce, R. R. Bush, and E. Galanter (eds.), *Handbook of mathematical psychology*, vol. III. New York: Wiley, 1965.

Bush, R. R. A survey of mathematical learning theory. In R. D. Luce (ed.), *Developments in mathematical psychology*. New York: Free Press, 1960, pp. 123–70.

Bush, R. R., Galanter, E., and Luce, R. D. Characterization and classification of choice experiments. In R. D. Luce, R. R. Bush, and E. Galanter (eds.), *Handbook of mathematical psychology*. New York: Wiley, 1963.

Bush, R. R., and Mosteller, F. *Stochastic models for learning*. New York: Wiley, 1955.

Bush, R. R., and Mosteller, F. A mathematical model for simple learning. Psychological Review, 1951, 58, 313–23.

Calfee, R. C., and Atkinson, R. C. Paired associate models and the effect of list length. Journal of Mathematical Psychology, 1965, 2, 254–65.

Campbell, N. R. *Physics: The elements*. London: Cambridge Univ. Press, 1920. (Reprinted as *Foundations of Science*. New York: Dover, 1957.)

Carterette, E. Book review of R. D. Luce, R. R. Bush, and E. Galanter (eds.), *Handbook of mathematical psychology*, vol. I, pp. 491 and xiii; vol. II, pp. 666 and vii. New York: Wiley, 1963. Psychometrika, 1965, 30, 207–33.

Cartwright, D., and Harary, F. Structural balance: A generalization of Heider's theory. Psychological Review, 1956, 63, 277–93.

Christian, J. J. Endocrine adaptive mechanisms and the physiologic regulation of population growth. In W. Mayer, and R. Van Gelder (eds.), *Physiological Mammalogy:* vol. 1, *Mammalian Populations.* New York: Academic Press, 1963.

Clarke, F. R. Constant-ratio rule for confusion matrices in speech communication. Journal of the Acoustical Society of America, 1957, 29, 715–20.

Clarke, F. R., Birdsall, T. G., and Tanner, W. P., Jr. Two types of ROC curves and definitions of parameters. Journal of Acoustical Society of America, 1959, 31, 629–30.

Clarkson, G. P. E. *Portfolio selection—a simulation of trust investment.* Englewood Cliffs, N.J.: Prentice-Hall, 1962.

Cohen, B. P. Conflict and conformity: A probability model and its application. Contemporary Psychology, 1964, 9, 273–76.

Cohen, E. A. *Human behavior in the concentration camp.* Trans. M. H. Braaksma. New York: Grosset & Dunlap, 1953.

Cohen, J. E. Information theory and music. Behavioral Science, 1962, 7, 137–63.

Cohen, J. E. *Chance, skill and luck.* London: Penguin, 1960.

Cohen, J. *Behavior in uncertainty.* New York: Basic Books, 1964.

Cohen, J., and Hansel, C. E. M. *Risk and gambling: The study of subjective probability.* New York: Philosophical Library, 1956.

Cole, M. Search behavior: A correction procedure for three-choice probability learning. Journal of Mathematical Psychology, 1965, 2, 145–70.

Coombs, C. H. Thurstone's measurement of social values revisited forty years later. Journal of Abnormal and Social Psychology, 1967, 6, 85–91.

Coombs, C. H. *A theory of data.* New York: Wiley, 1964.

Coombs, C. H. An application of a nonmetric model for multidimensional analysis of similarities. Psychological Reports, 1958, 4, 511–18.

Coombs, C. H. On the use of inconsistency of preferences in psychological measurement. Journal of Experimental Psychology, 1958, 55, 1–7.

Coombs, C. H. Psychological scaling without a unit of measurement. Psychological Review, 1950, 57, 145–58.

Coombs, C. H., and Komorita, S. S. Measuring utility of money through decisions. American Journal of Psychology, 1958, 71, 383–89.

Coombs, C. H., and Pruitt, D. G. Components of risk in decision making: Probability and variance preferences. Journal of Experimental Psychology, 1960, 60, 265–77.

Coombs, C. H., Raiffa, H., and Thrall, R. M. Some views on mathematical models and measurement theory. Psychological Review, 1954, 61, 132–44.

Creelman, C. D. Discriminability and scaling of linear extent. Journal of Experimental Psychology, 1965, 70, 192–200.

Cross, D. V. An application of mean value theory to psychological measurement. In *Progress Report No. 6*, Report No. 05613-3-P, Ann Arbor: The Behavioral Analysis Laboratory, Univ. of Michigan, 1965.

Cross, D. V. Metric properties of multidimensional stimulus control. Unpublished Ph.D. thesis, Univ. of Michigan, 1965.

Davidson, D., Suppes, P., and Siegel, S. *Decision making: An experimental approach*. Stanford, Calif.: Stanford Univ. Press, 1957.

Dawes, R. M. Memory and distortion of meaningful written material. British Journal of Psychology, 1966, 57, 77–86.

Dawes, R. M. Cognitive distortion. Psychological Reports, 1964, monograph supplement 4–VI4.

Debreu, G. Review of R. D. Luce, Individual choice behavior: A theoretical analysis. American Economic Review, 1960, 50, 186–88.

Debreu, G. Stochastic choice and cardinal utility. Econometrica, 1958, 26, 440–44.

DeSoto, C. B., and Bosley, J. J. The cognitive structure of a social structure. Journal of Abnormal and Social Psychology, 1962, 64, 303–7.

Duncker, K. On problem solving. Psychological Monographs, 1945, 58, no. 270.

Edwards, W. Conservatism in human information processing. In B. Kleinmuntz (ed.), *Formal representation of human judgment*. New York: Wiley, 1968.

Edwards, W. Behavioral decision theory. In P. R. Farnsworth, O. McNemar, and Q. McNemar (eds.), *Annual Review of Psychology*. Palo Alto, Calif.: Annual Reviews, Inc., 1961, pp. 473–98.

Edwards, W. Probability learning in 1000 trials. Journal of Experimental Psychology, 1961, 62, 385–94.

Edwards, W. Probability-preferences among bets with differing expected values. American Journal of Psychology, 1954, 67, 56–67. (*a*)

Edwards, W. Variance preferences in gambling. American Journal of Psychology, 1954, 67, 441–52. (*b*)

Edwards, W. The theory of decision making. Psychological Bulletin, 1954, 51, 380–417. (*c*)

Edwards, W. Probability-preferences in gambling. American Journal of Psychology, 1953, 66, 349–64.

Edwards, W., Lindman, H., and Phillips, L. D. Emerging technologies for making decisions. In *New directions in Psychology*, vol. II. New York: Holt, Rinehart & Winston, 1965, pp. 261–325.

Edwards, W., and Tversky, A. (eds.). *Decision making*. Harmondsworth, Middlesex, England: Penguin, 1967.

Egan, J. P., Schulman, A. I., and Greenberg, G. Z. Operating characteristics determined by binary decisions and by ratings. Journal of Acoustical Society of America, 1959, 31, 768–73.

Eijkman, E., and Vendrik, A. J. H. Detection theory applied to absolute sensitivity of sensory systems. Biophysical Journal, 1963, 3, 65–78.

Erickson, J. R. On learning several simultaneous probability learning problems. Journal of Experimental Psychology, 1966, 77, 182–89.

Estes, W. K. Probability learning. In A. W. Melton (ed.), Categories of human learning. New York: Academic Press, 1964, pp. 89–128.

Estes, W. K. Learning theory. Annual Review of Psychology, 1962, 13, 107–44.

Estes, W. K. Component and pattern models with Markovian interpretations. In R. R. Bush and W. K. Estes (eds.), Studies in mathematical learning theory. Stanford, Calif.: Stanford Univ. Press, 1959.

Estes, W. K. Of models and men. American Psychologist, 1957, 12, 609–17.

Estes, W. K. Toward a statistical theory of learning. Psychological Review, 1950, 57, 94–107.

Estes, W. K., and Burke, C. J. A theory of stimulus variability in learning. Psychological Review, 1953, 60, 276–86.

Estes, W. K., and Hopkins, B. L. Acquisition and transfer in pattern versus component discrimination learning. Journal of Experimental Psychology, 1961, 61, 322–28.

Estes, W. K., and Straughan, J. H. Analysis of a verbal conditioning situation in terms of statistical learning theory. Journal of Experimental Psychology, 1954, 47, 225–34.

Evans, S. H. Redundancy as a variable in pattern perception. Psychological Bulletin, 1967, 67, 104–13.

Fechner, G. T. Elemente der psychophysik. Vols. I and II. Leipzig, Germany: Breitkopf and Hartel, 1860.

Feigenbaum, E. A., and Feldman, J. (eds.), Computers and thought. New York: McGraw-Hill, 1963.

Feller, W. An introduction to probability theory and its applications, vol. I. New York: Wiley, 1957.

Festinger, L., and Thibaut, J. Interpersonal communication in small groups. Journal of Abnormal and Social Psychology, 1951, 46, 92–99.

Fey, C. F. An investigation of some mathematical models for learning. Journal of Experimental Psychology, 1961, 61, 455–61.

Fishburn, P. Decision and value theory. New York: Wiley, 1964.

Fisher, I. The nature of capital and income. New York: Macmillan, 1906.

Fitts, P. M. Foreword to M. I. Posner's An informational approach to thinking, IST Technical Report No. 2814–9–T. Institute of Science and Technology, Univ. of Michigan, 1962.

Fitts, P. M., and Switzer, G. Cognitive aspects of information processing: I, the familiarity of SR sets and subsets. Journal of Experimental Psychology, 1962, 63, 321–29.

Fitts, P. M., Weinstein, M., Rappoport, M., Anderson, N., and Leonard, A. J. Stimulus correlates of visual pattern of recognition. Journal of Experimental Psychology, 1956, 51, 1–11.

Fouraker, L. E., and Siegel, S. *Bargaining behavior.* New York: McGraw-Hill, 1963.

Friedman, M. P. Transfer effects and response strategies in pattern-versus-component discrimination learning. Journal of Experimental Psychology, 1966, 71, 420–28.

Friedman, M. P., and Gelfand, H. Transfer effects in discrimination learning. Journal of Mathematical Psychology, 1964, 1, 204–14.

Friedman, M. P., and Savage, L. J. The utility analysis of choices involving risk. Journal of Political Economy, 1948, 56, 279–304.

Gardner, M. Mathematical games. Scientific American, 1965, September, 222–32.

Garner, W. R. *Uncertainty and structure as psychological concepts.* New York: Wiley, 1962.

Garner, W. R., and McGill, W. J. Relation between uncertainty, variance, and correlation analyses. Psychometrika, 1956, 21, 219–28.

Gerard, R. W. Neuro-physiology: An integration. In *Handbook of physiology*, vol. 3. Washington, D.C.: American Physiological Society, 1960.

Gerard, H., and Fleischer, L. Recall and pleasantness of balanced and unbalanced cognitive structures. Journal of Personality and Social Psychology, 1967, 7, 332–37.

Gergonne, J. D. Essai de dialectic rationelle. Annales des mathematiques pures et appliques, 1817, 7.

Goldberg, D., and Coombs, C. H. Some application of unfolding theory to fertility analysis. In *Emerging Techniques in Population Research. Proceedings of the 1962 Annual Conference of the Milbank Memorial Fund.* New York: Milbank Memorial Fund, 1962.

Grabbe, S. R., and Woolridge, D. *Handbook of automation, computation, and control*, vol. I. New York: Wiley, 1958.

Grant, D. A., Hake, H. W., and Hornseth, J. P. Acquisition and extinction of a verbal conditioned response with differing percentages of reinforcements. Journal of Experimental Psychology, 1951, 42, 1–5.

Green, D. M. Psychoacoustics and detection theory. Journal of the Acoustical Society of America, 1960, 32, 1189–1203.

Green, D. M., Birdsall, T. G., and Tanner, W. P., Jr. Signal detection as a function of signal intensity and duration. Journal of the Acoustical Society of America, 1957, 29, 523–31.

Green, D. M., and Swets, J. A. *Signal detection theory and psychophysics.* New York: Wiley, 1966.

Greeno, J., and Scandura, J. All-or-none transfer based on verbally mediated concepts. Journal of Mathematical Psychology, 1966, 3, 388–411.

Greeno, J., and Steiner, T. Markovian processes with identifiable states: General considerations and application to all-or-none learning. Psychometrika, 1964, 29, 209–333.

Gregg, L. W., and Simon, H. A. Process models and stochastic theories of simple concept formation. Journal of Mathematical Psychology, 1967, 4, 246–76.

Gulliksen, H. A generalization of Thurstone's learning function. Psychometrika, 1953, 18, 297–307.

Gulliksen, H. A rational equation of the learning curve based on Thorndike's law of effect. Journal of General Psychology, 1934, 11, 395–434.

Guthrie, E. R. Psychological facts and psychological theory. Psychological Bulletin, 1946, 43, 1–20.

Guttman, L. A general nonmetric technique for finding the smallest coordinate space for a configuration of points. Psychometrika, 1968, 33, 469–506.

Guttman, L. A basis for scaling qualitative data. American Sociological Review, 1944, 9, 139–50.

Guttman, N. The pigeon and the spectrum and other perplexities. Psychological Reports, 1956, 2, 449–60.

Hack, M. H. Signal detection in the rat. Science, 1963, 139, 758–59.

Harary, F., Norman, R., and Cartwright, D. Structural models: An introduction to the theory of directed graphs. New York: Wiley, 1965.

Harsanyi, J. C. Approaches to the bargaining problem before and after the theory of games: A critical discussion of Zeuthen's, Hick's and Nash's theories. Econometrica, 1956, 24, 144–57.

Hays, W. L. Statistics for psychologists. New York: Holt, Rinehart & Winston, 1963.

Heider, F. Attitudes and cognitive organization. Journal of Psychology, 1946, 21, 107–12.

Hellyer, S. Supplementary report: frequency of stimulus presentation and short-term decrement in recall. Journal of Experimental Psychology, 1962, 64, 650.

Hochberg, J. E., and McAlister, E. A quantitative approach to figural "goodness." Journal of Experimental Psychology, 1953, 46, 361–64.

Hölder, O. Die Axiome der Quantität und die Lehre von Mass. Berichte über die Verhandlugen der Königlich Säclisischen Gesellschaft der Wissenschaften zu Leipzig, Mathematisch–Physische Classe, 1901, 53, 1–64.

Horst, A. P. The prediction of personal adjustment. Social Science Research Council, Bulletin 48, 1941, 455.

Hull, C. L. Principles of behavior. New York: Appleton, 1943.

Humphreys, L. Acquisition and extinction of verbal expectations in a situation analogous to conditioning. Journal of Experimental Psychology, 1939, 25, 294–301.

Hunt, E. B., Marin. J., and Stone, T. J. Experiments in induction. New York: Academic Press, 1966.

Hurwicz, L. Optimality criteria for decision making under ignorance. Technical report no. 370, Cowles commission discussion paper, Statistics, 1951.

Hyman, R. Stimulus information as a determinant of reaction time. Journal of Experimental Psychology, 1953, 45, 188–96.

Jarvik, M. E. Probability learning and a negative recency effect in the serial anticipation of alternative symbols. Journal of Experimental Psychology, 1951, 41, 291–97.

Jones, R. C. Quantum efficiency of human vision. Journal of the Optical Society of America, 1959, 49, 645–53.

Kaufman, H., and Becker, G. M. The empirical determination of game-theoretical strategies. Journal of Experimental Psychology, 1961, 61, 464–68.

Kemeny, J. G., Snell, J. L., and Thompson, G. L. *Introduction to finite mathematics*, 2nd ed. Englewood Cliffs, N.J.: Prentice-Hall, 1966.

Kendall, M. G. *Rank correlation methods*, 2nd ed. New York: Hafner, 1955.

Krantz, D. H. Measurement and psychophysics. In G. B. Dantzig and A. F. Veinatt (eds.), *Mathematics of the decision sciences*, Part 2. American Math. Soc. lectures in applied mathematics, 1968, 12, 314–50.

Kruskal, J. B. Multidimensional scaling by optimizing goodness of fit to a nonmetric hypothesis. Psychometrika, 1964, 29, 1–28. (*a*)

Kruskal, J. B. Nonmetric multidimensional scaling: A numerical method. Psychometrika, 1964, 29, 115–30. (*b*)

Lashley, K. S. An examination of the "continuity theory" as applied to discriminative learning. Journal of General Psychology, 1942, 26, 241–65.

Lashley, K. S., and Wade, M. The Pavlovian theory of generalization. Psychological Review, 1946, 53, 72–87.

Laughery, K. R. and Gregg, L. W. Simulation of human problem-solving behavior. Psychometrika, 1962, 27, 265–82.

Leary, T. *Interpersonal diagnosis of personality*. New York: Ronald, 1957.

Lewin, K. *Principles of topological psychology*. Trans. F. Heider and G. M. Heider. New York: McGraw-Hill, 1936.

Licklider, J. C. R. Three auditory theories. In S. Koch (ed.), *Psychology: A study of a science*, vol. I. New York: McGraw-Hill, 1959.

Lindman, H., and Edwards, W. Supplementary report: Unlearning the gambler's fallacy. Journal of Experimental Psychology, 1961, 62, 630.

Lingoes, J. C. An IBM program for Guttman–Lingoes smallest space analysis —RI. Behavioral Science, 1966, 11, 33.

Lingoes, J. C. An IBM 7090 program for Guttman-Lingoes smallest space analysis—I. Behavioral Science, 1965, 10, 183–84.

Lohrenz, L. J. Temporal factors in the recall of descriptions of balanced and imbalanced interpersonal events. Paper presented at the annual convention of the American Psychological Association, Washington, D.C., 1967.

Luce, R. D. Detection and recognition of human observers. In R. D. Luce, R. R. Bush, and E. Galanter (eds.), *Handbook of Mathematical Psychology*, vol. I. New York: Wiley, 1963.

Luce, R. D. A threshold theory for simple detection experiments. Psychological Review, 1963, 70, 61–79.

Luce, R. D. Detection threshold: A problem reconsidered. Science, 1960, 132, 1495.

Luce, R. D. (ed.). The theory of selective information and some of its behavioral applications. In *Developments in mathematical psychology*. New York: Free Press, 1960.

Luce, R. D. *Individual choice behavior*. New York: Wiley, 1959.

Luce, R. D. Semi-orders and a theory of utility discrimination. Econometrica, 1956, 24, 178–91.

Luce, R. D., and Raiffa, H. *Games and decisions*. New York: Wiley, 1957.

Luce, R. D., and Shipley, E. E. Preference probability between gambles as a step function of event probability. Journal of Experimental Psychology, 1962, 63, 42–49.

Luce, R. D., and Suppes, P. Preference, utility, and subjective probability. In R. D. Luce, R. R. Bush, and E. Galanter (eds.), *Handbook of Mathematical psychology*, vol. III. New York: Wiley, 1965, pp. 249–410.

Luce, R. D., and Tukey, J. W. Simultaneous conjoint measurement: a new type of fundamental measurement. Journal of Mathematical Psychology, 1964, 1, 1–27.

MacCrimmon, K. R. Descriptive and normative implications of the decision theory postulates. In K. Borch (ed.), *Risk and uncertainty*. New York: Macmillan, 1967.

Macworth, J. F., and Taylor, M. M. The d' measure of signal detectability in vigilance-like situations. Canadian Journal of Psychology, 1963, 17, 302–25.

McClintock, C. G., and Messick, D. M. Empirical approaches to game theory and bargaining: A bibliography. General Systems, 1966, 11, 229–38.

McGee, V. E. The multidimensional analysis of elastic distances. British Journal of Mathematical and Statistical Psychology, 1966, 19, 181–96.

Maruyama, M. The second cybernetics: Deviation-amplifying mutual causal processes. American Scientist, 1963, 51, 164–79.

Miller, G. A. The magical number seven plus or minus two: Some limits on our capacity for processing information. Psychological Review, 1956, 63, 81–97.

Miller, G. A., Bruner, J. S., and Postman, L. Familiarity of letter sequences and tachistoscopic identification. Journal of General Psychology, 1954, 50, 129–39.

Millward, R. An all-or-none model for noncorrection routines with elimination of incorrect responses. Journal of Mathematical Psychology, 1964, 1, 392–404.

Milnor, J. Games against nature. In R. M. Thrall, C. H. Coombs, and R. L. Davis (eds.), *Decision processes*. New York: Wiley, 1954, pp. 49–60.

Moore, M. E., Linker, E., and Purcell, M. Taste-sensitivity after eating: A signal detection approach. American Journal of Psychology, 1965, 78, 107–11.

Morrisette, J. O. An experimental study of the theory of structural balance. Human Relations, 1958, 11, 239–54.

Mosteller, F. A. Remarks on the method of pair comparison. I. The least squares solution assuming equal standard deviations and equal correlations. Psychometrika, 1951, 16, 3–11.

Mosteller, F., and Nogee, P. An experimental measurement of utility. Journal of Political Economy, 1951, 59, 371–404.

Nash, J. F. The bargaining problem. Econometrica, 1950, 18, 155–62.

Newcomb, T. M. *The acquaintance process.* New York: Holt, Rinehart & Winston, 1961.

Newell, A., Shaw, J. C., and Simon, H. A. Elements of a theory of human problem solving. Psychological Review, 1958, 65, 151–66.

Newell, A., and Simon, H. A. GPS, a program that simulates human thought. In E. A. Feigenbaum and J. Feldman (eds.), *Computers and thought.* New York: McGraw-Hill, 1963. (*a*)

Newell, A., and Simon, H. A. Computers in psychology. In R. D. Luce, R. R. Bush, and E. Galanter (eds.), *Handbook of mathematical psychology*, vol 1. New York: Wiley, 1963. (*b*)

Norman, D. A. Sensory thresholds and response bias. Journal of the Acoustical Society of America, 1963, 35, 1432–41.

Pavlov, I. P. *Conditioned reflexes.* Trans. G. V. Anrep. London: Oxford Univ. Press, 1927.

Peterson, W. W., Birdsall, T. G., and Fox, W. C. The theory of signal detectability. Institute of Radio Engineers Transactions, 1954, PGIT–4, 171–212.

Peterson, L. R., and Peterson, M. J. Short-term retention of individual verbal items. Journal of Experimental Psychology, 1959, 58, 193–98.

Pfanzagl, J. *Theory of Measurement.* New York: Wiley, 1968.

Platt, J. R. *The step to man.* New York: Wiley, 1966.

Pollack, I. Message uncertainty and message reception. Journal of the Acoustical Society of America, 1959, 31, 1500–1508.

Pollack, I., and Decker, L. R. Confidence ratings, message reception, and the receiver operating characteristic. Journal of the Acoustical Society of America, 1958, 30, 286–92.

Polson, M., Restle, F., and Polson, P. Association and discrimination in paired associate learning. Journal of Experimental Psychology, 1965, 69, 47–55.

Posner, M. I. Information reduction in the analysis of sequential tasks. Psychological Review, 1964, 71, 491–504.

Posner, M. I. *An informational approach to thinking.* IST Technical Report No. 2814–9–T. Ann Arbor: Institute of Science and Technology, Univ. of Michigan, 1962.

Postman, L. The present status of interference theory. In C. N. Cofer (ed.), Verbal Learning and Verbal Behavior. New York: McGraw-Hill, 1961, pp. 152–79.

Price, K. O., Harberg, E., and Newcomb, T. M. Psychological balance in situations of negative interpersonal attitudes. Journal of Personality and Social Psychology, 1966, 3, 265–70.

Price, R. H. Signal-detection methods in personality and perception. Psychological Bulletin, 1966, 66, 55–62.

Raiffa, H. *Decision analysis: introductory lectures on choices under uncertainty.* Reading, Mass.: Addison-Wesley, 1968.

Raisbeck, G. *Information theory: An introduction for scientists and engineers.* Cambridge, Mass.: MIT Press, 1964.

Ramsey, F. P. Truth and probability. In F. P. Ramsey, *The foundations of mathematics and other logical essays.* New York: Harcourt, Brace, 1931, pp. 156–98.

Rapoport, A. *Two-person game theory: The essential ideas.* Ann Arbor: Univ. of Michigan Press, 1966.

Rapoport, A., and Chammah, A. M. *Prisoner's dilemma.* Ann Arbor: Univ. of Michigan Press, 1965. (*a*)

Rapoport, A., and Chammah, A. M. Sex differences in factors contributing to the level of cooperation in the prisoner's dilemma game. Journal of Personality and Social Psychology, 1965, 2, 831–38. (*b*)

Rapoport, A., and Orwant, C. Experimental games: A review. Behavioral Science, 1962, 7, 1–37.

Rausch, H. L. Interaction sequences. Journal of Personality and Social Psychology, 1965, 2, 487–99.

Reitan, R. M. Principles used in evaluating brain functions with psychological tests at the neurolpsychology laboratory, Indiana Univ. Medical Center, Indianapolis, 1959 (mimeo).

Reitman, W. R. *Cognition and thought.* New York: Wiley, 1965.

Restle, F. The significance of all-or-none learning. Psychological Bulletin, 1965, 5, 313–24.

Restle, F. Sources of difficulty in learning paired associates. In R. C. Atkinson (ed.), *Studies in mathematical psychology.* Stanford, Calif.: Stanford Univ. Press, 1964.

Restle, F. The selection of strategies in cue learning. Psychological Review, 1962, 69, 329–43.

Restle, F. *Psychology of judgment and choice.* New York: Wiley, 1961.

Restle, F. A metric and an ordering on sets. Psychometrika, 1959, 24, 207–20.

Restle, F. A survey and classification of learning models. In R. R. Bush and W. K. Estes (eds.), *Studies in mathematical learning theory.* Stanford, Calif.: Stanford Univ. Press, 1959, chapter 20.

Restle, F. A theory of discrimination learning. Psychological Review, 1955, 62, 11–19. (*a*)

Restle, F. Axioms of a theory of discrimination learning. Psychometrika, 1955, 20, 201–8. (*b*).

Roby, T. B. Belief states and the uses of evidence. Behavioral Science, 1965, 10, 255–70.

Rorer, L. G. The great response-style myth. Psychological Bulletin, 1965, 63, 129–56.

Rose, R. M., and Vitz, P. C. The role of runs of events in probability learning. Journal of Experimental Psychology, 1966, 72, 751–60.

Savage, L. J. *The foundations of statistics.* New York: Wiley, 1954.

Savage, L. J. The theory of statistical decision. Journal of The American Statistical Association, 1951, 46, 55–67.

Scott, D., and Suppes, P. Foundational aspects of theories of measurement. Journal of Symbolic Logic, 1958, 23, 113–28.

Shannon, C. E. A mathematical theory of communication. Bell Systems Technical Journal, 1948, 27, 379–423.

Shaw, M. E., Rothschild, G. H., and Strickland, J. F. Decision processes in communication nets. Journal of Abnormal and Social Psychology, 1957, 54, 323–30.

Shelling, T. C. *The strategy of conflict.* Cambridge, Mass.: Harvard Univ. Press, 1960.

Shepard, R. N. Attention and the metric structure of the stimulus space. Journal of Mathematical Psychology, 1964, 1, 54–87.

Shepard, R. N. The analysis of proximities: Multidimensional scaling with an unknown distance function. I. Psychometrika, 1962, 27, 125–40. (*a*)

Shepard, R. N. The analysis of proximities: Multidimensional scaling with an unknown distance function. II. Psychometrika, 1962, 27, 219–46. (*b*)

Shepard, R. N. Stimulus and response generalization: Tests of a model relating generalization to distance in psychological space. Journal of Experimental Psychology, 1958, 55, 509–23.

Shubik, M. *Game theory and related approaches to social behavior.* New York: Wiley, 1964.

Siegel, S., and Fouraker, L. E. *Bargaining and group decision making: Experiments in bilateral monopoly.* New York: McGraw-Hill, 1960.

Simon, H. A. *Models of man.* New York: Wiley, 1957.

Simon, H. A., and Feigenbaum, E. A. An information-process theory of some effects of similarity, familiarization and meaningfulness in verbal learning. Journal of Verbal Learning and Verbal Behavior, 1964, 3, 385–96.

Sorkin, R. D. Extension of the theory of signal detectability to matching procedures in psychoacoustics. Journal of the Acoustical Society of America, 1962, 34, 1745–51.

Spearman, C. E. "General intelligence" objectively determined and measured. American Journal of Psychology, 1904, 15, 201–92.

Sternberg, S. Stochastic learning theory. In R. D. Luce, R. R. Bush, and E. Galanter (eds.), *Handbook of mathematical psychology*, vol. III. New York: Wiley, 1963.

Stevens, S. S. A metric for the social consensus. Science, 1966, 151, 530–41.

Stevens, S. S. Measurement, psychophysics and utility. In C. W. Churchman and P. Ratoosh (eds.), *Measurement: Definitions and theories.* New York: Wiley, 1959.

Stevens, S. S. On the psychophysical law. Psychological Review, 1957, 64, 153–81.

Stevens, S. S. Mathematics, measurement, and psychophysics. In S. S. Stevens (ed.), *Handbook of experimental psychology.* New York: Wiley, 1951, pp. 1–41.

Stevens, S. S. On the theory of scales of measurement. Science, 1946, 103, 677–80.

Stouffer, S. A., Guttman, L., Suchman, E. A., Lazarsfeld, P. F., Star, S. A., and Clausen, J. A. *Measurement and Prediction.* Princeton: Princeton Univ. Press, 1950.

Suppes, P., and Atkinson, R. C. *Markov learning models for multiperson interactions.* Stanford, Calif.: Stanford Univ. Press, 1960.

Suppes, P., and Ginsberg, R. A fundamental property of all-or-none models, binomial distribution prior to conditioning with application to concept formation in children. Psychological Review, 1963, 70, 139–61.

Suppes, P. and Zinnes, J. L. Basic measurement theory. In R. D. Luce, R. R. Bush and E. Galanter (eds.), *Handbook of mathematical psychology,* vol. I. New York: Wiley, 1963, pp. 1–76.

Swets, J. A. (ed.). *Signal detection and recognition of human observers. Contemporary Readings.* New York: Wiley, 1964.

Swets, J. A. Is there a sensory threshold? Science, 1961, 134, 168–77.

Swets, J. A. Indices of signal detectability obtained with various psychometrical procedures. Journal of the Acoustical Society of America, 1959, 31, 511–13.

Swets, J. A., Tanner, W. P., Jr., and Birdsall, T. G. Decision processes in perception. Psychological Review, 1961, 68, 301–40.

Tanner, W. P., Jr. Physiological implications of psychophysical data. Annals of the New York Academy of Science, 1961, 89, 752–65.

Tanner, W. P., Jr. Theory of recognition. Journal of the Acoustical Society of America, 1956, 28, 882–88.

Tanner, W. P., Jr., and Birdsall, T. G. Definitions of d' and η as psychophysical measures. Journal of the Acoustical Society of America, 1958, 30, 922–28.

Tanner, W. P., Jr., and Jones, R. C. The ideal sensor system as approached through statistical decision theory and the theory of signal detectability. In A. Manis and E. Porter Horne (eds.), *Visual Search Techniques.* Publication No. 712. Washington, D.C.: National Academy of Sciences, NRC, 1960.

Tanner, W. P., Jr., and Swets, J. A. A decision-making theory of visual detection. Psychological Review, 1954, 61, 401–9.

Tanner, W. P. Jr., Swets, J. A., and Green, D. M. Some general properties of the hearing mechanism. Technical Report No. 30. Ann Arbor: Electronic Defense Group, Univ. of Michigan, 1956.

Theios, J. Simple conditioning as two-stage all-or-none learning. Psychological Review, 1963, 70, 403–17.

Thorndike, E. L. Handwriting. Teachers College Record, 1910, 11, No. 2, 93.

Thurstone, L. L. The learning function. Journal of Genetic Psychology, 1930, 3, 469–93.

Thurstone, L. L. Attitudes can be measured. American Journal of Sociology, 1928, 33, 529–54.

Thurstone, L. L. A law of comparative judgment. Psychological Review, 1927, 34, 273–86.

Thurstone, L. L. The method of paired comparisons for social values. Journal of Abnormal and Social Psychology, 1927, 21, 384–400.

Toda, M. Book review of W. R. Garner's *Uncertainty and structure as psychological concepts.* Psychometrika, 1963, 28, 293–310.

Torgerson, W. S. Multidimensional scaling of similarity. Psychometrika, 1965, 30, 379–93.

Torgerson, W. S. *Theory and methods of scaling.* New York: Wiley, 1958.

Torgerson, W. S. Multidimensional scaling: I. Theory and method. Psychometrika, 1952, 17, 401–19.

Trabasso, T., and Bower, G. Presolution dimensional shifts in concept identification: A test of the sampling with replacement axiom in all-or-none models. Journal of Mathematical Psychology, 1966, 1, 163–73.

Treisman, M. Noise and Weber's law: The discrimination of brightness and other dimensions. Psychological Review, 1964, 71, 314–30.

Tune, G. S. Response preferences: A review of some relevant literature. Psychological Bulletin, 1964, 61, 286–302.

Tversky, A. The intransitivity of preferences. Psychological Review, 1969, 76, 31–48.

Tversky, A. Utility theory and additivity analysis of risky choices. Journal of Experimental Psychology, 1967, 75, 27–37.

Van Meter, D., and Middleton, D. Modern statistical approaches to reception in communication theory. Institute of Radio Engineers Transactions, 1954, PGIT–4, 119–45.

von Neumann, J., and Morgenstern, O. *Theory of games and economic behavior.* Princeton, N.J.: Princeton Univ. Press, 1944, 1947, 1953.

Weinstein, M., and Fitts, P. M. A quantitative study of the role of stimulus complexity in visual pattern discrimination. American Psychologist, 1954, 9, 490 (abstract).

Weintraub, D. J., and Hake, H. W. Visual discrimination, an interpretation in terms of detectability theory. Journal of the Optical Society of America, 1962, 52, 1179–84.

Williams, J. *The compleat strategyst.* New York: McGraw-Hill, 1954.

Young, F. W. Torsca,–9, a Fortran IV program for nonmetric multidimensional scaling. Behavioral Science, 1968, 13, 343–44.

Young, F. W., and Torgerson, W. S. Torsca, a Fortran IV program for

Shepard–Kruskal multidimensional scaling analysis. Behavioral Science, 1967, 12, 498.

Zajonc, R. B., and Burnstein, E. The learning of balanced and unbalanced social structures. Journal of Personality, 1965, 33, 153–63.

Zeuthen, F. *Problems of monopoly and economic warfare.* London: Routledge, 1960.

NAME INDEX

Adams, E. W., 16
Allais, M., 126–28, 137
Alluisi, E. A., 334
Anderson, N. H., 287–88, 327
Arieti, S., 97
Atkinson, J. W., 139–40
Atkinson, R. C., 139–40, 201, 289–91, 296, 299–303
Attneave, F., 307, 315–16, 322, 327, 330–31
Audley, R. J., 273–74, 305

Bartlett, F. C., 99, 105
Bayes, T., 146
Beals, R., 76
Beckenbach, E., 61
Becker, G. M., 115, 150, 196, 215–16
Behrend, E. R., 287
Bellman, R., 61
Bennett, J. F., 55

Bentham, J., 122
Berge, C., 85
Bernbach, H. A., 201, 300–301
Bernoulli, D., 118–19, 142
Binder, A., 305
Binford, J. R., 298
Birdsall, T. G., 165, 182–83, 185–86, 189–90, 197
Bitterman, M. E., 287
Bosley, J. J., 68–69
Bower, G. H., 240–41, 289, 291–96, 303
Bradley, R. A., 153
Braunstein, M., 109
Broadbent, D. E., 201
Bruner, J. S., 340–41
Burke, C. J., 286
Burnstein, E., 91, 93
Burt, C., 36
Burton, R. W., 305
Bush, R. R., 258, 261–62, 271, 274–76, 287, 296, 322

SUBJECT INDEX

A

Absolute judgment task, 333–37, 349
Absolute scale, 16
Absorbing Markov chain, 293, 301
Absorbing state, 237–38, 299
Achievement motivation, 139–40
Adaptation process, 291
Additive conjoint measurement, 25–29, 134–35, 162
Additive difference model, 65
Additivity (*see* Concatenation operation)
Admissible transformations, 15–17
Aggression, 249–55
All-or-none models, 239–40, 285, 293–94, 296, 298, 300, 302, 304
Alpha model (α model), 260–70, 272, 274–79, 286
Alternating reversal shift, 241
Ambiguity intolerant task, 333, 344–45, 349

Amplitude of response, 270
Amsterdam experiment, 157–59
Antisymmetric relation, 365
Armaments race, 243
Asymmetric relation, 365
Autocatalytic process, 257
Avoidance conditioning, 299
Axioms:
bisymmetry, 22–25
cancellation, 26–29
choice axiom, 149–56, 270, 274
connectivity, 123
decomposition, 154
existential, 29
independence from other alternatives, 151, 221, 261
quadruple condition, 156
reflexivity, 123, 365
simple, 29
solvability, 26–27, 125
solvability condition of Debreu, 156